THE ROUTLEDGE DANCE STUDIES READER

The Routledge Dance Studies Reader represents the range and diversity of writings on dance from the 1980s and 1990s, providing contemporary perspectives on ballet, modern and postmodern dance, South Asian dance, Black dance and dance on camera.

In an enlightening introduction Alexandra Carter traces the development of dance studies internationally and surveys current debates about the methods and methodologies appropriate to the study of dance. The collection is then divided into five sections, each with an editorial preface, and featuring contributions by choreographers, performers, critics and scholars of dance and related disciplinary fields. The sections address:

- choreographing
- performing
- writing criticism
- studying dance
- the place of dance in history and society
- analysing dance works

The Routledge Dance Studies Reader is an invaluable introduction to key dance texts, for the student, the practitioner, and all those interested in enhancing their experience of dance.

Alexandra Carter is Principal Lecturer in Dance at Middlesex University. She is on the editorial board of *Dance Theatre Journal* and is a regular contributor to dance and performing arts journals.

THE ROUTLEDGE DANCE STUDIES READER

Alexandra Carter

London and New York

First published 1998
by Routledge
11 New Fetter Lane, London EC4P 4EE

Simultaneously published in the USA and Canada
by Routledge
29 West 35th Street, New York, NY 10001

Typeset in Goudy by RefineCatch Limited, Bungay, Suffolk
Printed and bound in Great Britain by
TJ International Ltd, Padstow, Cornwall

British Library Cataloguing in Publication Data
A catalogue record for this book is available from the British Library

Library of Congress Cataloging in Publication Data
The Routledge dance studies reader / [edited by] Alexandra Carter.
p.   cm.
'Represents the range and diversity of writings on dance from the
1980s and 1990s' – P. [4] of cover.
Includes bibliographical references (p.   ) and index.
1. Dance.   2. Modern dance.   3. Dance – Philosophy.   4. Dance –
Sociological aspects.   I. Carter, Alexandra.
GV1594. R68   1998
792.8 – dc21   97–46643
CIP

ISBN 0–415–16446–X
0–415–16447–8

To Albert and Joan

CONTENTS

Acknowledgements   xi
List of contributors   xv

1 **General introduction**   1
   ALEXANDRA CARTER

PART I
Making dance

   Introduction   19
   ALEXANDRA CARTER

2 **Choreographers: dancing for de Valois and Ashton**   23
   ANNABEL FARJEON

3 **Torse: there are no fixed points in space**   29
   MERCE CUNNINGHAM with JACQUELINE LESSCHAEVE

4 **'No' to spectacle . . .**   35
   YVONNE RAINER

5 **Pina Bausch: dance and emancipation**   36
   NORBERT SERVOS

6 **Imaginary homelands: creating a new dance language**   46
   SHOBANA JEYASINGH

PART II
Performing dance

   Introduction   53
   ALEXANDRA CARTER

CONTENTS

7   Dancers talking about performance   57
    BARBARA NEWMAN

8   I am a dancer   66
    MARTHA GRAHAM

9   A dancing consciousness   72
    REBECCA HILTON with BRYAN SMITH

10 Spacemaking: experiences of a virtual body   81
    SUSAN KOZEL

PART III
Reviewing dance

    Introduction   89
    ALEXANDRA CARTER

11 Bridging the critical distance   91
    MARCIA B. SIEGEL

12 Between description and deconstruction   98
    ROGER COPELAND

13 Oh, That Pineapple Rag!   108
    ARLENE CROCE

14 Spring: Ashton's *Symphonic Variations* in America   113
    ALASTAIR MACAULAY

PART IV
Studying dance: conceptual concerns

    Introduction   119
    ALEXANDRA CARTER

15 What is art?   125
    BETTY REDFERN

16 A vulnerable glance: seeing dance through phenomenology   135
    SONDRA FRALEIGH

17 Dance history source materials   144
    JUNE LAYSON

18 Embodying difference: issues in dance and cultural studies   154
    JANE C. DESMOND

19 An introduction to dance analysis   163
    JANET ADSHEAD

20 Dance, gender and culture   171
    TED POLHEMUS

21 Choreographing history   180
    SUSAN LEIGH FOSTER

PART V
Locating dance in history and society

    Introduction   193
    ALEXANDRA CARTER

22 Myths of origin   197
    ANDRÉE GRAU

23 In pursuit of the sylph: ballet in the Romantic period   203
    DEBORAH JOWITT

24 Diaghilev's cultivated audience   214
    LYNN GARAFOLA

25 Women writing the body: let's watch a little how she
    dances   223
    ELIZABETH DEMPSTER

26 'Keep to the rhythm and you'll keep to life': meaning and
    style in African American vernacular dance   230
    JACQUI MALONE

PART VI
Analysing dance

    Introduction   237
    ALEXANDRA CARTER

CONTENTS

27 Dance and gender: formalism and semiotics reconsidered   241
    STEPHANIE JORDAN and HELEN THOMAS

28 Nijinsky: modernism and heterodox representations of
    masculinity   250
    RAMSAY BURT

29 Dances of death: Germany before Hitler   259
    SUSAN MANNING

30 Mark Morris: the body and what it means   269
    JOAN ACOCELLA

31 Dance and music video: some preliminary observations   278
    THERESA BUCKLAND

32 Two analyses of 'Dancing in the Dark' (*The Band Wagon*, 1953) 288
    RICHARD DYER and JOHN MUELLER

Bibliography   294
Index   305

ACKNOWLEDGEMENTS

I would like to extend my very sincere thanks to the following: Janet Lansdale for active support and constructive criticism on the editorial content; David Leonard, Anne Daye, Ann Nugent and colleagues in higher education who offered information and advice; Lydie Willem for her special help on dance in Europe; Carol Brown and Ralph Buck for their advice on the current situation in Australia and New Zealand; Michael Martin at Trent Park library for his patience with my requests. I also thank Middlesex University for allowing me to take research leave, and my friends and colleagues in the Dance department who shared my work in my absence. Finally, my gratitude to Albert and Joan Appleby for all their invaluable help with proof reading, and to Simon Dorling for his perceptive comments and critical questioning during the selection and writing process.

I am grateful to all the contributors to this volume who allowed their work to be abridged and who gave their support, goodwill and encouragement to the venture.

Most of the essays in this collection have been abridged. Readers who wish to pursue a topic in more depth might consult the original version where, in many cases, endnotes can be found which offer a guide to further bibliographic material.

Permission given by the following authors and copyright holders is gratefully acknowledged:

Joan Acocella, 'Mark Morris: the body and what it means' excerpted and revised from *Mark Morris* (New York: Farrar Straus Giroux 1993) © 1993 Joan Acocella. Reprinted by permission of Farrar, Straus & Giroux Inc.

Janet Adshead (now Lansdale), 'An introduction to dance analysis' abridged from *Dance Analysis: Theory and Practice* ed. Janet Adshead (London: Dance Books 1988) © 1988 Janet Adshead, Valerie A. Briginshaw, Pauline Hodgens and Michael Huxley

Theresa Buckland, 'Dance and music video' abridged from *Parallel Lines: Media Representations of Dance* ed. Stephanie Jordan and Dave Allen (London: John Libbey 1993) © 1993 John Libbey

ACKNOWLEDGEMENTS

Ramsay Burt, 'Nijinsky: modernism and heterodox representations of masculinity' abridged from *The Male Dancer: Bodies, Spectacle, Sexuality* (London: Routledge 1995) © 1995 Ramsay Burt

Roger Copeland, 'Between description and deconstruction' © 1997 Roger Copeland. Portions of this essay appeared in *Dance Theatre Journal* 10: 3 (1993)

Arlene Croce, 'Oh, that pineapple rag!' from *The New Yorker* 12 October (1981) © 1981 Arlene Croce

Merce Cunningham, 'Torse' abridged from *The Dancer and the Dance: Merce Cunningham in conversation with Jacqueline Lesschaeve*, Jacqueline Lesschaeve (London: Marion Boyars 1985) © 1985 Marion Boyars

Elizabeth Dempster, 'Women writing the body: let's watch a little how she dances' abridged from *Grafts: Feminist Cultural Criticism* ed. Susan Sheridan (London: Verso 1988) © 1988 Elizabeth Dempster

Jane Desmond, 'Embodying difference: issues in dance and cultural studies' abridged from *Cultural Critique* 26 (Oxford University Press 1993–4) © 1993 Oxford University Press

Richard Dyer, analysis of 'Dancing in the Dark' abridged from 'I seem to find the happiness I seek' in *Dance, Gender and Culture* ed. Helen Thomas (Basingstoke: Macmillan Press 1993). Reprinted with permission of St Martin's Press Inc. and Macmillan Press Ltd. © 1993 Macmillan Press

Annabel Farjeon, 'Choreographers: dancing for de Valois and Ashton' from *Dance Chronicle* 17: 2 (New York: Marcel Dekker Inc. 1994) © 1994 Annabel Farjeon

Susan Foster, 'Choreographing history' abridged from *Choreographing History* (Bloomington: Indiana University Press 1995) © 1995 Indiana University Press

Sondra Fraleigh, 'A vulnerable glance: seeing dance through phenomenology' abridged from *Dance Research Journal* 23: 1 (1991) © 1991 Sondra Fraleigh

Lynn Garafola, 'Diaghilev's cultivated audience' abridged from Chapter 10 'Paris: the cultivated audience', *Diaghilev's Ballets Russes* (New York: Oxford University Press 1989) © 1989 Lynn Garafola

Martha Graham, 'I am a dancer' abridged from *Blood Memory* (New York: Doubleday 1991). Used by permission of Doubleday, a division of Bantam Doubleday Dell Pub. Group Inc. © 1991 Martha Graham Estate

Andrée Grau, 'Myths of origin' abridged from *Dance Now* 2: 4 (Winter 1993–4) © 1993 Andrée Grau

ACKNOWLEDGEMENTS

Rebecca Hilton with Bryan Smith, 'A dancing consciousness' abridged from 'Knowledges/Practices', *Writings on Dance* 10 (Autumn 1994) © 1994 *Writings on Dance* and Bryan Smith

Shobana Jeyasingh, 'Imaginary homelands: creating a new dance language' from *Border Tensions: Dance and Discourse*, Proceedings of the Fifth Study of Dance Conference (Guildford: University of Surrey 1995) © 1995 Shobana Jeyasingh

Stephanie Jordan and Helen Thomas, 'Dance and gender: formalism and semiotics reconsidered' abridged from *Dance Research* XII: 2 (1994) © 1994 Stephanie Jordan and Helen Thomas

Deborah Jowitt, 'In pursuit of the sylph: ballet in the Romantic period' abridged from *Time and the Dancing Image* (New York: William Morrow 1981). By permission of William Morrow & Co. Inc. © 1981 Deborah Jowitt

Susan Kozel, 'Spacemaking: experiences of a virtual body' abridged from *Dance Theatre Journal* 11, 3 (1994) © 1994 Susan Kozel and *Dance Theatre Journal*, published by Laban Centre for Movement and Dance, London

June Layson, 'Dance history source materials' abridged from *Dance History: an Introduction* eds Janet Adshead-Lansdale and June Layson (London: Routledge 1994) © 1983, 1994 June Layson

Alastair Macaulay, 'Spring: Ashton's *Symphonic Variations* in America' abridged from 'Spring', *The New Yorker* 25 May (1992) © 1992 Alastair Macaulay

Jacqui Malone, 'Keep to the rhythm and you'll keep to life: meaning and style in African American Vernacular Dance' abridged from *Steppin' on the Blues: the Visible Rhythms of African American Dance* (Urbana: University of Illinois Press 1996). Used with the permission of the author and the University of Illinois Press © 1996 Board of Trustees of the University of Illinois

Susan Manning, 'Dances of death: Germany before Hitler' abridged from *Ecstasy and the Demon: Feminism and Nationalism in the Dances of Mary Wigman* (Berkeley: University of California Press 1993) © 1994 The Regents of the University of California

John Mueller, analysis of 'Dancing in the Dark' abridged from *Astaire Dancing: the Musical Films* (London: Hamish Hamilton 1986). Reprinted by permission of Alfred A. Knopf Inc. and Penguin Books Ltd. © John Mueller

Barbara Newman, 'Dancers talking about performance' extracted from *Striking a Balance: Dancers Talk about Dancing* (New York: Limelight Editions 1992) © 1982, 1992 Barbara Newman

ACKNOWLEDGEMENTS

Ted Polhemus, 'Dance, gender and culture' abridged from *Dance, Gender and Culture* ed. Helen Thomas (Basingstoke: Macmillan Press 1993). Reprinted with permission of St Martin's Press Inc. and Macmillan Press Ltd. © 1993 Macmillan Press

Betty Redfern, 'What is art?' abridged from *Dance, Art and Aesthetics* (London: Dance Books Ltd 1983) ©1983 Betty Redfern

Norbert Servos, 'Pina Bausch: dance and emancipation' abridged from *Pina Bausch: Wuppertal Dance Theatre or The Art of Training a Goldfish* (Cologne: Ballett-Bühnen-Verlag 1984) © 1984 Norbert Servos

Marcia Siegel, 'Bridging the critical distance' abridged and amended from *Looking Out: Perspectives on Dance and Criticism in a Multicultural World* ed. David Gere, co-ed. by Lewis Segal, Patrice Clark Koelsch and Elizabeth Zimmer (New York: Schirmer Books 1995) © 1995 Marcia Siegel

CONTRIBUTORS

Joan Acocella, author of *Mark Morris* and editor of *André Levinson on Dance*, is the dance critic of *The Wall Street Journal*. She also writes for *The New Yorker* and *The New York Review of Books*. She is currently editing the English edition of the unexpurgated diaries of Vaslav Nijinsky.

Theresa Jill Buckland is Head of the Department of Dance Studies, University of Surrey. She lectures and researches in the fields of dance anthropology, ethnochoreology and dance as popular culture and has published a number of articles in international dance and music journals.

Ramsay Burt wrote his doctoral thesis on representations of masculinity in dance, and this formed the basis for his first book *The Male Dancer: Bodies, Spectacle, Sexualities*. This was followed by *Alien Bodies: Representations of Modernity, 'Race' and Nation in Early Modern Dance* (1998). He is currently Senior Research Fellow in Dance at De Montfort University.

Alexandra Carter is Principal Lecturer in Dance at Middlesex University. Her teaching and research interests in feminist theory, history and dance analysis were combined in her PhD thesis on representation, hegemony and ballet in the British music hall. She has published regularly in dance and performing arts journals.

Roger Copeland is Professor of Theatre and Dance at Oberlin College. He has published well over one hundred articles about dance, theatre and film in a wide variety of journals. His books include *What Is Dance?* and the forthcoming *Cunningham's Legacy: The Repudiation of Primitivism in Modern Dance*.

Arlene Croce has been the dance critic of *The New Yorker* since 1973. Before that, she was the founding editor of *Ballet Review*. She has published *The Fred Astaire and Ginger Rogers Book* (1972) and three collections of critical essays: *Afterimages* (1977), *Going to the Dance* (1982) and *Sight Lines* (1987).

Merce Cunningham danced with Martha Graham's company from 1939–45 during which time he created many important roles, before establishing his own company in 1953. In creative partnership with John Cage, Cunningham is renowned for his radical questioning of what constitutes dances' processes, subject matter, structures and vocabulary. Renowned for working with chance processes, video and, more recently, computer programs, his influence on succeeding generations of dance makers is undeniable.

Elizabeth Dempster is a Senior Lecturer in Performance Studies at Victoria University, Melbourne. She is the founding and continuing co-editor of the journal *Writings on Dance*.

Jane Desmond, a former dancer and choreographer, is currently Associate Professor of American Studies and Women's Studies at the University of Iowa, where she also co-directs the International Forum for US Studies. She is editor of *Meaning in Motion: New Cultural Studies of Dance* (1997) and author of the forthcoming *Physical Evidence: Bodies/Identity/ Performance*.

Richard Dyer teaches Film Studies at the University of Warwick. He is the author of *Stars*; *Heavenly Bodies*; *Now You See It*; *Only Entertainment*; *The Matter of Images* and *White*.

Annabel Farjeon joined Sadler's Wells Ballet School at the age of twelve in 1931. She danced with the Company between 1933–41 during which time she started her first novel. For over twenty-five years she was ballet critic for the *New Statesman* and the *Evening Standard* and has published a biography, novels and children's stories.

Susan Leigh Foster, choreographer and scholar, is the author of *Reading Dancing: Bodies and Subjects in Contemporary American Dance* and *Choreography and Narrative: Ballet's Staging of Story and Desire* and editor of *Choreographing History* and *Corporealities*. She is Professor of Dance at University of California, Riverside.

Sondra Fraleigh chairs the Department of Dance at the State University of New York at Brockport. She is author of *Dance and the Lived Body* and numerous other articles; her book *Dancing into Darkness: Butoh, Zen and Japan* is in press. She directs the Core*Star Institute for Somatic Studies.

Lynn Garafola is the author of *Diaghilev's Ballets Russes*, editor/translator of *Petipa's Diaries*, and co-editor of *André Levinson on Dance: Writings from Paris in the Twenties*. She writes regularly for several journals, edits the Wesleyan University Press series *Studies in Dance History* and is currently preparing two new books on dance history.

Martha Graham studied and performed with Denishawn from 1916–23 before establishing herself first as a solo performer, then with her own company. Although she continued to choreograph after retiring as a performer in 1969, it is her early repertoire of expressionist psycho-dramas which is now seen as the most significant in terms of their choreographic innovation and historical influence. Graham's technique, now evolved, has formed the basis of the training of dancers in succeeding generations the world over.

Andrée Grau is a Benesh choreologist and anthropologist whose fieldwork includes working among the Venda (South Africa) and the Tiwi (Northern Australia). She is a Senior Research Fellow in Dance at Roehampton Institute and lecturers at Richmond, the American International University in London.

Rebecca Hilton is an Australian dancer, teacher and choreographer based in New York City. She was in the Stephen Petronio Company from 1988–95 and has performed in the work of numerous choreographers including Russell Dumas, Michael Clark and Lucy Guerin. Rebecca has taught and presented her own work in both hemispheres.

Shobana Jeyasingh, choreographer, directs the Shobana Jeyasingh Dance Company, which has received several major awards, including the prestigious Prudential Award for the Arts. Shobana has also worked for theatre and television. She was awarded an MBE, and holds an Honorary Doctorate from De Montfort University and an Honorary Masters from the University of Surrey.

Stephanie Jordan is Professor of Dance Studies at Roehampton Institute, London. Her books include *Striding Out: Aspects of Contemporary and New Dance in Britain* and *Parallel Lines: Media Representations of Dance* (co-edited with Dave Allen). She is currently writing a book on music and ballet, supported by a research grant from the Radcliffe Trust.

Deborah Jowitt has been principal dance critic for *The Village Voice* since 1967. She has published two collections: *Dance Beat* (1977) and *The Dance in Mind* (1985). Her *Time and the Dancing Image* won the de la Torre Bueno Prize in 1989. She is on the faculty of New York University's Tisch School of the Arts.

Susan Kozel uses choreography and writing to explore the impact of new technologies on dancing bodies. She has a PhD in philosophy and lectures for the Department of Dance Studies, University of Surrey. Publications for which she has written include *Dance Theatre Journal*, *Dance Research Journal* and *Performance Research*.

Janet Lansdale (formerly Adshead) is Professor and Head of the School of Performing Arts at the University of Surrey. Her publications include *The Study of Dance* (1981) and *Dance Analysis: Theory and Practice* (1988).

Current research interests lie in theorizing interpretative strategies in dance in relation to post-structuralist thinking.

June Layson retired from the University of Surrey where she established and led the first Department of Dance Studies in a British University. Her research interests are in early twentieth century British Modern Dance and dance history methodology. She has recently been honoured with the title Emeritus Professor.

Alastair Macaulay is chief theatre critic of the *Financial Times*, for which he also reviews dance and music, and is chief examiner in dance history for the Imperial Society of Teachers of Dancing. He was founding editor of *Dance Theatre Journal* in 1983 and was guest dance critic to *The New Yorker* in 1988 and 1992.

Jacqui Malone is an associate professor of drama, theatre and dance at Queens College, Flushing, New York, and a former member of the Eleo Pomare Dance Company. She has been a fellow of the John Simon Guggenheim Foundation, the Ford Foundation, and the Schomburg Centre for Research in Black Culture.

Susan Manning is an Associate Professor of English and Theatre and an affiliate of the Interdisciplinary PhD Programme in Theatre and Drama at Northwestern University in Evanston, Illinois. Her book, *Ecstasy and the Demon: Feminism and Nationalism in the Dances of Mary Wigman* won the 1994 de la Torre Bueno Prize.

John Mueller is professor of Film Studies and Political Science at the University of Rochester, New York. He has published extensively on dance, film and political science and produced twelve films. His book *Astaire Dancing: the Musical Films* (1985) won the de la Torre Bueno prize.

Barbara Newman is dance critic for *Country Life* magazine and covers all forms of musical theatre for *The Dancing Times*. She is the author of six books about ballet, including *The Illustrated Book of Ballet Stories* for children, published by Dorling Kindersley, and contributes regularly to international periodicals and reference works.

Ted Polhemus is a pop culturalist specializing in nonverbal communication and the expressive possibilities and meaning of the human body. His recent books include *Streetstyle*, *Style Surfing* and *The Customised Body*, and work in progress includes a book on contemporary dance.

Yvonne Rainer took dance classes with Martha Graham among others before engaging with the practitioners and principles of postmodernism during the early 1960s. As a reaction against the mythic spectacle of early modern dance, Rainer rejected all extraneous elements of dance in performance. Her philosophy was exemplified in her famous 'No' manifesto (included here) and her signature work, *Trio A* (1966).

Betty Redfern, after teaching in various schools and colleges, went on to study philosophy and became a freelance lecturer and writer. She obtained her doctorate in the field of aesthetics at Manchester University. Her published work includes *Dance, Art and Aesthetics* and *Questions in Aesthetic Education*.

Norbert Servos works as a freelance writer, choreographer and guest teacher in Berlin. He has published several books on Pina Bausch and modern poetry and since 1983 has created about ten choreographies in Germany and abroad. He is currently artistic director of Tanzlabor Berlin (DanceLab) at the Academy of Arts.

Marcia Siegel is the author of *The Shapes of Change: Images of American Dance, Days on Earth: the Dance of Doris Humphrey*, and three collections of dance writings. She is an internationally known teacher, lecturer and dance critic.

Helen Thomas is Head of Sociology at Goldsmiths College, University of London. She wrote *Dance, Modernity and Culture* and edited *Dance, Gender and Culture* and *Dance in the City*. Currently she is working on another book, *The Body, Dance and Cultural Theory* and a jointly-authored text *Culture, Representation and Difference*.

1

GENERAL INTRODUCTION

Alexandra Carter

The writings on dance collected in this book demonstrate the range and depth of late twentieth-century scholarship and show that dance can now fully claim its status as a culturally significant and intellectually viable field for study. In one sense, of course, dance has been 'studied' throughout the ages and in most cultures. In modern Western history, for example, in the courts of Tudor England and the European Renaissance, skill at dancing was a vital attribute and dancing masters formally disseminated the steps, patterns and essential social and performance etiquette. Dance was not only practised but also studied from various perspectives such as its social function; its anatomical basis; its educational value; the problems and potential of its aesthetics and the theoretical basis of its performance technique.[1] This theoretical tradition was sporadic, however, and by the end of the nineteenth century the Victorian moral backlash against dancing prohibited the development of a solid body of serious literature.

Other factors which contribute to the lack of a substantial heritage of dance study have been well rehearsed (Sparshott 1988). These include its very nature as an activity of body rather than mind and the Western dualism which privileges the cognitive over the corporeal; its population of predominantly women performers and resultant low status; the dubious moral character of any practice which not only involves women but also focuses specifically on their bodies; the lack of a substantial and stable canon throughout its theatrical history and, perhaps most significantly, the very ephemerality of the dance in performance.[2] Unlike music or drama, there is no score or script which can be revisited except for notation, the writing/reading of which is still a specialist skill. Two key inter-related concerns in the study of dance have been the search for ways in which the event can be recorded, and the nature of the translation between a physical and sensory activity and the written, aural or graphic form:

> One of the problems which has preoccupied certain dance scholars is the difficulty of determining or fixing in place the object of study. For dance practitioners, dance completes itself in the moment of its

1

disappearance, that is, in performance, and yet it is the nonreproduc-
ibility, the *tracelessness* of performance, which has been regarded as
the greatest impediment to its acceptance as a credible object of
research.

(Dempster 1994: 3)

The low social status of dance, the equation of its sensual nature with its
sexual potential and the difficulties of studying such a transient event have
all contributed to the lack of a substantial or seriously considered scholarly
heritage. Even today, when the study of dance has advanced considerably,
many people still find it difficult to comprehend how it is possible to 'study'
dance at all, especially in the elevated context of university or college education. The learning of technical skills is understandable though their relevance in a degree context less so; that the history of dance can be explored
seems reasonable but hardly substantial; that choreography has a craft that
can not only be implemented in practice but also studied in theory comes as
a surprise but is just within the realms of public comprehension. That
dance can be approached from many analytical perspectives, including
those of gender and semiotics; within anthropological, philosophical,
psychoanalytical and sociological frameworks; be explored for the potency
of its cultural significance; embrace a diversity of forms and functions and
deploy increasingly sophisticated resources, is almost beyond belief. Dance
still has a struggle for acceptance, in both common-sense perception of its
value and within formal institutional structures. Nevertheless, the twentieth
century has seen a vast growth in its popularity as leisure activity and theatrical art form, and modern technology has greatly increased the quality,
quantity and accessibility of resources. Dance scholarship has grown in
partnership.

Due to the tardy acceptance of dance by the academy and the initial
emphasis on the practice, rather than the theory, dance owes much of its
scholarly heritage to those writing outside of a formal institutional context.
As Cohen (Au and Peter 1989) notes, in the United States serious enthusiasts such as Kirstein on ballet, and Martin on modern dance turned their
advocacy into print. *Dance Magazine* first appeared in 1927 and in 1936,
Magriel published a bibliography of dancing.[3] In these early years of dance
study, 'the methodologies that were initially required came from other disciplines but only later began to be evolved from the nature of dance itself'
(Cohen in Au and Peter 1989: 276). This is an interesting observation in the
light of current interdisciplinary developments (see below). Societies were
established to promote research in dance, such as the American Congress on
Research in Dance in 1967 and the Society of Dance History Scholars in
1978. Each holds regular meetings and major conferences, and publishes the
proceedings of conferences, monographs and/or a journal. These organizations offer a regular forum for discussion and publication, and bring

together scholars, critics and researchers who work independently or in colleges and universities.

In Britain, writing on dance in the twentieth century was also initiated by individual enthusiasts such as Cecil Sharp who documented folk dance and in so doing was responsible for a resurgence of its popularity in education during the early part of the century. Currently, journals such as *Dance Studies*, the *Journal of the English Folk Dance and Song Society* and *Historical Dance* are among the serious repositories for research in folk and historical dance. In theatre dance, the London performances of the Ballets Russes from 1911 onwards gave rise to a new breed, the British amateur historian. With accounts often based on personal experience placed within an historical overview, these balletomanes shaped writing on British ballet from the 1930s to the 1950s.[4]

The establishment of the Society for Dance Research in 1982 and the publication of its journal *Dance Research* the following year, offered opportunities for independent scholars, as well as those aligned to educational institutions, to disseminate their work. Nevertheless, the study of dance in Britain has tended to be fragmented between those whose interests cohere around particular genres and functions such as theatre, social or historical dance. The development of a community of scholars is still an ideal rather than a reality.

There is a considerable amount of activity undertaken by independent researchers and those not working in dance departments of higher education. Furthermore, the notion of what constitutes the study of dance in professional training and the training of teachers for vocational work has broadened during the last decade, with a resultant expansion of curricula.[5] It is useful, however, to trace the changing nature and expansion of dance study throughout the twentieth century via its development in formal educational contexts. The United States and Britain form the focus of this brief historical overview; this is followed by a summary of the current situation in dance scholarship in mainland Europe, Australia and New Zealand.[6]

An exercise of the mind? Dance in education in the twentieth century

Is the subject suitable for Education? Is it an exercise of the mind? Is it not better left till Education is completed? Is it not sufficiently attractive to ensure a voluntary attention to it? Is it a convenient subject for Examination?

(cited in Marwick 1989: 55)

These questions, asked of the now respectable (if troubled) discipline of history when it was struggling to achieve academic status in the mid-nineteenth century, have also been asked of dance throughout its twentieth-century passage to academic credibility. In all disciplines, serious research grows on a bedrock of a comprehensive scholarly education. For dance, that bedrock has had a fractured and unstable history.

In the United States and Britain, dance found a home during the early part of the century within physical education, where it could be disguised as a form of exercise and made morally and educationally acceptable. It has a longer history in the United States; as Kraus notes, 'by the beginning years of the twentieth century, dance had become widely adopted in schools and colleges [. . .] With the exception of a few finishing schools or girls' academies or colleges where it might be taught essentially as a social grace, it was viewed primarily as a form of physical education' (Kraus 1969: 129).

During the early years of the century in the United States, the direct influence of, among others, François Delsarte and the indirect influence of Isadora Duncan introduced a more artistic and expressive element to the curriculum. Dance was offered to students as part of teacher training programmes in physical education, though as early as 1926, a key development was the establishment of a degree at the University of Wisconsin which offered dance as a Major in its own right. Although folk, clog and tap were taught in schools and colleges, they were superseded by forms which offered an outlet for the creative potential of the individual.[7] From the 1940s onwards, when these forms of 'creative dance', which lacked an artistic framework and systematic technical base, met the expanding professional world of modern dance which was needy of venues and audiences for its experimental work, the character of dance in education changed. In the United States, the influence of modern dance on forms of 'educational' dance gave rise to questions that were later rehearsed in Britain in the 1970s: what was the relationship between the 'educational' and the 'professional' models of dance? Did they share a body of knowledge, and what was the educational rationale for including modern dance in the curriculum?

By 1966, two surveys, although partial, indicated that just when British educators were being introduced to modern dance via the transformed Ballet Rambert and the newly established London Contemporary Dance Theatre, the opportunities for studying dance through to PhD level were already well advanced in the United States.[8] While dance scholarship should not, of course, be conflated solely with the professional world of theatre dance, the expansion of dance as a discipline in the academy has been largely contingent on the growing acceptance and popularity of modern (or, as known in Britain, 'contemporary') dance as a theatre art form.

As in the United States, in Britain it was the women's physical education colleges which disseminated dance in education through the training of teachers. In the context of physical education curricula, early forms embraced social, national and folk dancing as well as exercises and gymnastics with a more aesthetic element. From the 1920s, Duncan-inspired 'natural' movement offered a slightly more creative approach, but the most significant influence on dance in British education came from the modern dance of Central Europe. Laban's text on *Modern Educational Dance* (1948) provided not only a rationale for dance in the (mainly school) curriculum but also a systematic approach to its study. In practice, however, the distinction between 'dance' and 'movement' education was unclear, and the reliance on the individual's spontaneity and natural aptitudes undermined any notion that skills might be acquired through learning. Modern Educational Dance, therefore, provided a systematic basis for the curriculum both in schools and for teacher training, but it left those teachers with a sense that a dance education was almost solely about 'doing' and 'experience'. They were, therefore, wary of imposing too much in the way of technical or compositional craft and a dance lesson was not a dance lesson unless everyone had their socks off.[9] Such a characterization is not meant to do a disservice to Laban's work, for often the problem was in its interpretation, but it does demonstrate the unstable and confusing nature and status of dance study during the middle decades of the century.

From the 1960s, three inter-related developments contributed to the changing nature of dance in education in Britain. First, a questioning by philosophers such as Redfern (1973) of the concepts at the very heart of modern educational dance, including the confusion between self-expression and artistic expression. Second, the import of modern dance from America which re-established the connection between dance in schools and colleges, and dance in the theatre. Third, the introduction of Bachelor of Education degree courses from the late 1960s which necessitated, for their validation, the identification of a theoretical framework and theoretical aspects of study. Degree courses began to be established which offered dance not solely for teacher training but as part of creative or performing arts curricula.[10] The study of dance had to be reasoned and articulated not only in order to compare and compete with other disciplines in academia, but also so that teachers in all educational sectors could justify its existence on the curriculum. Since then, the inclusion of dance in the National Curriculum (ironically, within physical education), national examinations at secondary school level, and a wide range of opportunities to study dance for a first degree, all provide the potential for a series of albeit intermittent steps towards advanced dance scholarship. Though precarious in its funding (but here dance is not alone), such scholarship thrives in Britain today.

A survey of dance in higher education in mainland Europe (Adshead-Lansdale 1994a) reveals the sparse institutional provision for its systematic study.[11] Opportunities do exist in what could generally be termed the private sector, but these tend to be of a vocational nature; that is, training for careers as professional dancers or teachers. With a tradition rooted in rationalist philosophy, university programmes favour the sciences; the arts, apart from literature, tend to be small departments. Degree courses are rare in which dance is a sole or major component, either at undergraduate or postgraduate level. In Italy, for example, there are no degree level courses but a doctoral thesis can be submitted under the umbrella of another subject. In Germany, as in other European countries, dance can be found within theatre studies. In Greece, it is offered within BA courses in American colleges. Although many European countries have a healthy tradition of theatre dance practice, the survey concludes that there is still a significant split between dance education in a professional context and in universities. (There are, however, some collaborative ventures. For example, the University of Utrecht has collaborated with a dance academy in Rotterdam in the provision of a new course in choreography.) Nevertheless, there is a battle to be won in mainland Europe in order to demonstrate that dance can take its place within the university system. Without such a sub-structure, opportunities for research and the overall development of dance studies are sporadic. There are, of course, exceptions, and individual dance scholars, institutionally aligned or otherwise, make an important contribution to the development of the field. Reflecting its empiricist/physical education tradition, the research emphasis tends to be on bio-mechanical and/or psychological aspects of dance, with some work in theatre studies. Each European country has, to a greater or lesser extent, its own opportunities, organizations and specialist collections of resources but there are trans-European bodies such as the *Association Européenne des Historiens de la Danse* (European Association of Dance Historians) based in Paris, which holds conferences and study days. ELIA (European League of Institutes of the Arts) attempts to facilitate contact across the Community; there are occasional conferences, a newsletter and other publications, and the organization acts as a lobby group for dance in the European Community.

In Australia, the establishment of the Australian Association for Dance Education (now Ausdance Inc., the Australian Dance Council) in 1977 marked a key point in the recognition of dance as an important element of educational and cultural activity. Dance is now fairly well established at tertiary level and each state has its own university dance degree programmes, all of which exist within performing arts (rather than physical education) departments. Opportunities to study within a formal institutionalized system are catalogued in the Ausdance/Tertiary Dance Council of the Australian publication, *Further Studies in Dance*.[12] The growth of dance in the tertiary sector in Australia is evidenced by a large student demand for courses. However, current cutbacks in Federal University funding are having a big impact on all arts courses and at least one dance programme (in Adelaide) has had to close.

Opportunities for the study of dance *per se* to higher level are developing, with three institutions offering research degrees.[13] The research community in Australia appears healthy, embracing a wide range of interests. Forums for the presentation of practical and theoretical scholarship are offered by, for example, the Green Mill Project, which organizes annual conferences on specific themes. Latterly, these have drawn a broader international delegation, thus demonstrating that Australia is an increasingly fertile home for the dissemination of dance research. In addition to the popular magazine *Dance Australia*, there is a quarterly publication, *Writings on Dance*. This journal encourages research-based articles, but the interpretation of research is broad and often arises from the perspectives and practices of dancers and choreographers, as well as more conventional 'academic' sources.

In New Zealand, there has been no solid infrastructure for dance practitioners and scholars, though with the establishment of DANZ (Dance Aotearoa New Zealand Ltd) in the mid-1990s opportunities are now more readily available for networking via conferences and a journal (also called DANZ). Amongst the limited opportunities for dance study are programmes offered by, for example, the New Zealand School of Dance which offers training for performance and/or educating teachers in the ballet genre. The only opportunity to study contemporary dance within an institutional context is currently at Unitec in Auckland which plans to offer dance within a three-year degree programme of Performing and Screen Arts. To date, there are no Masters' programmes in dance as a single subject, though the University of Auckland offers a post-graduate diploma which embraces theoretical and practical courses. Opportunities for research are limited and can generally be found within the context of physical or general education programmes, such as those offered by the University of Otago. There are, of course, active independent scholars, and choreographers who undertake text-based research to inform their practical work are a vital part of the research community.

Whether as training for performance or as an embodiment of a philosophy of education, the development of the 'scholarly bedrock' of dance has been problematic and varied in its pace of development. Historically, it has been identified as a form of physical training which had the potential to develop good posture, graceful carriage and a healthy body. The rationale for creative dance, or 'educational' dance, reflected the 'child-centred' approach of the 1940s to the 1960s. It has now come to be valued as a discrete body of knowledge within an arts curriculum and, more recently, as a phenomenon worthy of study for its contribution to, and embodiment of cultural belief and value systems. Its focus remains on practice in the primary/elementary and secondary sectors, while undergraduate programmes tend, increasingly, to embrace a range of theoretical as well as practical concerns. During their studies, students are not only familiarized with the increasingly wide body of literature and visual sources, but are equipped with procedures and methodologies in order to undertake their own research. Not surprisingly, it is at graduate and doctoral level, when specialisms cohere, that the impetus for the advancement of dance study has been located. External factors such as the need for tenure in the United States and the Research Assessment Exercise in Britain have spawned a flurry of research activity and publications from academics.[14] Although, for the public at large, the very notion that dance can be studied without dancing is still received with perplexity, theorists, critics and scholars fought long and hard to establish dance as a discipline. Having done so, the nature of that disciplinary status is now in question – not from the outside world, but from within dance itself.

Dance as a discipline

The conceptual basis of dance as a discipline can be traced through its pedagogic literature. From the 1940s to the 1970s, the use of the term 'movement' caused slippage in just what constituted the area of activity and its very vagueness undermined aesthetic and artistic considerations.[15] My own studies at undergraduate level in 1970s Britain exemplified a period of transition; staff were attempting to broaden the perspectives we brought to bear on dance and make links with the professional world, yet there was little connection between the modern dance we studied as a theatre art form and the modern educational dance we were learning in order to work in schools. Furthermore, the literature placed our studies in an historical and aesthetic vacuum. It was rare to find research which located dance in its cultural context, except some key anthropological texts which seemed to bear little relationship to any world we knew.[16] There was barely any literature which explored the hegemonic role of dance in our own society. Even the application of aesthetic concepts to dance works was ultimately frustrating because of the almost complete lack of attention to dance in the philosophy of art. While this resulted in a broader education in aesthetics which, on reflection, was extremely valuable, I was suspicious about the uncritical transfer of concepts from one art form to another. Specialist texts on the history of dance were more plentiful but tended to be descriptive and, as noted above, were thoroughly researched but placed dance in a cultural vacuum. As in philosophical texts, general history books ignored the existence of dance, no matter how popular it was in practice or how significant within the web of social customs. A limited number of videos were available and we spent many happy hours in front of the screen, discussing our perceptions in a rather random way. These classes were wonderful, but unstructured, for we had no analytical skills with which to develop our debate. Furthermore, if there was a dislocation between the 'modern' dance of our technique and composition classes and the 'educational' dance of our pedagogic work, yet another disparity was introduced in dance appreciation sessions. The visual sources for these tended to draw upon the ballet world, as only a very limited number of modern dance works were available on video.

8

I characterize my own experience as an example of what constituted the study of dance during the 1970s, as reflected in the curriculum and the amount and nature of the sources available. The invisibility or marginalization of dance in all kinds of general texts and the paucity of its own literature were acknowledged by those teaching and learning in higher education but the prospect of dance ever having a solid identity and a wealth of sources of its own, let alone being acknowledged in other disciplinary fields, seemed remote indeed. No matter how deep our commitment, the notion of what we were studying, how we were studying it and what we were doing it for was vague indeed.

Throughout the 1970s and into the 1980s, the conceptual basis of dance study began to change. As mentioned above, debate in philosophy and developments in the theatre moved studies in secondary schools and teacher training away from modern educational dance and into modern dance. The development of degree courses which were not training teachers, and the changing nature of school examinations in dance, necessitated a clear rationale for its disciplinary status.[17] Although having moved from a 'process' base, the 'product' influenced curriculum, in terms of a 'hard', usually Graham-derived technique, seemed limiting and unsatisfactory. Debate continued about the relationship between the theatrical, social and educational worlds of dance and the nature of what constituted the study of dance. A model began to evolve, in accordance with developments in other arts curricula, which identified three inter-related concepts which were central to the study of dance. These cohered around the activities of dancing, making dances and appreciating dances.[18] Performance, choreography and appreciation, although not always expressed in such terms, became the core concepts and basis for its claim to disciplinary status.[19]

The newly articulated disciplinary model for dance required resources and the knowledge of how to use them. In the United States, the New York Public Library had an extensive dance collection. In Britain, organizations such as the National Resource Centre for Dance at the University of Surrey were established in order to catalogue, produce and disseminate resources. Professional companies began to develop their educational work and produce literature and videos. Dance on television and commercial videos expanded the accessibility of professional dance and, most importantly, offered the opportunity for repeated access to works.

While academia was attending to its own rationale, a dance explosion was taking place in the outside world. The popularity of many forms of dance grew in different contexts: in the theatre; in clubs and social gatherings; on the streets and in the media. The world of dance always had, of course, been wider than its formal scholarship, but that wider world began to infiltrate curricula and the interests of scholars. The notion not only of what constituted the study of dance but also the appropriate methodologies for that study began to be questioned. Most fundamentally, new ways of conceiving the very nature of knowledge itself had their impact. If the development of dance internationally has always been more sporadic than the previous overview suggests, from the mid- to late-1980s dance scholars deliberately rocked their own disciplinary boat, had it manoeuvred by others, steered it off course and found new worlds for exploration.

Disciplines, discourses and recent developments in the study of dance

In 1995, two conferences were held, one in Guildford, England and one in Montreal, Canada, with shortened titles of 'Border Tensions' and 'Border Crossings'.[20] Such accidental but convergent transatlantic nomenclature reflects one of the most significant current trends in the study of dance: that borders are being crossed not only in what constitutes dance, and therefore its study, but also what strategies can be employed and from what perspectives that study can be approached.

As suggested above, if dance in society has always been more varied and complex than its scholarship has addressed, recent years have seen a foregrounding of the many forms and functions of dance. The reconceptualization of the nature of knowledge itself has also expanded our 'knowledge' of dance. Postmodern perspectives resulted in claims that the formation of disciplinary boundaries are not only unnatural but contribute to the controlling and constraining meta-narratives of what counts as 'knowledge'. New historiography, sociology and cultural studies expanded the targets of scholarly attention, claiming the broad span of culture as not only legitimate but essential for any understanding of human society. Studies in the arts were 'moving away from art historical and literary discussions of style and of internal characteristics of works of art [attempting] to interpret the meanings of these works in terms of the social and ideological categories represented in them' (Wolff in Leppart and McClary 1987: 8).

Feminist studies made a major contribution to the debate on how knowledge is formed and controlled, exploring the construction and hegemonic functions of gender. Linguistic theories subverted the traditional relationship between the world, language and the users of language in the production of meaning, and a similar relationship between text, meaning and recipient of the text was reconfigured in literary theory. Furthermore, poststructuralism looked not just to language but to other signs and signifiers as carriers of meaning. Of these, attention to the body has created opportunity for the conception of dance as discourse. As Thomas claims,

> poststructuralism, postmodernism and feminism have instigated their respective attacks on the human subject [. . .] they have revealed the centrality of the body as a site of discourse and of social control. They have elucidated how bodies have been objectified and

subjectified through a range of discourses [and therefore] have contributed further to the possibility of dance being afforded a more substantial cultural voice.

(Thomas 1995: 20)

These ways of thinking about the world and the cultural phenomena it comprises have infiltrated the study of dance. All theoretical approaches have their particular debates and, however loose, their own parameters, but 'what they share is the belief that all artifacts and processes of life, including the arts, are embedded in culture. Scholarship, then, becomes a search for the meanings of culture and, in some cases, a critique of cultural values and trends' (Daly 1991a: 50).

As Daly stresses, not all scholarship is critique and some intentionally not so (see, for example, Ralph 1995 and Sparti 1996). She cites recent works which exemplify this broadened perspective from which dance is viewed and which use cultural or critical theories to inform debate. Among these are Foster (1986) on semiotic approaches to analysis; Jowitt (1988) and Garafola (1989) on contextualizing dance history and Novack (1990) on broadening the subject matter of anthropology. To this list can be added examples of British scholarship such as Adair (1992), Burt (1995) and the contributors to Thomas (1993) who have broadened the field of gender studies, and Thomas (1995) who turns her sociological perspective to dance.[21] Although dance studies have appropriated other epistemological modes of enquiry, the traffic has tended to be one-way. Some scholars with other backgrounds have come to dance but the area still tends to be ignored, even though it has the potential to contribute so much substance to their debate.[22]

Despite the expansion in resources (an expansion only relative, however, for written sources on dance still command less shelf space in libraries and bookshops than literature on, for example, the other performing arts), these are still lacking. It could be argued that in the excitement of looking out into the wider world, dance writers, perhaps afraid of being accused of modernist tendencies, have neglected to develop literature in crucial areas of study. For example, although there are recent publications, many texts still in regular use on the craft of choreography were published some time ago. (It is, admittedly, a challenge to write a 'how to' book in the light of the diversity of current choreographic practice.) Another area where there is a dearth of literature other than the autobiographical or physiological is performance. Now that the boundaries between 'training' and 'education' are being blurred both conceptually and institutionally there is a need for literature on, for example, psychological aspects of dance performance.[23] There is the opportunity for experiential learning to be reflected upon and contextualized, and an exploration of not just the technical training of the dancer but the whole realm of the dancer in preparation for, and in, performance.

11

Post-disciplinary debate

The consorting of dance with other critical and cultural perspectives has, undoubtedly, enriched the field of study but it has also given rise to much self-reflection. Has too much dancing with strangers resulted in not just increased popularity but an unwelcome promiscuity? Issues pertinent to the current state of dance scholarship can be summarized into questions concerning the nature of what is studied, how it is studied and for what purpose. What are the parameters of 'dance' and therefore dance study? As Kozel (1994) in Part I demonstrates, research in activities which involve the body moving in virtual reality comes into its domain. Is 'the body', in its corporeal or metaphorical usage, now a central organizing concept for dance study? Anthropologists have long since struggled with the question of what constitutes 'dance' in cultures that perhaps do not even have a term for it, but even if we are sure of the nature of the activity, long-held aesthetic, artistic and cultural assumptions about what constitutes dance need to be reconceptualized (see, for example, Ness and Martin in Morris 1996).

A further arena for debate concerns the question of appropriate methodologies for study. If the concept of dance itself is malleable, so are ways of looking at it. There appears to be a tension, false though it might be, between the formalist analysis of dance which focuses on the components and structures of the work itself, and approaches which read dance within other theoretical frameworks. Are there analytical strategies which are necessary for the study of dance, or are they merely sufficient, depending on one's intent? Dance can be used to support a pre-existing argument or paradigm but the danger can arise of losing sight of its specificity when dealing with its generality. (A *prima facie* case here is feminist studies, wherein all ballerinas are seen to represent the sylph or white-gauzed figure, a misrepresentation which negates not only the variety of the Romantic period in dance but also 90 per cent of the remaining past and current repertoire.)

A personal experience encapsulated a seemingly intractable dilemma for dance in relation to the nature of the activity and how it is 'studied'. I was asked to make a response to an American scholar's 'paper' at a well-known London venue.[24] Her exposition was delivered not in words – but in dance. How should I have responded? Most obviously, by a verbal discussion of issues raised in the 'performance', yet what was the nature of the translation between serious, scholarly 'physical' ideas and their verbal response? The tension between the traditional mode of expression in the study of any field of human activity, the written/spoken word, and the physical/sensory nature of dance has long been acknowledged and, as discussed, has been partly responsible for the latent development of dance study. But as Dempster suggests, in an academic field dominated by linguistic paradigms dance suffers from what might be termed its textual instability or insufficiency. But perhaps the difficulty lies not simply with the intractability of dance, with its refusal to conform to existing theoretical paradigms and procedures. One of the key questions ... concerns the appropriateness and adaptability of those current models of research: how responsive are they to the challenges of contemporary dance/performance practice?

(Dempster 1994: 3)

Is performance practice, Dempster continues, 'in danger of colonisation by the word'? As Foster (1995 in Part IV) indicates, post-structuralist theories of language and communication have paved the way for an exploration of this relationship between experiential knowledge of/in the dancing body and the propositional knowledge of the mind.

For the young student or general reader who is new to dance, much of the new writing emanating from the above debates provides either an intellectual challenge or a murky mystery. If some of Martha Graham's or Isadora Duncan's own words seem, to us today, to lose touch with reality because of their metaphysical style and sentiment, some current writing in dance is even more inaccessible. The question arises as to how familiar anyone engaging with dance study has to be with concepts and theoretical frameworks which have been thoroughly conceived elsewhere. It is not only a question of understanding these analyses, but trusting the paradigms within which they are presented.

The breaking of boundaries in the subject matter of dance, its methodologies and its research methods can be seen as a potential erosion of its identity. We are now aware, however, that the concept of identity is an unstable one. Dance is studied for different purposes and different questions are asked; it moves within an expanding arena of knowledge, forging its own pathways and interweaving with those of others. Instead of being under the traditional pedagogic, historical or anthropological spotlights, the study of dance is now revealed in all kinds of theoretical sidelights, uplights, downlights and all manner of overall washes. Sometimes it leaves its disciplinary stage altogether, performing in new spaces. The scholar/researcher/student may promenade, constructing all kinds of meaning within the parameters of their chosen perspective. The very self-reflexivity of dance studies today is a sign of its confidence, maturity and on-going vitality.

Guide to the reader

Dance can be discussed, debated, written about, analysed and explored from a wide variety of perspectives. This anthology presents many of those perspectives, drawing on contributions by choreographers, performers, critics and scholars. Most of the writing has been abridged with permission of the authors; original versions may include further bibliographic details and notes which would repay consultation for those who wish to probe an area of study in more detail.

The extracts are selected mainly from recent writings and organized in six Parts. Parts I and II address the making and the doing of dance. The chronological presentation is a deliberate attempt to reflect changing perspectives and practices but it is not intended as a teleological nor evolutionary view of twentieth-century dance history. The postmodern de-bunking of history-as-progression applies as much to dance study as to any other human endeavour. That is, whilst aesthetic stances are of their time, their relevance is not redundant when that time is passed. Part III addresses the appreciation of dance as formalized in critical reviews. 'Appreciation' is also the fundamental concern of the following three Parts but here some different critical approaches are addressed directly. Part IV offers discussion of concepts, methodologies and disciplinary stances which are either integral to, or can illuminate, the study of dance. From the broad perspectives of writing which deals with dance in its the social and historical location in Part V, more detailed analyses of dance works or choreographic *oeuvre* are presented in Part VI.

Although the Parts are separate, they are not discrete. Even the most personal writing, which arises from contemplation of direct experience, embodies a 'critical perspective' of some kind, albeit, perhaps, unselfconscious and unarticulated. Conversely, the concepts of 'making' and 'performing' are central to all the writing which analyses and contextualizes dance, for it is choreography (of whatever genre) in performance which constitutes the dance itself. Similarly, although each Part deals with a different kind of engagement with dance they are also inter-related in their concepts and methods. For example, a truly comprehensive analysis of a dance work or form (Part VI) cannot be undertaken without locating it within its cultural context (Part V). Those who are choreographing (Part I), performing (Part II) or reviewing (Part III) all analyse dance and share its concepts (Part IV). Such an organization for the book is not arbitrary, for it does reveal how theory can address the many different modes of engagement, but all the extracts have commensurate as well as specific concerns.

The very fact that extracts have seen selected from an increasingly large range of writing on dance takes away any notion of editorial impartiality. The introduction to each Part, however, attempts to identify the main issues and characterize the debate without taking any personal stance. These introductions, however, only partially contextualize the writings and the ideas embodied in them, for literature on the history and cultural context of dance is now easily accessible. A rewarding project might be for the reader to explore the relationship between ideas and the social and artistic circumstances within which they were produced. Even writing style and subtextual sentiment is of its time; compare, for example, the certainty of modernism in Graham (1991) with Foster's (1995) self-conscious wariness.

Notes on further reading

The introduction to each Part concludes with a guide to further reading. It is a tribute to the development of dance studies that this guide is very selective; the focus is on recent key texts and includes journal articles. Further substantial bibliographic details can be found in computer data bases (such as the New York Public Library catalogue's CD-Rom, *Dance on Disk*) and in bibliographic collections such as Bopp (1994) and Getz (1995). Further primary sources can be found in anthologies such as Cohen's *Dance as a Theatre Art* (lst edn. 1974) and Copeland and Cohen's *What is Dance?* (1983). The appendices in Adshead-Lansdale and Layson (1994) include a useful annotated guide to anthologies, encyclopaedias, journals, etc. Finally, as noted above, extensive references are often given in the original texts from whence the extracts are drawn.

By presenting writings which engage directly with the activities of making, performing and reviewing dance, followed by a variety of other perspectives from which dance can be studied, the book parallels the way in which the discipline tends to be encountered. It is usually the act of dancing, seeing dance in performance and/or choreographing which constitutes the first entry into the dance world. For those taking formal courses of study, these are often the activities which are privileged in the structure of the programmes and in the students' own minds. Critical reflection and engagement with theory tend to follow. In one sense, therefore, the structure of the book parallels a journey, but one in which the traveller can roam back and forth. It is also a journey in which we are reminded of our starting point and our destination – the dance itself. Whether studied in order to reveal its component parts and structures; to open up the possibilities for interpretation; to explore its function in society; to claim its significance as mode of personal aesthetic engagement, or as a cultural and artistic phenomenon; to exemplify its potential as subject for many kinds of critical discourse – it is the dance itself which is central. The theories developed within or appropriated by dance are exciting and thought-provoking and the debates and arguments are elegant and engaging for their own sake, but the main aim of the study of dance is to enhance our experiential engagement. As Best (1985) argues, the dualism implied in the notions of 'feeling' and 'reason'; the distinction between the body and the mind and, it may be claimed, the separation of practice and theory in dance are no longer tenable. The aim of this anthology is to open up many of the ways in which 'theory' relates to practice for all those who are engaged with dance, whether they are makers or doers; students, teachers or researchers, or informed, responsive audiences.

NOTES

1 For an overview of the development of dance study in the United Kingdom pre-twentieth century, see Adshead 1981.

2 Manning (1993) reminds us, however, that no performance texts are 'complete'; all performances are ephemeral and so, in this respect, dance may not be such a special case as is often claimed.

3 See Cohen in Au and Peter (1989) for an overview of key developments in documentation, especially the publication and content of dance journals in the United States.

4 Cyril W. Beaumont, Richard Buckle and Arnold Haskell are examples of these British writers. Garafola (1989) acknowledges the value of their work as key sources but notes the lack of any critical framework or broader cultural perspective. Although discussing literature on the Ballets Russes, her comments could also be applied to most of British dance history writing of this – and subsequent – periods.

5 For example, History and Anatomy are now required subjects for study on the syllabus of the Royal Academy of Dancing and the Imperial Society of Teachers of Dancing.

6 The desire for engagement with dance at higher levels of study in other countries, particularly in the Far East, must also be acknowledged.

7 See Kraus (1969) for a more detailed account of the early years of dance in American education.

8 One survey reported that 277 colleges in the United States offered dance either on performing arts programmes or as part of general education curricula. Modern dance was at the core of the majority of programmes. In the same year another survey reported that out of 99 colleges listed, 32 offered dance as a significant part of graduate programmes and 9 offered doctoral programmes (Kraus 1969).

9 I fully remember my own education as a teacher, when my studies veered vertiginously between tackling the cosmological and deeply metaphysical concepts at the heart of Laban's philosophy of human movement; getting totally lost in imaginary dodecahedrons around my body – and flicking and dabbing in the gym. (Flicking and dabbing were two of Laban's eight 'effort actions' which comprised four pairs of polarized, qualitative aspects of movement.)

10 See Adshead (1981) for an analysis of the nature and development of British degree courses in dance.

11 The survey, initiated by the Dance Section of the European League of Institutes of the Arts (ELIA), was admittedly partial as it relied on responses from members of ELIA and those within the European dance network. The cited examples are quoted within the survey but recent developments may have modified the situation.

12 *Further Studies in Dance in Australia* is available from Ausdance (National), P.O. Box 45, Braddon 2612, A.C.T., Australia.

13 The University of Melbourne; Queensland University of Technology and Western Australia Academy of Performing Arts offer postgraduate degrees in dance.

14 Higher education institutions are accountable for the public outcome of research activity, and these outcomes have significant funding implications for those institutions.

15 For example, government documents which included guidelines on dance curricula bore titles such as 'Moving and Growing – Physical Education in the Primary

School' (1952) and 'Movement – Physical Education in the Primary School' (1972).

16 Traditional anthropology broadened the cultural context of dance but it was rarely part of undergraduate curricula, especially for the training of teachers.

17 Since 1966, when the Certificate of Secondary Education in Dance was introduced in Britain, a linked route through qualifications has been established. Currently, dance can be studied in the public sector, either as a discrete subject or within the performing arts, at General Certificate of Secondary Education 'Ordinary' and 'Advanced' level; in B. Tech., Access and Foundation courses; for the Higher National Diploma, on undergraduate and postgraduate taught courses and for research degrees of M.Phil. and PhD.

18 Various writings identify these strands but Adshead (1981) explores in detail their application to dance as a discipline.

19 As a further biographical note, I did not feel secure about teaching dance, even at secondary school level, until I had completed a Masters degree in 1984. On reflection, this was due not only to the general increase in confidence that further study can give, but the content of the degree reflected a particularly exciting time in dance studies, when the specific concepts, methods and claims for dance as a discipline had been recently consolidated.

20 *Border Tensions: Dance and Discourse* (1995), University of Surrey, Guildford and *Border Crossings: Dance and Boundaries in Society, Politics, Gender, Education and Technology* (1995), Society of Dance History Scholars, University of California, Riverside.

21 As an example of the interdisciplinary nature of dance study, see Thomas (1995: Appendix) for an overview of how dance anthropology, aesthetics and studies in body symbolism have informed a sociology of dance.

22 For example, see Koritz in Morris (1996) for a discussion on the potential of interdisciplinary exchange between dance and cultural studies.

23 Increasingly, vocational courses in Britain are being validated by universities. Conversely, in 1994, Middlesex University offered a BA (Hons) degree in Dance Performance.

24 Presentation by Susan Leigh Foster, 'The Ballerina's Phallic Pointe' at the Institute of Contemporary Arts, London, 16 October 1995.

PART I

MAKING DANCE

In terms of its scholarship, dance has suffered from an assumption, based on contentious notions about the nature of artistic expression, that it is the 'outer' manifestation of 'inner' experience. Such an idea, wherein dance is seen as 'an outlet for intuitive or unconscious feelings inaccessible to verbal (intellectual) expression' has cultivated a 'sanctimonious mutism' (Foster 1986: xiv) on the part of dancers and choreographers. In recent years, however, the deconstruction of 'natural' bodies and an analytical approach to methods of creating have resulted in a more self-conscious reflection on the activity of choreography. If artists have always implicitly recognized the nuts and bolts of their craft they are now more willing to expose those mechanics publicly and to share their personal manifestos about what they do.[1] The extracts presented here are grouped chronologically not in order to present a teleological progression, but to exemplify some different approaches to choreography or, lest that be seen as too constraining an activity in the light of current multi-media contexts, to 'dance making'.

Although an attempt has been made to let the dance makers speak for themselves, there are two exceptions. Annabel Farjeon's writing is of special interest in that she describes the choreographic approaches of Ninette de Valois and Frederick Ashton from the perspective of a company member of the Sadler's Wells Ballet in the 1930s. Inevitably, the personalities of these choreographers were reflected in two very different modes of dance making which still have relevance in some contexts today. De Valois came to the studio fully prepared. Her dancers were 'puppets', there to execute her 'private imaginings', and they knew little about the meanings or even the subject matter of the work in progress. Some laxity of interpretation was accorded to the principals, but the *corps* was allowed little deviation from de Valois' intent. Ashton, on the contrary, often appeared at rehearsal having thoroughly researched his theme but apparently with little choreographic material. He drew upon the dancers 'as though we were shapes with whom he was playing or experimenting'.

Merce Cunningham, a continent and a genre away, also engaged in choreographic play, but with a far more premeditated approach. Although discussing a specific work (*Torse*, 1975), Cunningham's general choreographic principles which govern most of his *oeuvre* can be extrapolated. These include the democratization of both the stage space and the kine sphere of the body; the layering of movement phrases and tempi and the resultant, constantly changing flux of movement through time and in space. Although Cunningham is renowned for his use of chance procedures[2] this interview reveals the amount of forethought and preparation before the rehearsal stage, especially in the creation of dance phrases and the general structuring of the work. This exposition of the creation, selection and rejection of movement illustrates how Cunningham is able to work with chance, yet retain a distinct choreographic style. His procedures may appear to be 'play', but the playground is delineated and the rules are strict.

Yvonne Rainer attempted to do away with 'rules' altogether, although, paradoxically, the negation of traditional methods and products of dance making resulted in the affirmation of another kind of approach, perhaps equally constraining (or enabling, depending on one's view). Her statement of denial of the theatricalism of theatre dance exemplifies one of the postmodern imperatives to strip dance down to its essential components. This philosophy of dance was followed in spirit, if not exactly in letter, by the generation of choreographers/performers working during the 1960s and early 1970s. As Banes described, 'movement itself became like an object, something to be examined coolly without psychological, social or even formal motives' (1986: 43).

An antithesis to the cool examination of movement can be found in the work of Pina Bausch. Here is the second exception to the choreographer's own voice for, although Bausch has discussed her work in interview (Servos 1995), the exposition by Norbert Servos which is presented here is a useful and illuminating one. When existing terminology is inadequate to describe a genre which has transgressed its boundaries, a new description evolves; Servos notes Bausch's key role in the development of 'dance theatre'. This kind of work draws upon elements of both dance and theatre, juxtaposing, for example, choreographed gesture, the spoken word and popular song. It echoes her heritage of *Ausdruckstanz* ('dance of expression') but extends that tradition in a radical approach to form, content and subject matter. In impulse, Bausch has much in common with the postmodernists: in her rejection of illusion; her reconceptualization of what constitutes dance and the imperative to make it 'aware of itself'. But her retention of realism, wrapped in a theatrical though fragile framework, results in a very different mode of dance making and performing. The movement may be examined, but not 'coolly', for the seeming authenticity of the performers' experiences on stage and the unapologetic presentation of everyday bodily experience demand a reciprocal sensory response from the audience. Servos identifies further key constituents of Bausch's aesthetic, including the use of montage and the fragmentation of structure which offers potential for pluralistic readings of the work. The stark presentation of gender conflict, both within individuals and between women and men, and the raw and gutsy energy of performance which demands a visceral response, seem to hold a special attraction for a young audience, particularly in Europe. Despite the fact that there has been little opportunity to see Bausch's work in live performance outside of Germany and Belgium, this popularity bears testimony to its potency and appeal.

Similarly, international audiences have also had little opportunity to see the work of Shobana Jeyasingh with any regularity, and her dances have been less fully disseminated on television or video.[3] The issues she deals with, however, are pertinent to all dance makers (and audiences) who work and live in today's multicultural societies. As a preface to her discussion of three recent works, Jeyasingh enters into the debate about so-called 'cross-cultural' collaborations and highlights some of the paradoxes she encounters as a choreographer working in Britain, with a dance vocabulary that is rooted in the South Asian form of Bharata Natyam. She acknowledges that, in the process of dance making, she is a choreographer who tends to direct her dancers, although their contribution and the device of improvisation play an important part. She faces the same problems as any artist dealing with a classical language, that of how to personalize the vocabulary without losing its 'strength and its power to communicate with sureness and confidence'.

Although the above choreographers represent ballet, modern/postmodern and South Asian-influenced dance, contrasts and commonalities can be discerned which are independent of genre. Furthermore, while each extract has been chosen for its encapsulation of the choreographic approach with which that artist is identified, it must be recognized that an individual's aesthetic preferences and beliefs have the potential to change. Dance making is a dynamic activity which allows for personal exploration, experiment and alternative approaches.

NOTES

1 Artists have 'spoken' through the writings of others or in edited collections. See, for example, Choreographers' testimonies, p. 22.
2 One of the first works in which Cunningham used chance procedures was Suite by Chance (1953).
3 The Company's first New York performance was in 1997.

PART I

FURTHER READING

Choreographers' testimonies: Morrison Brown (1979); Banes (1980); Kreemer (1987)
Frederick Ashton: Vaughan (1977); Kavanagh (1996)
Pina Bausch: Servos (1984 and 1995); collection of articles in *Drama Review* (1986)
Merce Cunningham: Lesschaeve (1985); Kostelanetz (1992); Regitz (1996)
Ninette de Valois: de Valois (1957); Sorley-Walker (1987)
Yvonne Rainer: Hecht (1973/4); Rainer (1983); Banes (1980, 1986)
Shobana Jeyasingh: Jeyasingh (1990). Video and monograph of *Romance ... with Footnotes* available from the Shobana Jeyasingh Company, Freepost (WC 5501), London, WClH 9BR

2

CHOREOGRAPHERS: DANCING FOR DE VALOIS AND ASHTON

Annabel Farjeon

When I was a dancer with Sadler's Wells Ballet Company through the 1930s I was first a student in the school and then, two years later aged 14, given the roles of a Snowflake and a Biscuit in the original London production of *Casse Noisette*. From that time began more *corps de ballet* work, learning such classics as *Giselle*, *Le Lac des Cygnes*, and *Les Sylphides* from the regular repertoire. For this we students were paid five shillings a performance until, suddenly, there was a salary of £3 10s a week and one was in the company. By 17 I had a flat of my own in Canonbury Square, Islington, and was independent.

Ninette de Valois and Frederick Ashton were the two main choreographers who worked on me – and at me – when I was a dancer. In their manner of composition, in their manner of getting what they wanted out of artists, they had very different methods. De Valois was cold and reserved, outwardly sure of herself, so that one was never exposed to her personal feelings or a sense of participation in the creation of a ballet. Ashton was hot and subject to violent emotional whims which would sometimes hinder, sometimes forward, his work, but with which nobody in the company could resist sympathy, so exposed and tender were his sensibilities.

Of course, we members of the *corps de ballet* were of minor importance as far as the choreographer was concerned, save as a group, being expected to do what we were told without fuss. But this subservient state gave all the more opportunity for observation with a curious and critical eye. It is the same with servants, who are generally far more astute and accurate in assessing their masters than is any equal friend or relative, since servants' judgments are not nearly so swayed by personal prejudice or sentiment. Thus I watched de Valois and Ashton carefully, judging each mood, each decision, each joke, and each *pas de chat*.

Although the prospect of a new ballet such as *Checkmate* or *The Wise Virgins* was obviously of great importance to the company, both financially and artistically, it always seemed to me odd that nobody, or practically nobody, in the *corps de ballet* knew what this creation was to be about: either the story or who had composed the music or who would design the décor. We were never told. The title with a cast list would be pinned to the notice board by the stage door – that was all. In the case of Ashton, this lack of information stemmed from a kind of unconcern; his feelings were so intense that he thought the theme must almost immediately become apparent without the bother of an explanation. In the case of de Valois it was partly her secretive nature, partly her policy of separating director from work force. She needed solitary power, for her own satisfaction and for the management of the company. From our point of view both methods had at least one advantage: they lent excitement to every new discovery, to every new rumour.

At the first rehearsal de Valois would remain cool, concentrated, and often humorous. She was already primed with ideas and knew what she wanted: it had been written down in a notebook. Save for a pianist or merely using the score, she had marked out the details of the whole ballet in private. She inclined to use dancers as puppets to be manipulated and there was little elasticity to the system. Now and then she would alter some step, rearrange a pattern, or bring a character more to the fore, but it was seldom necessary. Her private imaginings had been pretty accurate.

De Valois never ranted and raged at rehearsals of her own work as she did when dealing with that of other choreographers. Then she would abuse dancers for lack of vitality, lack of technique, of being 'perfectly hopeless'. Once, in the fullness of exasperation, she cried to the young girl dancing Clara in *Casse Noisette*, 'Haven't you any temperament? You stupid little Anglo-Saxon!' For her own ballets impatience was merely at some slowness of understanding or forgetfulness of a move, which is common enough in newly fledged dancers who are expected to memorize the choreography of twenty or more ballets at an early stage in their career.

De Valois stumped into the Wells Room for the first rehearsal of *Checkmate* with her feet, as usual, well turned out and a determined look on her face. It was a surprise to learn that she knew nothing about the game of chess or the moves of the pieces, since the story concerned a battle on a chessboard. The fact that the designer dressed us in red and black as opposing forces made me suspect that he did not know the game either.

Hilda Gaunt sat at the battered upright piano, a cigarette drooping from her mouth as she gossiped in a husky, smokey voice. Often she was the only filter through which information about a new ballet could be sifted. Now it seemed that the music was by Arthur Bliss and the décor by E. McKnight Kauffer. De Valois sat down in the middle of the long bench with her back to the window that looked on to Rosebery Avenue. 'Come along! I want the eight Red Pawns,' she said in a voice as sharp as the snip of scissors.

Now, I was understudy for the six Black Pawns. It was lucky that one of them, Margot Fonteyn, was almost immediately elevated so that I took her place. But first, as understudy, there was time to watch, admire and criticize.

The Red Pawns were ranged down one side of the room, the smallest girl in front, graded up to the tallest at the back. 'Fourth position, right foot in front, left hand on your hip, right arm straight forward, hand turned down from the wrist. Now – like soldiers drilling! Music!' De Valois would stand up to demonstrate, then hurry back to her book, open on the bench where the hieroglyphics could be studied. Sitting on the end of the bench, I wanted to get my hands on that book to see how her notation looked, but I never dared peep. When one of the Pawns yet again got out of line and then lost her way I gave an involuntary gasp of exasperation. De Valois turned in surprise, then gave a quick nod and lift at the corners of her mouth as a sign of recognition, so that I felt we were momentarily allied in the same cause.

The plot of the ballet evolved jerkily, for scenes were not rehearsed in their final order. Every detail of footwork, each turn of the head and arms had to be fixed to de Valois' satisfaction before she would move on. With soloists in whom she put her trust it was different; they were allowed to interpret movement almost in their own way – almost. But as the Red King, Robert Helpmann took the character entirely into his own hands. He became a dithering senile old man, pushed in every direction by his Queen and his Knights. Unable to make up his mind, with arms shaking, he tottered from square to square as though blown by a violent storm, to be ultimately hoisted prostrate on the staves of the Black Pawns and carried to his checkmate. I enjoyed every minute of being a Black Pawn.

To dance in de Valois' finest ballets, such as *Job*, *The Gods Go a-Begging*, or *The Rake's Progress*, was another delight. Technically the steps were not difficult, but to get the style correct – that balance between restraint and display, that sense of period and character – was a problem that these ballets always posed. In *Job* it was a mixture of Blake and the Bible, in *The Gods Go a-Begging* Watteau and neoclassicism, in *The Rake* unadulterated Hogarth. During the brothel scene, when we chorused with the street singers 'Oh deary me, I do want to pee, and I don't really care who sees me!' (words not intended to carry, composed by Constant Lambert), I stuck my tongue out at the audience one night. A moment later I grew nervous that de Valois might pounce as I came into the wings and tick me off with one off her magnificent tirades for deviating from her choreography.

Frederick Ashton arranged his ballets in quite another fashion. He loved the feel of dancers, both physically and mentally, and he greeted them with warmth. His long face and sad eyes would light up with joy as readily as a child's when we danced well. But there were days when he would turn up to rehearsal seemingly without an idea in his head, and in my experience he never wrote anything down. Sitting on the bench before the window, his cheeks and neck would turn peony pink with anxiety. There was stillness and silence in the room.

At last he would go to the piano and, leaning over the music to hide his embarrassment, say, 'Play this bit, Hilda.' Hilda Gaunt would lay her cigarette on the fingerboard and play. After a moment he would pick on a favourite dancer. 'Do something! Go on, darling, do something!' Then he, too, would start swooping about the room, drag a couple standing at the side by the hands. 'Try it like this. Try lifting her – no, one leg like this! No – yes! Lovely! Now reverse the whole thing.' It was as though we were shapes with whom he was playing or experimenting, as a little boy might.

On other occasions he knew just what he wanted, but movements were always open to improvement. 'Look at the way Wenda flopped her head then. I want you all to flop your heads like that; it looks charming. Flop your heads!' So we all flopped our heads as Wenda had done.

In *Le Baiser de la Fée*, a ballet first produced for Ida Rubinstein with music by Stravinsky and choreography by Nijinska, then in 1935 by Ashton, I remember at the age of 16 the misery of not being strong enough on pointe, and how kindly forebearing Ashton was to me. There was a terrible quick-change in the wings from the first peasant scene into a new costume plus pointe shoes, which added to my agony. Pearl Argyle, as the wicked fairy, looked divine and danced with a numb elegance that left me longing for a spark of imperfection. The prologue of the mother and baby floundering back and forth in a snowstorm struck me as sentimental and incongruous. It would be interesting to know how Nijinska coped with this scenario.

Ashton taught us the peasant dance during one long afternoon but then, next day, arrived in a frenzy of dissatisfaction and scrapped the whole thing. He had thought up a new plan in the night. This, of course, was a dismal waste of rehearsal time, which time was hard enough to come by, what with the opera rehearsals, our regular repertoire, and classes for both company and students. All day every room in the theatre was filled with dancers leaping and singers shrieking, while the auditorium resounded with the players of music and the tap of a conductor's baton on his desk as he stopped the orchestra mid bar, saying, 'Now, go back to C, I want those five notes much softer.'

During an early stage of *The Wise Virgins*, which we rehearsed on tour in Brighton at the start of the war in 1940, Ashton produced a book of photographs of baroque churches in southern Germany, with their curlicued plasterwork and the asymmetric poses of saints and madonnas who look at the same time so beautiful and so unnatural. He explained how our limbs should express the formality and elegance of Bach's music, how they should match the pinnacles around which cherubs spun, the altars of fluffed clouds, and angels disporting themselves with such absurd affectation.

'You see,' he said, smiling at Fanny's charming pose as she aped a saint, 'Fanny understands. She sees herself like this in the afterlife, floating about heaven with beautiful thoughts, laid out on a mauve cloud.'

Fanny's face expressed distress. She was one of the few serious Christians in the company. Quickly Ashton showed his contrition by turning attention away from the sensitive one, to cry, 'Pamela, you shall massage my dowager's hump after the rehearsal!'

In this ballet, where I played the Bride's Mother, he would say, 'Come on now, what about your ancestors, Annabel? Let the Jewish momma in you take over – your daughter is getting married so howl, howl from head to toe! Go on – HOWL!' That a mother might howl at the marriage of her daughter had not occurred to me before, but immediately I saw drama in this sorrow and it affected every gesture I made.

Often, after searching for clues among his dancers, Ashton would suddenly begin a flow of movement that seemed to take hold of choreographer and dancer alike, until both became instruments on which his imagination would improvise for hours with a facility and professionalism that entirely belied all that early agony and dither.

Ashton was no moralist, but there was one socially conscious ballet he produced at the beginning of 1940. The war with Germany had begun, although so far there had been no direct attack on Britain. Ashton, the romantic, chose as his subject the battle between the forces Good and Evil, set to Liszt's *D'après une lecture de Dante*, arranged for piano and orchestra by Lambert, and called the ballet *Dante Sonata*. With awareness of Nazi concentration camps, with photographs of Jews being abused in German streets, revulsion surged up in him, always a man full of sympathy for the underdog. Unlike de Valois, he was not a natural autocrat. Again we were shown a picture book, this time of engravings by Flaxman of Dante's Inferno, where bodies happily spiralled up to heaven or tumbled in agony down to hell.

As so often, Constant Lambert, our conductor, collaborated with the planning and suggested the music. In a broadcast he later explained, 'The general layout, by which I mean not the dancing as such but the association of various characters with various themes and the general dramatic sequence, was then established by Ashton and myself. I played the piano at almost all the rehearsals while the choreography was being created, so that when it came to finally orchestrating the ballet, I had the whole stage picture in mind.'

We danced *Dante Sonata* barefoot on the stage, the choreography designed in a free, almost Martha Graham style, though as I remember with a wider scope of movement. It was a release from the restrictions of classical ballet and pointe shoes, for so-called 'modern dance' is far easier to execute.

Fonteyn and Somes were the leaders of the Children of Light, while Brae and Helpmann led the Children of Darkness. Of course Fanny was one of the Good, while I was one of the Evil group. Ashton cast his dancers with care. We fought and parted without a victor and in the final tableau there was no triumph. On opposite sides of the stage, mounted above their followers, Helpmann and Somes hung as though crucified. Some critics found this ending trite, while others felt it to be a step toward a much needed social consciousness within the Sadler's Wells Ballet Company.

Certainly, this ballet, fraught with emotion, was appreciated by us who interpreted the tortured ecstasy that runs through Liszt's music. And the sorrow and anger we expressed seemed to identify us more closely with the terrible drama surging across Europe. We the dancers thought that *Dante Sonata* would be a creation to last through generations, as it was handed down by example and word of mouth. Some years later, with a different cast, a larger stage, and changed attitudes, the ballet failed and has not survived. There was probably too much passion in it and not enough artistic decorum. But I still remember Ashton's choreography as marvellously balanced, full of power and romance, and above all – beautiful.

Frederick Ashton aimed at beauty. Ninette de Valois aimed at truth. That was the difference between them.

3

TORSE: THERE ARE NO FIXED POINTS IN SPACE

Merce Cunningham with Jacqueline Lesschaeve

JACQUELINE LESSCHAEVE: *Merce Cunningham, the choreography for classical or modern dancers follows often predictable sequences: mainly soloists doing variations in relation to (or against) a background of a group of dancers. You deliberately broke with that procedure of repeating familiar sequences, and you involved yourself in exploring the range of possible movements. Starting with one of your recent dances, could we take note in some detail of what differentiates it from the older, more traditional forms?*

MERCE CUNNINGHAM: Imagine going to the other extreme of what you described. Say you have eight people each of whom is doing different sequences, all of whom are being soloists. That is immediately far more complex. Think of how they divide the *corps* in classical ballet: you have eight girls on each side of the stage, eight girls moving symmetrically which you can perceive at a glance. If you have these two groups of eight girls doing totally different phrases, that's not very complicated but it's already more unexpected. Now go further still, take each eight. Have four do one thing, four something else. You immediately see that you can go to the extreme: you can take all sixteen and have each dancer doing clearly different movements. That would be done not just to be complex but to open up unexplored possibilities.

Further: in classical ballet as I learned it, and even in my early experience of the modern dance, the space was observed in terms of a proscenium stage, it was frontal. What if, as in my pieces, you decide to make any point on the stage equally interesting? I used to be told that you see the centre of the space as the most important: that was the centre of interest. But in many modern paintings this was not the case and the sense of space was different. So I decided to open up the space to consider it equal, and any place, occupied or not, just as important as any other. In such a context you don't have to refer to a precise point in space. And when I happened to read that sentence of Albert Einstein's: 'There are no fixed points in space', I thought, indeed, if there are

29

no fixed points, then every point is equally interesting and equally changing.

I began to work in that direction, for it opens up an enormous range of possibilities. As you're not referring one sequence to another you can constantly shift everything, the movement can be continuous, and numerous transformations can be imagined. You still can have people dancing the same phrase together, but they can also dance different phrases at the same time, different phrases divided in different ways, in two, three, five, eight or whatever. The space could be constantly fluid, instead of being a fixed space in which movements relate. We've grown up with ideas about a fixed space in the theatre to which spectator and dancer refer. But if you abandon that idea you discover another way of looking. You can see a person not just from the front but from any side with equal interest.

Taking nothing else but space, you see how many possibilities have been revealed. Suppose you now take the dimension of time. Our eight dancers can be doing different movements, they may even do them to the same rhythm which is all right, there's nothing wrong with any of it! [laughter] – but there is also the possibility that they can be doing different movements in different rhythms, then that is where the real complexity comes in, adding this kind of material one on top of and with another. One may not like it, but it seems to me anyway that once one begins to think this way, the possibilities become enormous. One of the points that distinguishes my work from traditional choreographies, classical and modern, is certainly this enlargement of possibilities.

JL: *Your dancers often enter into unison groups and break up from them. These movements give a sense of exploding or changing in time and space, but it's disconcerting to those used to more linear changes.*

MC: But just think of a group of six people walking along on the sidewalk together. At any moment they can all walk off in different directions, at different rhythms.

JL: *It's especially visible when you see children, grouping and separating, walking off, going off, in very different dynamic modes. The same holds for flights of birds, at once fluid and abruptly changing.*

MC: One of my recent works, *Torse*, is very clearly made in that way. The groups of dancers are constantly changing. I finished it in 1975. The whole piece was done using chance operations so as to have the possibility of any formation of the dancers appearing.

Say, for example, that you had two groups, not with the same number of dancers, one downstage and one upstage, somewhat diagonal, and say they were simply to exchange places, though they're doing two different phrases. Now obviously they could pass through each other, but say the movement wouldn't allow for it. Let's suppose that this group's tempo is slower, and that I want both groups to end at the same time (that could happen, yes . . .). I could for instance have the first group start, stop for a while, start the second one that would pass through the first one. Because of the different rhythms, they could end together, as the first one would start more rapidly to go to a stop and then go on, while the other group would go more slowly but regularly.

The other fact in that dance that I like very much, actually, is that if you saw the whole dance – it is fifty-five minutes long when the three parts are danced one after another – you would see that each one of the ten dancers appears at some point as a soloist. You have to watch, really use your eyes, but if you see it a few times, you see that each one comes out separately at one point, some way, back or front, as a soloist. And though the general feeling throughout is that the dance remains a dance of ensembles, it is very individualized as well, each dancer at one point or another has a chance to appear outside the group. It's subtle enough; it doesn't happen in an obvious way or place, but I'm sure it's felt. Or it may come about that there are no groups on stage, just two solo dancers. That was decided as well through chance means, which included this constant appearance of soloists. And as I worked it out from step to step, I didn't decide any of it ahead of time. As chance made a solo possible, long or short, I would see which dancer could do it, and in what way.

JL: *I especially admired one of the sequences where, leaving them all very distinct, you set a whole group of dancers in a small part of the stage, leaving the rest empty, which by comparison seems much bigger; after which you shift them all on the other side in a continuous flow, which gives the feeling of much more space than if the dancers had been spread about all over.*

MC: If you don't divide a space classically, the space remains more ambiguous and seems larger.

JL: *I think* Torse, *because of the many questions it brings up, would be a good basis for studying the composition process.*

MC: I'm going to give it in a workshop. I will not be able to show it the way my dancers do it, but I will show students the basic process. What's interesting in it is that all the elements were dealt with simultaneously, and even though to some people *Torse* looks like classical work, it isn't really. The movements do have a certain emphasis on line but the line is not at all a classical ballet line.

JL: *The coherence of a certain type of movement through* Torse *gives the impression that the way it seems to float in space is achieved by means that are very précise and used throughout, and that gives the flowing sensation that is so beautiful.*

MC: I figured out the phrasing and the continuity ahead of time, before the dancers came to rehearsal. Not, of course, the way they would dance the phrases, but the phrases themselves. It took a long time. I worked on it by myself with the help of video. There are sixty-four phrases, because that's the number of hexagrams in the *I Ching*. The phrases are formed like the numbers themselves. For example, one has one part in it, two has two, three has three, up to sixty-four. But I didn't make it as though one were one rhythmic beat, and so forth, metrically. Let us take the second phrase, it will be clearer. The counts are related to *weight changes*. That is, if you stand on your foot, that's one; if you bend your knee, that's a weight change, so that's two. Now that could be done slowly or quickly. At sixty-four, you have sixty-four weight changes. Or say, in phrase ten, for example, you have to produce ten weight changes, which means you're on one foot or both or whatever – but you might stand on one foot for a long time and circle the arms, which is not a weight change but changes completely the structure of time for this phrase. I figured them all out ahead of the rehearsal period with the dancers or I never would have been able to finish the piece in the rehearsal time available. And I allowed for repetition within a phrase, for instance: thirty-six is nine times four, or six times six.

That was for the sixty-four movement phrases. But then you take the space and you have a similar process. I numbered the space with sixty-four squares, eight by eight. Then I used the *I Ching* as it comes out: the hexagrams come out double most of the time, one over the other, for example thirteen over fifteen, that means phrase thirteen along with phrase fifteen. Then I would toss to see how many people did each phrase among the men, the women or both. Gradually all the combinations would come out and I would see them more and more clearly and try them out. Most of the paperwork had to be done ahead. But the crucial moment is when you try it out physically.

Sometimes you would have all the dancers doing the same phrase. That was decided by chance, the number forty-nine, for instance, comes up a couple of times alone, and in that case they danced in unison. Let's look at all this more closely: for instance, this is hexagram thirteen over hexagram twelve, and say that the following one is by chance the five or seven. I had prepared what would be phrase five, and working on it with the dancers I would see how it could move through the space, starting from where they stood before. I did the same with the space they occupied, numbered as you remember from one to sixty-four: someone was standing in space thirteen and someone in space twelve. I would choose how many dancers would come in those two spaces, and to go to forty-nine in terms of space – forty-nine is a specific place – they all go in that direction, but they can do it by such or such a detour according to the phrase they have to dance. This last point is important, as the dancers may as well go straight there as go while forming circles or whatever figure is suggested by the dance phrase to get them there. The dance phrase itself was generated, as you remember, by its own number.

So I made a space chart and a movement chart, both in sixty-four distinct units, and I had to deal with them both, this chart and the movement chart. Then there would come up the possibility of exits or entrances or the possibility of a duet and that's done by tossing coins, according to which some dancers leave the stage or not. I would toss a coin to see what to do. That's how those trios and duets appear in the piece. What it amounted to was a *continual change*.

JL: *There are only about ten dancers, but one gets the impression of a flock of them. This constant shifting makes them seem to be everywhere.*

MC: I know. A lady saw *Torse* once and said, 'But you must have sixty dancers'. For a lot of people, especially people accustomed to classical ballet, it's very difficult to watch. They're disturbed because they realize it's clear but they can't see it, can't deal with it at first sight.

JL: *It's at once precise and strict, and in constantly shifting motion. I understand better now why someone I know well, who is a mathematician, liked* Torse *so much. He literally saw* numbers *at work. To give this continual sensation of flux, you must have been quite selective in the choice of the movements themselves.*

MC: I did leave certain movements out, you're quite right. I was thinking about the torso, as the title indicates, and I retained mainly the range of body movements corresponding to five positions of the back and the backbone, positions with which I mostly work: upright, curve, arch, twist and tilt. Those five basic positions are very clear and the leg and arm positions in relation to those are clear, too. When you assemble all this to form the phrases, the possibilities are numerous though they stay within a certain vocabulary. It's wide but strict. I remember, though, when the dancers danced *Torse* for the first time, they found it very difficult to do. Now they're used to it, some of them even do it extremely well, the ones who've danced it often like Chris Komar, Robert Kovich, Ellen Cornfield and Meg Harper.

JL: *To what extent do the dancers know the complexity of the structure they're working on?*

MC: I think they're aware of it, because even if you're only dancing a part, after a while, you begin, if you're at all conscious, to develop a sense about what the others are doing, and you realize they're doing something else. You have to begin to know where the other dancer is, without looking. It has to do with time, the relationship with the timing. If you paid attention to the timing, then, even if you weren't facing them, you knew they were there. And that made a relationship. It depends also on how you think something can be created, too. If you always think that relationships are only one way, then that's the way you do it. But if you think relationships can be many ways, then that comes into your possible perception. It's like a cat. It doesn't have to turn around and look at something, it knows it's there. In human beings, it comes by experience, and certainly my pieces develop this faculty.

JL: *A word about the music for* Torse.

MC: The music is by Maryanne Amacher. I don't know how to describe it, you almost don't hear it. Sometimes there are no sounds at all. Every once in a while I hear a railroad train. It's quite like subliminal sounds. It's very quiet. Sort of still.

JL: *What indications did you give for the music?*

MC: None. I asked John [Cage] who he thought might make some music for *Torse*, and he suggested Maryanne.

JL: *Did he know of the piece you expected to do?*

MC: I'm trying to remember . . . I think he must have known somewhat, because I was working on it so much before I did the piece, making all those charts.

JL: *I'd like us to jump ahead to your work with video, by talking about the splendid film (double screen) of* Torse *that you made with Charles Atlas, and for which you were one of the cameramen!*

MC: Yes, it's a colour film of the whole piece, fifty-five minutes long as well. We chose the double screen because of the nature of the choreography. It wouldn't have been possible with one screen. We did the shooting in a large theatre in Seattle where the dance company was in residence, that allowed for very good camera work. And in that case, too, we prepared all the takes in advance. The shooting itself only took three days. The idea is that on the two screens you see everything that happens on the stage. When half the company appears on one of the screens, the other half appears on the other – that's the simplest case. We didn't do much that way because the dance itself opens and closes so much. The other extreme case is where all the dancing can be happening on one screen for a few seconds, while the other screen is empty.

At first, I felt strange as a film cameraman . . . and I was afraid of having wasted film and time, but it turned out the camera wasn't working! . . . One of the three cameras was stationary and took the whole stage, and the other two, moveable, were placed slightly lower. The stationary camera was handled by a technician, the mobile ones by Charles Atlas and myself. We followed the groups of dancers and took what closeups were possible. After that Charles Atlas edited the film. In its final version it is projected on two screens using two synchronized projectors.

4

'NO' TO SPECTACLE . . .

Yvonne Rainer

No to spectacle no to virtuosity no to transformations and magic and make-believe no to the glamour and transcendency of the star image no to the heroic no to the anti-heroic no to trash imagery no to involvement of performer or spectator no to style no to camp no to seduction of spectator by the wiles of the performer no to eccentricity no to moving or being moved.

Original source: *Tulane Drama Review* (1965) 10, 2: 178. Also in Banes (1986)

5

PINA BAUSCH: DANCE AND EMANCIPATION

Norbert Servos

When Pina Bausch took over the Dance Theatre Wuppertal (formerly the Wuppertal Dance Theatre) at the start of the 1973/74 season, a change occurred in the stagnating development of the German ballet scene. Of course other choreographers before her – like Hans (Johann) Kresnik in Bremen and Gerhard Bohner in Darmstadt – had begun to break away from the limited framework of expression of both classical and modern dance, looking for new forms appropriate to the times. But the Wuppertal company, under Pina Bausch, was the first to establish the term 'dance theatre' – until then occasionally used in the names of dance companies – as a synonym for a new and independent genre. Dance theatre, a mixture of dance and theatre modes, opened up a new dimension for both genres. Basically the term stood for a kind of theatre that was aiming at something new both in form *and* content.

The Dance Theatre Wuppertal discovered and developed its unusual field of action in the midst of a ballet culture that – apart from the few experimental centres like Bremen, Darmstadt and Cologne – was essentially content with either preserving and gradually updating its classical heritage or with dealing with the modern dance being imported from the United States. The German *Ausdruckstanz* tradition, with names like Mary Wigman, Rudolf von Laban, Harald Kreutzberg and Gret Palucca, had been all but dead since World War II. Striving for an apolitical, supposedly timeless theatre, people avoided confrontation with the provocative ancestors whose radical rejection of pointe shoes and tutus as early as the 1920s had made a new understanding of the body essential. John Cranko, an innovator in spite of his classical background, stood as the exception. Now, for the first time, with Pina Bausch, contact was being re-established – indirectly – with this almost forgotten revolutionary tradition; without its *ecce homo* pathos, without its universal fatalism, and in a manner that was completely new. From piece to piece the Dance Theatre Wuppertal gradually blazed a trail towards a goal to which *Ausdruckstanz* had probably always aspired but had failed to

36

achieve: releasing dance from the constraints of literature, relieving it of its fairytale illusions and leading it towards reality.

Pina Bausch's training with Kurt Jooss at the Folkwang School in Essen had acquainted her with the *Ausdruckstanz* concept of movement, and periods of study in New York had familiarized her with modern dance, so with her first pieces, the most outstanding perhaps the choreography of Stravinsky's *Rite of Spring*, Pina Bausch created a highly original synthesis between German tradition and American modernism. Even in these works, which were quite within the conventional framework, the special quality of her dance theatre was obvious. On the stage, her dancers unleashed a raw new energy, their bodies telling the stories with honesty, freed from any superimposed connotations. Although *Rite*, and the two Gluck operas *Iphigenia on Tauris* and *Orpheus and Eurydice*, and later *Bluebeard*, were still based on original plots, Pina Bausch had already gone beyond any previous concept of the 'interpretation' of librettos. She did not 'choreograph material', but took instead individual elements from the plot as a point of departure for her own wealth of associations. While other choreographers toil to translate music into movement, dance theatre deals directly with physical energies. Its story is told as a history of the body, not as danced literature.

However, the real significance of Pina Bausch's work lies in the way she broadened the concept of dance, releasing the term 'choreography' from its narrower definition as a series of connected movements. Increasingly, dance itself became an object to be questioned. Outdated forms of expression were no longer taken for granted. Dance theatre developed into something one could define as 'theatre of experience', a theatre that by means of direct confrontation made reality, communicated in an aesthetic form, tangible as a physical reality. By simultaneously rejecting literary constraints and concretizing the abstraction of dance, the Dance Theatre Wuppertal made dance – perhaps for the first time in its history – aware of itself, emancipated it to its own modes.

Labouring on the flat: theatre of experience

Pina Bausch's very first dance evening in Wuppertal was given an extremely mixed and controversial critical reception. This début of dance theatre innovation was not easily integrated into the canon of existing values and categories. It contrasted sharply with the customary concept of dance. The reactions ranged from astonishment and perplexed acknowledgement of its existence to open rejection. The confounding novelty of Bausch's work apparently demanded – and the works that followed made this increasingly obvious – a new understanding of dance. The manner in which the barriers between the genres were broken, and the demarcation lines that traditionally separate dance, spoken theatre and musical theatre were abolished, resisted any attempts at standard categorization. The pieces stood defiantly at right angles to the stream, causing a friction that at first hardly anyone was prepared to acknowledge as productive. Initial reception reflected a hard battle against critics who are extremely reluctant to change their established patterns of viewing and of absorbing what they see. On the one hand people were certainly prepared to admit that the 'artist Bausch' had fantasy, imagination and genius, but, on the other hand, the content of her works remained largely mysterious and inaccessible. The distinction between the (talented) personality and the ('hermetically sealed') work proved to be a decisive feature of her early reception, and, with the increasing popularity of the Dance Theatre Wuppertal, provided the arguments for the simultaneous appeal and rejection.

One steady source of irritation is the principle of montage, which has developed into the overriding stylistic principle of dance theatre. The linkage of scenes in free association, without the need for continuity of plot, psychology of character, or causality, also refuses to be deciphered in the normal way. It defies interpretation. Elucidation of every detail of a piece from a *single* universally applicable viewpoint is as impossible as encompassing the individual elements in an arc that declares them, in combination, as having a clear-cut 'meaning'.

The elements of content and form in the pieces are interlocked in a simultaneity that is so complex as to be scarcely apprehensible at a single glance. Merely recounting the chronological sequence of the scenes is equally inadequate. The events on the stage can barely be reconstructed in words. One can describe them, and must be content with an approximation. The complexity of the elements that make up the living theatrical process cannot be defined in terms of a *single* meaning. Since Bausch's pieces have no 'fables' in the Brechtian sense, and do not pursue the systematic variation of a *single* theme, the coherence only becomes apparent during the process of reception. In this sense, the pieces are not 'complete'. They are not self-sustaining works of art because, in order to develop completely, they require an *active* onlooker. The key lies with the audience, who are asked to question their interest and their own everyday experiences. These should, and indeed must, be collated against the happenings on the stage and related to them. A 'sense connection' can be made only when the corporeality (the physical awareness portrayed) on the stage relates to the physical experience of the onlooker. This connection is dependent upon the concrete (physical) expectations of the onlooker, which are disappointed, confirmed or confounded by the activities on the stage, and thus provide the opportunity to learn new lessons. By leaving literature aside, dance theatre, with all its physical, mimetic, and gestural possibilities, again sets theatre in motion as a communication of the senses.

The starting point for Pina Bausch's works are the daily social experiences of the body, which she translates and alienates into objectifying sequences of images and movements. The daily experiences of the individual, the physical constrictions and restrictions, even reaching the point of tragicomic self-regimentation, are demonstrated on the stage by means of provocative repetition, duplication, etc, and are thus made *experienceable*. The point of departure is authentic, subjective experience, which is also demanded of the audience. Passive reception is impossible. 'Theatre of experience' mobilizes the affects and the emotions because it deals with undivided energies. It does not *pretend*. It *is*. Because the viewer is affected by the authenticity of these emotions, which confuse both sense and the senses but are simultaneously enjoyable, he must also make a decision, must define his own position. He is no longer the consumer of inconsequential pleasures, nor is he witness to an interpretation of reality. He is included in a total experience that allows the experience of reality in a state of sensual excitement. The dissemination of knowledge is secondary to the experience. Dance theatre, however, does not seduce us with illusions; it puts us in touch with reality. Its point of reference is a universal social structure of affects which, in each case, can be clearly localized historically.[1] Theatre in the 1960s attempted to scale the difficult heights of abstraction. Dance theatre is now 'labouring on the flat'.

On the art of training a goldfish: how the new dance theatre tells its story

The Dance Theatre Wuppertal provided for the first time material for the discussion of the meaning of reality on the ballet stage. This kind of 'theatre of experience' not only changes the reception conditions by involving all the senses of the onlooker, the transference of dance from an aesthetically abstract level to one of everyday physical experience becomes not only a matter of style, there is also a difference in terms of content. Whereas dance previously was regarded as the domain of 'attractive illusions', as a refuge for self-satisfied technique or for the abstract treatment of existential themes, Bausch's works refer the onlooker directly back to reality. Making dance aware of itself also means burdening it with the whole spectrum of real phenomena. The special quality of dance, the fact that it tells its story through the sensual presence of the bodies, now is given the chance to portray a reality that is defined by physical conventions. Even Bertolt Brecht must have had an idea of these possibilities when he wrote in his *Kleines Organon*,

> choreography, too, is again given tasks of a realistic kind. It is a
> mistaken belief of recent times that it has nothing to do with the
> illustration of 'people as they really are' [. . .] At least a theatre that
> takes everything from the Gestus cannot dispense with choreo-
> graphy. The very elegance of a movement and the grace of a

formation alienates, and the pantomimic invention helps the fable
a great deal.

(Brecht 1977: 698)

Even if Pina Bausch's theatre of movement does not communicate its content through fable, indeed distinguishes itself in its rejection of a literary
thread of plot – the use of epic theatre modes is not excluded. Applied to
the individual process, the individual scene, these are, as they were for
Brecht, essential elements of realistic (dance) theatre. Some of the key
definitions of didactic theatre can be rediscovered in the Dance Theatre
Wuppertal, although no claim to didacticism is made; the 'Gestus of indication', the conscious exhibition of processes, the technique of alienation, as
well as a special use of comedy, have increasingly become characteristic
means of portraiture. Together with the motifs borrowed from the world of
everyday experience, these serve to illustrate 'people as they really are', as
postulated by Brecht.

Pina Bausch's principle of montage, which she has not borrowed from the
spoken theatre or from literature, but instead has developed from the less
reputable traditions of her own medium like vaudeville, music hall and
revue, acquires its reality in individual incidents and situations, in the process disregarding any conventional dramaturgy of plot. Instead of every
detail being absolutely interpretable, the dominant features of the pieces are
a multidimensionality and complex simultaneity of actions that offer a wide
panorama of phenomena. The pieces do not claim to have the kind of integrity in which every element can be questioned as to its individual significance in relation to a continuous story line. Instead, the principle of the
structure of dance theatre resembles that of music, in that themes and coun-
terthemes, variations and counterpoint are woven around a basic idea. The
beginning and conclusion do not mark temporal limits in the psychological
development of its characters. Its overriding principle is that of a dramaturgy of individual numbers, which deals with the motifs in a free but, at the
same time, precisely calculated and choreographed order.

These are 'field studies' aimed at the depths of physical conventions and
emotions and what they find there is brought to the surface. Groups of
motifs can be illuminated from different angles and approached from various directions. At the same time dance theatre abandons any obvious 'position' which pre-requires an unequivocal interpretation of reality. It does not
claim to know where it cannot have knowledge. Instead it takes what it finds
and makes it worth questioning, in the most positive sense. In Pina Bausch's
dance theatre realistic material is dealt with in the open and can be observed
in all its varying constellations. It is theatre in its original sense: a scene of
transformations. But the transformations are intended neither to deceive the
onlooker like cheap conjuring tricks nor to console him nor to make him
oblivious. Dance theatre does not anaesthetize the senses. It sharpens them

for that which 'really is'. The theatre is a laboratory in which the author/ choreographer allows the reagents to work together, to contradict and complement each other, to combine to provide new insights. The observer takes part in the process *as a whole*, is not pacified with mere effects, as in pure entertainment theatre. And still the expeditions of the Dance Theatre Wuppertal are enjoyable adventures. Their 'entertainment value' is provided by curiosity, by the hunger for experience.

No moral judgements are made. Whereas the conventional narrative dramaturgy equips its characters with morals, of whatever kind, be they politically motivated or on the basis of human reasoning, dance theatre refrains from making such judgements. It presents its findings and the onlooker is able to experience for himself the extent to which these deform the original needs or help them to achieve recognition. In these 'field studies' samples are taken from everyday life and the general forms of social intercourse are tested for suitability. Preconceived opinions do not exist. The freedom of an experiment allows curiosity to be reawakened. Pina Bausch asks questions. Her pieces are the outcome of the explorations she has undertaken with her company.

Because the exercises and variations on a theme are not subject to logical stringency, the usual linkage according to the principles of causality is also missing. No taut thread of narrative stretches between beginning and end for the audience to grasp and follow towards a destination predetermined by the author. How and why the people on the stage behave as they do is not determined by any psychological driving force. The freely associated images and actions form chains of analogies, spin a complex web of impressions that are connected, as it were, 'beneath the surface'. If a logic exists, it is not a logic of the consciousness, but of the body, one that adheres not to the laws of causality but rather to the principle of analogy. The logic of emotion and affects does not depend on reason.

Consequently, no differentiation is made between leading roles and minor characters in the Dance Theatre Wuppertal. When protagonists appear – as in *Rite of Spring* or *Bluebeard* – they are 'anonymous'. Their fate represents that of *every* man, *every* woman. The onlooker can no longer identify with the histories of individual characters, and is thus forced to find the tension of the piece not where he is accustomed to seek it, but elsewhere. And this tension is no longer directed towards a single tension-releasing climax, but instead exists in every moment, is provided by the combination of different tools and moods. Loud alternates with soft, fast with slow, sadness with joy, hysteria with moments of quiet, isolation with tentative approaches. Pina Bausch does not investigate *how* people move, but *what* moves them.

The field of vision is enlarged to reveal the greater correlations that exist. No character takes on the function of the deputy who acts in exemplary fashion. The individual aspects and the social ones are directly reflected in

41

the theatrical panorama of the passions. No need for interpretation exists in order to discover the social conditions behind the figures on the stage. The unfulfilled desires that are the subject of Bausch's pieces are formulated without deviation. For the first time, the dancers appear not as technical personnel performing the roles; they appear unprotected with their entire personalities. Their fears and joys possess the force of authentic experience. While dance theatre is recounting the universal history of the body, it is also always telling something of the actual life story of the people on the stage. Although Bausch makes use of the most varied theatrical tools, borrowed from every genre, the autonomy of the individual media is preserved. The dissonance and friction between them are – quite in the Brechtian sense – not united into a 'total work of art', but rather 'their interaction with each other lies in the fact that they mutually alienate each other' (Brecht 1977: 699). However, in a theatre that appeals less to the cognitive than to the emotive abilities of the onlooker, alienation is given a different function. Since theatre of movement makes no use of fables 'as the heart of the theatrical performance' (Brecht 1977: 693) to pass on information, its goal can only be regarded as the communication of a reality that has been personally experienced. The immediate effect is more important than rational elucidation. Where Brecht's epic theatre serves to create an 'appropriate consciousness', dance theatre offers us experience. Its opposition is not organized on the basis of rational insight, but on the turmoil of the affects. Whereas didactic theatre's attention is directed primarily towards the social context, and arranges the phenomena according to a preconceived view of the world, Bausch starts from the internalized norms and conventions. In her theatre of movement, the 'conditions' can be read in the individuals' behaviour.

As in Brecht, her theatre takes 'everything from the Gestus'. However, here the Gestus refers to the sphere of physical actions. It does not support or contrast a literary statement. Instead it 'speaks' through itself. The body is no longer a means to an end. It has itself become the subject of the performance. Something new has begun in the history of dance: the body is telling its own story. When, for instance, a man carries a woman draped around his neck like a scarf as a sign that for him she is no more than a decorative accessory, such a scene needs no further interpretation. It must not be examined as to its meaning. Again and again, the body is revealed to be in a state of weakness. The whole scope of human affects is shown as constricted and confined to conventions, but the pleasure involved in breaking the restricting taboos is also seen. These limitations, which have become second nature to us, are made more obvious by alienation. Things that are regarded as generally accepted norms are dissected out of their familiar contexts and can thus be experienced anew. The alienated image allows the everyday and often deformed language of the body to be 'recognized, but still at the same time appear strange' (Brecht 1977: 680). Things that in daily

42

life have become a matter of course are perceived for the first time from the distant perspective of this new alienation.

Often alienation is achieved with comedy that makes use of cinematic tools. Whole series of movements are performed in slow motion or are reeled off at slapstick speed. But the result is not roars of laughter at the expense of a single person. The humour does not denounce the real needs, but reveals something that has been buried by the deformation. The humorous moments always have an undertone of sadness which makes a tragedy of the grotesque egg-dance of bourgeois etiquette. The self-righteous logic of conventions is demolished. The matter-of-fact gestures are invalidated in order to show what has been lost and reveal a longing that is worthy of preservation. As he laughs, the onlooker recognizes on the stage the reality of his own behaviour. The difference between this and boulevard theatre is that it is no longer the plight of someone else that causes the amusement. Pina Bausch reduces the distance and brings the 'reality of the wishes' into uncomfortable proximity. Revelation can result when the public and the private spheres – in daily life carefully separated – unexpectedly collide. A couple stands at the front of the stage, smiling happily while, behind their backs, they mistreat each other with vicious little pinches and kicks. This comic-serious scene demonstrates, in the simplest form, the contradiction between hypocritical harmony in public and the reality of the battles that are fought in private. The smiling mask is not the true countenance.

The explorations of dance theatre are equivalent to repeated checks on the forms of behaviour acquired and accepted without thought. Increasingly Bausch makes use of the popular fantasies propagated by Hollywood films, comic strips, pop songs, and related media like operetta and revue. She takes from them not only the basic elements of her theatre of movement (like the chorus line, the revue formations, the principle of repetition), she also takes their ideals of beauty, partnership and happiness literally. But the idealistic concepts cannot stand comparison with reality. Through them, the internalized conformity is revealed as a physical self-regimentation. The polished, Hollywood-style embrace is a failure. The stiff gestures of the partners refuse to fit together. The popular myths cannot keep their promises. The tacit agreements prove to be valueless. Behind them the true need that can no longer be obscured by the shining façade is visible. With a nudge and a wink, the onlooker is made an accomplice to the unmasking; laughing together makes it easy to shrug off the compulsions.

But not just the 'outside world', the theatre, too, is included in the reflexions. The conventions of the theatrical apparatus, with its distinction between stage activity and audience passivity, are attacked in furious runs towards the front of the stage, and by extending the action into the auditorium. The audience are also made a direct subject of what is going on on the stage. At the end of the piece of the same name the dancers entice the audience to 'Come dance with me'.

The Dance Theatre Wuppertal resists the demands for superficial attractions, for inconsequential, purely aesthetic edification. As in *Ausdruckstanz*, which dispensed with elaborate sets and costumes in favour of concentration on the body and the dance, for Bausch, stage design and properties are subordinate to her intended statement. Her simple, poetic sets refuse to allow a passive, culinary, consumerist attitude. Their fragile beauty is always in danger, like the mass of flowers in *Carnations*, which is guarded by tethered dogs. The sets are 'tangible' (the original cast of a street, an oversized room in an old house, a cinema), far removed from any naturalism. They are poetic playgrounds (a lawn, a frozen painted sea, a huge pool of water), that stretch the 'realism' of dance theatre into a Utopian reality, a realistic Utopia. But, above all, they are spaces in which to move, whose structures impose certain prescribed movements on the dancers, that make those movements audible (for instance leaves or water on the floor), offer resistance.

The costumes, simple dresses and suits, high-heels and street shoes, or glittering, extravagant evening dress, are borrowed from reality. They are the 'typical' clothes of men and women and, instead of serving as mere decoration, they are questioned as to their function. They are the outer skin of a society trapped in rigid roles and frequently prove to be instruments of physical torture. Especially for the women, dressed as man-eating vamps or naive nymphets, clothes are, in line with the male ideals of beauty, tailor-made in the form of constricting identities. They leave no doubt as to what the men and women are selling. The openness of the stage, which is usually stripped to the fire walls and extends over the orchestra pit to the apron, is continued in the works themselves. In contrast to the usual consistency and continuity of communication, dance theatre thematizes the contradictions of the theatrical conventions. It refuses to accept the compulsion to exhibitionism or the audience's mute attitude of expectation. Theatre does not stand apart from reality. Dance theatre attacks what theatre embodies, as an institution – the rigidity – in order to make it once again a place of living experience. In the process, the frontier between rehearsal and performance is no longer recognized. The end product is revealed as what it really is, namely a product of development. The actors/dancers explain the next passage, discuss the coming scene, make no secret of their bad temper, or of their enjoyment of their work; they step forward with the words, 'I've got to do something', and are unsure of themselves. Just as the public and the private spheres converge, so the distinction between the production process 'behind the scenes' and the finished artistic product 'onstage' is no longer valid. By baring the creative process and its tools to view, dance theatre destroys the slick theatrical illusion. Theatre is brought back to life as an ongoing process of comprehending reality. It charges itself with the contradictions of reality and deals with them in full view of the public.

In one scene, a dancer tells of the tragi-comical process of training a goldfish to become a land animal, with the outcome that the creature, its environment having become alien to it, threatens to drown in water. The process of civilization – it would seem – leaves people high and dry in exactly the same way: in a physical reality that is like a foreign element.

Translated into English by Patricia Stadié

NOTE

1 The sociological concept of 'structure of affects' ('*Affektstruktur*') is taken from Elias (1976) who sees this as the dimension of the 'inner nature' of the individual, the modification of his physical behaviour and instincts, in relation to the 'outer nature', the social and economic conditions of certain forms of society.

6

IMAGINARY HOMELANDS: CREATING A NEW DANCE LANGUAGE

Shobana Jeyasingh

I have called my paper 'Imaginary Homelands'. This will probably be the only paper in this conference which has as its starting point a tube of shaving cream. This particular one was my gift to my brother and it bore the legend 'Mysore sandalwood shaving cream', and since our childhood home was not a million miles away from Mysore I thought it was a rather well chosen little gift. On receiving it, my brother rather unsubtly, I thought, started reading the small print. 'But it says made in England,' he exclaimed in a rather accusing tone of voice. So there you have a living everyday example of 'border tensions' as two supposedly mutually exclusive territories encroached on each other's terrain, producing a wail of dismay at the loss of authenticity and integrity. (Ironically, my brother is part of that international community of computer professionals whose culture brooks no limits of geography.)

Despite the multiple compass points of modern urban life, there are areas where a simpler mythical version seems to be preferred. You notice this in many areas and I suppose an area that immediately springs to mind is politics. In politics, definitions of national identity are often a denial of the sort of complex present in favour of some nostalgic, eternal and much purer past. Advertising, that ultimate myth-making machine, for example, makes easy fictions whether they be of ideal families or exotic holidays. These are, I think, all symptomatic of a refusal to see the changing borders raging all around. This refusal to see or to be allowed to see does not come about in a haphazard manner; rather it follows established patterns of power and discourse. The advertiser obviously wants to sell you his holiday, the politician wants the supreme power of all, to shape the story of the past – what we call history – in order to shape your present. One such established discourse is that between the East and the West. What we really mean is the 'colonized' and the 'colonizer' and the unequal power relationship between them. (See

Edward Said's book *Orientalism*, which deals with this whole area in great depth, as do the writings of Paul Gilroy, Homi Bhabha, and Salman Rushdie.)

So I can only talk about my personal experience in this area. In fact, whenever I hear the phrase 'East–West collaboration' used about what I do I have a very strange sensation. It is a sensation of being a baby wanting to be born but being pushed back into the uterus, of not being allowed to be born. 'You cannot come out,' says the midwife. 'Not as a common or garden British choreographer you can't, specially if you don't have any particular mission. Yes, you *can* have a mission – I mean to update Bharata Natyam. You can come out if you want to give voice to non-Western cultures or to oppressed minorities or Indian women or Third World issues. You can be a social ambassador, but not just a choreographer. You can come out if you make perhaps a colourful dance about arranged marriages, told entirely through hand gestures, of course. And this is very important – before you actually perform it, you have to explain each one because, of course, each one has a specific meaning and . . . What? You mean you want to work with a white composer? That will be a "cross-cultural collaboration". Never mind that he lives next door to you in Stamford Hill. But of course, if *he* wants to work with *you* that will be different, that will be "influenced by world music and his rich eclecticism". And what do you mean "West–East collaboration"? That just never happens. No, no, *we* engage in deeply ironic postmodern quotations but never collaborations, so in you go.'

I find this kind of experience as a citizen of a country where I want to be born, where I am labouring to be born, to be deeply undemocratic. I think it is very undemocratic to be prescribed your areas of concern, the issues that you want to deal with as a choreographer and as an artist. So I suppose what I reject about these categories is perhaps the best prologue to talking about what I do or what people like myself do. Central to these frustrations is not that I resent being an ambassador, because I think all dance work is representative of its maker's life and concerns and I think in that way all artists are ambassadors to their own private countries. I think what gets me is the sheer inaccuracy of the country I am supposed to be representing. The country I represent, I admit, is difficult to chart. It is definitely not India, especially that fictional incarnation of India as a place entrenched in deep spiritual and cultural certainties, if that exists. It is difficult to chart the landscape of my country for the simple reason that it is being created and imagined even as we board the train. The journey and the destination are one and that is home. As Marina Warner says in her book *Managing Monsters*, 'Home lies ahead in the unfolding of the story in the future, not behind waiting to be regained.' There is nothing particularly radical about what I say about this dynamic, ideal home. I think it is the experience of most city dwellers, of anyone whose life is different to their parents. Those of us who have been part of the great post-war migrations are only an extreme example of this imaginary home making. In fact, Homi Bhabha says in his book *The Location of Culture*, 'The truest eye may now belong to the migrant's double vision.' Perhaps that is why the Booker Prize is won again and again by the Rushdies and the Ondaatjes and the Ishiguros – by those who illuminate the dynamism of journeys, the constant packing and unpacking, the constant loss and recovery and loss again. Those who illustrate a pattern of belonging that is multi-dimensional. However, this experience of 'unhomeliness' is not to be confused with 'homelessness'. Rather, I think, to these artists their unhoming has been a source of immense creative activity. It is also no surprise, I think, that Marina Warner in her last Reith Lecture where she talked about British national identity does not invoke Churchill or Shakespeare but Derek Walcott – a man of mixed parentage who is content to forget the injuries of history and 'the vain search for one island that heals with its harbour and a guiltless horizon'. Obviously what he finds joyful is that 'there are so many islands'. Late twentieth-century living, whether lived in Bombay, in London or in that imaginary homeland of the Diaspora, which is where people like myself belong, has made Captain Kirks of us all.

Choreography 1991–1994

I shall start first with *Making of Maps*, which I made in 1991. I suppose the first thing I thought about when I made *Making of Maps* was the question of heritage. One of the things that I found very frustrating about East–West collaborations and crosscultural ventures was that they seemed to prescribe to me a very static view of my own heritage. For me, my heritage is a mix of David Bowie, Purcell, Shelley, and Anna Pavlova, and it has been mixed as subtly as a samosa has mixed itself into the English cuisine in the last ten years or so: impossible to separate. But it is surprising how to many people my heritage could only be things Indian.

About two years ago I asked Richard Alston to make a piece for my dancers, and he chose the music of Purcell. In one of the reports that I got from the Arts Council observers was the comment, 'The dancers are now dancing to *our* music, Purcell. It is wonderful that they have made it their own.' What I think the person did not know or did not care to know was that someone like myself from the age of 12 in my school assembly in Malaysia heard nothing but Purcell. So, for me, Purcell, like Shelley, like David Bowie, is not 'the other' – it is part of my heritage. And in dance terms Rukmani Devi *and* Merce Cunningham are also part of my heritage. So, *Making of Maps* really started in a way as a process of inventing my own heritage. One of the first things I did was to commission two composers to make the music. One, Alistair Macdonald, who lived in Birmingham, and the other R.A. Ramamani, who lived in Bangalore. One of the images that I had for *Making of Maps* was someone sitting in a room and playing different cassettes and different CDs into their machine or sitting in front of a radio and twiddling the knob. It seemed to me that one of the things that characterized the way my peers and I lived was the amazing accessibility and openness of the universe which was there for the taking. I also wanted sounds of everyday life, of station announcements, of church bells because, again, as Homi Bhabha says in his book, 'The recesses of the domestic space become sites for history's most intricate invasions.' So that was the kind of logic behind this work *Making of Maps*.

When I started *Making of Maps*, obviously I had to also look at what I did with the dance language. The dance language that I was given was Bharata Natyam and the reason *why* is rooted in certain historical events. The reason I learned Bharata Natyam was a direct result of the British presence in India. One of the movements in India which led to Independence came to be known as the 'Self-Respect Movement'. I suppose when the psyche of a country has been bashed around for over a hundred years, one of the things that actually happens when you want to break free is that you begin to re-evaluate and re-find your own culture. The struggle towards political independence was paralleled by our struggle for cultural credibility against the predominance of Greece and Rome. Therefore, for my parents, who were typical of their generation, it was important that their daughter learned Bharata Natyam, the classical dance of India. The idea was that by doing that we kept faith with something ancient and precious about Indian culture. In fact, as I grew up and started reading about the history of Bharata Natyam, I found that its antiquity was only half the story. It had suffered a great neglect and was rediscovered and rejuvenated in the early decades of this century – a process in which even Anna Pavlova had a part to play. It is a far more interesting and more subtle story than sometimes one is led to believe.

The advantages of a classical dance language are its strength and its power to communicate with sureness and confidence – and its objective technique that you can fit your body into. The things that I wanted to change were the rigidity that is there in lots of classical dance, the almost mechanical quality. You work very hard to attain a kind of virtuosic quality for no other reason except to be virtuosic, and I think in a way classical dance also has this feeling of a kind of impersonality which did not suit me. I wanted in some ways to introduce a strain of idiosyncrasy to balance this non-personal feeling, and I suppose, most importantly, it did not offer me those domestic spaces where those historically intricate moments happen. So we as a company looked at vocabulary, and I also looked at composition because I think in a way in *Making of Maps* more things happen in the area of composition than in the area of vocabulary, although obviously both cannot but be interconnected. Often, when one simplified the dance language – because obviously it started off as solo dancing and it has an immense density of structure but within one body – if one wanted to unpick that structure from the individual body, then one found that in fact one had to compensate by compositional layerings. Otherwise, you just ended up with something extremely flat and one-dimensional.

In the area of emotion, the floor seemed to beckon me in a very passionate manner. It is a very logical thing actually for a Bharata Natyam dancer to think about the floor. Bharata Natyam takes the body from the erect standing position and it wants the dancer to turn out at the hips and then lower the body along the central median into a demi-plié. Eighty per cent of the dance is actually done that way. The depth of plié is a very important part of Bharata Natyam. It is a dance which very much obeys the pull of gravity. It is very aware of the floor, but the way it actually relates to the floor is very contained, very formal. I wanted to make the dancers roll on the floor and embrace it in a much looser way than doing Bharata Natyam footwork. One of the things that I know, being a Bharata Natyam dancer, is that because it is quite a cerebral, quite an academic dance language, Bharata Natyam dancers become great experts at marking. It was good to have a movement which was outside the normal terminology of Bharata Natyam and which could not be marked. I think the formal qualities which I like about Bharata Natyam are still there in *Making of Maps*. The whole way I think about space and about bodies in space and their relation to time is very influenced by the formality in Bharata Natyam.

In the work *Romance . . . with Footnotes*, I was trying to see how much emotion I could get out of formal movement. For me touch was something that I and my dancers played around with because, again, we come from a solo tradition where the body is extremely self-sufficient. It is also very much in command of the space that it performs in. With each piece that I make, I try and go further – to go further into an emotional relationship which the dancer has with the space around or with the person with whom they are dancing. *Romance* starts off with certain iconic positions which are there in Indian dance, and I have tried to change them and give them much more of an incidental feel, a much more friendly feel.

Raid, which we are touring at the moment, is based on a game that is played in the streets of India and Birmingham and Glasgow, called 'Kabbadi'. I suppose it is the sheer perversity of the game really that interested me because although there are two teams, the 'raiding' is done by a single raider who runs into the opponents' territory and takes on the entire team singlehandedly. All the time they are in the enemy territory they have to hold their breath and chant 'Kabbadi, Kabbadi' to prove that they are holding their breath. While they are holding their breath they have to try and touch one person on any part of their body and then run as fast as they can back home. Once they have actually touched somebody, all seven of the opponents can tackle the raider, piling on top of them and holding them down until they lose their breath. The other thing that intrigued me was that even though it was a game of territories the border line was there for crossing. It was crossed and re-crossed the whole time and all the interesting things happened when the raider actually crossed and went over to the other side. While they were in their home ground nothing much dynamic happened at all. I find sport an interesting area because with all this talk about East and West, sport is one area where post-colonial discourse does not seem to happen. People are quite happy for Linford Christie to be extremely British as long as he is winning, and I sometimes wonder whether if Linford Christie were a choreographer or a painter, his ethnic origins would be more of an issue.

Raid is a piece about two territories, and because I am called Shobana Jeyasingh, people assume that these two territories must be East and West. In fact, they are not. They are sport and dance. I suppose the prosaic and the poetic. One of the things that I had in mind when I choreographed it was something that I had read a very long time ago in that book *A Hundred Years of Solitude* by Gabriel Garcia Marquez where he goes from describing something very, very ordinary, a scene in somebody's kitchen, to then looking out of the window where he says 'and then there was a rain of marigolds'. I thought it was really a brilliant way of one territory very slowly going into another with perfect credibility. In my own humble way I also wanted to go from the kitchen into that rain of marigolds.

Questions received from Conference delegates

QUESTION: *What type of things do you do in the studio with your dancers? Can you describe the process?*

SJ: The process actually changes from piece to piece and from year to year because I don't have a permanent company. In fact, each year there is always a change to the people in the company so in a way a lot depends on who the people are. For example, for this particular piece *Raid* we started by watching lots of videos of the game and looked at the rules of the game and the type of movements. On the whole, I suppose I am quite a directive choreographer in that I have a picture in my head when I come to the studio of roughly what I want to do and where I want to go. With this particular company that I am touring with at the moment there have been more instances of me handing phrases which the dancers actually developed or played around with. We would look at it and see whether it would fit or not. Obviously, one of the things that characterizes the way I work is that all the dancers are trained in Bharata Natyam so that gives us a common language as far as things in that area are concerned. However, when the movement is personal and invented, we do not have that common terminology and have to make up our own.

QUESTION: *I am curious how you take from that traditional vocabulary.*

SJ: It is really trial and error. Sometimes I have an image in my head of what it could look like and then I ask the dancers to try something. I use improvisation in a way as a process of communicating rather than as a way of getting vocabulary out of the dancers. So sometimes I set up a particular problem or a particular thing to solve and by doing it I hope they understand what I want them to do. It might not actually be what they have been doing, but it is a way of showing the road which I want to take – which I often do in the studio.

QUESTION: *Do you see yourself in the future seeking a new, third language, say, designating a movement so that this is movement number 1. Not so much finding a terminology as a movement vocabulary, so that you could say to your dancers, 'Do movement number 1 or movement number 2.'*

SJ: I think it's difficult when you make contemporary dance work actually to find that way of signalling because it changes from year to year. If I put a name to it, then I'll be doing what I'm trying to get away from. Because when you put a name to it, that's when you make it rigid. In some ways it's good to be rigid, I'm not saying it's all bad – but that it would be the problem because one year I might want to call it X and the next year I might want to call it Y. Very confusing for the dancer!

QUESTION: *In Indian film music, there are all kinds of influences; they have Mozart's 40th Symphony or popular songs, for example. Do you think that the ritual and general nature of the history of Bharata Natyam is one of the reasons why people, Indians in particular, think it's so sacrosanct, not to touch it or tamper with it?*

SJ: I think it goes back to what happened in India in the 1930s and 1940s. I think it has to do with those political reasons why Indians such as my parents felt that in dance and music one had some image of India which they wanted to hold very precious. Obviously, to recover Bharata Natyam took a lot of effort by various people, so there is a very natural inclination to conserve. But when one has the confidence that comes out of that conservation – and I'm saying that it's a very important process – then the next step is to say, 'Well, actually, now that I'm sure and free, I need to take a step forward.' I'm not saying that Indians have a very specific culture and therefore they won't find the relevances. I'm saying the opposite, actually. I'm saying that in cities in India, as you say, there is an amazing mixture of influences. So I think Indians are not any more particular than anyone else in any other country where there is also a mixture of past and present, of juggling various elements. We're all jugglers now.

PART II

PERFORMING DANCE

> Silently executing steps and manipulating the body, obediently complying with the teacher's or the choreographer's demands, the dancer moves through space – both stage and studio – often without uttering a sound, denied the conventional means of attracting attention: the human voice.
>
> (Lunn 1994: 26)

Here Jonathan Lunn, British choreographer/dancer, is making a plea against the 'mutism' of modern dance when he implores dancers to be more verbally articulate in order to play a full and active role in the creative process and in their profession at large. Since the Judson era (see Banes 1980), more and more dancers are 'speaking up', not necessarily in order to politicize their status but to share their views and experiences. Nevertheless, compared with their colleagues in other forms of theatre whose job rests on the spoken word, dancers are understandably still reluctant to be self-reflective in speech or writing. In fact, whereas in other Parts of this Reader the challenge was to find representative work from the wide selection available, for this Part, the difficulty was in finding writing by dancers at all, especially on their experiences of performance.

Barbara Newman's book from which the following extract is drawn is a collection of interviews with performers who work predominantly in the ballet genre. The juxtaposition of four of these dancers' attitudes to how they prepare for a role, and their creation/interpretation of those roles, produces a fascinating comparison. With reference to Tudor's dramatic *Pillar of Fire* (1942), Nora Kaye discusses the relationship between dancer and choreographer, and her need to be fully prepared before starting work on a new role. Her difficulty with the character of Giselle can be compared to Alicia Alonso's enthusiastic reading of the story of this Romantic ballet. Both agree, however, on the importance of dancers immersing themselves in the context of the work, its narrative and its stylistic features. In contrast, Tanaquil LeClercq takes a very businesslike approach to Balanchine's *The Four Temperaments* (1946) and Peter Martins tussles with the problem of how to deal with a quasi-narrative ballet, yet retain the abstraction of a neo-classical work such as *Apollo* (Balanchine 1928).

It is fortunate for our heritage that one of the most important figures in the development of modern dance, Martha Graham, has been eloquent in the expression of her beliefs. In her personal manifesto for the dancer (and, by implication, the choreographer), she allies the experience of life with the experience of dance. Learning, in both, is acquired through practice; the dancer becomes 'an athlete of God'. The training of the dancer requires a holistic approach to body/mind and the cultivation of the whole being. Graham pleads for openness to the past, the 'blood memory' of the body, and to the present. The dancer must be 'reborn to the instant', permitting feeling and vulnerability.

Graham's writing, not only in its content but also in its metaphysical style, reflects the aesthetic beliefs which are embodied in her choreography. Working at the time of the artistic movement of abstract expressionism, Graham attempted to deal with the 'inner landscape' of humankind and the role of the subconscious and of memory. For Graham, the dancer/choreographer was a unique, special individual, an Artist. For the next generation of post-modernists, 'Art' became 'art' and a more pragmatic sensibility pervaded their writing.

During the last decade or so, one of the significant changes in how dancers in theatre art perceive their work is hinted at by Rebecca Hilton, who, at the time of interview, was working with Stephen Petronio's company in New York. In smaller scale, independent modern dance companies today, performers no longer expect just to perform or to be 'someone else's tool'. They aspire, or are expected to make a direct contribution to the development of choreographic material, mainly through improvisational processes.[1] The democratic aspirations of the postmodern/New Dance movement, the entry of dancers into the profession who have studied the craft of the making as well as the doing of dance, and the trend towards devised work have all contributed to these changing demands on the dancer. Hilton reflects on other long-held assumptions about how dancers prepare themselves for performance, including the questionable imperative of the daily technique class. She acknowledges the range of alternative approaches from which the professional dancer can choose in order to develop the 'physical intelligence' of the body. Hilton also argues that it is important for the dancer to acquire knowledge about the anatomical basis of movement in order to understand the needs, constraints and potential of each individual body.

The very concepts of 'dance', 'dancer' and 'performance' are tested in Susan Kozel's writing on her experience in a virtual reality performance in Amsterdam in 1994. Kozel offers a phenomenological account of moving in technological space, and through her cognitive reflection upon her kines-thetic experience, social and philosophical issues relating to dance and virtual reality emerge.

It is, perhaps, fitting that this Part should end with Kozel's account, for here is an example of writing which addresses two significant developments in dance practice and study. First, the age-old human activity of dance and the futuristic technology of the virtual world are united; it remains to be seen how much impact each will have on the other and how technology will expand conceptual boundaries as well as the practice of dance. Second, in Kozel's writing, the actual/virtual experience of dancing is imbued with a scholarly perspective to the mutual enrichment of both.

NOTE

1 Lauren Potter (1993) notes how during her professional dance training in London in the late 1970s, 'improvisation' was almost a dirty word. Even in modern dance, 'the emphasis was on training and perfecting the body in recognised techniques, alongside assimilating the "technique" of choreography' (Potter 1993: 60).

FURTHER READING

To date, very little substantive literature exists in the area of dance performance. Books on the techniques of various dance forms, improvisation or choreography may address the technical and interpretative skills required by a dancer, and interviews with dancers in journals and magazines can provide useful insights. For 'inside accounts' autobiographies are a fascinating source.

Autobiography/biography: Seymour (1984); Kirkland (1987); McGehee (1989); Farrell (1990). Collections of primary sources on dancers/choreographers' perspectives on dance: Newman (1992) on ballet; Morrison Brown (1979) on modern dance
Performance: Adamson and Lidbury (1992); Koner (1993). Journals such as *Contact Quarterly* (USA); *Writings on Dance* (Australia) and *Dance Now* (UK) often include articles by dancers on performance
Dance and technology: Trotter (1995)

7

DANCERS TALKING ABOUT PERFORMANCE

Barbara Newman

NORA KAYE *discusses characterization in* Pillar of Fire (*Tudor 1942*) *and her attitude to some of the roles in the traditional repertoire.*
When [Tudor] actually started rehearsing, he started with the three sisters, and even before he started the actual steps, the choreography, he talked so much and so clearly about our characters and the small town in which we lived, and he even described the wallpaper of our house. It was so clear in our minds that we couldn't have done a wrong movement if we had tried. It felt absolutely right because were so absolutely sure of our characterizations. By discussing it and immersing ourselves in those characters, it became part of us.

If there's time, I always like to have that period first, of discussing why the characterization has to be this particular thing. I don't like to find it during the process of working; I like to do it all before. And I like to learn the music, so I know it before I start with the choreography. For the most part, *Pillar* was choreographed sequentially. We did little pieces here and there, but he tried to do it as the music went. Some choreographers don't work that way. They work right on the floor and they don't necessarily start from the beginning – they jump around. I've worked both ways, but I prefer Tudor's way. He just has ideas in his head but no movement at all.

It's very difficult to say where the creator and the interpreter take on and leave off. The dancer becomes an instrument, and also it's a physical thing, that you move in a particular way. Let's say he was the author and the director and I was just the instrument, the actor. You're not an automaton; you automatically personalize things that you're told to do. It happens with actors and actresses all the time; I see that now that I'm in that field. There's always the play, but there's always what the actor brings to the lines. I never changed anything he wanted me to do and never questioned anything. I made myself very malleable.

I approached all the Tudor ballets the same way I approached *Pillar*, and I tried to do the same thing with the classical ballets but it was more difficult for me. For instance, I thought Giselle was a silly girl. I could never under-stand her. And I thought the ballet was silly. It made no sense to me as a narrative ballet, and I had a great deal of trouble with it. I went to Paris with Margot Fonteyn and we studied with (Olga) Preobrajenska, because Margot had trouble with it too before she made some weird step with it I could never figure out. I never got it right. There was so much you had to close your eyes to in terms of it making sense to you as a performer, and I never could. I did the best I could with it but I was never happy with it. I didn't mind doing mime at all, because you were doing that kind of ballet. I liked the rigid, traditional aspect of the mime. I just couldn't bring myself to understand the whole character of Giselle.

You can play with *Swan Lake* because it isn't realistic. It's camp, in a funny kind of way. The third act is really your idea of Pola Negri and the silent screen stars – but that's fun – and the second act is very lyrical and lovely and romantic. That I understood much more than I did *Giselle*.

I never went at those roles with awe. It was just a challenge, and either got through it to the best of my ability or I didn't. I never thought I did *Giselle* properly. I never liked *Firebird* – we didn't do the Fokine version, we did another version by (Adolph) Bolm. And I certainly never liked *Petrouchka*, not because it was a silly ballet but because the Ballerina wasn't a very satisfying role. I just didn't like it.

In the abstract ballets you concentrate on your technique, your line and trying to do what the choreographer wants. It's just another approach. I was never particularly happy doing that kind of ballet because I wanted something with a little more emotion and not just steps.

ALICIA ALONSO *on the role of* Giselle
In our company, in Ballet Nacional de Cuba, we try definitely to understand the Romantic style, definitely to understand in what time was that ballet done, what is the story about, what kind of person each of them was. And then, out of that work, to put their personality into it. This is very important. And that's what I have to decide and try to do with myself.

That role is very special. I think it captures the essence of Romanticism in a very beautiful way. It has a definite style, it has a story that is eternal, and it has a contrast of the First Act to the Second Act – they're so different – that to the audience becomes very beautiful, very entertaining. And also, I think *Giselle* is one of the classics that has the right length as a spectacle, and it combines music, a style of dancing, choreography, pantomime.

Something that every dancer likes is that it's very definite, clear. The expression of a dancer is not just technique. The art is how skilfully the technique is used. It's skill, like a doctor with the operating table, how skil-fully he manages those instruments. The dancer has to be that skilful, to have a technique and at the same time to be able to use it in an extremely expressive way.

At the beginning at Ballet Theatre, the Romantic style was new to every-one [. . .] I learned the style through books, and reading old write-ups. And from then on I've been reading everything about the Romantic era, looking at lithographs and critics of the time. I started then, and I have never fin-ished. I'm still doing it. I still read about different dancers of the *Romant-isme*, their different styles. Not only because I like that epoch, no. I read about all of ballet. Before I do any ballet in my life, I try to know the most about it that I can.

I think all the background material gives you richness, richness to under-stand the part and to take the most advantage of it. I think it's most import-ant when we do any part. When you dance *Giselle*, whether you're a *corps de ballet* or a soloist or prima ballerina or premier danseur, you should know all about it. You should read and research the most you can about it, so you can portray the style and believe in what you're dancing. Today when you see a company, you notice not that they do it automatically, not that they do it because they have been told what to do, when to do, but that one of the most difficult things for them is to believe in what they're doing when they do it.

In Act I, when she comes out of the door, Giselle is life itself! She's not exactly doomed, but slowly, as you look at this person, you begin to under-stand that she's not just like all the other women, that there's something different on her, something more fragile. You cannot put your actual finger on it, but there's something about her that doesn't quite let go. It should make the audience hold their breath looking at her, because they don't know what will happen.

There are different versions of *Giselle*. In some versions, the audience gets the feeling that she knows Loys, and everybody around already knows him. In our version, Ballet Nacional de Cuba, we do it she's introducing him for the first time to her friends, to all the peasants. They don't know him. Because they are there, because they are celebrating this special once-a-year festival of the harvest, and are going to make Giselle their queen for the festival, they find her for the first time with him. Maybe, in the story, one of them has seen him, another one saw him another time, but not all of them could have seen him. And they analyse that this man is not a peasant. If he were, they would ask the logical question: 'Where does he live? He's not one of us.' All the peasants cannot know him, because they ask instead, 'What work does he do for a living? I don't see him picking the grapes. I don't see him working the earth.' That's why she presents him to the friends and says, 'I will dance for him.'

But that doesn't mean this is the first time *I* see him. Not Alonso – it's Giselle we're talking about. She's known him long enough to love him. There is no time when you know that you love – I mean, a pure love. There is not one moment that you say, 'There it is.' You cannot talk about time, about counting dates, being very practical, when you're talking about art.

When I say that I work on Giselle, I'm not only working on the person of Giselle, on the main role. For me, everything that surrounds. Giselle is most important to understand, the why of the existence of Giselle, the problems of Giselle, what happens to Giselle. You cannot do Giselle alone. You have to do it with a frame, with a company, with every detail.

I have worked this version based on the original. Every person and everything that's part of the story has a place in it and has a why, a reason. Even the Wilis; each Wili has a story in herself. They know why they are dead and why they are here. Each of them! We make it like this because this makes the frame and makes the story, and this goes into the audience. It's like . . . if you see a painting of a great master, but he only started, he only drew one person, and the rest is just a sketch, then you say, 'Oh, why didn't he finish it?' That's what I think when you see *Giselle*. You have to see every part finished so you can enjoy the whole thing.

Giselle's own story is right there onstage. If her story is not told onstage, then you cannot believe any of the other Wilis. If you read the poem of the Wilis by Heine, which is where Gautier got the idea of the story, then you realize that the other ones are just an old German legend. But you see her actual story.

But go back to Act 1. She feels sorry for Hilarion. If you knew Giselle, she can never feel that anybody would be a nuisance. She doesn't want to hurt him; she doesn't want to hurt anyone. She's incapable of hurting anyone. But she's fragile, and that's why she can be hurt. She loves to dance because she loves life itself. She loves everything that's around her, and when she dances, she portrays everything. She's happy, she's tender, she's gay. A very, very happy person, very alive, and yet she's fragile. But sometimes when people are ill, they are the people who enjoy life the most. Because in every bit of it, they realize the value of it. That's her a little bit too. So, just to say that she likes dancing because of dancing seems to me not to show the real person that we're studying: Giselle, in a Romantic era, surrounded by people who love her and believe in her, and so fragile.

Of course, she's ill from the beginning, of course. When you have studied this story as I have studied, deeply, to be able to portray it, you do it in this way, artistically and realistically. Now, you study a person who is sick with a heart, trouble with a heart, who can die like a bird, so quick. It must be a person who must have trouble at certain times; she must be weak. It's not the first time that Giselle had anything wrong with the heart. Because why does the mother not want her to dance? You must follow this story logically, and then create the artistic surroundings, the atmosphere of it. But you must base yourself in something real of life, with logic, and you have to base the pantomime in reality too. You have to have a logic in your pantomime, a logic in the people you present on the stage, and after that comes your artistry. Then you create. You put on the clothes you should, the make-up you should, the gesture. You study it, and then you melt it together, and that *becomes*.

Because, first of all, you're not dancing for yourself – you're dancing for an audience. You believe the part, but they must believe in it too. Therefore, in a theatre, and especially in our theatre today, you have to use every little bit of theatrical technique to be able to create the atmosphere that you want. You must study: if a person is sick of a heart, how sick could she be? How long has she been having this illness? Why would her mother not want her to dance? You must ask a doctor, 'What kind of heart did she have? What kind of feeling? How does she feel physically when, for instance, she dances too much? *What* does she feel?' You ask the doctor, who will say, 'You feel heart beat faster than usual, faster. It loses timing. And then, when you take it easy, it goes back again. She feels well, normal.' Well, for me it helps. And I've studied, I've studied. Some other dancers have not, and they're beautiful! But to me, it's like that.

It's about time that all dancers learned theatre. They have to learn it. They have to know what is drama, and they must read the history of art. And when they're going to do any ballet, they must read all about it, in every way.

TANAQUIL LECLERCQ *on her creation of the 'Choleric' section in* The Four Temperaments (*Balanchine 1946*)
You don't get pushed around so much in that section [of *Four Temperaments*] even when the four boys promenade you. You give your arm to one, you do arabesque, then you do *soutenu* on your own, then you give your arm to another one, and if he's good, he stays out of your way. You do your arabesque minding your own business, unless he's a lump and knocks you off. And then there are the two boys under your arms for that lift in the finale, and it's only done twice. So you feel secure – no problems. When you're young, you don't think as much as you do later on, when you've danced more and you realize all the awful things that could happen. You just go in and do it.

I'm not sure about the different finales. I don't think the soloists were involved in that; it was the other people who had different things. I think the couples always did the glissade, jeté across, and we always did that massed group, kick, lean. At one point he had it like a circle and they used to go up and down in waves. He said it was 'my Radio City Music Hall number', sort of Florence Rogge style. I remember it distinctly, but it doesn't seem to me that I was in that circle. I wouldn't swear, but I have a feeling it was all the corps people. But my part always remained exactly the same as he originally staged it.

As we continued to do it and we got out of those costumes. I wouldn't say I danced it differently, but I danced it better because I was better technically. I could take more chances, throw myself around. I knew the music like the palm of my hand. It was very comfy, and it was a nice fast thing – I wasn't on

61

the stage for hours. You zipped in and zipped out and made an impression. In other words, I liked dancing it very much. I don't say that I had a different interpretation when I didn't have a costume – it was the same thing. I had the choreography and how it should look. It should look maximum, 100 per cent everything: move 100 per cent, turn 100 per cent, stop dead. Kick legs as much as you can, straight knee, pointed toe. Zip round. Fast. Nothing slow, no adaaaggio. [. . .] Kick, wham, fast, hard, big. You have certain steps that you have to do in a certain amount of time, and the certain steps give it a certain flavour. But you can't interpret because you'll be late, you won't be with the music.

I had no sense that any part of what I was doing was any more important than any other part, or that any step was pulling anything together. And if people write about it that way, I think they're wrong. I think they're just writing because they have to write. If you said to George Balanchine, 'Those three ronds de jambe pull the ballet together,' he would faint. He would absolutely faint. I know from having sat with him and read reviews. He said, 'What is this man talking about?' Third movement Bizet (Symphony in C), all they're doing is plié and up, plié and up, and someone wrote something about 'The Danes did it a certain way'. George said, 'What the hell is he talking about? All they're doing is demi-plié, up, demi-plié, up.' People read into something. Everybody takes away a different impression. Fine. But they're all private citizens, and it doesn't make it so. It's very nice in *Serenade* – she falls down. And somebody thinks it's death and somebody thinks it's life and somebody thinks it's so-and-so. Fine. But to write and say, 'This pulls it together' – that I think is idiotic. It's certainly not true from the dancer's point of view, unless you're a very pretentious dancer and say, 'I'm doing three ronds de jambe and I'm pulling the whole ballet together.' It's nothing like that. It's very primitive, banal. You go on and you do the best you know how, and you don't worry about other things, other this, other that, anything. And if Balanchine has a master plan, he doesn't tell you that he has it.

PETER MARTINS *on his interpretation of the title role in* Apollo (*Balanchine 1928*)
As a rule, I prefer not to look at too much or do any reading. If you have to do *Romeo and Juliet* or *Hamlet*, you have to know what it's all about, and then you read about it. It's nice to know the story. But *Apollo* is a Greek myth, and what more do you need to know than this is a young god? You need to know he's the son of Leto? Fine, all right, so you know that. You look that up and you see a picture . . . But what pictures do you look at? Michelangelo's Apollo? Who do you look at? There's a wonderful story about Balanchine – he told it to me. After the première of *Apollo* in Paris, somebody said to him, 'How could you make Apollo look like this, walking on his knees and all awkward? Apollo is a god. He doesn't look like that and he shouldn't do stuff like that.' And Balanchine said, in response, 'How do

you know what Apollo looks like? Who knows? [. . .] As long as you know he's the god Apollo, he has the three Muses, he chooses, that's all you need to know.' I personally always resent – not resent – but I try not to get too analytical, because the role can lose its spontaneity and its flavour.

The music is what you dig into, especially when you work with Balanchine, because that says a lot. I got a record of *Apollo* and I listened to it a lot, and I think several things were revealed to me by listening to the score. But you don't have to analyse story lines or meanings. With *Four Temperaments*, you might ask, 'What does this movement mean?' But the minute you hear the music, you know. You think, 'Ah, this is why he made that movement,' and often it's not because he's trying to tell a story.

I don't mean to analyse and tell a story about *Apollo*. I'm sure Balanchine has a story in his mind, but I don't know and I don't really care to know what it is. I don't want to have him sit there and explain in terms of a story. I'd much rather discover it myself through the steps. What he wants to convey is so obvious and so clear in the steps. But where the ballet starts now, in the new version, Apollo is already – in *my* mind anyway – in command. He's not a child; he's a god. Therefore, you have no development of a character, which for somebody like me who's done it so much is maybe too bad. It's nice to do the little child and grow up and build the character to the end. But this is just as valid; you already are when the curtain goes up and, you remain the same person throughout.

Something like *Apollo* is so simple, so rich in itself, that you don't have to add anything. It's all there. To me, the less you add, the stronger it becomes. Anything you add becomes an obstruction, gets in the way. There's no need to add – I hate to say, but I can't find better words – anything of your own. To say consciously 'I'm going to add something of me' is wrong. You just have to do it the way you are; that's why you were chosen to do it in the first place because the choreographer sees the way you are. There's no need to do more than is required; the interpretation is already in the pure dance-design. That's again why I so much prefer Balanchine ballets over anybody else's, because they're pure dance-designs that don't need fuss.

There is a big difference between *Violin Concerto* and *Apollo*. The minute you start adding to *Apollo*, you would tend to add a story. Maybe not a story, but feelings and emotions. What else could you add? But there's no feeling or emotion or thought to add to *Violin Concerto*, so what you add is purely physical; maybe you do a jump differently. But also, when he choreographed *Violin*, he used my dancing. He said to me, 'What can you do here? Do what you can do.' So *Violin* is much more me than *Apollo*. I dance *Violin* the way *I* dance, and that's *why* I dance it. In *Apollo*, I'm doing somebody else.

I want you to see a child being born. He comes out of the bandages, he's born, and he screams. And he simply cannot stand up at all. The two maidens take his hands and teach him to play the lute. Then there's a blackout, and the next thing you see is him starting out dancing. It's as if you're seeing ten or fifteen or two years roll by, just in the first variation, the 'birth' variation I call it. He's actually discovering his two legs, like a little animal, like a horse when it's just born. The solo is like the first time you see a little child walk. Progressively, he becomes more secure; the first step he cannot walk, the fifth step he all of a sudden can sense the solid ground with his feet. Essentially, the variation finishes as it begins, with him playing lute. But there's a big difference. Now – not to over-analyse and not to interpret to the last detail – now there's a slight . . . not authority *per se*, but now he knows what he's doing. And as he does that, the three Muses come on. He plays the lute, and there they are. This is how I see it. It has never been explained, never been told, it's not written anywhere why he calls them, but you want to select the one for you. You want to select your Muse.

I wouldn't say you challenge them, but you play with them. That's a very difficult part of the ballet, because there you shouldn't be too mature already. Even though at the end of the variation you're not a little boy any more, you're still playful with them. He pulls them after him, he takes two away, he takes one away, he plays. One is already selected in the choreography, when he splits the two from the one. Already there you get the idea of selection, but it's basically playfulness.

Now I want to see what they are offering. I give one symbol to each of them, and I essentially say, 'Dance for me. Show me you have to offer.' Then I sit down, and the way I am sitting is . . . now I have authority. Without a doubt, the most difficult part of the ballet, to me, is when I sit there and watch the three variations, because you cannot act. You cannot sit and emote. Even though the first girl is playing all to me, I cannot pull away and I can't lean towards her. It's still a neoclassic, abstract ballet. And yet I cannot sit slumped. There has to be a certain presence and a certain awareness of what they're doing, yet without acting. And you cannot do it in your face at all. This is my view of it – I'm not talking for Balanchine; he never told me this. But you cannot show in your face dislike or happiness or pleasure or any emotion at all. You have to show everything in your neck, in your spine, and in your being. And you have to show very little, or else your sitting there becomes ridiculous. When you're dancing, then you are using your body, and the choreography expresses what you are supposed to express. But when you're sitting there and you have really nothing to do, that is the most difficult thing.

I do my solo right after, and now I am a man or a young god. I'm not a boy any more – now I know what I am doing. I have already selected Terpsichore and I am dancing for her, I suppose. That solo is very strong, very powerful, and very masculine in a sense. There isn't any more to it than the fact that I am now completely in charge, I have selected my Muse, and I dance.

It's a love *pas de deux*, like any other pas de deux. We're expressing our love for each other. It's not a difficult *pas de deux* at all. I wouldn't say any of

Apollo is technically difficult. The plasticity of it, the shaping of it, is what's difficult. I mean, *entrechat six* or *entrechat cinq* or double pirouette turned in is not difficult, but it's difficult to make that look interesting. I've always found the most difficult part about *Apollo* is not to fall into the temptation to act the ballet. I have seen people do that, and it looks wrong. It's too much. I don't mean you can dance the steps without being there, and without believing that there's something behind them, but I don't think you should start acting in your face and putting in a character that you have analysed beforehand. That'll ruin it all. That's why it is very difficult to talk about, also.

8

I AM A DANCER

Martha Graham

I am a dancer.

I believe that we learn by practice. Whether it means to learn to dance by practising dancing or to learn to live by practising living, the principles are the same. In each it is the performance of a dedicated precise set of acts, physical or intellectual, from which comes shape of achievement, a sense of one's being, a satisfaction of spirit. One becomes in some area an athlete of God.

To practise means to perform, in the face of all obstacles, some act of vision, of faith, of desire. Practice is a means of inviting the perfection desired.

I think the reason dance has held such an ageless magic for the world is that it has been the symbol of the performance of living. Even as I write, time has begun to make today yesterday – the past. The most brilliant scientific discoveries will in time change and perhaps grow obsolete as new scientific manifestations emerge. But art is eternal, for it reveals the inner landscape, which is the soul of man.

Many times I hear the phrase 'the dance of life'. It is an expression that touches me deeply, for the instrument through which the dance speaks is also the instrument through which life is lived – the human body. It is the instrument by which all the primaries of life are made manifest. It holds in its memory all matters of life and death and love. Dancing appears glamorous, easy, delightful. But the path to the paradise of the achievement is not easier than any other. There is fatigue so great that the body cries, even in its sleep. There are times of complete frustration, there are daily small deaths. Then I need all the comfort that practice has stored in my memory, a tenacity of faith.

It takes about ten years to make a mature dancer. The training is twofold. First comes the study and practice of the craft which is the school where you are working in order to strengthen the muscular structure of the body. The body is shaped, disciplined, honoured, and in time, trusted. The movement becomes clean, precise, eloquent, truthful. Movement never lies. It is a barometer telling the state of the soul's weather to all who can read it. This

66

might be called the law of the dancer's life – the law which governs its outer aspects.

Then comes the cultivation of the being from which whatever you have to say comes. It doesn't just come out of nowhere, it comes out of a great curiosity. The main thing, of course, always is the fact that there is only one of you in the world, just one, and if that is not fulfilled then something has been lost. Ambition is not enough; necessity is everything. It is through this that the legends of the soul's journey are retold with all their tragedy and their bitterness and sweetness of living. It is at this point that the sweep of life catches up with the mere personality of the performer, and while the individual becomes greater, the personal becomes less personal. And there is grace. I mean the grace resulting from faith . . . faith in life, in love, in people, in the act of dancing. All this is necessary to any performance in life which is magnetic, powerful, rich in meaning. In a dancer, there is a reverence for such forgotten things as the miracle of the small beautiful bones and their delicate strength. In a thinker, there is a reverence for the beauty of the alert and directed and lucid mind. In all of us who perform there is an awareness of the smile which is part of the equipment, or gift, of the acrobat. We have all walked the high wire of circumstance at times. We recognize the gravity pull of the earth as he does. The smile is there because he is practising living at that instant of danger. He does not choose to fall. At times I fear walking that tightrope. I fear the venture into the unknown. But that is part of the act of creating and the act of performing. That is what a dancer does.

People have asked me why I chose to be a dancer. I did not choose. I was chosen to be a dancer, and with that, you live all your life. When any young student asks me, 'Do you think I should be a dancer?' I always say, 'If you have to ask, then the answer is no.' Only if there is one way to make life vivid for yourself and for others should you embark upon such a career . . . You will know the wonders of the human body because there is nothing more wonderful. The next time you look into the mirror, just look at the way the ears rest next to the head; look at the way the hairline grows; think of all the little bones in your wrist. It is a miracle. And the dance is a celebration of that miracle.

I feel that the essence of dance is the expression of man – the landscape of his soul. I hope that every dance I do reveals something of myself or some wonderful thing a human being can be. It is the unknown – whether it is the myths or the legends or the rituals that give us our memories. It is the eternal pulse of life, the utter desire. I know that when we have rehearsals, and we have them every day, there are some dancers, particularly men, who cannot be still. One of the men in my company is not built to be still. He has to be moving. I think at times he does not know what he is doing, but that is another matter. He's got the essence of a man's inner life that prods him to dance. He has that desire. Every dance is a kind of fever chart, a graph of the heart. Desire is a lovely thing, and that is where the dance comes from, from desire.

Each day of rehearsal for a new ballet I arrive at a little before two in the afternoon, and sit alone in my studio to have a moment of stillness before the dancers enter. I tease myself and say I am cultivating my Buddha nature; but it is really just such a comforting place for me to be – secure, clear, and with a purpose. It is that order of these elements together that led one writer to call dance 'glorified human behaviour'. I sit with my back to our large mirrors so that I am completely within myself.

Outside my studio door, in my garden, is a tree that has always been a symbol of facing life, and in many ways it is a dancer. It began as a sapling when I first moved here and although a wire gate was in its way, it persisted and grew to the light, and now thirty years later it is a tree with a very thick trunk, with the wire embedded within. Like a dancer it went to the light and carried the scars of its journey inside. You traverse, you work, you make it right. You embody within yourself that curiosity, use that avidity for life no matter whether it is for good or for evil. The body is a sacred garment. It's your first and your last garment; it is what you enter life in and what you depart life with, and it should be treated with honour, and with joy and with fear as well. But always, though, with blessing.

They say that the two primary arts were dance and architecture. The word 'theatre' was a verb before it was a noun – an act, then a place. That means you must make the gesture, the effort, the real effort to communicate with another being. And you also must have a tree to shelter under in case of storm or sun. There is always that tree, that creative force, and there is always a house, a theatre. The spine is your body's tree of life. And through it a dancer communicates; his body says what words cannot, and if he is pure and open, he can make of his body a tragical instrument.

I am absorbed in the magic of movement and light. Movement never lies. It is the magic of what I call the outer space of the imagination. There is a great deal of outer space, distant from our daily lives, where I feel our imagination wanders sometimes. It will find a planet or it will not find a planet, and that is what a dancer does.

And then there is inspiration. Where does it come from? Mostly from the excitement of living. I get it from the diversity of a tree or the ripple of the sea, a bit of poetry, the sighting of a dolphin breaking the still water and moving toward me ... anything that quickens you to the instant. And whether one would call that inspiration or necessity, I really do not know. At times I receive that inspiration from people; I enjoy people very much and for the most part feel it is returned. I simply happen to love people. I do not love them all individually, but I love the idea of life pulsing through people – blood and movement.

For all of us, but particularly for a dancer with his intensification of life and his body, there is a blood memory that can speak to us. Each of us from our mother and father has received their blood and through their parents and their parents' parents and backward into time. We carry thousands of years of that blood and its memory. How else to explain those instinctive gestures and thoughts that come to us, with little preparation or expectation. They come perhaps from some deep memory of a time when the world was chaotic, when, as the Bible says, the world was nothing. And then, as if some door opened slightly, there was light. It revealed certain wonderful things. It revealed terrifying things. But it was light.

William Goyen, in *The House of Breath*, wrote that 'we are the carriers of lives and legends – who knows the unseen frescoes on the private walls of the skull.' Very often making a dance springs from a desire to find those hidden frescoes.

In Burma, on our second Asian tour in the 1970s, I had been asked to present flowers at the tomb of the Burmese Unknown Soldier. This I did in the presence of our ambassador and the Burmese minister of culture. When I had finished, there was a tremendous stir, great sounds of conversation. The Burmese wanted to know who had coached me to present the flowers in precisely the correct manner, steps, and gestures that would be appropriate to a Burmese woman of my age and station. No one had. Just as no one had taught Ruth St Denis to touch back generations in East Indian dance to find the true path and spirit for her solos which even the Indians at that time had lost.

But for this you must keep your vessel clean – your mind, your body; it is what the Zen masters tell their students who get too full of themselves, too wrapped up in theory and too many thoughts. They ask them, 'That is all very good; but have you cleaned your dish?' For the Buddhist student lived by begging food; and how could he receive it if his bowl was not clean? He is being asked if he is ready for his next meal. A clear instruction to get back to basics. It is so easy to become cluttered.

I think that is what my father must have meant when he wrote to me when I was away from home. 'Martha,' he said, 'you must keep an open soul.' It is that openness and awareness and innocence of sorts that I try to cultivate in my dancers. Although, as the Latin verb to educate, *educere*, indicates, it is not a question of putting something in but drawing it out, if it is there to begin with.

Dancers today can do anything; the technique is phenomenal. The passion and the meaning to their movement can be another thing.

At times I will tease my dancers and tell them that they are not too bright today, that all of their jumping has addled their brains. And yet they move with grace and a kind of inevitability, some more powerfully than others. This moment of rehearsal is the instant that I care about. This is the very now of my life.

The only thing we have is the now. You begin from the now, what you know, and move into the old, ancient ones that you did not know but which you find as you go along. I think you only find the past from yourself, from what you're experiencing now, what enters your life at the present moment. We don't know about the past, except as we discover it. And we discover it from the now. Looking at the past is like lolling in a rocking chair. It is so relaxing and you can rock back and forth on the porch, and never go forward. It is not for me. People sometimes ask me about retirement and I say, 'Retire? Retire into what?' I don't believe in retirement because that is the time you die.

There are always ancestral footsteps behind me, pushing me, when I am creating a new dance, and gestures are flowing through me. Whether good or bad, they are ancestral. You get to the point where your body is something else and it takes on a world of cultures from the past, an idea that is very hard to express in words. I never verbalize about the dance as I create it. It is a purely physical risk that you desire to take, and that you have to take. The ballet I am doing now is a risk. That is all I can say because it isn't fulfilled yet. I let no one watch, except for the dancers I am working with. When they leave I am alone with the ancestral footsteps.

Somewhere very long ago I remember hearing that in El Greco's studio, after he died, they found an empty canvas on which he had written only three words: 'Nothing pleases me.' This I can understand.

What I miss some days in a dance class is not perfection, because some of them will never achieve that moment of technical expertise. I don't demand, at the beginning, any vestige of perfection. What I long for is the eagerness to meet life, the curiosity, the wonder that you feel when you can really move – to work toward a perfect first or a perfect fifth position. There comes an excitement, an avidity, a forgetfulness of everyone about you. You are so completely absorbed in this instrument that is vibrant to life. The great French poet St John Perse said to me, 'You have so little time to be born to the instant.' This I miss in class very much. I miss the animal strength, the beauty of the heel as it is used to carry one forward into life. This, I think more than anything, is the secret of my loneliness.

I do not feel myself unique by any means, but I do know that I agree with Edgard Varèse – and I'm going to use a word that I never use regarding myself or anybody else. And that word is genius. Varèse, a wonderful French composer, who wrote some music for me, opened up new areas of musical strength in the way he used percussion that I had never experienced before. He said, 'Martha, all of us are born with genius, but most people only keep it for a few seconds.'

By genius he meant that curiosity that leads to the search for the secret of life. That is what tires me when I teach and I come away alone. Sometimes you will see a person on the stage who has this oneness with himself – it is so glorious it has the power to stop you. It is a common gift to all of us but most people only keep it a few moments.

I can never forget the evening I was staying late at the school, and the phone rang. I was the only one there and I picked it up to hear a mother ask about classes for her child. 'She is a genius. Intuitive. Unique. It must be nurtured now.' 'Really,' I answered. 'And how old is she?' Her mother replied, 'Two years old.' I told her that we only accepted children at nine (today much earlier, thanks to vitamins and computers and home training). 'Nine!' she cried. 'But by nine she will have lost all of her genius.' I said, 'Madame, if she must lose it, it is best she lose it young.'

I never thought of myself as being what they call a genius. I don't know what genius is. I think a far better expression is a retriever, a lovely strong golden retriever that brings things back from the past, or retrieves things from our common blood memory. I think that by every act you do – whether in religion, politics, or sex – you reveal yourself. This, to me, is one of the wonderful things in life. It is what I've always wanted to do – to show the laughing, the fun, the appetite, all of it through dance.

In order to work, in order to be excited, in order to simply be, you have to be reborn to the instant. You have to permit yourself to feel, you have to permit yourself to be vulnerable. You may not like what you see, that is not important. You don't always have to judge. But you must be attacked by it, excited by it, and your body must be alive. And you must know how to animate that body; for each it is individual.

When a dancer is at the peak of his power he has two lovely, fragile, and perishable things. One is the spontaneity that is arrived at over years of training. The other is simplicity, but not the usual kind. It is the state of complete simplicity costing no less than absolutely everything, of which T. S. Eliot speaks.

How many leaps did Nijinsky take before he made the one that startled the world? He took thousands and thousands and it is that legend that gives us the courage, the energy, and arrogance to go back into the studio knowing that while there is so little time to be born to the instant, you will work again among the many that you may once more be born as one. That is a dancer's world.

My dancer's world has seen so many theatres, so many instants. But always I have resisted looking backward until now, when I began to sense that there was always for my life a line through it – necessity. The Greek myths speak of the spindle of life resting on the knee of necessity, the principal Fate in the Platonic world. The second Fate weaves, and the third cuts. Necessity to create? No. But in some way to transcend, to conquer fear, to find a way to go on.

How does it all begin? I suppose it never begins. It just continues.

9

A DANCING CONSCIOUSNESS

Rebecca Hilton with Bryan Smith

Rebecca Hilton graduated from the Victorian College of the Arts Tertiary Dance Course in 1983. Following two years of intensive work and study with Russell Dumas' Dance Exchange, she performed and taught throughout Australia and New Zealand with Danceworks. She was awarded an Australia Council Travel Study Grant and travelled to New York in late 1987. Shortly after her arrival she was invited to join the Stephen Petronio Company with which she has danced ever since, assisting Petronio in resetting work and teaching extensively throughout Europe, South America and the United States. In 1992 she performed her own work at the Judson Memorial Church under the auspices of Movement Research and she continues to teach regularly in New York City through the Movement Research Program.

What is it like dancing in a company in New York? How do you organize your working life as a dancer there?
Working in Stephen's company, even though we have a lot of work, is still really precarious because the amount of work we have changes drastically and dramatically from year to year. Last year we were on the road a lot. I was working with Michael [Clark] as well. I was away from New York for eight months out of twelve last year. When we're in New York we only work for sixteen hours a week. So we work four hours, four days a week, which leaves me with the option to work with other people I'm interested in. I've been getting more and more interested in improvisation, so whenever I'm in New York for a period of time, I've been concentrating on that. There's a real freedom for me, at this stage in my life, to have other options and not just be absolutely focused on the company. It changes though; as I say last year it wasn't possible to do many other things but this year it may be a little looser. That's why being in a city like New York is great, the options abound. In the spare time I have I can do whatever I want as far as dance goes. That is basically what New York is about, and why people gravitate there. There is this huge community. It is not like anyone there is better than anyone else, or more talented. It is that the community is so much bigger; the options are so much broader.

But it's a real problem for me being in a company. This company has Stephen's name on it and it's his company and his work. I've always had a bit of an authority problem and there are still times where I get completely frustrated by feeling like I'm someone else's tool. On the other hand he is very appreciative of us and our work and tells us so. He lets us know. As a dancer in Stephen's company I make lots of decisions. A lot of the work is made through improvisation and through playing with manipulating phrase material that we've been running for a year and that we know inside out and back to front. I have a lot of artistic control and input into the work.

We officially start at 2.30, so it's a three and a half hour work period actually. Usually we will start by running a piece of rep as soon as we get in. Lately it's been different because we have had two new members join so a lot of rehearsal time has been taken up with teaching. We have a break and the second half of rehearsal, if we're in New York, is for working on a new piece, which we do in a variety of ways.

The whole thing is based on trust and mutual respect and the sharing of information between me and the other dancers, Stephen and I, Stephen and the company and so on. The more familiar I am with him and the more he knows me, the more the mutual trust is growing. There's a real feeling of working with peers. I care for the work as much as he does. That's great, it's what makes it worth it. His work is pretty full on and pretty hard. Without caring for and having a respect for my body I couldn't do it. I couldn't bash it. My body has changed a lot. I've got stronger and broader. My body has more power than it had and I know it better. It's another four years of examining, finding out more about it, allowing it to change, becoming familiar with it all over again every day because it's a different body everyday.

What do you do about training or informing your body? I presume it is not training in the way we know it in the company system here.
A lot of time I don't go to class. We have an hour at the beginning of rehearsal that we can use to warm up. So a lot of time I'll do my own warm up. People in the company do all sorts of weird and strange things; a lot of people are into aerobics, some go to the gym, do swimming, or yoga. It goes in phases. People are doing yoga at the moment. I swim a lot. You get to a certain age and you have a wealth of knowledge and you know what's best for your body. You wake up in the morning and you know what you need. The whole idea of company class is really bizarre to me. It's just not part of my lifestyle. New York is a place where there are a thousand classes to choose from in the morning and whatever you feel like, you do. I might go and take one of the ballet for modern dancer classes or I study with Susan Klein and Barbara Mahler as much I can because I find that information continually inspiring. It's basically a stretch and alignment technique. In a lot of techniques I've studied there's been that difficult transitional moment between standing still, focusing and imaging and putting that into moving.

Being able to take that with you into rehearsal and use it. Susan and Barbara's work immediately sets you in motion with images, so the transition is easy. They have a pretty set series of exercises, I suppose you'd call them, they're very simple but they're all about movement, immediately. It's not a cerebral process; it goes directly from your brain into your body memory because you're already moving.

I've done so much study lying in constructive rest and imaging, but I've always had a real problem with the leap from that into Stephen's rehearsal which entails dancing around hysterically and aerobically. I have a great respect for techniques like the Alexander technique and I've seen them work incredibly for other people but that just wasn't the route for me. I've always responded to things that I can take into motion. I know a lot of people who work with the Alexander technique (Feldenkrais is a little different because it's already pretty much based in motion), they say the idea is to retrain your body in those simple positions, like sitting and standing. Gradually you retrain all your patterns, so that when you go into complex movement, they're already there retrained. But for me, my problem was that I've been a professional dancer since I left school so I can go and do Alexander work but then I have to go and jump around like a maniac, so I don't have the time to integrate it in that way. Now after four years I can actually work with a simple image, like having my tailbone motor me through space, something that simple, and I can think about it as I'm doing this very complex movement. Before I could never make that connection. With Susan and Barbara all the imaging is very anatomical, and that's imagery I could always relate to more easily than images like 'your spine is a river' or something. I'm a realist. Stephen's work is hysterical; it's really fast and pushed and I can actually apply concerns I learn from Susan and Barbara while I'm dancing.

I've always been attracted to body work that is initiated in movement. It's still a really long period of integration but it happens gradually in the dancing rather than lying on your back on the floor imagining and then forgetting about it while you reaffirm your bad patterns every afternoon in rehearsal and then trying to get rid of them lying on your back in the morning. That was a big discovery for me.

What kind of physical intelligence are you seeking to develop in your body and hence in your moving/dancing? What, now, do you think are the important things for dancers to understand physically?
The kind of physical intelligence I'm building is really in all those kinds of basic alignment things we have been talking about; like allowing your weight to do the work for you rather than muscling it. That doesn't mean I'm not a muscular dancer, I am, I use my muscles a lot. Finding an impulse for moving from a weight base and finding ease, strength and a centre by connecting to the floor allows me to take risks that I feel I wouldn't be able to take if I didn't have that, that connection and familiarity with the floor. From the

thrust I get from the floor, the amount of weight I let drop into the floor, I get an equal and opposite amount of thrust that can send me in the widest possible arcs through space that are possible for my body. It's sensual and exciting; I like feeling the breeze rush against my face. I like to be out of control, but in control of being out of control.

I find the particular techniques I've been studying allow me to do that. I think you need a fairly comprehensive knowledge of your skeleton and the way joints work. Then I think you need to be aware of the limitations of the body, the skeletal limitations. That's really important, knowing the kinds of movement possibilities you have in the joints. I've studied anatomy since I was young at school and pretty much consistently since then.

Knowing your body means knowing it in an intellectual sense as well, knowing how your body functions. The opposite would be moving from an emotional base, the movement quality you can get from feelings and emotions rather from the way your body moves mechanically.

Can you talk about the process of making work? For example how does the conceptual framework arise? How is the work actually made? How do you rehearse a work that you are making? Where does the movement come from and how long does it take to make a new piece?

Often you'll find that in the piece before there's a germ that goes on to become the focus of the next piece. Stephen's development is very linear in that way. He makes his work for himself. He is very excited by dance and making work. He doesn't labour under the pressure of 'are people going to like it?' He takes a year to make a piece. Stephen has only made three new pieces in the whole time I've been in the company. And they're usually 25–35 minutes long.

We don't have a solid block of time; this is where it's different from companies working here. We take work when and where we can get it. We're on the road. When we do have time in New York we develop a series of phrases and they're usually quite long, up to five minutes long. He'll make three or four of them and throughout the year we'll just run those. Where we are on tour, we'll run the new phrases before the show or during the day we'll run the phrases and he'll change them over a period of eight months to a year. It turns out by the time we get to make the piece, when there is a period to make it, which might only be a month long when we're in New York uninterrupted, the material is so in our bodies, the fabric with which he is going to wend the piece is so known, that it's like a dream. The basic phrases are a part of our neuro-muscular patterning. I don't have to think about them, I don't have to think about what comes next or how to do this or that. It's in my body so thoroughly because I've been doing it for a year. It's like you have all the ingredients lined up on the shelf, you don't have to keep going back to the cupboard, as when you make a cake. The places are so familiar, they are like this solid thing you can depart from and come back to without it having moved. It's still where you left it, a weight in the centre of the piece from which things can move out and in.

He makes material by standing in front of us and improvising and then seeing who caught it. The process of making the phrases is a very long and involved one. I might have caught a particular thing that he was doing with his lower body, someone else might have caught his upper body and then we'll go through the stage of working till there's something there he's interested in. He doesn't make the phrases and come in and teach us at all. They are made in the studio on us basically. Over that period of running those phrases the idea for the piece is gestating, along with the material. By the time he comes to make the piece he has a really solid idea of what he wants to do with it, what it is about if you like. The actual time of making the piece is fairly short. In that month we do a number of different manipulations of the material, or not even working with the material at all but working with the physicality that has been developed over the year in terms of the material.

The last piece we made, MSG, was very much about manipulating each other. There was a lot of partnering in it . We played this thing that we called 'the game' where rôles changed, but it was basically one person being manipulated by the group. That person could either be very passive or very active. They could be leading the group or the group could be leading them. We would improvise and if he saw something that he liked we would spend time trying to get it back, till eventually we had this long and complex series of events. We each often have a personal variation of the material ourselves, which can be very simple like take this phrase and keep it moving through space in the way that it is already but jump, turn or whatever. He works a lot with these simple things.

We work a lot with imagery, which I love. One of his main concerns is in showing forms, as in line, then breaking them down. He made a whole piece called *Walk In*. 'Walk in' is something that happens when you die and your spirit leaves your body but then you get resuscitated and your soul 'walks' back into your body. In that piece we worked a lot with photography. Re-creating, motorizing and moving photographic images. And film techniques; he's always talking about zooming in and out and cutting from one thing to another so the transitions are almost invisible. I've found that really useful for teaching. It's a great way to teach people material because it gives it a base that isn't about put your leg there, put your arm there, put your head there. With imagery a shape can be alive in a different way, each time you do it, it can be subtly different. We do things like be angles and run into brick walls. Yeah, we use a lot of imagery.

The other day you were saying how you enjoy making steps and movement phrases but that just doing that doesn't make a choreographer. So, what is the difference between someone making steps and someone being a choreographer?

I think it's about concepts and ideas. A piece of art, a dance, needs to have a context. The steps operate like individual notes in a piece of music. Individual notes aren't by any means the piece of music. Spatial design is important, so is the rhythm of a piece, its rises and falls. Mostly I think it's about having an idea or a concept and you don't resolve or clarify *that* merely with steps. They are one means, one single element amongst a host of other things. I see work that is just steps; they're pretty but they're out of context. People try to contextualize steps by putting everyone in the same costume, or having a long piece of music turned on or doing it with lighting but it's still not a piece, it's just steps that are dressed up.

What is your perception of the difference between the dance you are involved with in New York and the kind of work that is coming to the fore in Europe?
Just before I left New York to come here a few of the old Judson Church group, Trisha Brown, Steve Paxton, Simone Forti, and Yvonne Rainer got back together for a talk. Judson twenty years later kind of thing. The talk gradually got onto their perceptions of what's going on in dance at the moment in New York. People have been talking about New York as if it's no longer the centre of dance, and the new dance centre has shifted to Europe, France and Belgium. They were saying something really interesting, that is, a new form comes when you reject the old. That seems to be the pattern with dance, starting way back with Isadora and then on down the track. This group of luminaries were suggesting that as a community in New York we haven't rejected the forms they set up in the sixties. They had all these forms to break down, they just went for it. Whereas we, because we're still labouring under the set of aesthetics they set up, haven't reacted and we still basically embrace those concerns. The reaction's happened in Europe. So in a way it has shifted, which is not to say there's not still interesting work going on in New York, there is, but the new movement has shifted really for the first time from America to Europe. The response to what they were doing twenty years ago has happened and there's lots of interesting work going on, having those two centres – having the centre of form still in New York and the romantic centre in Europe. And you can see the struggle between those two things in the work. The postmodern has really affected the work in Europe through things like repetition and spatial design. They are still drawing on concerns that have been kicking around in New York for twenty years or so.

So work in New York is still very much influenced by the concerns set up in the postmodern era. Dance in New York is a very big scene and I'm only involved in a particular section of it, the downtown scene, and that's what I'm talking about here. People are still very much concerned with ideas in New York. A lot of work is still coming from a very intellectual place, and from thinking about the body. New York is still very much into pure dance, dance as a form unto itself. Dance, movement and the body. In Europe the work is much more emotionally based, a lot more dramatic. It's much more theatrical, more about intense feeling or something and the body is an instrument for drama and for creating passion. It's not that people in New York don't have elements of that too, but I think it's because they've been influenced lately by the Europeans; it's not a movement that's springing up in New York.

It's hard to separate what you're interested in doing with your own body and what is 'interesting'. I often really like something if I want to do it and I can feel my body responding. A lot of European work seems to be about the constraints society sets up. Anna Teresa De Keersmaeker, for example, does a lot of things where she'll set up a simple phrase that is incredibly repetitive; it goes on and on and on until you think you're going to go mad watching it. It's emotionally manipulative. She has women in tight dresses and high heels trying to dance. I remember seeing her doing a really long series with women in their tight dresses and high heels and they couldn't get their knees apart. They were doing this specific, structured dance, but they couldn't get their knees apart. I get a really visceral and physical response to her work; I get so tense and then after about twenty minutes I realize I'm on the edge of my seat, clenching every muscle. It's amazing when work can do that to you, make you respond physically and it doesn't have to be in a pleasant way. Wim Vandekeybus' work is like that too; you respond in a visceral way.

But a lot of European work is for me frustratingly heterosexual. Another interesting thing about Stephen's work is that the women are strong, we do a lot of lifting, partnering and so on; the roles aren't traditional in that way. In Europe all those ballet role models are still operating. When we tour Europe and England and we have the 'meet the choreographer' thing afterwards and the audience asks questions, people are fixated on the fact that the women aren't built like sylphs and do a lot of the lifting and are strong. I don't think of myself as this really tough she-man thing. It's just what I do, it's always been one of my skills.

We don't tour much in America, we're not very popular. I mean we're popular in New York and the bigger cities but a lot of the touring network in America is through the universities, middle and general America and I think it might be that Stephen is definitely out as a lot of his work is about his sexuality and our sexuality. There are many different varieties of sexuality in the company and it's not the heterosexual, I love you I hate you, between a man and a woman thing. It's anything but that. Sexuality is one of his major concerns. Gender and the representations of gender are important issues too; challenging them. His work just isn't about that traditional male–female relationship and people find that threatening and hard to deal with.

I've been horrified by the depiction of women in a lot of European work. Absolutely horrified. It's so incredibly sexist. Work made by both men and women, but mostly men. Most choreographers are men. People think of dance, of all the arts, as the female art, but it is still men in control I think.

Have you experienced your movement patterns changing significantly since you've been away?

I can tell now that my dancing has changed incredibly over the period of time I've been in New York but the process of change isn't one I can really put my finger on. I've been to a number of places. At a certain point a couple of years ago I really allowed myself to go so far with movement that I would end up flat on my back or flat on my face. I definitely noticed that I was changing; I was falling over all the time. That was a stage I needed to go through to discover my limitations and I allowed myself to go through it. It was kind of weird and unstable and scary in a way, plus I was performing the whole time. I didn't have time to just work in a studio. But Stephen's work allows that too, it's about the extreme. The more extreme you can be the better, and if that means you're flat on your face then he's cool about that. It was great to have an avenue to allow myself to do it in. It was a funny period. In the company we seem to go through some of these things together. We're together a lot of the time; we all study pretty much with Susan and Barbara. We became the 'falling down and standing back up again company' for a while. Stephen's work can soak up some of that. It's really exciting for me that my job, which is what it is, can support me in my life and the decisions I'm making about my dancing in that way.

What is it like being in that dancer-choreographer relationship in the company you're working in? What sort of give and take is operating there?

For a start the kind of relationship Stephen has as a choreographer with the dancers he chooses to work with and who choose to work with him, it's a two way street, everyone has a choice, there's a real freedom for us in that. He basically thinks, and I agree, that whatever information we have we bring to his work. We have to be able to meet the needs that *we* have in order to function fully and happily in the situation we're in with him.

But no matter what you think of someone's work and no matter how much respect I have for Stephen's work, that isn't enough to completely inform me and my dancing. I need to gather and garner information from other places and New York gives me the opportunity to do that in a real way, going to classes, seeing performances, taking workshops and so on. Our company operates as a group of people who are all focused on and interested in Stephen's work but we all have different backgrounds and interests that we bring into the situation. Rather than getting into the company and closing all those off we seem to have kept the channels open for learning and experiencing other things.

So, it's not that Stephen's work feeds me perfectly but it's like I've found something that is right for this time in my life and that's more lucky than a

79

lot of people get. A lot of it is about risk-taking, pushing my body further aerobically, and in every way almost than it would go of its own volition. A lot of it is finding a group of dancers who I can learn from. I look at these dancers who I'm working with, every day they can stun me with something beautiful, something amazing. I had that here also but I was young when I worked in Australia. I left here when I was just 23. I'm 27 now; I don't think I could walk into Stephen's audition and be blown away the way I was when I was 23 and had just left Australia. I don't think I could surrender myself in that way now. At a younger age I think you're much more likely to want to hand yourself over lock, stock and barrel to someone else; the older you get the more you know yourself.

One of the most incredible dancers I've ever seen is a woman called Jennifer Monson, who's an improviser in New York. We decided to get together and dance, it's really that simple. We split the cost of hiring a studio a couple of evenings or mornings a week. Some people you meet you just dance with easily. Jennifer and I are like that. We have performed, there are a variety of places to do that. But mostly we just dance. I'm really into it because there's no one telling me what to do. Even in a situation like the one I'm in with Stephen where I'm basically having a great time with it, it's still someone else's vision and someone else telling me what to do and how to move. I've definitely gone further with my body in a different way through improvising. It's a different body experience. We work quite a bit with improvisation in the company to develop movement, but it's much more goal-oriented.

Does improvising bring you in touch with new understandings in your body?
I've learnt a lot about my movement patterns, the kinds of things I like to do, what my body will do naturally if left alone and a lot about my rhythms. Discovering patterns that I have that I wasn't aware of has been very inter-esting. It's all a process of rediscovery and you never get there, that's what keeps you going. If you ever got there you may as well just lie down and die. I'll never know my body utterly, it's changing daily, each day it's a new body. Did you know, every seven years every cell in your body is completely replenished? Isn't that amazing? I spent a lot of time when I was younger trying to be someone, trying to be something very particular. Once I got over the hump of accepting that'll never happen, I got this incredible feeling of freedom and release.

10

SPACEMAKING: EXPERIENCES OF A VIRTUAL BODY

Susan Kozel

Virtual reality is a new materiality. For four weeks I performed in Paul Sermon's *Telematic Dreaming*, an installation which was part of a large exhibition of contemporary art in central Amsterdam called *I + the Other: dignity for all, reflections on humanity*. Spending several hours a day over a period of weeks in virtual space allowed me to explore in greater depth the relation between my 'cyber-body' and my fleshly body, and gave me greater insight into some of the sexual and political implications of the technology.

With *Telematic Dreaming* Sermon created a space for interaction between a performer and members of the public using a technology called telepresence. Using video projectors and monitors people in two separate rooms were drawn together. There was a bed in each room. I was alone on a bed in a room well removed from the public visiting the exhibition. My image was projected onto the bed in the room which was open to visitors, where they had the option to join me. Then video cameras in the public room transmitted the actions of the person on the bed with my image back to me in my room upstairs. I was able to interact with the person on the bed downstairs by watching both of our images on the monitors placed around my bed. The bed became my performance space. Our movement occurred in real time, but in a space which was entirely created by technology. I was alone on my bed, moving my arms and legs in physical space as if in some sort of hypnotic ritual dance, yet in virtual space I carried on intense physical improvisation with other unknown bodies.

Virtual reality (VR) is associated with image manipulation technologies that create the illusion of being immersed in an artificial world, or of being present in a remote location in the physical world. In many VR applications, such as architectural design, medical imaging and flight simulation, the virtual space is reached by placing a head-mounted display (HMD) on your head and donning a dataglove. The HMD looks like a large scuba mask and replaces your view of the world with a digital three-dimensional computer graphic depiction of a world, while the glove contains the controls which allow you to navigate in the computer generated space. This was not the space of *Telematic Dreaming*, for my body was not abandoned while my consciousness travelled in an all encompassing 3-D space. Yet my body did take on an electric state, for the only way I could move was by relying on the video images of both myself and the others.

Trust

In *Telematic Dreaming* human interaction was reduced to its simplest essence: touch, trust, vulnerability. Movement usually began in a hesitant way with hand contact taking on excessive importance. The impact of slow and small movement became enormous. Great care and concentration was required to make intricate web patterns with the fingers of a stranger, or to cause one fleshly finger to meet up with one video finger. When the movement progressed from these early stages to a sort of full body choreography the piece became an emotional investment which shocked and sometimes disturbed people. Some people simply froze, and fled the installation once they realized what it was about.

The occasions when the movement worked well felt very much like good contact improvisation: a hypnotic feeling of not knowing what is coming next but letting the strong flow of movement carry you onward. When the movement moved through us in this way, based on openness and trust, the distinction between which bodies were real and which were virtual became irrelevant.

Performing the piece was emotionally taxing as well as enriching. For a time I worried that by being drawn into tender and intimate interchanges with dozens of strangers who got on the bed I would be desensitizing myself to the detriment of relations with my real loved ones, exhausting myself, rendering myself mechanical or cynical. This concern in itself is an indication of the strong physicality of the piece, of the powerful link between the body on the screen and the bundle of emotions, thoughts and movement which makes up my material body. The mechanization or computerization of human experience is generally thought to diminish the physical and emotional sides of life, yet in the virtual world of *Telematic Dreaming* questions of privacy, intimacy and identity were central. This was not just my experience as a performer, many members of the public were overwhelmed by their experiences on the other bed. Some felt protective toward me, or stayed on the bed because they didn't want me to be alone in my virtual world. Others claimed to have been 'changed' by the experience. The installation was paradoxical for not only using technology to provide a forum for experiencing the basics of human intimacy, but for situating this private interaction within a public domain.

Pain

My back and neck rebelled after two days of performance, forcing me to evaluate the relation between my physical self and my virtual body through that ultimately corporeal experience: *pain*. I felt as if I was disintegrating. Through pain I was able to see a link between the seemingly abstract image of myself and my flesh. My pain was discernible in my image, giving my movement a peculiar stiffness.

At the same time I became obsessed with the invisible side of my body: digestion, intestines, breathing. When to eat, what to eat, how it affected my moods and the way my body felt. It was as if my involuntary organs could not be counted upon to perform their usual roles unassisted by my conscious self. They called attention to themselves through pain and cramps. My real body asserted its presence as a response to the virtual image which had come to dominate my movement while performing. The invisible elements of my body began to take on a new, demanding significance, as if needing to assert themselves to balance the scale. The more I ventured into the visual, virtual world the more my non-virtual body called attention to itself like an anchor, like ballast. I seemed to be pulled between the two extremes of an imaginary spectrum: the abjection of flesh and the sanitization of technology.

Sex and violence

Someone took out a knife. Not in a threatening way, yet I felt the predictable shiver and set of alarm bells in my mind. The most he could do was slash the duvet, but I still felt uncomfortable. The knife is a loaded item, it entered the virtual space of *Telematic Dreaming* as a heavily inscribed object, meaning that it could not be separated from a code of behaviours and a set of emotional and physical responses, particularly since the knife wielder was a man and I was a woman on a bed.

Someone elbowed me hard in the stomach and I doubled over, wondering why, since I didn't actually feel it. But I felt something. I was shaken for a while; it was a betrayal of trust. The famous claim associated with virtual technology is that the body is futile, replaced by an infinitely enhanced electronic construct. If this is so, then why did nastiness or violence enacted upon my image hurt? How could the body be futile yet still exert a basic visceral control over my movement?

The potential for violent as well as highly pleasurable interchanges was inherent to *Telematic Dreaming*. Frequently I allowed myself to play, and at times I luxuriated in the physical intimacy and sheer decadence of it all. After a tender and intimate quarter of an hour of improvised movement, a man returned with a rose. He presented it to me in virtual space so there was no way I could take hold of it, beyond tracing its outline or passing my hand

83

through it. It became a metaphor, and fundamentally immaterial. It occurred to me that what preserves the distinction between materiality and immateriality in the technology is movement: as moving beings people take on an alternative materiality, while objects become immaterial in their inertia.

An unlikely character dressed in blue and green, wearing philosopher's glasses calmly stroked my thigh, brushed delicately over my hips and up my torso. He remained partly detached, or at least quizzical, and his movements were languid but not overtly sexual. I felt little electric shocks pass through my body as I accepted the caresses. Not five minutes after this, I experienced the worst cyber-sexual violence of the entire time. Two men in leather jackets jumped my image on the bed. One attacked my head and the other my pelvic area. After three or four body-twisting blows they fled. It was a back alley scenario. What did I feel? Very little. This amazed me, after my body had felt so much in the subtly erotic context and through earlier acts of aggression. I believe that the extreme violence of the attack caused me to separate my physical self from my virtual self. A split-second after they began to hit me I found myself watching my image in the video monitor, paralysed with horror at what they were doing to the woman's body – no longer my body. This was the only moment in the entire four weeks when I divorced my two selves, and it was the result of an involuntary act of self-preservation – a primordial reaction in a sophisticated technological context.

The virtual sex I experienced was based on the energy, intimacy and rhythm of lovemaking: a tender beginning, playfully building up, making shapes with our bodies, improvised rolling through one another – a different sort of interiority at play – followed by a slow and intimate denouement. I was so involved in the flow of improvised movement that it was only once the cycle drew to a close that I recognized it. It was not a substitute for sex, it was a mimetic version with strong physical and emotional qualities. It was a variation or extension rather than a technological replica. Moreover, it was undeniably real, not a compromise. As with the question concerning the reality of theatre, that of the reality of virtual experience becomes spurious, with no adequate grounds upon which to test it. In some respects, the advancement of virtual technology will help to render the claim that theatre is an artificial reproduction of reality even more nonsensical. The designations between the virtual and the real in our media-soaked world become blurred. It becomes more and more difficult to sustain a clear distinction between truth and falsity when the phenomenology, or direct experience, of technology is taken into account; when, according to Marshall McLuhan, the contours of our own extended bodies are found in our technologies (1964: 6–7).

My virtual lover visited me several times. The times we met in person were wooden, stilted, since our preferred mode of interaction was virtual intimacy, not chatting over a cup of coffee in a crowded gallery. Although both contexts were real, our virtual relationship seemed to be more meaningful. The difference between our ages and cultures lost significance, but *not* because our bodies were digitalized and abandoned. It was just the opposite. Our virtual rapport had a greater physicality and intimacy than our real engagement.

The body electric

As a dancer, hearing anyone claim that virtual technology demonstrates the futility of the body makes me want to dig my heels in, theoretically and practically. Yet this is a commonly held belief, based on the recognition that in much of the technology consciousness is drawn out of the body and into an electronic construct. Yet for me the experience was one of extending my body, not losing or substituting it. My intuitive conviction that the virtual body is entwined with the fleshly body was reinforced by my experiences of intimacy and violence in *Telematic Dreaming*. I discovered a theoretical basis for this intuition in the debate between 'intelligence amplification' and 'artificial intelligence'.

Frederick Brooks, one of the most prominent virtual reality researchers in America, makes this distinction, insisting that intelligence amplification (IA) is more interesting than artificial intelligence (AI). AI refers to a field of research which seeks to replace the human mind by machines. IA is different since it aims to build systems which amplify the human mind by providing it with computer-based auxiliaries to do the things that it has trouble doing (like enormous sums), thereby freeing it to scale new heights at more creative tasks (Rheingold 1991: 37). Translated into the debate concerning virtual technology and the body, an AI approach substitutes the body with a digitalized one, or sees it as a hindrance and tries to lose it entirely. IA, on the other hand sees technology as an extension of the body's existing abilities, a building upon what exists, rather than a digital replacement.

In *Telematic Dreaming* my body was always the ultimate ground for the image, it was the final reference point and the source of meaning. Like the difference between three-dimensionality and four-dimensionality, the image provided my body with another dimension rather than rendering it obsolete. Initially I was disorientated in virtual space: left became right, up became down and right left. Someone would touch one hand and I would move the other in response. My disorientation was a symptom of how moving was entirely mediated by my sense of sight. The way I overcame this was by drawing my attention back to the pattern of my body in physical space. Instead of moving my arm according to the logic of our images in the monitor, I would look at my body and move the hand on the side of the bent knee, or I would move my arm up towards my head. Once I directed myself according to my body pattern I was able to overcome disorientation and avoid shattering an intense sequence of improvisation by moving the wrong limb. In this sense my electric body was an extension of my physical body, it could do things which the latter could not, such as map itself onto another or disappear, yet it could not exist independently.

Still, the virtual space of *Telematic Dreaming* was not an unqualified amplification of physical space. Under normal circumstances, dancing engages the senses in a non-hierarchical and kaleidoscopic way. Sight, hearing and touch play obvious roles; taste and smell, although less obviously defined, are still active participants in the whole experience. *Removing one of these senses does not bring the movement to a grinding halt.* However, if I lost sight of the monitors (as happened occasionally since there were only three, leaving one side of the bed blind), I lost myself as well as the other person: interaction became impossible. When interaction is dependent upon one sense, it becomes inherently fragile.

And the gaze *is* fragile, like crystalline channels between people conveying emotions or information. There were times when I would become only gaze and movement, making shapes with my body on the bed while taking no notice of anything except the figures in the monitors. Then without warning the flesh of my body would reassert its presence, recalling my focus from its temporary engagement four feet from my natural frontier within space. On one occasion, while thoroughly absorbed in interaction with another body I passed my hand over someone's leg, he placed his hand on my leg, when I followed his hand I touched my own leg – and was taken aback by its bulk. For an instant I didn't know what obstacle my hand had encountered after moving so freely in visual space. With vague feelings of guilt I realized that this foreign body was in fact my own! When I momentarily experienced my own body through my sense of touch it did not coincide with my body according to my sense of sight. The disorientation made me reassess what I took to be the frontier of my own body. Could it still be called a frontier if it was no longer fixed, but highly flexible and constantly changing?

The ability to disappear is central to the experience of the body electric. According to media philosopher Mark Taylor, the 'power of erasure' reaches near perfection with computers, and the way the presence of a person or a text can be transformed into seamless absence is fundamentally unsettling (Taylor and Saarinen 1994). I could disappear by wrapping myself in the chroma-key sheet which covered the bed or by sliding off the bed and out of the line of the video camera. I could also make a part of my body disappear in order to leave another bit, like a foot, floating in digitalized space. This now-you-see-me-now-you-don't quality is central to the physicality of *Telematic Dreaming* since it implies a departure from and a return to the body as a whole. The unsettling quality is not merely, as Taylor suggests, the erasure of substance, but its reappearance.

Telepresence has been called an out-of-body experience, yet what intrigues me is the return to the body which is implied by any voyage beyond it. Once plunged back into flesh, what has changed? Theorists and artists such as

Randall Walser and Myron Krueger who claim that virtual technology changes what it means to be human, that it radically alters human perception, are not simply referring to the voyage out, but the inevitable return and the lasting effect that the outward motion leaves on the reunited body. It is here that the political dimension of VR resides.

Sexual inscription

There is much hype in intellectual circles over the cyber-feminist claim that virtual technology is ultimately liberating because in cyberspace you can leave your age, sex and race behind and interact in a disembodied space, or in a space where you select another body as a persona. This was not my experience. There were times when I was dismayed by how strong cultural influences seemed to be, by how my actions as well as those of the people who moved with me were so shaped by codes of sexual and social interaction. I felt that this was the great limitation of the piece – the fact that it took place on a bed meant that much of the engagement was predefined. Yet, I came to realize that this was also its great strength. Banal sexual responses, such as grabbing and poking, were not open to a new vocabulary of movement since they fell into a sort of automatic code of behaviour. And they were basically very boring. Sometimes I wanted to get rid of the bed, to see how the technology would work in a physical context which was not immediately recognizable so that a new social and movement vocabulary could be created. I had visions of a strange sculptural set in which bodies could be suspended, inverted and layered. But I realize that in order to create a new space, and a new movement and cultural vocabulary, the old one needs to be fully identified and understood, not simply sidestepped. By confining the interaction to the bed, Sermon challenged visitors (and myself) to identify their cultural formation and to overcome it.

Virtual space is not a blissfully undetermined area, an easy answer to sexual and racial inequality, an effortless digital Utopia. By recognizing that gender roles can filter through to cyberspace, we are put on our guard against expecting any simplistic technological solutions to entrenched chauvinism. Yet it is undeniably an opening of potential: a space for us to recognize the tendency for our prejudices and conditioning to be carried forward, and to work at creating a new way to inter-relate. In this sense *Telematic Dreaming* created a social and cultural space as well as a virtual one, and as we decided through our movement how to chart it, we became spacemakers.

Where aesthetics and politics coincide

The aesthetic concern which animated my movement was the creation of shapes with bodies, where the bodies had varying degrees of physicality depending on the perspective adopted. For the people in their room I was an image and they were flesh; the monitors which showed the action in both rooms transformed them into images and me into the image of a projection; from my perspective if I decided to ignore the monitors I was flesh and my dance partners simply did not exist. These varying physical states swirled and danced while we did the same. From a formal, choreographic perspective the piece was a delight, as unexpected shapes made by our bodies appeared on the screen, challenging existing ideas of what it was possible for two bodies to do. We could pass through one another, I could be projected onto the other, or even disappear by placing my body within the frontier of another body. If the other wore dark clothing my pale, spectral image would be swallowed up until I let an arm or a sliver of my profile slide off their shape. It was easy to become a goddess of many arms, or to use the frame of the projection to act as a guillotine and slice away sections of our bodies. Standing on the bed brought us closer to the fixed overhead cameras, making our heads huge balloons above tiny feet. Our bodies seemed to be infinitely mutable, while they never ceased to be *our* bodies.

The amplification or distortion of physical experience is central to the politics as well as the aesthetics of virtual reality. Walser distils the political essence when he claims that 'more than any mechanism yet invented, it will change what humans perceive themselves to be, at a very fundamental and personal level [. . .] In important ways, cyberspace goes beyond all previous forms of expression' (Rheingold 1991: 191). Perception (how we perceive ourselves in our environment) and expression (how we communicate with others) are basic ingredients of a political community. Once these are radically transformed by altering or distorting the substance and space of a body the worlds of politics and science converge with that of art, for art is where the radically new is first transformed into experience.

Walser asserts that knowledge of theatre, sports, dance and film will be as important as programming to the development of VR, since in these areas altered states of consciousness and physical experience combine to provide the grounds for a new way of life. Krueger also emphasizes that in developing VR systems much will be learned from the existing arts, and by inventing new art forms (Rheingold 1991: 116). The collaboration between dance and VR technology is a new art form, or at least a hybrid made by uniting different ways of spacemaking. If dance is able to play a role in the future development of VR technology we could end up with radical new directions for materiality within virtuality, as well as the basis for a poetics of virtuality that centres on the dancing body.

PART III

REVIEWING DANCE

This Part presents a slightly different format from the others in the Reader, in that it includes two debates about criticism followed by two examples of criticism. Marcia Siegel tackles issues which are crucial not just for the work of the critic, however, but for any dance spectator. Notwithstanding the multicultural nature of many societies, we are still often faced with dance events which initially appear alien to us; in what ways, she asks, is it possible to distinguish, describe, interpret or evaluate the work of cultures with which we are unfamiliar? Furthermore, how is it possible to judge what is 'authentic' in any culture, or is this quest for authenticity doomed logically to fail when culture itself is dynamic, ever-changing? Although Siegel argues that, however ideal an immersion into the context of a work may be, critics cannot be anthropologists, she offers ways of looking at dance which can help focus attention on the unfamiliar. An acceptance of the many different functions of dance other than the theatrical, can also engender a more open perspective and contribute to a celebration of dance in all its diversity.

Roger Copeland takes issue with what he sees as two extremes of critical writing: the over-descriptive and the over-theorized. He acknowledges the value of the former, wherein the writer tries, in effect, to capture the moving dance on the still page. Copeland notes how this kind of writing is commensurate with formalist work which appears (wrongly) to be devoid of contextual significance. Furthermore, seemingly self-sufficent as dance-for-its-own-sake, it appears to make redundant any interpretative or evaluative comment. Nevertheless, Copeland argues that descriptive writing can reveal a 'bias against ideas'; the mutism in the face of the sensory experience of dance that is discussed in the Introduction to Part I. There is a place for writing which directly addresses this sensory experience, but the danger is that it can 'remain intellectually insular, virtually estranged from the realm of ideas'. On the other hand, the tendency to extreme theorization, using deconstructive and other strategies, does not necessarily embody ideas but often replaces or certainly obscures them. Theory should not remain in the realm of the abstract but should arise as a result of experiential and contemplative engagement with the dance.

The two brief examples of writing by practising critics exemplify Copeland's argument that 'description is a necessary, but not sufficient, component of the critical task'. They include observant analysis of action and structure in order to support the writers' interpretation of the works and, in addition, each review is pegged to an idea or discursive line. For Arlene Croce, it is the marriage of the literal and the abstract in Tharp's *The Catherine Wheel* (1981) which frames her discussion. Overloaded with symbolism and extrinsic references, the work is nevertheless 'always and only about itself'. It invites, suggests Croce, the engagement of the intellect yet is also precognitive in its effect. Whilst Croce draws our attention to the dance values which are central to a narrative work, Alastair Macaulay offers the reverse approach: how seemingly 'abstract' works are resonant of time, place and atmosphere. Exploring the concept of classicism, one to which he returns in later writing (e.g. 1987; 1997), Macaulay notes how classicism in dance, as in all art works, is not a transcendent aesthetic but is moulded by the personality of its creator and the socio-historical context of its creation. In *Symphonic Variations* (Ashton 1946) characteristics of classicism are identified: the paring away of subject matter 'until only pure-dance essence remains' with a resultant 'radiant legibility . . . beaming forth with affecting kinesthetic impact'.

As all cultural artefacts and activities are imbued with time and place, so, too are the writings of cultural commentators. Siegel's concerns most obviously reflect the multi- and inter-cultural nature of society today and how the writer (and spectator) engages with its manifestation in dance. Copeland's debate encompasses elements of a recent history of the aesthetics of both critical writing and dance itself. In Croce's and Macaulay's reviews, the dance works are conjured up in rich and evocative language. The very use of that language and the contextual references they employ can be seen as reflective not only of the 'time and place' of the dance but also as an embodiment of the personal histories of the writers themselves.

FURTHER READING

Criticism and/or the experience of the critic: Copeland (1990); Banes (1994); Brennan (1993/4); Theodores (1995/6); Martin in Morris (1996)
Cross-cultural approaches to appreciation: Best (1986a) and see Further Reading, Part V
Authenticity: Berg (1993)
Recent collections of critical reviews: Jowitt (1985); Croce (1987); Siegel (1991)

11

BRIDGING THE CRITICAL DISTANCE

Marcia B. Siegel

The following essay is adapted from two talks given at the conference of the Dance Critics Association which took place in conjunction with world dance perform-ances at the 1990 Los Angeles Festival. They were published in slightly different form in Looking Out – Perspectives on Dance and Criticism in a Multi-cultural World (*ed. David Gere, New York: Schirmer Books 1995) and in* Ballett International, *July/August 1991.*

There have been some underlying themes of this conference, and one of those themes is fear. Fear of the Other is one form of it. And I don't just mean racist fear, which we've elaborated on quite a lot during the confer-ence. I mean that in Euro-American culture many people think the business of a critic is establishing and protecting norms. To acknowledge high art in another culture is to threaten 'our' standards (i.e. whatever it is we endorse to our readers). And it also threatens how those standards are determined, which is something we don't normally examine. Where did we get them from? What are they based on? How much do they influence what we write? If we open ourselves up to the Other, on equal terms, we'll have to give up our position as standard-setters, because it means acknowledging that someone else has set some other standard that's equally . . . standard.

When we step outside our Euro-American framework, we experience a desperate need for criteria. We demand formulas, rules, contexts, signs of the exceptional. We want to be responsible and not misinterpret, but we hate to give up what we see as our evaluative job. Understandably, we're nervous being out there on our own, confronting an immediate, unfamiliar experience, and dealing with it inside ourselves, let alone playing judge over it.

And then we have to think and be interesting in 700 words.

It seems to me the matter of criteria is very problematic. For one thing, you can't always know what the criteria are. No matter how hard you try and how many people you consult, or how many times you've seen that dance form before, you can't always know what that culture is accepting as good or bad. (If you're in the Good-or-Bad business.)

And even if we could learn some of the basics of a culture, or of its cultural forms, are we really sure we'd know what the whole range is? Can we say that the dance we're seeing here in Los Angeles is *the* Javanese court dance? Is this the only way to perform that dance or style? Is this the only context in which that style is seen? In places with very strong cultural styles, like Java, everything from tourist performance to the most classical, private and high-context high art can use the same elements. These basics, in any culture, get manipulated by the culture and within the culture. We may see only one example of a given dance in our lifetime, so how can we say we know if it's characteristic?

Another fear, and it's related to that, is the sense that we ought to establish some sort of historical, aesthetic, or stylistic authenticity for our subjects. When you travel, you realize what a huge variation there is among what seem to be the normative genres within any culture. Style, or technique, or form, isn't just one thing. Although it may be ever so much simpler for us to identify a classical style or a folk dance form that someone has conveniently researched, it's folly to expect that it will look exactly the same as what the researcher described.

Western critics have hierarchies, though we may not admit it. Going from the bottom up, we esteem social dancing, pop dancing, jazz dancing, theatrical dancing, concert dancing, ballet. Classical ballet dancing seems accepted as the crowning achievement of dance art in Western culture. And within that hierarchy, we also tend to respect old work more than we respect new work, and an 'accurate' reproduction of an old work over a reinterpretation.

Now even if these hierarchies are justified (I don't think they are), even if you were going to rank things by levels and categories, how do you figure out a comparable scale for some other culture? How do you discriminate the best dancing or whatever, without imposing an imagery that may not apply to it? And then, supposing you follow some guidelines issued by the local authorities, standards established by scholars or academies, can you be sure these most meticulously researched and preserved forms mean the same thing for all time and for everyone in that culture?

I find the interplay between preservation and inevitable change very poignant and very distressing. I also love old dances and I wish we could preserve old traditions and I know we can't. I think that is true in every single culture. It's true in ballet and modern dance. I've seen those two forms change drastically just in the twenty-five years I've been writing. And that's right in front of our eyes. So how can we talk about The Tradition or 'the authentic' in a culture that's thousands of years old and has been undergoing change over all those years? Much of that change having been instituted from outside, by colonial powers as well as other forces like trade and technology.

I like the idea of reincarnation. The idea that to talk about change in culture is not to talk about terminality. It's not to talk about something being destroyed or something decaying, but something that's in a process. The natural process, the process of nature, is, yes, trees die, but other trees grow out of what dies, and everything is in a constant state of metamorphosis and rebirth.

Everything is authentic something. And if we weren't so diligently seeking out how this compares to some norm that we don't really know very much about anyway, we might really *look* at what is being done, and try to determine what that is.

I think this conference has concentrated quite a lot on traditional forms. Those high-art traditions, those codified stage forms that are culturally endorsed, the things that come here touring, like the Wayang Wong. We're very lucky to have it. But it alone doesn't represent Indonesia. It doesn't represent Java. It's one form, and a very high-art, officially sanctioned, intentionally visible form that is to some extent molded in an image of what such art should be. I don't think they're going to bring some of the seedier forms over here, or the airport art, or the vernacular shows that people put on in the backyard, which for me would be just as interesting. As a matter of fact, certain governments apparently withheld funding for groups appearing at this festival because they considered them vulgar or lowbrow.

The emphasis on high traditional forms is easier for us critics because more interpretive and background material is made available to us about them. More scholarly writing and analysis has been done. They may superficially resonate with things we call 'classical' in our own system of values because they're likely to be linked to historical or religious phenomena, to have clear encoded vocabularies, sequences and musical accompaniments, and to emerge from rigorous training processes. But these 'classics' are changing, and they are much too complex and multi-faceted to be matched against our equally complex but differently formulated traditions.

We also have a great fear of making a mistake. We might say the wrong thing, and I must say that a great deal of intimidating sanctions have been issued in the last four days from this platform along the lines of: Non-Natives Keep Off. I certainly take to heart everything that's been said, but it's not going to deter me from doing my work, with the most informed and open spirit I can bring. And it shouldn't deter you. Get the tools. Get the ability to look. Open your mind, and do it.

Although what we do has some similarities to ethnographic field work, we cannot be anthropologists. Any of us might want to go into one particular culture and immerse ourselves in it, and we could make that choice. But realistically, that would eliminate other choices. To me being a critic is a great privilege because I can see a lot of things. I can experience many different things and address them. And I don't want to sacrifice that, much as I might want to spend more time in cultures that I find especially congenial and learn more about them first-hand. We just can't work intensively enough with any one thing to become anthropological experts.

An anthropologist is also going to try to get direct information from the doers, from the culture itself. As critics, we'd like to have that, but we don't. We usually have access to the artists only through their press representatives and their presenters. We get little useful information from them. And if we can get in direct contact and speak to the performers, the teachers, the choreographers, we have to surmount problems of language, problems of interpretation, problems of what is it that they really mean and do they understand what we really mean when we're trying to get this information.

But even if we could assume maximum accuracy and utility from our verbal sources, my best information is in the dance. My observation of the dance, which in a sense is my participation in the dance, allows me to connect the performance with my writing. I'm aware that it's controversial to assume we can learn something nonverbally from a culture whose deepest traditions we can't read. But I'm very unsure about the fashionable tendency to discard the idea that there might be 'universals' – qualities or expressive behaviours that all people share. I do know that physicality is universal. It underlies all performance, certainly all dance performance, and it contains basic information. I am fully aware that physicality always takes place in reference to a context and that the context is not universal. We can't ignore that context, if we have access to it in some form. But the performance itself is also a context.

I am Laban-trained and I certainly believe that Labananalysis and Choreometrics direct us to useful information. The Laban systems draw attention to dynamics, the use of space and time and weight, to phrasing, transitions, the shape of the movement, parts of the body used or not used, and to the performer's sense of the space through which he or she is moving. There are interpretive problems with Choreometrics, but its movement researchers, Irmgard Bartenieff and Forrestine Paulay, did come up with basic tools and ways of organizing observational data that would help us in these unfamiliar situations.

I would say that all of the Laban systems – Labanotation, Labananalysis and Choreometrics – though they are probably the largest body of analytical work anybody has ever done with movement, are Eurocentric. Laban theory centres on the body and conceives of movement from the performer's point of view, not from the audience's point of view. It doesn't really concern itself with choreography, with the overall form of a dance piece or the process of a performance. It doesn't address the group. It leaves out a lot of things that aren't paramount in Western choreography. So even though it's useful, I don't find it is everything. I'm going to suggest a few other things that I've been working with, and that seem to encompass the performance as a whole experience.

The first one is *lexicon*. That is, if we take note of the actions, energies, objects, places, people, sounds that the dance immediately draws our attention to, we can come up with a sort of vocabulary belonging to that dance. The lexicon is like the raw materials of the dance. As soon as we consciously begin assembling a lexicon, we start to track how it gets manipulated, interwoven and elaborated on during the dance. We do this unconsciously always, I think, but looking for it more purposively leads us to structure, conventions, typical ways of moving that we might not be so clear about otherwise, or that we might overlook because they're unfamiliar.

The *beat and rhythm* are essential. I don't see how you can look at any dance form without understanding what its rhythm is and how that rhythm is expressed, musically, physically, spatially, its colour, its energy, its variety.

We in the West tend to see dance as a unified entity, where everything serves one choreographic end, or is meant to be in one form – Aristotelian if you will. Not all dance is like that, and we should discover what the *orchestration* is, how it works, what it serves. How are all the parts of the piece orchestrated? How do the individuals go together with the other individuals, the dancers with the music? What are the segments in the dance and how are they marked off? What are the changes, what triggers them, and how does the dance change from one section to the next, from the beginning to the end?

What are other *structural elements*? For example, is the dance a progression or is it a series of things that occur on an equal level all the way through? How is this structure or progression communicated? Who dictates when things change, and what does he or she dictate? Is the sequence learned on the spot? Is it spontaneous, or is it learned ahead of time and always repeated the same way, or does it blossom extemporaneously out of a set pattern?

What is the *performance practice*? Is it filled with artifice and how is artifice stated and where does it come from? Or is it very naturalistic? What are the patterns or conventions of visual focusing?

These things are all in play as we watch a performance. Out of all the possible ways to perform, they have been selected and refined by the culture which performs them, and their development during the course of the dance is a kind of text that we can read without extensive knowledge of the other texts out of which it arose. In many ways, we learn from the dance just what the dance is, and how to respond appropriately to it. I encourage you to be more confident of your ability to discern the workings of these movement texts. I think we have to recognize and compensate as best we can for our personal biases and lapses in information. We can't go to see one performance of something and understand it. Mark Morris may have gone and looked at one Kathak performance for a long time and 'gotten it'. But what he got he translated into some personal expression. Our job as critics is to communicate on behalf of those performers, not to express our creative fantasies. If you think you got it, you can only admit to the limitations of what it is you got, on one viewing. But express that. Describe that. Address that. Don't just sort of say well, this is *it*.

Multiculturalism and eclecticism have been confused here. I don't think they're the same thing. For a long time in this country we considered ourselves a melting pot, and in that sense eclecticism is not at all new. It's not new for a dancer to appropriate from other cultures. The whole twentieth century has been doing it, from Ruth St Denis to Mark Morris. But recognize that when we're looking at their work, we're looking at a Western form, into which these elements have been inserted to make it more interesting, give it a twist, or pay an homage to something that the artist has been taken with. I submit that though benign and well-meaning, that's nevertheless a form of cultural imperialism. The end product is still ballet. It's still modern dance. No matter what Balanchine took from this culture and that culture, he still made ballet and we can recognize it as ballet. I'm not putting down ballet or Balanchine. I'm just saying, it's not multicultural, it's not intercultural. It's using cultural material to revitalize an ongoing form. I am dismayed by Arlene Croce's idea that multiculturalism and all the imperatives that surround it just now can be answered by the appropriation and subsuming of any culture's bric-a-brac into Western forms. And that that answers all our conscience problems about recognizing the rest of the world. It doesn't for me.

Art or dance, or however you want to define this experience we're looking at, is more than that, and can be more than that. I don't just mean it can have different colours or that it can have different cultural styles, I mean it can address other things, entirely, and still be wonderful, and still be worth our true attention and love. Western dance forms are built on individual creation, personality, the assertion of personal skills. They are theatrical, self-contained, mostly transitory events in proscenium spaces, they provide entertainment in a highly developed aesthetic tradition. We in this country have almost no knowledge of dance as ritual, dance as a spiritual lesson, dance as a historical memory, dance as a means of communal celebration – at least, our arts pages don't recognize them.

That doesn't put the multiculture out of bounds for us as critics, but if we admit these possibilities, we will have to relinquish some of our accustomed critical behaviours. One reason multicultural performances are so popular is that they often aren't framed in closed, one-way presentational structures. They're often more inclusive and spontaneous, more participatory and personal. Even Western audiences find them accessible, not esoteric as ballet and modern dance can be for the lay person. They give us access, temporarily, to community, to spirituality, a longed-for social bonding that seldom occurs in a Western, high-art encounter.

Work on your editors; get them to see the expanse of non-theatrical spectator dance, participatory dance, ritual dance, and all kinds of other venues and forms. Even if there are no imported companies touring through town, the public festivals and entertainments of transplanted minorities and indigenous non-Anglo populations are part of every city's culture today. Can't we write about them as vibrant performance activity and experience? Isn't that at least as important to us as sitting in a theatre and being constantly stunned with new tricks and new ideas?

One reason multiculturalism is such a tense issue now is that it is perceived as a major force in the weakening of Western high-art traditions. In a pluralistic, postmodern society, no monolithic art form can satisfy everyone, and even those of us who grew up on the high arts – I certainly did – may welcome other reflections of what has become a very complex lifestyle, other models for solving the confused ethical debates in which we're involved. I listen to Mozart; I also listen to gamelan and samba and West African drumming. Why not?

Ballet and modern dance as we've understood them seem to be going through a fallow period, and not only because of competition from the multicultural sector. We're seeing a lot of imitation, a lot of desperate claspings on to what remains of these older traditions, and not very much 'authenticity' of feeling about it, and certainly not very much creativity within those forms. The phase will undoubtedly pass, but I'm not so interested in looking at those mainstreams or writing about them at this point.

I don't mind if I get labelled an anthropologist, or a journalist, and not a critic. I've been interested in non-Western forms for a long time, writing about them since the early 1970s, and I find them more and more interesting, and more and more of a challenge. And very much to my surprise, some fascinating contemporary forms are getting invented – and they're not even forms. They're little ideas, poking up here and there, from people who have not been totally overcome by the massive infiltration of ballet and modern dance training around the world. Assimilating those and other influences, often recovering their own buried cultural heritage, some choreographers have come to a new resolution of dance identity for themselves, or are dancing out the colliding, still unassimilated elements of what is contemporary life for them.

I think the questions surrounding what is anyone's identity in anyone's culture are deep and affecting. They are going to result in creative work. I personally want to be around to see that work too, and to write about it, and I hope you'll be there with me.

12

BETWEEN DESCRIPTION AND DECONSTRUCTION

Roger Copeland

We had the experience but missed the meaning,
And approach to the meaning restores the experience
In a different form . . .
                    (T.S. Eliot, *The Dry Salvages*)

If one were to summarize the essential differences between the best nineteenth- and twentieth-century dance criticism (the differences between the writing of say, Gautier on the one hand and that of Denby or Jowitt on the other), the key contrast would surely be the latter's greatly improved capacity for describing the exact contours of the body in motion. Gautier provides the reader with a wonderfully vivid sense of the mental images the dance evoked in his mind's eye ('Taglioni reminded you of cool and shaded valleys where a white vision suddenly emerges from the bark of an oak'), but alas, very little sense of what the choreography itself actually looked like. The best twentieth-century dance critics haven't – by any means – abandoned the evocative phrase or the visual analogy, but unlike Gautier, they also strive to provide the reader with a palpable sense of the dance as a thing-in-itself, independent of the imaginative faculties of the perceiver.

Few would fail to applaud this new emphasis on description. And who would underestimate the immense difficulty of the task? The ability to see movement clearly and to describe it evocatively is a rare and wonderful gift. Good dance criticism is a multi-faceted endeavour. It involves – at a minimum – description, interpretation and value judgment. To see something clearly and then describe it evocatively may sound less glamorous (intellectually speaking) than brainy exegesis. But accurate and evocative description are probably the rarest of all critical achievements. As John Ruskin once wrote,

The greatest thing a human soul ever does in this world is to see something and tell what it saw in a plain way. Hundreds of people

can talk for one who can think, but thousands can think for one who
can see. To see clearly is poetry, prophecy and religion – all in one.

(Ruskin in Braudy 1976: 2)

Unfortunately though, in dance criticism, this sort of 'seeing' is too often
achieved at the expense of other, more 'reflective' critical activities. It often
seems as if good descriptive dance criticism demands a laser-beam intensity
of vision that 'locks on' to the work so tightly that it prevents the mind
from taking the next step, and arriving at generalized conclusions that are
interpretive, theoretical and contextual. The best descriptive criticism (e.g.
Deborah Jowitt's weekly columns in *The Village Voice*) most often takes the
form of impressionistic connoisseurship – vividly, even lovingly attentive to
visual detail, but virtually devoid of ideas and fearful of arriving at general-
izations (on the assumption that to do so is to vitiate the sensory immediacy
of the work). As a result, the dance world has produced very few 'practical'
critics whose work compares favourably with that of Harold Rosenberg,
Clement Greenberg, Lionel Trilling, R.P. Blackmur, Eric Bentley or Charles
Rosen – critics of painting, literature, drama and music whose talent for
empirical description is enhanced by a love of ideas, an awareness of social
context, and a willingness to generalize about the significance of highly
particularized experiences.

This is one of the reasons why the publication, in 1988, of Deborah
Jowitt's *Time and the Dancing Image* was an event of no small importance.
Jowitt's book is a splendidly written introduction to dance history, concentrating on the way in which the image of the dancer and the very shape of
the dancing body changes in response to transformations of the culture-at-
large. But the broader significance of the book has less to do with its
intrinsic merit (or even with its specific arguments) than with what it tells us
about Jowitt's own evolution as a dance writer. For the past quarter-century,
Deborah Jowitt has personified (both as practising critic and as peripatetic
teacher of criticism) the dominant 'school' of descriptive American dance
writing. But early in the preface to her book, she endorses a very different
view of criticism:

> dancers and choreographers don't exist in a vacuum, however cut
> off from life their rigorous daily discipline can make them appear to
> be. Those of us who write about dance sometimes find that in our
> anxiety to capture and chronicle a notoriously ephemeral art we do
> it an inadvertent disservice: we focus so intently on it that we sever it
> from the culture that spawned it and which it serves.

(Jowitt 1988: 7)

Not exactly a Mea Culpa, but a confession – however belated – that criticism
of an essentially descriptive nature can perform an 'inadvertent disservice'. I

suspect it's modesty rather than guilt that prevents Jowitt from admitting the extent to which her own example has perpetuated this 'disservice'; but one can only hope that her new critical orientation will prove as influential as her earlier one. Alas, one book does not a movement make, but it's encouraging that similar murmurings can be detected in other quarters as well.

To what can we attribute this growing dissatisfaction with a criticism myopically focused on description? Well, in one sense, dance writing is merely trying to keep pace with dance: consider the extent to which American choreography of recent years has repudiated many of the 'formalist' impulses that were reasonably well served by a descriptive criticism. Descriptive critics like Jowitt and Marcia Siegel came of age during the formalist heyday of Balanchine, Cunningham and Paul Taylor. An aesthetic that emphasizes movement-as-an-end-in-itself has more to gain (and less to lose) from an essentially descriptive criticism than does the dance theatre of Pina Bausch or those non-Western dances, so central to today's multicultural mandate, which cannot be adequately 'described' without paying a great deal of attention to the cultural fabric into which they are woven.

But it's my belief that the descriptive bias – however well it may have served the needs of formalist dances in which movement is declared autonomous of meaning – was never principally a response to formalism. It was also in part a consequence of the unique conditions under which dance criticism is written. (That is: unlike painting, sculpture, or literature, choreography does not 'sit still', inviting the critic to examine it in a spirit of leisurely detachment. Thus 'mere' description – which can seem so pedestrian in the criticism of the other arts – is an important means of lending the dance some semblance of permanence.)

But there's more to this story. Traditionally at least, the bias toward description has been part and parcel of another, even deeper bias: a bias against ideas. As we'll soon see, many people – including many dance critics and intellectuals – are attracted to dance precisely because the experience of viewing it generates an intense pleasure that has the effect of inhibiting, rather than promoting, the impulse toward reflection.

Now, at this point, I need to make a confession: I speak as someone fundamentally unsympathetic to the sort of jargonized, overly methodologized 'theories' that have come to dominate academic approaches to the arts over the past fifteen years. Perhaps it's a blessing in disguise that dance studies – despite the steadily increasing influence of deconstruction, poststructuralism, and gender-politics – remain comparatively 'under-theorized', that they haven't gone the way (or at least not *all* the way) of film and literary studies, where graduate students are infinitely more conversant with Lacan, Kristeva and Derrida than with Antonioni, Mizoguchi and Bresson or with Proust, Joyce and Dostoevsky. (When Oscar Wilde wrote that critics would become the artists of the future, his tongue was planted in his cheek. But when the pioneer of deconstruction, Paul de Man proclaimed that 'Poetry is the foreknowledge of criticism', he wasn't kidding.) I for one am not eager to see the sensuous surface of the dancer's body vaporized beneath the blowtorch of deconstruction (which typically produces more heat than light). Still, for better or for worse, the fact remains that the relationship between dance and theory is very different from the relationship of say, literature and theory, or the visual arts and theory. Before we decide whether this state of affairs is a good thing or a bad thing, we need to try to explain why it exists in the first place.

Against interpretation

Susan Sontag's notorious essay of 1964, *Against Interpretation*, never directly mentions dance, but it has great implications for both dance and dance writing. Consider this central paragraph:

> In a culture whose already classical dilemma is the hypertrophy of the intellect at the expense of energy and sensual capability, interpretation is the revenge of the intellect upon art. Even more. It is the revenge of the intellect upon the world. To interpret is to impoverish, to deplete the world – in order to set up a shadow world of 'meanings' . . . The world, our world, is depleted, impoverished enough. Away with all duplicates of it, until we again experience more immediately what we have.
>
> (Sontag 1966: 7)

Clearly, for Sontag, it is the peculiar achievement, perhaps even the spiritual mission, of certain art forms to hold interpretation and reflection at bay, to impede them – or even ward them off. What they offer us (in its stead) is something infinitely rarer and more valuable: sensory immediacy. ('What is important now is to recover our senses. We must learn to see more, to hear more, to feel more', adds Sontag (1966: 14).)

Alain Robbe-Grillet, one of Sontag's intellectual heroes, makes a closely related argument in *For a New Novel*:

> At every moment, a continuous fringe of culture (psychology, ethics, metaphysics, etc.) is added to things, giving them a less alien aspect, one that is more comprehensible, more reassuring. Sometimes the camouflage is complete: a gesture vanishes from our mind, supplanted by the emotions which supposedly produced it, and we remember a landscape as austere or calm without being able to evoke a single outline, a single determining element.
>
> (Robbe-Grillet in Hall and Ulanov 1967: 274–5)

Both Sontag and Robbe-Grillet are prescribing an antidote to what Ortega y Gasset once called 'the progressive dis-realization of the world', the cannibalizing of the world by consciousness. 'What we decidedly do not need now', wrote Sontag in the same essay, 'is to further assimilate Art into Thought' (1966:13). Sontag and Robbe-Grillet both seek to reinvest the physical world with a sense of 'être-là' or sheer 'thereness'.

But how does one embark upon this arduous, if not Utopian, task? For Robbe-Grillet, the answer was a style of excruciatingly detailed description, virtually devoid of anthropomorphizing adjectives. That's what he's getting at when he complains that 'We remember a landscape as austere or calm without being able to evoke a single outline, a single determining element'. By contrast, his legendary paragraph describing the surface of a tomato (in his novel *The Erasers*) keeps our attention focused obsessively on the physical characteristics of the object. ('The peripheral flesh, compact and homogeneous, of a fine chemical redness, is uniformly thick between a band of shiny skin and the semicircular area where the seeds are arranged . . . ' (1953: 48).)

Sontag recommends a similar strategy for criticism:

> What kind of criticism, of commentary on the arts, is desirable today? For I am not saying that works of art are ineffable, that they cannot be described or paraphrased. They can be. The question is how. What would criticism look like that would serve the work of art, not usurp its place? What is needed first, is more attention to form in art. If excessive stress on content provokes the arrogance of interpretation, more extended and more thorough descriptions of form would silence [. . .] Equally valuable would be acts of criticism which would supply a really accurate, sharp, loving description of the appearance of a work of art. This seems even harder to do than formal analysis.
>
> (1966: 12)

Ultimately, she calls for 'essays which reveal the sensuous surface of art without mucking about in it' (1966: 13). Has anyone ever provided a better description of what critics like Denby and Jowitt do so brilliantly? The best descriptive dance criticism may well offer us the clearest example of what Sontag was advocating. It's especially instructive to compare the current state of dance writing with the current state of writing about film. We might begin by noting the privileged place in her aesthetic pantheon that Sontag assigned the cinema in *Against Interpretation*. Remember, this was 1964, long before the semioticians and the post-structuralists had launched their (now successful) invasion of film studies. Here's what she says about film:

> Ideally it is possible to elude the interpreters [. . .] by making works of art whose surface is so unified and clean, whose momentum is so

102

rapid, whose address is so direct that the work can be [. . .] just what it is. Is this possible now? It does happen in films, I believe. This is why cinema is the most alive, the most exciting, the most import-ant of all art forms right now [. . .] In good films there is always a directness that entirely frees us from the itch to interpret.

(1966: 11)

But now in the Age of Theory – aided and abetted by the availability of video cassettes and the resulting ease with which one can conduct frame by frame analyses – film too has been caught up in the hermeneutic net. And for many intellectuals, this amounts to nothing less than a loss of innocence, a fall from grace. One thinks of Pauline Kael's classic dismissal of Siegfried Kracauer's *Theory of Film: The Redemption of Physical Reality*:

Siegfried Kracauer is the sort of man who can't say 'It's a lovely day' without first establishing that it *is* day, that the term 'day' is meaning-less without the dialectical concept of 'night,' that both these terms have no meaning unless there is a world in which day and night alternate, and so forth. By the time he has established an epistemo-logical system to support his right to observe that it's a lovely day, our day has been spoiled.

(Kael 1965: 269)

It may well be that dance is now the only art that still serves the anti-interpretive function formerly assigned to film. (As Martin Leonard Pops once put it, 'Anatomy presupposes a corpse, but the living body of dance is never still enough for a proper dissection'.) The descriptive bias insures that dance will continue to perform that anti-interpretive function. But it also, perhaps inadvertently, insures that dance writing remains intellectually insular, virtually estranged from the realm of ideas that routinely enliven discussion of the other arts.

Dance and the thoroughly modern intellectual

Writing about dance rarely appears in magazines geared toward generalist intellectuals (e.g. *The New York Review of Books*, *Harper's*, *The Atlantic*, *The New Republic* and so on). This is not, I hasten to add, because the readers of these publications are afraid of coming into contact with so 'physical' an art form. Dancers and choreographers often envision intellectuals as people who are uncomfortable with their own bodies and thus fundamentally unsympathetic to dance. We like to believe that existing bodies of know-ledge exclude a knowledge of the body. What a charmingly dated caricature! It ignores the reality of that peculiarly contemporary intellectual who is breathlessly eager to establish his or her Dionysian credentials – the sort of intellectual who, upon hearing the word culture (as defined by Matthew Arnold) is more likely to reach for his popcorn than to brush up his Shakespeare. The choice, for such people, is not between Milton and Madonna. The point is to embrace both without compromising one's seriousness or one's funkiness. Like the angels in Wim Wender's film *Wings of Desire*, this sort of intellectual has grown weary of the ethereal and hungry for the material.

Certainly, among the fabled 'New York Intellectuals', a passion for Balanchine is *de rigueur*. Granted, their commitment to (and knowledge of) dance may not extend beyond the obligatory seasonal pilgrimage to the New York City Ballet. But my point is that such people are by no means dance-o-phobes (although they may be ballet-o-manes). In fact, they would feel incomplete, or at least impoverished, without their periodic Balanchine fix. *Concerto Barocco*, *Agon*, and *The Four Temperaments* offer the promise of instant access to a realm of 'pure' wordless physicality.

Thus a passion for dance is absolutely essential for the modern intellectual. But is there a comparable passion for *ideas* about dance? No, not as long as dance is viewed as the art that holds interpretation in check, the last remaining link to some lost, pre-verbal, Dionysian paradise. This brand of anti-intellectualism is of course very different from the sort that Doris Humphrey attributed to the dance community when she wrote, 'The person drawn to dance as a profession is notoriously unintellectual. He thinks with his muscles; delights in expression with body, not words; finds analysis painful and boring; and is a creature of physical ebullience' (Humphrey 1959: 17).

In fact, this is a mode of anti-intellectualism peculiar to intellectuals; and it has little or nothing to do with old-fashioned philistinism, 'no-nothing-ism' or traditional forms of Anglo-American empiricism and positivism. Philip Rieff was describing this condition when he complained that 'Many (intellectuals) have gone over to the enemy without realizing that they, self-considered the cultural elite, have actually become spokesmen for what Freud called "the instinctual mass"' (1966: 8–9). And when it comes to writing about dance, we find something upon which the least intellectual members of the dance world (those who've never known the life of the mind) and the hippest, most 'advanced' intellectuals (those who feel that they've *outgrown* the life of the mind) can agree. When it comes to writing about dance, these two varieties of anti-intellectualism merge into a single stream.

Practical proposals

But surely, there must be some middle ground between anti-interpretative description and dauntingly theoretical 'deconstruction'. Unfortunately – at the moment – the only existing alternative to the descriptive bias would seem to be the triumph of 'theory'. Here we pause for my favourite joke of recent years: 'What do you get when you cross a deconstructionist with a mafia hit man?' Answer: 'You get an offer you can't understand!' In the 'age of specialization' – where the generalist reader or writer is automatically regarded as an amateur or a dilettante – one's 'public' becomes an extension of one's self: a small cabal of other like-minded specialists. And compounding the sense of folly is the fact that today's esoteric theoretical apparatus is so often deployed in the service of the cultural left – which displays an 'anti-elitist' hostility toward the traditions of high art – and correspondingly, an egalitarian embrace of popular culture. What a ridiculous paradox! The very people who complain most vociferously about 'elitism' are themselves the real elitists when it comes to the utterly private language in which their ideas are encoded.

The great literary critic R.P. Blackmur once said that the best sort of writing about the arts is 'the discourse of an amateur'. And by 'amateur' Blackmur did not mean 'uninformed'. He meant the true connoisseur, someone motivated by a deep love of the art and a desire to communicate his or her enthusiasm to the widest possible public. This motivation is rather different from the activist goals of gender-politics or the tenure-driven pressures of publish-or-perish. (Which is not to imply that these motivations are mutually exclusive. Today, the impulse to 'politicize' and the pressure to 'professionalize' are often part and parcel of one another.)

Perhaps what's really called for is not the sort of writing that today's excessively 'professionalized' academics would regard as theoretical, but rather something closer to the now vanishing tradition of *belles lettres* (which at its best, effortlessly synthesized description, interpretation, theoretical reflection and value judgment). I don't know that we even possess a name for such writing today. We might refer to it as accessible scholarship, erudite journalism, or serious but non-specialized prose aimed at a broad-based, well-educated readership. Call it what you will; but there's no denying that writing of this sort has gone, or is rapidly going – the way of the spotted owl, the snail darter, and other endangered species. This sort of writing is more interested in *ideas* than in theory *per se*. But, I hasten to add, this is not an argument on behalf of popularization or dumbing-down. As Frank Lloyd Wright once wrote: 'Things should be made as simple as possible, but no simpler.'

With the possible exceptions of André Levinson and Lincoln Kirstein, dance writers have rarely achieved – or even aspired toward – criticism of this sort. Although at their best, Arlene Croce, Joan Acocella, and Alastair Macaulay can all lay claim to this 'belletristic' tradition. Here, for example, is Arlene Croce on Balanchine's *The Four Temperaments*:

> When, in the opening statement of the ballet – the first part of the Theme – we see a girl, supported on her points, turning from side to

side and transferring her weight from one foot to the other as she turns, we see her do it with a finicky grace: she lifts and lowers the free foot, curls it around the standing leg, and carefully flexes it before arching to full point. We see, in short, a foot becoming a point – nature being touched to artificial life [. . .] The 'story' of *The Four Temperaments* is precisely that story – the subjection of persons to a process and their re-emergence as human archetypes.

(Croce 1977: 187–8)

Or – for a more recent example of what I have in mind – consider Joan Acocella writing about the way Twyla Tharp's dances have benefited from the participation of Mikhail Baryshnikov:

What she (and he) achieved was a kind of apotheosis of her disorderly order. Plump-line pirouettes suddenly melting off sidewise, grands battements so grand, so forceful, that they knocked the body off balance – not so much, however, that it didn't recover in an instant, and launch itself into some other feat of embattled perfection – and this moreover, while sliding and diving down the beat like an otter down a snowbank; it looked like a dream. And what Tharp learned with Baryshnikov she brought back to her company, pushing her dancers to greater heights of skill and daring. It *was* a dream – a symbol, an idea. And that fact, not just the wit and beauty of the dancing, accounts for Tharp's immense popularity with audiences of the seventies. Her work was an idea about America: that you could indeed have freedom and order at the same time. It was also an idea about history: that you could question the past without losing it.

(Acocella 1992: 166–7)

Note how effortlessly Croce and Acocella move from precise, evocative description to the realm of generalization. They offer us a sensuous portrait of the *ideas* at the core of Balanchine's and Tharp's achievement. And note that in praising Croce's and Acocella's work, I'm not suggesting that dance writing will benefit from becoming less descriptive (only that it shouldn't *settle* for description). The ideal dance writer regards description as a necessary, but not sufficient, component of the critical task.

Similarly, the ideal critic realizes that theory need not, should not, *must* not, become synonymous with abstract system-building. Alvin Gouldner once defined theory as 'the capacity to make problematic what had hitherto been treated as given; to bring to reflection what before had only been used' (Gouldner in Culler 1982: 11). The real function of theory is simple: it promotes reflection. And 'dance theory' should examine the ideas that are generated when one reflects systematically upon the sensory experience of dance; it shouldn't bury dance beneath ready-made notions purchased from the mail-order catalogues of Derrida, Foucault and Company.

In conclusion, I fear it may sound as if I'm trying to have it both ways – or perhaps every which way. That's because I'm arguing on behalf of the centre or middle ground between two equally undesirable extremes. Dance writing today is either too descriptive or not descriptive enough. And in academia, dance writing has leapt from description to the rarefied realm of theory without having passed through the humble, but more fertile intermediate stage of *ideas*. Ideas require thinking. Today's theoretical heavy artillery often functions as a pre-fabricated, follow-the-numbers substitute for thought. What we really suffer from is a shortage of genuine dance intellectuals, whom we might define as critics for whom *ideas* are as palpable as pirouettes.

13

OH, THAT PINEAPPLE RAG!

Arlene Croce

When choreographers take real life as their subject, they usually take it in the abstract. Literal intentions are almost always suicidal; even when they succeed they generally don't succeed at a high level, and the choreographer is accused of trying to think, as if cogitation and choreography were mutually antagonistic. Twyla Tharp's newest work, *The Catherine Wheel*, which she is showing at the Winter Garden, manages to be literal and abstract at the same time, so that the turn of a thought and its realization in dance are more often than not presented together. But they are also presented in separate systems that are elaborately cross-referenced. Tharp's use of semi-abstract mime and semi-literal dance is one such system. She also uses the straight varieties of dance and mime, an array of props and costumes, a sophisticated and highly theatrical rock score by David Byrne, and the ingenious stage technology of Jennifer Tipton and Santo Loquasto. *The Catherine Wheel* is schematically overloaded, but then Tharp tends to be excessive. She's like a juggler piling Pelion on Ossa on Mount Saint Helens on the tip of her nose. When the elements are harmoniously integrated, as in *Deuce Coupe* and *Push Comes to Shove*, we get magic. When the overload collapses, as it did in last year's *When We Were Very Young*, we get cacophony. *The Catherine Wheel* holds together. Unlike *When We Were Very Young*, which was a playlet with dances, it is a multilevel poetic fantasy that discharges its deepest meanings through music and dance. On one level, it is a reworking of *When We Were Very Young*: some of the characters from that piece are back doing some of the same things; Tharp seems determined to reduce the American nuclear family to a pile of smoked turkeys. This time, though, she zips through her catalogue of abuse, adds a twist of scalawag comedy and a suite of social dances through the ages, and gets on with the main objective of the show, which is to enlarge the turkey story to the dimensions of a fable. It's a little like interleaving the *National Enquirer* with *The Golden Bough*, but Tharp does it, and brings it off as an uncluttered, intensively lyrical experience. And keeps it going for eighty minutes without interruption.

The Catherine Wheel is so completely systematized that although it encloses a story about the modern world, it is always and only about itself.

From time to time, lyrics are sung to the music which seem to relate to the action. For instance:

> Well the bride bride and the groom
> Run in a circle around their house
> They're goin' out they're comin' in
> Inside a circle around their house.

That's about as explicit as the lyrics ever get, and we do see a bride and groom. Yet at no time are the words used as a functional element in the staging. They're in dream language to begin with, and then, as part of the processed studio sound that makes up Byrne's taped score, they're largely inaudible. When a word drifts out of the sonic haze, it strikes us as pre-articulate speech – closer to the sources of pain and emotion than normal speech is. The cryptic sound goes with the various pieces of primitive machinery which Loquasto has fashioned out of what look like scraps from a Victorian bicycle shop. The wheels turn but they don't go anywhere. Another contraption, which is lowered from the flies, has a use that may be guessed from its retractable prongs: it is a torture rack. One may with cause think of Saint Catherine impaled on her wheel or of Lear's 'I am bound upon a wheel of fire, that mine own tears do scald like molten lead'. But one isn't given time to ponder wheel symbolism, or even wheel non-symbolism; there's more going on. *The Catherine Wheel* has wheels within wheels.

It also has pineapples. The wheel is a perfect symbol for the spectacle that has been devised by Twyla Tharp and her collaborators; the music, the decor and props, the costumes, the lighting, the staging and the choreography are spokes radiating meaning from the hub of conception. And when the wheel spins and gives off sparks, it really is a pyrotechnical accomplishment. The pineapple is not a self-referential symbol; it's more in the nature of what Alfred Hitchcock used to call the MacGuffin. In Hitchcock's movies, what people chased after – secret formulas or uranium ore in wine bottles – was the MacGufffin, and, as Hitchcock told François Truffaut, the meaning of the MacGuffin is always beside the point: 'The only thing that really matters is that in the picture the plans, the documents, or secrets must seem to be of vital importance to the characters.' In *The Catherine Wheel*, the characters worship pineapples; they need and want and love pineapples, they steal pineapples, make sacrifices of pineapples. At the start of the show, a cluster of pineapples glows through the gloom like a Christmas tree, like the tree of the knowledge of good and evil, like the burning bush. A vestal virgin (Sara Rudner) extracts one fruit; it brains a coy bridegroom (Tom Rawe). So we witness the fall of man, the rages and quarrels, the cretinous offspring (Katie Glasner, Raymond Kurshals), acts of brutality and of bestiality. A furry dog (Christine Uchida) is sexually abused; later she kills her tormentor. A monster mother (Jennifer Way) pimps for her daughter. A young poet (John

Carrafa) shows some interest in the girl but he'd rather sleep with a pine-apple. A pineapple isn't the Holy Grail; it isn't sex or money or power, although at different times it seems to be those things, and if you think it looks like a grenade it is that thing as well. It's an absurdist symbol, a symbol of absurdity, and a dumb device all at once. It's active, whereas the wheel symbolism is passive; pineapples, and not wheels, turn the plot and at the same time turn our minds to thoughts of illusion and degradation, of slav-ishness and cultishness and obscene greed. The pineapple is Tharp's pretext for showing us the harsh and depressing world we live in. As the frenzy reaches its climax and tapers off, Rudner, as the priestess, returns bearing a golden wheel with a pineapple at the hub, and the inner and outer thought systems of the ballet are merged; at least, they're meant to be. But, like the 'sacrifice of the pineapple' that occurred a moment before, the moment of the merger is largely a mystifying one. In the sacrifice scene (Tharp calls it 'The Leader Repents'), Rudner takes her precious pineapple, now reduced to a bag of (Styrofoam) chunks, and shoves it – literally impales it over and over on the torture rack. Although the scene is repeated many times and played alongside another 'loop', of the monster family at its most Jukes-like, we don't get a chance to sort out the meanings or to relate the two scenes. We haven't drunk deep enough of the pineapple – we've been too busy discarding hypotheses – to know that it is capable of dying for our sins.

The last quarter of the ballet is a dance apotheosis of astonishing beauty and power. Tharp's title for it is 'The Golden Section', and it rises like an Atlantis from the murk of the pineapple world, transforming it into a para-dise of new feelings and visionary exploits. Tharp's abrupt alchemy substi-tuting harmony for chaos is almost painful in its honesty. It's as if she were substituting art for life, knowing that no solution to the palpable terrors she has invoked is possible. Art less than a solution yet more than a consolation, offers terms she can settle for; it's the great alternative to the dilemma of life, the only other reality that isn't death. 'The Golden Section' is the clas-sical 'white' ballet, with all its implications of redemption intact. In the old ballets, though – *Giselle* and *La Bayadère* and *Swan Lake* – death was the condition of redemption. In 'The Golden Section', the dancers are dressed not as incorporeal figures in white tulle but as acrobats in gold tights, launch-ing themselves against a honey-gold backdrop. The characters of the previ-ous scene return transformed and dance wonderfully, and the choreography reaches supersonic speeds as it passes from one prodigious episode to the next, until suddenly, in the middle of a leap, the lights go out. The dance ends in midair, which is to say it does not end. 'The Golden Section' is a glimpse of infinity; it's a celestial version of those moments of Tharpian continuity in other works (like *Baker's Dozen*) when the dance leaves the stage and returns, having continued behind the scenes. Tharp keeps the energy level climbing and the invention flowing, but she doesn't create a compulsive, inhumanly brilliant atmosphere, as she did in last year's *Brahms'*

Paganini. 'The Golden Section' seems to rise effortlessly above the negotiations of virtuosity and to ride along in a kind of relaxed ecstasy. For the first time, Twyla Tharp attains grandeur.

The world of *The Catherine Wheel*, half in darkness, half in light, has the completeness of Elizabethan cosmogony and the aura of myth. The rude mechanicals and their swinish and sleazy existence, the supernatural priestess and her entourage, the innocents (the Poet, the Pet, the hysterical Maid danced by Shelley Washington) occupy their classic positions as forms of life and dramatic counterweights. And in 'The Golden Section', when they dance, dance, dance, they are all one race, neither gods nor human beings but the gilded beasts of the Greek fables. The ballet is a running frieze of stags and hinds and winged colts, with some broncos and circus ponies cut into the herd. It's a Circean transformation, and as an image it's true to the rough, inarticulate nature of the parable that precedes it. For all its polished surfaces and moments of blinding lucidity, *The Catherine Wheel* is an experience of mute sensations; we look and wonder, and are lifted we know not how, and at the end our blood is changed.

But to say that the experience is mute is not to say that it is incoherent. No; feeling about in the dark, we are able to sense and then grasp with conviction the relationship of things, and whether we accept pineappleism as mystical wisdom or tactical whimsy we are bound to follow the pattern it imposes – we can't get lost. The climate of Twyla Tharp's best work has usually been so spartan that the plush fancies of *The Catherine Wheel* are overdazzling at first, and one may be inclined to mistrust them. But you could strip away the symbolical apparatus; you could cancel Tipton's shadows and scrims, her shimmering blacks and ashen greys and warm golds; you could delete Loquasto's fierce little engines, and even his forest of poles, through which the whole first section of the piece is danced, and stage the work, as Tharp often staged her early dances, in a school gym. And still the piece would work, on the strength of its current of rhythm. The choreography has no trouble sustaining rhythmic tension over an improbably long span of time; the flat-out driving attack of 'The Golden Section' only accelerates the excitement – Tharp has been in high gear right along.

Byrne's music is the first rock score to pull solid weight in a theatrical-dance context. It has real rhythm, not just a beat. The deficiencies of rock as dance music were noticed long ago by Paul Draper, who pronounced it 'rhythmically more arid than the Sahara', and went on to define rhythm as 'visual or aural patterns which live within the framework of the beat and the time'. Byrne's brand of concert rock must, I suppose, be accorded the status of serious music. Its werewolf-and-charnel-house sound imagery is not the kind of seriousness I care for, but there is no doubt that working with Tharp has sharpened Byrne's sensitivity to the variety of pulse and mood a dance score has to have. The horrendous chill that I take to be characteristic of Byrne's music – it is there in his records with the Talking Heads as well – is perfectly suited to the dark side of Tharp's world, where dads rape dogs, devils writhe in women's bodies, and public assassins creep in the shadows. In 'The Golden Section', the brilliant metallic clang of the music is appropriately circusy; then it changes into a choir sweetly chanting

> Oh I don't understand
> Oh it's not just a sound
> Oh I don't understand
> It doesn't matter at all.

For a thinking choreographer's comment on the world, *The Catherine Wheel* is strangely precognitive. One would have to go back to Paul Taylor's *Orbs* to find a work of comparable scale, purity and charm. But even Taylor did not attempt an uninterrupted dance epic. Nor did he use a commissioned score. *The Catherine Wheel* is a major event in our theatre.

14

SPRING: ASHTON'S SYMPHONIC VARIATIONS IN AMERICA

Alastair Macaulay

When we call a work of art classical, we imply that it is made of perennial stuff. And yet dance classicism is immensely fragile. *That* was *Divertimento No. 15?* You should have seen *Monotones* when it *was Monotones.* We cannot know how much will survive for future generations or for our own old age. In terms of creative talent, this is the worst recession ballet has endured since at least the thirties. What a tonic, therefore, to go back to an era when ballet classicism was being defended, restored, rebuilt and intensified – to the forties. American Ballet Theatre opened its current spring season with a programme including *Theme and Variations*, which George Balanchine created for the company in 1947, and a newly acquired production of *Symphonic Variations*, which Frederick Ashton made in 1946 and which for more than thirty years was a signature work of the Sadler's Wells – later Royal – Ballet.

Balanchine's classicism pours forth in all its majestic power in *Theme and Variations.* The ballet takes us from the fountainhead's first eruption to the surging torrent of the river mouth. It keeps proclaiming 'Petipa!' with a high-density brilliance way beyond that of Petipa's own ballets. In 1947, Russia, France and Britain posed major alternatives to Balanchine's vision; in 1992, there are no challengers. New ballets everywhere have 'Balanchine on My Mind' stamped all over them. This is right and proper; Balanchine was the towering genius of his art. But it is time to insure that Ashton – who was merely a great choreographer – is not eclipsed. Ashton, only eight months younger than Balanchine, was the first major choreographer to take inspiration from Balanchine's ballets, to use it in his growth as an artist and, in several ways, to dissent. As *Theme and Variations* and other works show, Petipa is often the only choreographer in Balanchine's view of classicism. In *Symphonic Variations*, however, Ashton's view takes in Petipa, Balanchine, and more. For that reason, among several, its presence in the A.B.T. repertory refreshes the springtime climate of ballet at Lincoln Center. And spring, by the way, is part of its theme.

Ashton's classicism had its peculiarities. Ballet is urban, and his was often Arcadian. Ballet is hierarchical, and his inclined to egalitarianism. Ballet is sexist, and his gave parity to male and female. Ballet is movement, and his often featured an unusual degree of rest. (Not that Ashton's classicism was markedly eccentric – it was no more peculiar than Bournonville's, and less so than most others'. It is the grand orthodoxy of Petipa and Balanchine that is truly rare.) Naturally, Ashton interpreted classicism in the light of his own temperament, and in the light of his place and time. I cannot imagine that even Balanchine could have produced the unchecked continuity and reinvigorated tradition that shines through *Theme* if he had spent the war years in Europe. In the work of every European artist in the forties we can feel the threat that the war posed, how close it came to shattering accepted traditions, and how profoundly and permanently it altered European life. *Suite en Blanc*, made in occupied Paris for the Opéra by its director, Serge Lifar, is classicism as sheer façade or couture. The elegance that it defiantly proclaims is not expressive; it's defensive, a shell. *Symphonic Variations*, made in London immediately after the war, is classicism as haven.

The war elicited a new, expressionist streak in Ashton, who had previously tended to choose frivolous or sentimental themes as the seeds of his brilliant constructions. His most famous ballet of the war years was *Dante Sonata*. What would we make now of its conflict between the Children of Light and the Children of Darkness? Or its two tableaux of crucifixion? Well – it was loved once. The war didn't rob Ashton of humour; the one dance of his that survives from those years is the hilarious Foxtrot that he added to his 1931 hit *Façade*. The tension between his new seriousness and his more familiar frivolity is caught in a passage from Margot Fonteyn's autobiography:

> One night, in our theatrical lodgings, over cold meat, apple pie and hot tea, Fred Ashton announced that he was going to read the Bible from beginning to end, and that by the time he finished it the war would be over. Finding some passages monotonous and heavy going, he made a further announcement: he would read it aloud to us. Billie Chappell protested, saying: 'Freddie, you can't do that to your friends.' Nevertheless, Freddie did, but he miscalculated by about four years, and was to read a great many other books before the holocaust ceased.

That further wartime reading included, Ashton said, 'lots of mystical books, Saint Theresa of Avila, Saint John of the Cross, and so forth'. He also listened repeatedly to the Symphonic Variations of César Franck.

Ashton's ballet to this score began in his mind as another expressionist work. The music's progress was to have taken the ballet from winter to summer, from darkness to light, from chastity and vigilance to love, fertility

114

and marriage. But working on *Symphonic Variations* taught Ashton something like what Stravinsky's score for *Apollo* had taught Balanchine in 1928: to eliminate. Ashton pared subject matter away until only pure-dance essence remained. Consequently, by suppressing the many things he originally meant to say, he made a ballet that says far more. It is easy to feel how *Symphonics* takes its place in the line of English lyric poetry. Its dances, to use Milton's (and Mark Morris's) terms, are both allegro and penseroso, active and contemplative. The ballet's pastoral spirit is like Marvell's garden: 'Annihilating all that's made To a green thought in a green shade.' And its quiet mysteries are those of Keats's Grecian urn. *Symphonics* is also near in spirit to Eliot's *Four Quartets*: 'the still point of the turning world', 'in my beginning is my end', 'the time of the seasons and the constellations'. The ballet is both Hellenistic and English; it refers to the perpetual stillness of Greek statuary, to the expressive vitality of pure geometry, to the chain dances of the Greek and mediaeval eras, to the flowing arabesques and attitudes and the glowing tableaux of *The Sleeping Beauty*, to the white virginity of *Swan Lake*, to the primitive footwork and extreme oppositions of Nijinska's dances, and to the creative union of male and female in *Apollo*.

Above all, *Symphonics* is a Vitruvian ballet – an exposition simply of how pure dance to music, without props or scene changes, can radiate from the area of space onstage into the larger, taller facing arc of an auditorium. In 1946, Ashton was obsessed with Covent Garden. The old theatre, which had so often presented Russian ballet before the war, was now, for the first time, the home of British ballet. *The Sleeping Beauty*, with which Covent Garden reopened, was a Russian ballet that he had helped to make English and to make register to the depths and far distances of the opera house. And *Symphonic Variations* was the first ballet of his own in which he continued that process.

Six dancers are standing onstage when the curtain rises, small at first against the verdant expanse behind, and they remain onstage throughout. Their stance – arms calm by their sides, one foot crossed over and resting on its point, head turned toward one shoulder, eyes lowered – is the most characteristic motif of the whole ballet, and it shows a facet of classicism usually ignored by ballet: repose. Upright, the body is relaxed and harmonious. The orchestra calls out metrical figures in brief phrases, and the piano calls out quietly the main theme of the music, like a roll call of the original cast's names ('Margot *Fon*-teyn ... Moira *Shear*-er ... '; then 'Michael *Somes*; Brian *Shaw*; Henry *Dan*-ton'). Though Franck quickly embroiders variations on the theme ('and *Pam*-ela May'), he keeps returning to devout announcements of it. The three women, plotted in a row along the front, dance first, to the first piano statement; and their chaste unison – arms often crossing over the body's centre in drastic lines – represents the winter of Ashton's original conception, as they dance to and fro along the stage's horizontal

115

foreground. It is the central man who brings the spring. Turning to face us, he slowly advances through a series of piqué fourth positions, raises an arm, and holds a long, limpid gesture that aims past and above the women's zone into the theatre's heights.

The quartet that follows is the ballet's main reference to *Apollo* (3f, 1m) but the relations of male and female are not Balanchinean. When the two other men start to move, from sentinel positions in the stage's rear corners, they stretch their arms to the audience and then open them out, as if parting curtains and letting in new light and air. All this has a sense of ritual. The movements are still tied closely to the music's phrases. Gradually, as the dance grows more complex, it also becomes musically more surprising. You see lifts and jumps that correspond to no audible beat, and a unison stand-still while a trilling musical crescendo begins. Though the sense of ritual never quite evaporates, the dance shows an accumulation of spontaneity, even of ecstasy. Many moments shine out, like the second male dancer's multiple pirouettes in the centre of the stage: in passé, he starts to turn like a gyroscope, with one arm curved above his head and then he arches back and continues to turn in renversé. (This is the most elusive step in the ballet. With A.B.T., Wes Chapman came closer to bringing it off ideally than anyone I have seen in years. The renversé can make you feel as if the world had briefly spun off its axis.) Or like the highest and most jubilant of all the lifts: the central ballerina is high in the air and fully extended in écarté when suddenly the piano adds its acclaim.

That American Ballet Theatre now dances this ballet is in several ways remarkable. In his lifetime, Ashton allowed no foreign company to dance it. Perhaps as a result, at Covent Garden it became enveloped by the same Holy Grail aura that has blighted many companies' accounts of *Les Sylphides* and *Apollo*; and during the last ten years of his life it died (died standing up). Since his death, the Royal has not revived it. But, to much British surprise, Michael Somes – long the chief régisseur of the Ashton repertory – has staged it for a European and now an American company.[1] A.B.T.'s performances, light and free, are the best *Symphonics* has seen in fifteen years. As was to be expected, it does not read perfectly in the vast, hangarlike space of the Met – no ballet does – but it is an ideal work for teaching A.B.T. dancers how to make a dance breathe into the house and how to shape a serene dance phrase to the music. It teaches much else, too: to keep the waist pliant and the base of the neck Praxitelean. And it asks for line, line, line. Academic steps and positions find their perfect resolution in the address of the eyes, the angle of the head, the gentle opening of the hands.

The A.B.T. version lacks something in sculptural detail, focus and (Ashton's word for this ballet's essence) breath. There are, however, numerous gains. The ease of the women in pirouettes frees the ballet from an element of strain it often had at Covent Garden, and the combination of upper-body fullness and precise unison in the two side women (in the first cast, especially) lightens the whole work. In the central role, Christine Dunham has the greater poise and more expressive head positions, but in phrasing and plastique I prefer Cynthia Harvey. *Symphonics* is no longer exclusively a British ballet. The warm glade-like green of Sophie Fedorovitch's back-drop is now as much New England as it used to be Arcadia or Ashton's Suffolk.

In the mid-sixties, Ashton made *Monotones*, the pair of pas de trois to Satie music that have long been international currency. *Monotones* is Ashton's ultimate distillation of his personal classicism. It takes the old British mastery of flowing adagio to its purest form. And it refers to *Symphonics*, to *Apollo*, to *La Bayadère*, and to Greek imagery. It does not, however, efface *Symphonics*, which is, in some ways, its opposite. All Ashton's plotless works are, in a broad sense, ballets d'action; each one carries a specific sense of time, place and character. Both parts of *Monotones* are encompassed by darkness; one thinks of the Stygian gloom in which the *Bayadère* Shades scene begins, and of the surface of the moon. *Symphonics* is danced in sunlight. Though Sophie Fedorovitch's décor, with its grand parabolas running across the green backdrop, is the most abstract that Ashton ever employed, the choreography always make you feel that these dancers are people in a pastoral landscape. And whereas *Monotones* is daringly sustained in a single slow tempo, *Symphonics* is bright with internal contrast. Its movement is almost all in various kinds of allegro moderato, and is repeatedly set against the motionlessness of one or more dancers.

Sometimes it is the dancers at the centre who scarcely move or are still, and the dancing passes around them. At such points, you sense the pattern of suns, planets, and moons – what A.V. Coton, reviewing the original production, called 'an imagery of infinities'. One of the features – first seen in that opening female trio – that most reminds me of *Four Quartets* is the way the dancers look ahead, then behind. Late in the ballet, the women – backs to us – cross the stage and, just as they step into piqué arabesque, looking forward, they turn to look back; then the men, jumping in second, do the same. This alternation is at its most heart-catching in the brief pas de deux. The leading man carries the ballerina in a soft circuit of floating lifts around the stage ('the enchainment of past and future'); in one she is looking ahead, in the next behind. There is no suggestion of regret. Simply, you sense contemplation even in the midst of action.

I owe this ballet much. Eighteen years ago, it formed the centrepiece of the first programme of ballet I ever saw at Covent Garden; and it was this and *The Sleeping Beauty*, as they were performed there in the seventies, that first addicted me to ballet's radiant legibility. Sitting far away, I would feel how extraordinarily those dances filled the theatre, beaming forth with affecting kinesthetic impact.

NOTE

1 *Symphonic Variations* was subsequently revived at the Royal Opera House in 1994 ·
and in later seasons. It has also been staged for other companies.

PART IV

STUDYING DANCE: CONCEPTUAL CONCERNS

It could be argued that one of the key developments in dance studies during the second half of this century has been an increasing tendency toward self-reflection. That is, as the nature and status of knowledge has been questioned in all areas of scholarly and cultural activity, so writers in dance have identified, explored and critiqued the epistemological frameworks with which they are dealing. Such an enterprise allows for assumptions to be teased out and terminology clarified; it can present arguments for what is distinctive about the conceptual and methodological basis of dance study and what it shares, or has the potential to share, with other fields of enquiry.

The invisibility of dance in these 'other fields of enquiry' has been, perhaps, nowhere more evident than in the realm of philosophy. Even if the instability of knowledge is recognized and the search for any definitive wisdom now argued as futile, Betty Redfern demonstrates how traditional conceptual analysis can expose many of the assumptions buried in both scholarly and everyday discourse. Tackling the concept of art and exemplifying her argument with dance, Redfern raises issues which cohere around the nature of the activity: what kinds of movement, by whom, and where, count as 'dance' – and who says so? Other issues concern the very nature of the debate itself. For example, does the singular form of the question 'what is art?' (or 'what is dance?') preclude a pluralistic response? Is the traditional quest for a definition one that is doomed from the start? Exploring these issues through a model of logical argument, Redfern acknowledges the socio-historical construct of art but suggests that it is the very debate about 'what is art', and the essentially complex and contested nature of art, which sustains the construct. It is the instability of 'art' which accommodates variation and change in practice and in theory.

Sondra Fraleigh also examines the contribution of a branch of philosophy to dance, but from a very different perspective. Dealing with existential phenomenology, she characterizes it as a concern with 'human experiences arising always in particular contexts of being-in-the-world'. Though concerned with individual experience, this philosophical perspective does not remain at the level of the unique or idiosyncratic, but seeks to identify shared, collective experience. The interdependency of 'self' and 'other' is stressed, whether that 'other' comprises people, objects or the natural phenomena of the world at large. A phenomenological approach to dance, therefore, considers both the individuals' sense impressions of each dance and the consciousness which 'transcends separate acts of perception' and unifies our experience of all dances. Subjective experiences of the dance are celebrated, but located within the wider world of dance-consciousness and knowledge.

Although disciplinary boundaries are now blurred, the ways in which dance has changed in its concepts and its practices, and the reasons for those changes, have traditionally been the business of the historian. The status of history as a discipline, the role of the historian, the concept of historical 'truth' and the very nature of what constitutes evidence from the past are among some of the many questions which currently pervade this field of enquiry. While being alert to these debates and their impact on any historical project, it is useful to be reminded of the basic ways and means of classifying and categorizing source material. June Layson makes the distinction between primary and secondary sources; identifies the three general categories of written, visual and sound materials, and considers their problematic nature. Questions concerning their status as witting or unwitting testimony, their authenticity, reliability and relative value can be asked in order to evaluate their merit and usefulness for the particular study in which the historian is engaged.

The remit of what constitutes our study of society, as found in the kind of traditional historiography which focused on 'important' people, activities and events in history, has been expanded by a comparatively new field of scholarship, that of cultural studies. As the name implies, it embraces all kinds of activity undertaken by all kinds of people, currently as well as in the past. Jane Desmond sees an important place for dance within the inter-disciplinary embrace of cultural studies. By placing kinesthetic activity under scrutiny, the realm of what constitutes 'culture' can be expanded and the relationship between the 'micro' levels of activity such as the dancing body and the 'macro' readings of that activity (its social, historical and ideological signification) can be explored. Dance can reveal 'in codified fashion, socially constituted and historically specific attitudes toward the body in general, toward specific social groups' usage of the body in particular, and about the relationships among variously marked bodies'. If social distinctions such as those of gender, class and ethnicity are produced, mediated and circulated by dance, then analysis of how dance styles; their performances; their meanings and concomitant attitudes toward them spread and change, the 'shifting ideologies attached to bodily discourse' can be revealed. Such analyses require, however, appropriate tools and methodological approaches which can shift between the particular and the general, between dance and society.

It is the importance of dance analysis, for a whole variety of purposes, which is argued for by Janet Adshead. The activity of analysis in the arts has been treated with suspicion, particularly by those who believe that our artistic encounters are fundamentally emotional and therefore experiential (see Introduction, Part I). Any kind of analytical intervention might militate against the primacy of that experience. This belief, even though it is rarely articulated or pursued rationally, has been instrumental in hindering the academic development of all the arts, but of dance particularly. Adshead points out, however, that analysis is embodied in any form of appreciation of the arts; it is the basis of knowledge and experience and serves to extend that knowledge and enrich that experience. Not only audiences, but choreographers, performers, critics, reconstructors and notators all utilize analytical skills and share common concepts even though their eventual usage may differ. A model for analysis is offered which recognizes the specificity of dance. Although the contribution of related disciplines to the study of dance is acknowledged, this model places the dance itself as central. It does not remain, however, at the level of movement analysis, but accommodates issues of context, function, meaning and value.

Any analysis of dance and culture, whether specific or general, rests upon an understanding of the fundamental inter-relationship between those two concepts. Culture, Polhemus argues, not only produces shared customs and beliefs, words and artefacts, but also movement styles and activities. Movement behaviour is not 'natural', therefore; it does not transcend culture but is rooted in it. Dance can be seen as a stylization of the physical culture of society. As such, it embodies one of the most significant subjective and social distinctions in any culture – that of gender. The construct of gender has proved highly profitable for those who have wished not only to place dance fully within its cultural context but who have aspired to claim its political dimensions. Dance reflects and produces both dominant (and, as Polhemus exemplifies, sub-cultural) notions of what it is to be male and female in a society. Thus, 'at the most fundamental level of analysis, dance, gender and culture are one and the same thing'. The study of the relationship between gender and the dancing body has led to one of the most recent concerns and commonly used concepts in dance scholarship: that of 'the body'.

The extract by Foster is taken from an anthology which draws together writings from various disciplines, all of which take the body as their central concern. Alerting us to the significance of the actual corporeal body and its cultural construction, Foster points to its neglect in Western scholarship. She also uses the body as metaphor in order to problematize the historiographic project. Issues addressed include the notions that the historian (the body that writes history) intervenes in the creating of the past; that the corpus of history seduces us by its authority into believing in its stability; that theoretical structures are necessary in order to produce meaning but theories cannot accommodate all phenomena. Those bodies which write on history but cannot be framed within existing paradigms 'fall into a no-man's-land between the factual and the forgotten'. What, asks Foster, is the relationship between past history and the mode of recording it? That is, between experience, especially the untranslatable experience of dance, and the written word? The historian cannot replicate history, but must create it. Foster likens the interchange between the bodies of the past, bodies of historians and the body of knowledge to a choreographic process – never static, conspiratorial and creating mutual signification.

Foster's writing is significant in that she addresses key concerns in historiography, including the neglect of the history of the body at the expense of mind and ideas, the 'objective' status of the historian and the logical tenability of simply recording history in opposition to the notion that all history is interpretation. Furthermore, she stretches the conventional writing style of scholarly discourse and the words of different 'voices' dance along in compliance with their subject matter. In the final section of her Introduction, Foster's imagination takes flight in an extended analogy of the apparent polarities between rhetoric (the spoken word) and movement, or the dancing body. Two muses duet: Clio, the muse of history, who 'realises the need to bring movement and fleshiness into historiography' and Terpsichore, the muse of dance, who 'senses the need to rationalise choreography as persuasive discourse'. Foster's analogy is apt, for being a dance rather than a fight, the duet calls for co-operation rather than competition, and, like the advancement of all knowledge, any resolution is only temporary.

FURTHER READING

General: Adshead (1981); Au and Peter (1989); Daly (1991a); Thomas (1996)

Philosophy: Redfern (1983); Sparshott (1988); McFee (1992); Carroll (1992); three articles in *Dance Research Journal* (1982)

Analysis: Adshead (1988); Foster (1986); Adshead-Lansdale (1994b). Jackson (1994) examines Adshead's and Foster's approaches to dance analysis

On *interpretation* as a component of analysis: Lavender (1995); Sayers (1992).

History: Chapman (1979–80); Brown (1994); Foster (1995); Adshead-Lansdale (1996); Sparti (1996). An interesting debate on the study of dance history is raised by Ralph (1995) and responded to by Adshead-Lansdale (1997)

Phenomenology: Sheets-Johnstone (1979); Fraleigh (1987 and 1991); Rothfield (1994); Kozel (1995a)

Anthropology and Ethnography: Sklar (1991); Kaeppler (1992); Grau (1994)

Cultural Studies: Desmond (1994); Koritz (1996)

Gender and Dance: Daly (1987 and 1991b); Adair (1992); Thomas (1993); *Writings on Dance* (1993); Brown (1994); Burt (1995); Carter (1996)

Collected conference papers provide a useful cross section of writings which reflect recent developments on dance study and research. Recent collections include:

Dance and Technology: Moving Towards the Future (1992) CORD (Congress on Research in Dance), Madison, USA

Retooling the Discipline: Research and Teaching Strategies for the 21st Century (1994) Society of Dance History Scholars, Riverside: University of California

Border Crossings: Dance and Boundaries in Society, Politics, Gender, Education and Technology (1995) Society of Dance History Scholars, Riverside: University of California

Border Tensions: Dance and Discourse (1995) Proceedings of the Fifth Study of Dance Conference, Guildford: University of Surrey

15

WHAT IS ART?

Betty Redfern

BOSWELL: Sir, what is poetry?
JOHNSON: Why, Sir, it is much easier to say what it is not. We all
know what light is; but it's not easy to *tell* what it is.

(James Boswell: Life of Johnson)

It is not unusual for those interested in the arts – though not, so they may
think, in philosophy – to ask nevertheless as a result of that interest questions which are of an indisputably philosophical kind. These are often of
the form, 'What is . . . ?'; for example, 'What is rhythm?', '. . . form?',
'. . . dance?', and, not least, 'What is art?'

It may further be asked: 'Are ceremonial and ritual dances art? What
about folk dances, American square dancing, ballroom and tap dancing? Is
popular art a branch of art in general, or not art at all?' Or it might be said:
'Suppose someone creates a dance but never shows it to anyone – is that
art?' Perhaps even more interesting, philosophically speaking, is an
undiscovered dance or music score. In other words, for something to count
as art must it be publicly accessible or can art be private?

Then what of talk of animals dancing, singing, painting, etc.? Can there be
animal art, or is art something created and presented only by human beings?
Must there be the intention to produce something to be seen as art? What
of objects found, say, on the beach (*objets trouvés*)? How is it that soup tins,
firebricks and so-called Readymades such as a bicycle wheel or a urinal have
been displayed – and apparently accepted – as art? Is it simply a matter of
someone declaring certain things to be art? Are 'happenings' in the theatre
to rank as art? What of accidents – stumbles, falls, collisions, and other
chance occurrences on the part of dancers? Are extemporized dance and
music to rank as art, or must there always be some repeatable final form? Is
the term 'artwork' interchangeable with 'art', and does it imply excellence,
or can there be bad works of art?

I am not able, nor shall I even attempt, to deal fully with all these (and
similar) questions. Rather, I shall seek to identify the major philosophical
problems they raise in connection with the question, 'What is art?'

It may be noted first that this question is apt to be construed as a request for a definition of the term 'art' – a definition, moreover, of the sort that seeks to sum up the nature or essence of the thing in question in terms of a certain characteristic or set of characteristics that make it just what it is and not something else. Now if what is wanted here is a verbal definition that sets out both necessary and sufficient conditions for the correct application of the term, the request itself is of doubtful merit, for it suggests that something can be said in a brief space that is adequate for the thing that is up for definition. The very form of the question, 'What is . . . ?', tends to place constraints on the kind of answer that is sought: it is expected to be all-embracing, but concise. Yet to attempt this in the case of a phenomenon as complex and varied as art would seem an impossible task.

Even within a limited period and within the same culture the manifest-ations of what is commonly regarded as art are extraordinarily diverse. Like 'beauty', 'aesthetic appreciation', 'form', and many other terms, 'art' would therefore seem to be precisely the kind that resists satisfactory definition in neat epigrammatic form, although examples of just such formulae abound: 'Art is expression of emotion', ' . . . is significant form', ' . . . is objectified subjectivity', and so on.

The problem is not, however, simply one of brevity. Rather, the question is whether 'art' is the kind of term that can be defined (in the strict sense) at all. It has certainly been the view of many philosophers in the second half of the twentieth century that it cannot; that the task is not merely as a matter of fact difficult, but logically impossible. The traditional quest for answers to 'What is art?', 'What is beauty?', and the like, has therefore been widely rejected as a proper subject for philosophical enquiry. To ask such questions, it has been insisted, is to misunderstand the kind of concept under review: no condition can be found necessary, let alone sufficient. Fur-ther, to prescribe a set of defining properties of art would restrict future development.

Traditional theories nevertheless often have the virtue of pinpointing aspects of art that are worthy of attention yet may have been neglected or distorted by previous accounts. Some definitions, often advanced with the express intention of revising an existing idea of art, might indeed be regarded as instances of 'persuasive definitions' – formulae that endow a word which has strongly emotive overtones with a particular meaning that the author tries to get others to accept as the 'real' or 'true' meaning.

What, however, were the purposes of traditional accounts of art? Many, if not most, would seem to have been principally concerned with the excel-lence of artworks, and with what makes for that excellence (the possibility of bad art was not usually considered – perhaps implicitly ruled out). Although, then, a strict definition might not be possible, it does not follow that nothing can be said about the character of whatever is under discussion. Some theories were attempting, for instance, to explain what sort of a phenomenon art is: for example, to make a case for the idea that it is a kind of play.

Thus what appear to be pithy definitions are often no more than short-hand summaries of substantial theses, which may provide important new insights into the subject. The extent to which traditional theories may still affect professional art criticism, as well as the responses of lay people, should not indeed be underestimated. Thus traces of doctrines derived from, for example, Wordsworth, Coleridge, Tolstoy, often remain deeply ingrained in people, even if their origins or wider implications are unknown.

What, however, have philosophers critical of traditional theorists them-selves had to say? Two major recommendations have been proposed. First, instead of asking 'What does "art" (or "work of art") mean?' we should consider how the word or phrase is commonly used and accepted in every-day language. Second, instead of trying to discover some property or prop-erties common and peculiar to the various instances of (say) art, we should look for *family resemblances*. The model here is Wittgenstein's well-known advice in respect of a game:

> Don't say: 'There *must* be something common or they would not be called "games" – but *look and see* whether there is anything common to all.
>
> (1953: para. 312)

What we shall find, rather, is 'a complicated network of similarities overlap-ping and crisscrossing'; somewhat like a rope held together by a vast number of fibres, even though no single fibre runs from one end to the other (Wittgenstein 1958: 87).

To take the first suggestion then: a highly abstract term such as 'art', unlike 'table' or 'tree', for instance, will be found to have a plurality of uses. This, of course, is evident from any dictionary. But listing 'skill', 'guile', 'craft', 'painting', etc. does not usually help when we ask, 'What is art?' Rather, we should examine how the word or phrase in question, along with its correlates and derivatives, is used in a range of familiar contexts, and compare and contrast those uses not only with one another but with those of other abstract terms that are relevantly similar.

We are then obliged to think more carefully about which sense we have in mind and to put forward reasons for or against a particular usage in a par-ticular case. In striving to make clear what we mean, and thereby to achieve better understanding and communication with others, we shall probably soon find that we begin to draw parallels, to make distinctions, to notice interesting and significant differences and similarities. We are likely, too, in gaining a clearer idea of other people's conceptions of art, to become more precisely aware of what our own consists in, and to see what other perspectives we have (*must* have) in order to maintain this perspective consistently; we might even come to modify or change it altogether.

As regards the second suggestion, namely of family resemblances, a serious criticism often levelled at the model in general is that in the case of an actual family, one of whose members might resemble another in respect of the nose, another the lower lip, or the hair, gait, and so on, we already have the family determined for us. These traits are family likenesses because the individuals concerned belong together in the first place by virtue of genetic ties: if someone not related by blood happens to look like a Hapsburg or a Mitford, say, s/he could not be said to bear a *family* resemblance. But in the case of artworks, as well as many other things to which the model has been applied, how are we to identify the individuals between which likenesses are to be traced? What corresponds, that is, to the genetic tie? However, if we knew this, we might want to say, the puzzle as to what is to count as art would not have arisen in the first place.

One answer might be that we have to start with central cases which would seem indisputably to be art and then work outwards, so to speak. If, for example, *King Lear*, *Giselle*, *The Birth of Venus*, *The Magic Flute*, the *Eroica* symphony are not art, what is? We seek, that is, relevant similarities between such cases and other particular cases. But what is to count as relevant? For of course not any kind of similarity will do; it has to be of significance. For, given a little ingenuity, we could find likenesses between almost any two things. Yet if such a set of likenesses were to be worked out this would ultimately impose unacceptable limitations. It might be possible in principle – though in practice the task would be of overwhelming magnitude – to trace significant similarities among the vast body of items already acknowledged as artworks. But the exercise would be pointless; for even as we did so, some artist (especially a well-established artist) could come along with a new 'offering' which would cast doubt on any such scheme. This is not to say that no important similarity or similarities – as well as important dissimilarities – could be found between the new arrival and the rest; indeed, if it were otherwise, as I shall discuss further in a moment, there would be no reason to see it as art at all. But a particular set of resemblances laid down here and now, or at any other point in time, would be likely to exclude later candidates.

One aspect of the problem of resemblances which certainly requires elucidation has to do with the qualities or properties that are to be compared. For the terms 'qualities', 'properties', 'features' and such like are apt to give rise to a major problem, namely what is available to ordinary perception. For instance, several critics of traditional theories of art would seem to have supposed that what the authors of those theories had in mind when they spoke in 'essence' terms were qualities or properties of a directly observable kind – or what they thought was directly observable. Perhaps in some cases this was so, especially among those of a formalist persuasion, whose accounts do sometimes sound as if, for example, form, beauty, unity, harmony are actually *there* to be seen *in* the work. Yet such qualities have rarely been considered discernible in the way that features such as redness, hardness or circularity are thought of as discernible; moreover many traditional accounts of art focused not so much on artworks themselves as on, say, the (alleged) effect of art on the percipient; or on what was thought to be the creative artist's activity or mental state; or on the relationship between the artist and the public.

What might be more significant, therefore, are not directly manifested, but non-exhibited characteristics. Similarities and relationships between various objects, performances, etc. might, for example, be established in respect of origin, function, intention or purpose. We cannot, for instance, know that a dance is a work of art just by examining the movements involved; indeed we cannot even know that it is a dance. Rather, artworks are to be distinguished by their central role in a whole complex of social activities and practices that includes creating and producing, performing and presenting, criticizing and reviewing, marketing and financing, and so forth. The problem, of course, is how to provide a sufficiently precise characterization of such activities and practices so that they pertain specifically to art and not to other things as well. Nevertheless, the recognition of art as a social and historical phenomenon, quite unlike, say, sun, darkness, cold or stickiness, would seem vital for any satisfactory analysis of the concept. It is one of a vast host of concepts that require for their understanding a grasp of a whole culture.

To see something as a work of art then is not to recognize a brute fact, but depends on what can be known or taken for granted about the context of the object in question; and that context is of an *institutional* kind. As with, for instance, booking a ticket for a theatre – which may seem a very ordinary occurrence, yet in fact involves an intricate web of assumptions and beliefs that normally are not made explicit – so the knowledge needed to regard something as an artwork and to appreciate it *as* art requires acquaintance with the institutional framework in which such practices and activities are embedded.

Thus we are able, for example, to understand a set of bodily movements in terms of the art of dance and not (whatever outward similarities there may be) of, say, a magic ritual, a gymnastic display, or a set of therapeutic or physical fitness exercises, because we belong to a society in which, typically, one group – the audience – watches, and may pay money to watch, another group or an individual give a performance in a special space such as a theatre or *quasi*-theatre (e.g. a park, a school hall), where the proceedings are regulated by certain conventions. These conventions may, of course, be modified to a greater or lesser extent: audiences may be invited to participate themselves in some way; stages, lighting and special costumes may be dispensed with; a street may become, temporarily, 'the boards'. But no matter how experimental or revolutionary the presentation, either in terms of what is presented or how, there have to be sufficient likenesses between the old and the new frameworks for us to be able to accommodate any innovations within our existing concept of art. When we question whether something is a new form of art or not art at all, it is precisely when the institutional framework is strained to breaking point. But as long as a few conventions remain it is possible that our concept of art, or of a particular art form, is expanded and enriched, perhaps even drastically revised.

One of the most valuable points insisted on by writers who draw attention to the institutional character of art is that just as there cannot be a private language, so is art essentially public. What is art cannot be determined according to personal whim or even the serious reflective judgment of a single individual. As with moral questions, nobody can set himself up as a solitary arbiter in respect either of his own 'works' or anyone else's – which is not, of course, to say that revolutionaries do not bring about change in the realms of both conduct and art, merely that no individual can ever be entirely independent of the standards of the culture to which s/he belongs. The most free-thinking radical is radical only in the light of what is generally accepted; revolutionaries and innovators have to be familiar with certain norms in order to revolt against them.

Recognition of the essentially public nature of art enables us to indicate answers to some of the questions raised at the beginning of this discussion. It will be evident, for example, that manuscripts and scores remaining unpublished, perhaps undiscovered, and choreographic inventions performed exclusively in private, are not art, though it is merely fortuitous that they have not so far acquired this status. Neither are songs, poems, etc. as yet only 'in the composer's head', though this time for the very different reason that they *cannot* (logically cannot) be. For whereas in the first case it is only a contingent matter that what may be art is so far not known about, yet *could* be, in the second case there is nothing in sensuous form that is available for public scrutiny. Only when these two conditions (at least) are fulfilled can something be a candidate for art status, though success is not, of course, thereby automatically guaranteed.

This is sometimes apt to strike people as rather strange. Surely, it might be said, if something is an artwork it has always been an artwork, and always will be. How can the nature of something change simply as a result of its being regarded in a particular way? But, as should now be clear, a work of art is more than a physical phenomenon. The same physical object (which may be a set of movements, sounds, etc.) can therefore rank as art at one period of time, but not at another; in one place, but not elsewhere. Any sense of strangeness occasioned by this idea indicates a failure to grasp the significance of what has been discussed in the last few paragraphs, namely the social and historical character of art and the need, in any analysis of the concept, to take account of non-exhibited features of things, and of the customs and attitudes of a society in respect of certain objects and activities, the kind of *regard* in which they are held.

Once this is appreciated, however, we may begin to see how it is that such things as weapons, domestic utensils, masks, or articles of clothing, whether from the everyday life of our own or another civilization, of our own day or of the past, may, appropriately treated, *become* art; how dances and songs, once an integral part of worship, say, or the celebration of some other occasion, can – again, appropriately treated – be, as it were, transformed, enter the domain of art. Removed from their normal context, such phenomena can take on a different character; they can acquire a new status, a new role in the life of the society that accords them this different treatment. And that society is thereby itself modified; for art not only derives its 'being' from the culture in which it emerges, but in turn contributes to, and indeed in some measure constitutes, that culture.

As with knowledge of any kind, we cannot start from scratch but have to begin from where we already are, with what we already know. Thus in the case of art our taking-off point has to be those instances which are meant to be seen as art, that is, which have been produced intentionally under the concept of art (even if an individual artist may not be explicitly aware of what that concept involves or be able to articulate it). Further candidates are considered in relation to acknowledged artworks against a background of established or, we might say, inherited standards and traditions – inherited inasmuch as we are brought up in a society in which human beings engage in art activities (in the wide sense referred to earlier).

A point made during the discussion of family resemblances perhaps needs to be stressed again here, however, namely, that to recognize something as art is not a matter of searching for a *prescribed* set of similarities. The standards and traditions of art, far from being fixed or static, are constantly being enlarged and revised, as new dances, novels, films, operas and so on (as well as combinations of some of these) achieve the status of art, perhaps using new materials and new techniques and demanding new kinds of response and behaviour on the part of those who watch or listen or read.

Reference to what has gone on in the past as a necessary part of any satisfactory account of art does not, therefore, imply a rigid concept. Paradoxically perhaps, it is the continuity of certain cultural practices and norms that makes for its flexibility and elasticity; without them innovation would not be possible, for, as we saw earlier, traditions are necessary for there to be fresh developments. Modern dance, for example, originated as a direct consequence of classical ballet, and could be understood as a new kind of dance only against that background. Its exponents might have thought they were overthrowing everything, but they did not for some time attempt to dispense with, say, music or some other sort of sound accompaniment, or with stages, audiences who sat in their seats to watch, and the like. And while some of these conventions, along with a number of others, have from time

131

to time been abandoned by later choreographers, some connections with previous presentations remain, and have to remain (though it need not be the same connections that persist). Otherwise, as emphasized previously, these pieces could not be seen as art at all, maybe not even as dance.

Moreover artists are always limited not only by the nature of the medium (what can be 'said' in the dance cannot be said in literature, what is express-ible in music is not expressible in sculpture, and so on); but also by the particular milieu in which that medium is used. For artistic techniques do not develop independently of the general cultural climate or of previous uses of paint, movement, words, etc.; the work of even the most highly creative artists grow out of the habits of thought and feeling integral to the society to which they belong and the language and art forms which both shape and enshrine that thought and feeling.

The fact that it is only in the light of what has already been accepted as art that new departures can be seen *as* new departures, means that newly admit-ted candidates – and most especially, perhaps, candidates presently seeking admission – are intelligible as art only to those with some knowledge of its history. This is not necessarily, or even usually, 'history of art' as a formal subject of study, however, but rather, first-hand acquaintance with indi-vidual artworks and art practices – in particular, of course, those belonging to the art form and the genre to which the newcomer most closely approxi-mates. For they bring to their looking a store of experience that enables them to make significant comparisons such that a judgment is possible as regards the art (or non-art, or borderline art) status of whatever is in ques-tion. Indeed the knowledgeable spectator, listener, or reader – perhaps a critic, an art historian, a collector or a biographer – can often find a certain coherence between the items of an individual artist's total output, or that of a group, better than can the artist or group concerned.

Conversely, it is the man- and woman-in-the-street who are apt to be most resistant to change in the arts and to be puzzled by new developments. For they have literally lost their bearings; the fewer points of reference there are to existing artworks, the more restricted and the more readily upset are people's responses and expectations. What is required in such circum-stances is someone who can latch on, as it were, to what is familiar: to repeat, we have to start with what *can* be seen as art. But all depends, as already indicated, on both parties being able to take for granted a whole range of shared concerns and values. The would-be appreciator will be able to grasp whatever similarities and comparisons a guide may point out only in so far as s/he is at home in the cultural milieu within which such similarities and comparisons make sense.

Once the point is established that the central cases of art are those inten-tionally produced under the concept of art, another of the questions posed at the beginning of this discussion may be taken up, namely the possibility of art among animals other than humans. For it now becomes evident that such a suggestion is hardly plausible. Certainly an observer or listener might find marks or movements or sounds made by birds, insects, etc. aesthetically interesting and might indeed display them in conditions normally reserved for art. But we cannot attribute *artistic* activity to non-human animals even in the case of, say, the singing of whales, or the movements and paint daubings of apes when these are intentionally produced and seem to be selected and arranged in some manner. For we are unable to say whether the intention and ordering in question involve the idea of making and presenting something which is primarily to be looked at or listened to, something which is typically altered, revised, improved upon or even scrapped altogether in order to make a better song, dance, painting or whatever.

The possibility of *dis*satisfaction on the part of an artist in respect of the look or sound of what s/he is doing is in fact as important as is that of satisfaction. In other words, critical appreciation goes hand in hand with making and performing: the artist pays attention to what s/he does not only (normally) in terms of taking care with movements, marks or sounds, but also in terms of what emerges, what makes for certain effects. S/he looks or listens reflectively, discriminatingly, and proceeds in the light of this assessment; s/he knows what s/he is doing and is able to imagine how others might respond. That is, s/he works against the background of certain criteria – though not a set of fixed criteria that can be laid down in advance, but criteria applied in relation to this particular effort.

Both the making and the looking or listening then take place not *in vacuo*, but in the light of other sounds, marks and movements that the artist has seen and heard, and has noticed other people, especially those known as *artists*, looking at and listening to, as well as talking about, displaying and presenting in particular ways: in short, against the background of what s/he has learned to conceive of as art. As a social activity of this kind, art is clearly outside the range of non-language users. An ape is no more *dancing* in the sense in which a human being dances than is a budgerigar *talking* when it imitates sounds of human speech. For that matter, neither are human beings dancing if they merely reproduce movements taken out of any context that makes those movements intelligible as dance.

To have a grasp of the concept of art, however, is not (as also with many other concepts) an all-or-nothing affair: there can be degrees of understanding ranging from the rudimentary to the more fully-fledged; and it seems clear that this is a concept that goes on developing throughout childhood and, indeed, beyond. Even those individuals who go on to learn very little about art inevitably absorb a good deal about the forms and traditions of their own culture or sub-culture. For the idea of art is one that permeates our experience and plays an important part in shaping it. Indeed if it were to die out in a particular society, that society would not remain the same except for that single change: the whole fabric of its customs and practices, its habits of feeling and thinking, would be radically altered.

133

The way then in which debate about art tends to flow freely back and forth among specialists and non-specialists alike, indicates that the answer to the question 'What is art?' is, in some sense, already known. The question presupposes that examples of art have already been identified. Moreover, as will have been evident throughout this discussion, we are also able to take for granted a great deal about art in general – for instance, that it is a complex phenomenon, that its manifestations are amazingly diverse and that it constantly undergoes change.

It has also become clear that the status of artworks is determined by history. Nevertheless, as Diffey argues (1969: 147), there are occasions, especially in periods (such as our own) when the arts are subject to rapid change, when the question whether something is a work of art is not an idle one. For while this has *normally* been settled, it does not follow that the decision can *never* be contested, though neither does the successful contesting of a particular case mean that *nothing* is settled. There is thus every reason why philosophers should continue to pursue their enquiries into the question 'What is art?'

The concept of art would certainly seem to be a classic case of the sort known as 'essentially complex and essentially contested' – a concept, that is, lacking full elaboration, yet nevertheless in general use. It is one that does not *as it happens* occasion endless disputes, but is *in the nature of the case* contestable; and will, as a rule, actually be contested. Although not resolvable by argument, such concepts are sustained by argument; they are essentially *appraisive* concepts, involving some kind of valued achievement which always admits of variation and modification. They therefore benefit, rather than suffer, from the constant scrutiny to which they are subjected.

16

A VULNERABLE GLANCE:
SEEING DANCE THROUGH
PHENOMENOLOGY

Sondra Fraleigh

When phenomenology is true to its intent, it never knows where it is going (Merleau-Ponty 1962: xxi). This is because it is present-centred in its descriptive aims, accounts for temporal change, and does not have appropriate and inappropriate topics. It might move from Zen to dance to baseball to washing dishes, and even isolate a purity of attention that under certain circumstances connects them all. Phenomenology develops unpredictably, according to the contents of consciousness. This is its first level of method. Its second level develops philosophical perspectives from the seed of consciousness. It holds that 'philosophy is not the reflection of a pre-existing truth but, like art, the act of bringing truth into being' (ibid.). Here I will discuss phenomenology as a way of describing and defining dance, shifting between the experience of the dancer and that of the audience.

Experiential truth

Phenomenology depends on immediate experience, but includes more. It hopes to arrive at meaning, perspectives on the phenomena of experience (dance in this case) which can be communicated. It is not devoid of past and future, since both are lived as part of the present. Present time takes its meaning in part from past and future. Heidegger (1962: 164) described time as belonging to the totality of being, as 'the horizon of being.' He chose the vulnerable image of *falling* to describe the lived dimension of present time. Falling is both a movement and a symbol of our existential mode of being-in-the-world.

Existence is not static. It moves always just beyond our grasp. It has no specific shape, no texture, no taste (because it is nowhere). Yet we assume it is something. We can't see it (because it is everywhere), and we feel its perpetual 'dance' inside us. It is of the essence of vulnerability. It surfaces to attention through reflection in literature, history and philosophy, with the urgency of word and gesture, formulations of concrete materials, the actions and passions of drama and the infinite combinations of sound and bodily motion in the various arts. Here psychic life, visible form, and experiential truth merge; thought and feeling converge, and meaning arises. Art is an attempt to give substance to existence, that we may gain insight through distilling life's ongoing nature, repeating selected gestures, motions and sounds, moulding and maintaining certain shapes. Art in its various forms holds these before our senses. It allows us to absorb the textures, meanings and motions of a perishable bodily existence. Art and existence are both within the context or 'horizon' of time. Both are subject to the ways in which time is lived – compressed, elongated, endless, a long time, a short time, barely enough time, etc. Lived time does not refer to clock time, but to how time feels. Falling in love may take 'an instant', for example, and some chores may 'never' get done.

When I use the term phenomenology I mean existential phenomenology, the development of Edmund Husserl's phenomenological philosophy by later twentieth-century existentialist philosophers: Martin Heidegger, Jean Paul Sartre, Paul Ricoeur, Maurice Merleau-Ponty and Gabriel Marcel. The common concern of these philosophers was to describe existence from the 'horizon' (Husserl's term for the 'context' in which experiences arise) of being-in-the-world. Existential philosophy originated primarily in the thinking of men – with the exception of feminist Simone de Beauvoir. As a revolt against traditional Western philosophy, it developed several concerns consistent with feminists (see Addendum on Phenomenology and Feminism p. 142). Of particular interest is that the body (mythically associated with woman and the mystery of birth) has been ignored and denied by traditional philosophy, but is important in phenomenology, and is a central theme in existential phenomenology.

Existential phenomenology is vulnerable because it rests on experiential descriptions of the lived world; more precisely, human experiences arising always in particular contexts of being-in-the-world. While much of male-dominated philosophy has striven for invulnerability through logic and reason, phenomenology took up the risky position of experiential description. But phenomenology does not rely primarily on the uniqueness of experience. Overall, it is propelled by a universalizing impulse, since it hopes to arrive at shared meaning, recognizing that this world is indeed 'our world', that our being-in-the-world is conditioned by the existence of others. Self and other are terms that take on meaning in relation to each other. Individual subjectivity is therefore understood in view of its intersection with a surrounding world, constituted by other objects, natural phenomena and other human beings.

If there is a single guiding principle behind phenomenology, it derives from Husserl's repeated assertion that 'consciousness is always consciousness of something'. Consciousness, he held, was the necessary condition for experience, or experience is presupposed by consciousness (Husserl 1931). Experience has both immanent and transcendent levels. Immanence is that which is held within consciousness, a memory in a stream of experience, for instance. Transcendence is not a mystical term here, nor does it necessarily mean an ecstatic level of consciousness. Transcendent consciousness is active since it unifies impressions, grasping phenomena in their entirety. (A phenomenon is anything that appears to consciousness.) Consciousness is transcendent because it refers beyond itself, attesting to a world of objects and the reality of others. It is the ground or possibility of our recognition of a world outside ourselves.

Central to phenomenology is the understanding that we never perceive a phenomenon in static unchanging perspectives, but rather as existing through time. Time and motion are ever-present conditions influencing attention and perspective. Nevertheless, consciousness can unify experience. For example, when one considers a particular phenomenon such as a dance, one not only has changing sense impressions of the dance as it flows through time, but also insight into the essence of the dance. By essence here I mean that something is discerned which characterizes or typifies the dance, so that it is recognized as itself and not some other dance. The dance then becomes more than sense impressions of motion. The essence of the dance is not identical with its motion. It arises in consciousness as the motion reveals the intent of the whole and its parts. Consciousness transcends separate acts of perception to unify our experience of phenomena.

Essence: identity

When I look at a dance I perceive something of the work's identity, its individuality. Not only do I perceive it – I consciously construct it. That is, I imbue the work with the meaning I find there as a viewer (or critic). This requires both my perceptual grasp and conscious integration of the work.

For example, it is obvious that Cunningham's work *Eleven* takes its title from the eleven performers in the dance. It is also strongly identified with the mantra-like word/sound score. In the following description, part of the work's identity emerges for me:

> The text is sparse, with sound and silence coming at intervals and chanted in monotone, returning over and over, lending to the meditative quality of the whole. Duets, solos, trios and other groups collect and disperse without emotional impetus, like a hand plays easily with an intricate design when the design begins to lead the hand unconsciously into the next figure. However, the exact movement, its energies and space/time configuration, is unique to *Eleven*. At one point, there is a long stalking sequence with body leans and

leg extensions. It finally develops into a reaching walk with the body twisting and turning on one foot, ending with the torso bending over the leg, and an arm dangling, the hand tracing a circle, actually outlining it on the floor.

This sequence contributes to the individuality of *Eleven* for me. Others may pay attention in a different manner, thus consciously constructing aspects I don't see. When I reflect back and relate this work to other Cunningham dances, I understand that their lack of overt expressiveness focuses my attention on intricate tangles of sound, movement, colour, lines of energy, shape and design. Thus, I see them as abstract and formal, or form become content. I further notice that my attention becomes cleared and concentrated toward the end of his dances, like the concentrated attention of the dancers.

The phenomenologist approaches the task of defining or describing a phenomenon (a dance or a dance experience, for instance) as though seeing it fresh for the first time. Of course this is not possible since we do have conceptions, attitudes and assumptions which colour understanding. Phenomenology is at best an effort to remove bias and preconception from consciousness. It aims to describe through some direct route, not to analyse and theorize (at least not in the beginning), but first to describe the immediate contents of consciousness.

Phenomenology strives to capture pre-reflective experience, the immediacy of being-in-the-world. I think of this initial impulse of phenomenology as poetic and subliminal, containing moments of insight into an experience when the details of 'being there' are vivid in feeling, but have not had time to focus in thought. The subsequent descriptive process may also be similar to the poetic: both are grounded in experience and require reflection, or a looking back on the experience to bring it to language. It is further significant that both poetry and phenomenological reduction seek the essence of experience, a re-creation in words of the living of the experience, as the most salient features arise in consciousness and others drop away. In this, the phenomenologist knows that finally she cannot strip away her own consciousness, nor would she want to however much she may rid herself of baggage in terms of previous knowledge or attitudes. Consciousness and, moreover, her particular consciousness, will be a part of the experience and its description. (See Addendum on Phenomenology and Ethnography p. 143.)

Meaning

Let's take an example again from Cunningham: I notice in general that his dances use the geometrically clean lines of ballet, even though they are overlaid with radical departures from typical ballet geometry, and that the performer is cool and detached (as others have also noticed). The male dancer is not simply a prop for the female as in ballet stereotypes since much of their dancing together develops unison and equality, but the partnering per se continues the classical/Romantic dependence of the female as she leans on or is held and lifted (however dispassionately) by the male. With comparisons to ballet, I am, of course bringing to consciousness my background in dance, and I move from the purely descriptive to the comparative and analytical. This comes about naturally as a result of first recognizing attenuated lines and geometric forms. However, I would miss what seems a major point of Cunningham's works if I let them rest with balletic influence. In *Doubles*, for instance, dancers are seen in problem-solving modes, and the balletic movement serves more as a background for this to occur, as my attempt to describe a part of the dance indicates:

> One movement motif develops out of a small leap stubbornly turned to the back at the landing, then stopped in a balanced position on one leg [. . .] An incomplete stop-action fall is the most memorable of the work's challenges to the dancer's skill and the choreographer's inventiveness. The dancer falls sideways without warning or preparation in a sudden drop to his hands. He recovers from the fall but not completely, getting up only halfway, reaching that difficult to control mid-zone between standing and falling, only to fall again and again from an incomplete recovery. The dance's repetition of this series draws upon my body's memory, touching those murky moments in experience where something is about to happen, but never quite breaks through.

The foregoing is an example of my consciousness of one aspect of *Doubles*. It is true for me, it contains both descriptive, interpretive and evaluative elements. One of the major purposes of phenomenological description is to build towards meaning. Then others may be able to see what you see, or at least understand what you see. The truths of dance are not scientific or irrefutable. They are of another order, created by the choreographer, the dancer, the audience and the critic. Good critics do phenomenology naturally, describing without prejudging and then drawing forth the meaning they find. They exercise their consciousness of the dance in writing about it, finally delineating its values (and disvalues) for them. Critics, like phenomenologists, try to speak the truth of their own experience clearly so that others may find meaning in it.

The admission of the primacy of consciousness is central to existential phenomenology, distinguishing it from scientific phenomenology, claims to distil (reduce) phenomena to pure essences of ideas (*eidos*) through 'eidetic reduction'. A phenomenology which takes for granted our being-in-the world owes more to insight than to an objective scientific stance. Existential phenomenology is vulnerable because it admits this level of subjectivity. It

allows for irrationality and accident as human concerns. It is also paradoxical. While it seeks to describe the essence of things, it acknowledges the
impossibility of knowing things purely as objects, since objects are relative
to our perception of them. It celebrates subjectivity without surrendering to
a view of a privatized or narcissistic world where individual consciousness is
isolated, understanding and community an impossibility. It is the desire to
reach beyond the boundaries of one's own consciousness to understand
how consciousness is human, which in fact motivates existential
phenomenology.

Definition

Merleau-Ponty (1962) held that phenomenology united the poles of subject-
ivism and objectivism in its philosophical approach. We know that it was
also an attempt, in its formulation of the existential concept of 'the lived
body', to mend the subject/object (mind/body) split in Western attitudes
toward the body (see Fraleigh 1987). When I turn to phenomenology, I am
aware of a non-dualistic way of using language and seek modes of expression that will most closely appropriate the experience I wish to describe. Out
of the descriptive process, I understand that I will be defining dance while
drawing my readers into the process with me. In its own way, a description is
a definition.

My process of phenomenological writing develops definitional anchors
and experiential description toward an overview. Otherwise, I would lose my
reader in a stream of consciousness which, however meaningful to me, may
seem pointless and rambling to the reader. My philosophical obligation is to
extract the meaningful essentials, to communicate to the reader well founded points of reference. These often come through questioning, even through
questioning the questions.

For instance, instead of asking the typical question *What is dance*, I might
get a fresh approach to my subject by asking another definitional question,
such as *When is dance happening*. If I can answer the second question I will
be answering the first and from a perspective that will not allow me to revert
to assumed definitions. I examine this question descriptively from the
dancer's experiential perspective:

> When I dance, I am subtly attuned to my body and my motion in a
> totally different way than I ordinarily am in my everyday actions.
> That is, I seldom take notice of my ordinary comings and goings
> [. . .] But, when I dance, I am acutely aware of my movement. I
> study it, try out new moves, study and perfect them, until I eventu-
> ally turn my attention to their subtleties of feeling and meaning.
> Finally, I feel free in them. In other words, I embody the motion [. . .]
> And in this, I experience what I would like to call 'pure presence,' a

radiant power of feeling completely present to myself and connected to the world [. . .] These are those moments when our intentions toward the dance are realized.[1]

Further questions crop up immediately. What kinds of intentions are
these? Is my intentionality in dance different from my intentionality in other
kinds of movement? The subject of 'the aesthetic' as it applies to performance would then become important, since one apparent distinction between
dance movement and everyday actions is that dance is 'performed' with
qualitative attention toward the movement. Or we could say the movement
is intentionally designed and performed, not merely habitual and functional
nor purely accidental. My description obligates me to look into these aesthetic distinctions and whether they might hold for all forms and cultures. It
is also apparent from the description that the movement is not only intentionally performed, but it is also performed for itself, for the experience of
moving this way. And there may be purposes beyond this intrinsic one that
appear in dance according to cultural contexts. Most of our movement
accomplishes some objective; it gets us some place or accomplishes a task.
Generally dance movement does not, especially theatre dance. Rather its
values are not utilitarian or practical; they are affective or aesthetic. In terms
of human movement, aesthetic intent implicates intrinsic values which
inhere in actions, be they appreciated for their beauty or for some other
affective quality. (My brief description included affective aspects of
freedom.)

Imagination

Still another aspect of aesthetic intent is involved. The dancer deals not just
with movement but with the motivational source, idea, or metaphor behind
the movement, that which the movement will bring to mind. Even if the
dance is stylistically abstract, it will draw our attention to its unique unfolding of movement patterns in space-time. Movement patterns are also
images, and they impress the imagination, as the word 'image' implies.

The imaginative, or meaningful, level of the dance may be the focus of
phenomenological description. Clearly there would be many ways into this,
and the description would be influenced by the full intent of the dance –
theatrical, ritual, social, etc. In the following description based on phrases of
original choreography, I carry through my consciousness of freedom as a
compelling experience in dance and discover that dance is less ephemeral
than I have supposed:

My dance contains an original structure all its own, however related
or unrelated to the world from whence it springs. As I move up,
down, or spin around, I feel the purity of these directions. As

movements, they take on specific identity. My own identity merges with the movement I experience. And I can repeat it. To a great extent, my dance is repeatable; it has permanence, but my life moves always into the future. I cannot relive it, nor any part of it, as I can my dance [. . .] There are certain dance phrases I like to do again and again. They strike my imagination. In one there is an upward reach that seems to pull down the stars. I can depend on this happening. It is there when I do it. It fills me with wonder, and l feel free in it. In another more complex phrase, l also feel free, but it is more precarious [. . .] This phrase always evokes feelings of tenderness and devotion in me [. . .] When I do it well, I feel peaceful, serene and free.

Since phenomenology seeks to get at the core of things (phenomena), it aims for simplicity in the initial descriptive process. For me it often comes to rest on a single word, such as 'freedom', as has come up thematically in the foregoing description, but much depends on where I begin, the point of entry into my own consciousness of a particular dance experience, and whether I am conscious of my own dancing or paying attention to the dances of others. I am also aware that what I already know experientially and theoretically eventually enters the picture, but it is questioned, expanded, reinforced or discarded in the process of extracting core values. Contrary to what might be expected, it is not easy to see (and give word to) the most basic constitutive elements of phenomena without the support of common assumptions and dualistic habits of thought which favour the objective status of phenomena apart from their manifestations in subjective life.

As a philosophical school, existential phenomenology returns to the traditional tasks of philosophy. Plato stated that 'philosophy begins in wonder', and indeed this is the point of beginning for the phenomenologist. As I step back from my own processes to better understand them, I confess to giving myself up to a quest and questioning with a kind of blind faith that something in me already knows the answers, if I can somehow get out of my own way (remove my conditioning) long enough to glance them.

Addendum on phenomenology and feminism

While I don't identify existential phenomenology directly with feminism, I am aware that the anti-philosophers at the foundation of existentialism, Nietzsche and Kierkegaard and the later twentieth-century philosophers who extend that foundation with phenomenology, are in revolt against the traditions – especially the logic, essentialism and idealism – of Western philosophy. They admit concerns into philosophy which are also important to feminists: the importance of individual consciousness, freedom and choice. They are against determinism, and against the Western body/mind dualism propagating the body as inferior that also concerns feminists. Indeterminacy, expressed by Sartre's familiar 'existence precedes essence', is at the root of existential self-responsibility and the existentially feminist assertion that biology is not destiny, as first taken up in the existentialist movement by Simone de Beauvoir in *The Second Sex*. Existential phenomenologists, like feminists, are deconstructing a Western hierarchy.

Addendum on phenomenology and ethnography

Culture develops as people relate to each other and build common understandings and traditions. The phenomenologist's admission of the subjective level of awareness is not clearly focused on the accumulated cultural knowledge that interests the ethnographer. Phenomenology aims first to describe immediately perceived features of anything, admitting the subjective character of perception. Cultural context inevitably arises in phenomenology in terms of 'the other', or the ever present understanding that subjectivity is conditioned by our relation to others – intersubjectivity. The very notion of a self depends on the notion of an other (or others) separate and distinct from the self. The concept of culture further assumes that distinct individuals can build relationships and share meaning. A general task of phenomenology would be to expose these notions and the constructs of culture as elements of human consciousness – or perspectives that we take on life as we literally 'make meaning' out of it.

NOTE

1 Sondra Fraleigh, 'Good Intentions and Dancing Moments: Agency, Freedom and Self Knowledge in Dance'. Emery Cognition Project with the Mellon Foundation, Colloquium on the Self, Emery University, Atlanta, Georgia, 5 May 1989.

17

DANCE HISTORY SOURCE MATERIALS

June Layson

Introduction

To be able to work efficiently and effectively with sources is a required tool of the dance historian's trade. Even though the use of computers has revolutionized documentation of historical sources the basic necessity remains to start from the extant evidence of dance. It may well be that as more advanced computer programs are developed so dance historians will need to re-tool and to re-appraise well-established practices, but the starting point for study is essentially with source materials, the bedrock of dance history.

Types and categories of source materials

In history generally a fundamental distinction is made between types of source materials, and it applies equally to dance sources. This is the separation of 'primary' from 'secondary' sources, which is crucial since it determines the nature and value of study in an area as well as any written outcomes.

Primary sources are those that came into existence during the period being studied: thus they are first-hand and contemporary, and provide the raw materials for dance study. Examples of primary source materials in dance are a dance performance, a choreographer's working score or log with all its amendments and annotations, actual costumes worn by dancers for known performances and eye-witness accounts of certain dance events. Secondary sources, as the term suggests, are second-hand, processed, after the event accounts, often using hindsight to trace developments in the dance over a span of time. All the standard dance histories, dance encyclopedias and dance reference books come into the secondary source category. Some of these texts are based on primary sources though the more 'popular' histories often use materials previously published in other dance history books.

Some sources can be regarded as both primary and secondary according to the purposes for which they are being used. An example of this is the Kinney and Kinney (1936) dance history book. This is now a primary source for early-twentieth-century European theatre dance but in its time and subsequently it has also been used as a secondary source since much of the text reviews the development of dance from ancient Egyptian origins by reference to other published works.

The relative importance of primary and secondary sources usually depends upon the kind of work being done and the person undertaking it. The beginner, faced with too many primary sources at once, may be confused by apparently conflicting evidence, but to use only secondary sources could engender the attitude that all the interesting work has been done and dance history is fixed, undisputed and boring. The exclusive use of primary sources is the mark of the experienced dance researcher who refers to good secondary sources to provide background, points of entry for further study, bases of comparison, and so on. On the other hand, concentrating solely on secondary source material by reading many dance history books can be rewarding, interesting and informative, but as such this means reading about dance history and neither getting involved in the methodologies of dance history nor actually contributing to it.

Generally then, a balance that is appropriate to the kind of study being undertaken has to be maintained between the use of primary and secondary source materials, and this must be based on the recognition that the former are of a particular period and the latter are about a particular period, that the former were produced during the period and the latter after the period.[1]

Given the crucial primary/secondary source divide, in dance history it is often useful to make further categories in order to group similar sources and to gain an overall impression of the kind of evidence they present. However, while the assigning of primary and secondary source status is a necessary first step, subsequent categorization depends largely upon the source base of the topic area selected. For example, the sources gathered for a study of an eminent dancer or dance teacher might usefully be placed in separate public and private categories, the first consisting of published material such as reviews and journal articles, the second of unpublished diaries and letters. Similarly, a focus on a particular dance style might suggest the grouping of written sources, such as class notes, monographs and textbooks, and non-written sources, including sketches, photographs and video.

The categories proposed here, of written, visual and sound sources, are broad but they have the merit of reflecting the classifications used in many dance archives and collections. Since the order in which these categories are presented is non-alphabetical it clearly signals some kind of hierarchy. In fact the order is based on current importance and frequency of use, it being the case that, in Western dance history scholarship, written materials have traditionally taken precedence over visual while, overall, sound sources are only minimally used. This reflects the hegemony of the printed and written word prior to the introduction of new technologies to record visual images and sound.[2] However, as 'new' dance history methodology develops and traditional practices and the outcomes they inevitably give rise to are questioned, it is likely that in the future more emphasis will be given to the use of visual and sound sources than hitherto. Furthermore, the need to use written sources in conjunction with visual and sound sources is becoming increasingly recognized.

1   *Written sources* – advertisements, autobiographies, bills, cast lists, choreographers' log books, critics' reviews, dance notations, diaries, edicts, journals, letters, literature, magazines, music notations, newspapers, parish records, posters, school records, theatre programmes, receipts, tracts, etc.

2   *Visual sources* – primarily the dance itself, also architecture, costumes, designs for sets, films, musical instruments, paintings, photographs, prints, properties, sculpture, videotapes, etc.

3   *Sound sources*:
    aural – music (live and recorded), sound accompaniment.
    oral – interviews (formal and informal), reminiscences.

These lists are by no means exhaustive, and some materials are such that they could be placed in more than one category depending upon their use. For example, a theatre programme is a written source but it may also be of value for its visual contents such as lay-out, photographs, typeface, etc.

The dance as a visual source in its own right is often taken for granted yet certain dances, even in the here and now of performance, are 'living history'. For example, a current standard performance of a ballet such as *Swan Lake* is but the latest presentation of a work that originated in 1877. Even though the choreography has changed, perhaps almost totally, its survival today is a modern manifestation of a theatre dance genre of considerable historical significance – as well as testimony to the manner in which the ballet tradition is 'handed on'. Thus a dance performance may itself contain the historical threads which can be traced back from the present through time to its inception or earliest records.

Problematic source materials

Most of the items given in the proposed three categories could readily be labelled as primary or secondary sources but some materials present problems in this respect.

Probably the easiest to deal with is photocopied material. The original item, such as a theatre programme, may be a primary source but a photocopy of it is clearly not. There may well be differences in quality of paper, size, colour, texture and so on, all of which may be of significance in the original. Therefore, a photocopy is just that, a photocopy of a primary or secondary source and it does not take on the status of the original. However, in the future current photocopied material will assume primary source status of a kind for the period in which it was produced.

Descriptions of village dance festivals and society balls often occur in historical novels and other fiction and appear authentic. Nevertheless, such literature is solely a primary source for the period in which it was written and cannot be regarded as evidence for the period about which it was written. There are, for example, several references to dance in Thomas Hardy's (1872) *Under the Greenwood Tree*, a novel set in early nineteenth-century southern England. In 1926 the then English Folk Dance Society asked Hardy about the accuracy of his dance descriptions. It transpired that in his novel Hardy had described dances that he himself had performed fifty or sixty years earlier. In this instance Hardy is recalling a personal experience, a primary source, but recreating and placing it in a fictional context.

Drawings, paintings, prints, sculptures and sketches of dancers by contemporary artists may at first sight be considered good primary source material; however, there is a need to be aware of prevailing artistic conventions and style. In her book *The Dance in Ancient Greece*, Lawler (1964) points to the consequence of not recognizing such practices in art.

> The Greek vase painter often draws figures without a 'floor line' – a convention which has led some modern interpreters to insert an imaginary 'floor line' of their own in a given scene, and then to deduce from its position all sorts of untenable conclusions, e.g. that the ancient Greeks engaged in something like ballet and even toe-dancing.
>
> (Lawler 1964: 21)

Even when it is known that a dancer co-operated with or posed for an artist, as in Isadora Duncan's case, it is necessary to realize that what is presented is seen through the artist's eyes. Sketches by Rodin and Bourdelle of Duncan dancing are very different in the impression they give of dynamism in Duncan's movement. The former are more static and robust, the latter more fluid and delicate. Therefore, although such material is primary, by virtue of its origins, it needs to be used with considerable care and understanding. Knowledge of artists' personal styles and the art movements or schools with which they identified is required. It may also be revealing to view them as witting or unwitting testimony (see Evaluation of Source Materials p. 150).

In the light of the difficulties that may arise in the use of visual works of art it might be assumed that photographs of dancers would be accurate and, consequently, impeccable primary source material. Yet this would not allow for the fact that many of the technical problems encountered in the early days of photography, such as exposure time and capturing movement accurately, remained unsolved until well into the twentieth century. Thus photographs (c.1855) of Fanny Cerrito, one of the famous ballerinas of the Romantic period, were of necessity posed, as were most of those of Denishawn dancers taken between 1915 and 1931. Therefore, in using photographs as historical evidence it is important to distinguish between posed and action photographs and to establish location. Posed portraits are usually taken in the photographer's studio, although occasionally outdoor and theatre locations are used, and the pose may or may not be from an actual dance. Action photographs, a comparatively recent development, may evoke a performance mood or quality, but even when captioned with the title of a dance it does not necessarily follow that such photographs were taken during an actual performance.

Film and video may also seem to be easily classified as either primary or secondary source material and, generally, this is the case but here, too, caution is needed.

Much of the early dance film available presents difficulties in establishing date, place of origin and subject matter simply because such details, even if recorded at the time, can readily become separated from the film itself. Laboratory analysis may establish approximate dating; nevertheless, dance film shot in the first decade or so of the twentieth century is invariably unstable and also difficult to use. The apparent jerkiness of the movement can be rectified in the transfer to video format but it needs to be appreciated that since the filmed event is seen through the eyes of the cameraperson it is inevitably a selected presentation.

Video recordings are easy to use and amenable to various analytical techniques. Even so, whether the video is a primary source, as in the recording of a dance event (where occasionally it is necessary to distinguish between actual performance and rehearsal), or secondary, as in a documentary television programme (although these often include primary source inserts), here, too, the element of selectivity has to be taken into account. It is rare, for example, for the whole performance area to be in frame throughout a video recording of theatre dance and, similarly, a processional carnival with dance elements is unlikely to be recorded in its entirety. Other matters which need to be allowed for when using dance video as a historical source are that the movement tends to be 'flattened', the space and dynamic can be distorted and the small dancing image depersonalized.

Sound sources may also be problematic in use. In this text 'sound sources' is the preferred category title although in general history texts 'oral sources' is used as the global term. This choice of terminology is deliberate here because it allows a distinction to be made between aural sources, such as music, and oral sources, which can then be reserved for the spoken word.

If the provenance of a music recording or disc can be established and the instruments being played identified then few problems will arise in the use of such materials, which are likely to be primary in origin. Nevertheless, if the current recording of a music work is being employed as a source for studying a dance choreographed to that music decades or even centuries ago it needs to be appreciated that such matters as tempi and other aspects of performance may well have changed during the intervening years. This is a further example of a secondary source which, although of value, cannot be used as if it had primary source status.

Oral sources are gaining importance as their unique significance in dance history is becoming increasingly recognized. Generally these sources are of two types. First, there is the oral tradition of a subgroup or culture which is passed on from one generation to the next and is liable to both embellishment or erosion but appears to retain essential features. Reference is made earlier in this chapter to the handing-on of roles in ballet. This is accomplished by means of a combined movement and oral tradition which is also an important element in social and traditional dance. Second, there are the oral histories which are concerned with first-hand accounts of events and experiences lived through. These are primary sources of potentially great importance to the dance historian since they offer material not readily accessed elsewhere or even unavailable by any other means. Consequently, oral history sources need to be used with a clear understanding of what they can yield rather than with an undue emphasis on their perceived shortcomings.

Whether live or recorded, oral testimony may range from reminiscences given as a monologue to highly structured interviews. When dancers and other witnesses speak freely of the past and their involvement in it as recollections this resembles a sound autobiography. Typically, it is likely to be multilayered and possibly anachronistic but its value lies, for example, in the accuracy of remembered details of choreography, particular interpretations and performances and perceptions of events. Such testimony is 'lived experience' and is properly regarded as phenomenological. While former choreographers, critics and dancers may have reliable movement memories (although this is not necessarily so), it is likely that, as in a written autobiography, events recalled and retold may be subject to selection and re-ordering. Facts and other evidence can be cross-checked with reliable contemporary accounts but primarily these personal accounts need to be valued for what they offer in terms of insights, impressions, feelings and the overall ambience of a period rather than for factual matters. Oral testimony of recent dance history has the merit of immediacy although long-term trends and developments may not be appreciated. Conversely a dancer reminiscing about events that occurred more than half a century ago may well be able to describe key events and personalities but the detail may be missing.

Since the monologue style may not always yield the specific material sought, an interview format is often adopted. In this the recollection and narrative process can be given a degree of structure and kept 'on track' and this may lead then and there or subsequently to a memory being triggered. Here again, though, there are pitfalls to be avoided and the interviewer needs to be aware that a potentially interventionist role may prejudice the gaining of unique insights.

Evaluation of source materials

With problematic source materials the need is to establish primary or secondary status and to understand the particular ways in which they can then best be used. In contrast some source materials can easily be categorized but they have to be judged by various criteria in order to determine their value to dance history study. Three examples illustrate the point.

Historical studies of dance that cross language divides necessitate using translations if texts cannot be read in their original form. Translations made by non-dance specialists may place the dance essence of an account in jeopardy; caution has to be exercised because some dance terms and nuances do not translate readily. In such circumstances the dance historian has to attempt to evaluate the translations to hand in order to determine, for example, how much credence should be given to one translated text in relation to another.

Autobiographies, the written counterparts of oral histories, are often seized upon as being central primary sources especially when emanating from a choreographer or dancer. Yet these, too, require evaluation. Occasionally authorship is contested and some recent autobiographies have been acknowledged as partially 'ghost-written'. Other factors which need to be taken into account are the time-gap between when the events occurred and their written description, and whether the text is based on diaries kept and notes made at the time or largely consists of memories retained over the intervening years. Some autobiographies are written in a narrative style with the intention of adding a personal viewpoint to well-known events, others are motivated by the desire to 'set the record straight' and to challenge existing interpretations of cause and effect, although such underlying reasons are rarely made explicit. In this respect autobiographies tend to be more deliberate and less immediate than oral histories simply because the written word is perceived as the more permanent testimony and, thereby, to offer the opportunity to refashion and even recast past events. Autobiographies are valuable primary source material for what is revealed about authors, their personal relationships, their perceptions and views about the particular events in which they were involved and the prevailing climates of opinion within which they worked. But, as chronicles of facts, autobiographies can be downright misleading and understandably so. Therefore, in order to extract the full value of an autobiography in dance history terms it is necessary to evaluate it as a primary source of a particular kind and to use it in the full understanding of its various attributes.

Biographies may be classified as primary sources when written during their subjects' lifetime, or immediately afterwards, and secondary sources when written much later. Nevertheless, in some respects a more crucial distinction is by reference to the materials upon which the biography is based. In this case judgements have to be made as to the value and merit of the primary and secondary sources used as well as the balance between them. Other factors which can inform such evaluations are, for example, whether the subject of the biography is still alive and if access to personal papers has been gained. Most biographies are of the chronological-narrative type, some are more thematic in structure and a few are written in the vein of other disciplines such as psychoanalytical studies. It is important, too, in arriving at judgements about the value of a biography to include a consideration of its author in terms of interest in, links with and knowledge of the subject matter.

While translations, autobiographies and biographies are just three examples of source materials where prior evaluation promotes effective use, there are four further guidelines which can aid this process. These are to do with testimony, authenticity, reliability and value.

In general history Marwick (1989) makes a distinction between 'witting' and 'unwitting' testimony which is also relevant to the evaluation of dance history source materials. The term 'witting' testimony is used to describe those primary sources in which the originator of the source sets out intentionally to convey the information that the source contains. Examples of witting testimony abound in dance history. Sachs (1933, trans. 1937) bases his classification of dance themes and types on the reports of European travellers who, from the seventeenth century onwards, saw various kinds of tribal dancing in the then remote areas of Africa, Asia and other parts of the world. Sometimes these eye-witnesses to the event give information over and above what they intended and this is then termed 'unwitting' testimony. In many of the accounts included by Sachs the use of words such as 'obscene' and 'hideous' convey far more about the attitudes of the European onlookers than the quality of the dance being described. Indeed, it is often this very failure to realize the culture-bound stance of observers and to ignore the unwitting nature of their testimony that makes the early dance history texts both suspect and difficult to use.

As well as eye-witness and participant accounts the official documents of national, regional and local arts organizations and dance companies offer particular examples of witting testimony and this is especially so when they include annual statements and financial accounts. In contrast, many of the photographs of women dancers taken during the first quarter of the twentieth century provide unwitting evidence which the dance historian can use to gain insight into the then prevailing attitudes both to the body and to women.

A second useful test in evaluating dance source materials is that of authenticity. This is to do with whether a source is what it purports to be in terms of its subject matter, date and provenance. Examples of this are Nijinsky's (1937) diaries and Duncan's (1927) autobiography, since both publications have been questioned on the grounds of authenticity. It has been suggested that the original writings of these dancers have been amended and altered and, in some instances, passages written by others inserted. However, unless the historical study is based on only one source, and this would be rare, questions of authenticity can usually be resolved or at least allowed for by reference to other primary sources.

The reliability or the degree to which a particular source can be trusted is a third important factor in making judgements about dance sources. A dance theatre programme can normally be relied upon to give accurate information. Nevertheless, when dancers are injured, last-minute alterations in casting and even in the dances presented may have to be made and therefore what is printed regarding certain dances and performers in a theatre programme may not always be accurate. Eyewitness accounts may also need to be assessed in relation to their reliability. It is often vital to know whether such a witness was an interested, although peripheral, observer or a key participant. But from this it cannot necessarily be assumed that the latter is likely to be more reliable than the former. Corroboration with other sources may confirm the reverse to be the case.

The value of a single item and the comparative value of several source materials is a fourth important factor in judging worth and usefulness. Shawn's (1954) book on Delsarte, the nineteenth-century movement theorist, is itself a secondary source but, since Delsarte did not publish his own work and the publications of his various pupils are largely unavailable, Shawn's text is often used in the initial study of Delsartean theory. It is important therefore to establish the value of Shawn's book as a means of gaining access to Delsarte's work. In this case, as in many others, the matter may be resolved to a certain degree by examining the bibliography and the references cited. Mere length in either case does not guarantee worth, but in Shawn's thirty-six-page bibliography 'with commentary' the Delsarte literature itemized consists almost entirely of primary sources and the annotations are particularly detailed. This is an indication of the book's value as good secondary source material to the dance historian studying Delsarte even though more recent studies have advanced knowledge in this area considerably.

The value of other sources may reside in their status. For example, the British *Dancing Times* (published monthly from 1910) and the American *Dancemagazine* (published monthly from 1926) are the leading 'traditional' publications of their kind in their respective countries. They derive much of their authoritative status from their longevity, continuous publication and the resulting vast written source which has accumulated. This does not, of course, confer special status on any single item published in one magazine:

rather it is the whole runs that cover many decades of dance history which are significant.

With some written material the value of the evidence it contains can be determined by relevant knowledge of the author and this is particularly so in using the work of the dance critics. Dance criticism at its best is objective and informative with the judgements made being supported explicitly by reasons and by references to the choreography, the performance and so on. Although dance critics may well enthuse and inspire, it is important in the study of dance history to be able to recognize the difference between matters of fact and matters of personal opinion in their writings. Beaumont's perplexed remark on first seeing Martha Graham dance in *Appalachian Spring* in London in 1954 – 'but why does she roll about on the floor . . . ? It breaks the line' (Beaumont in Roose-Evans 1970: 110) is understandable only in the light of the knowledge that Beaumont was an expert on ballet with scant knowledge of American modern dance. His remark as such is of little value to the dance historian trying to identify trends in Graham's choreography over time but it could be of considerable value to a dance historian interested in, for example, the development of different modes of dance criticism and the prevailing use of particular canons of judgement in theatre dance.

Summary

The importance of source material in dance history study cannot be overstated. All academic disciplines have their essential features, and in dance history one of these is its source base. Source materials in themselves do not constitute dance history but as the remnants of and commentaries upon the past they provide the basic starting point for study. It is, therefore, essential that students of dance history, at whatever level, understand the crucial importance of source materials and take steps to acquire proficiency in their use.

NOTES

1 It is important to note that, although the primary and secondary source distinction described here is that which prevails in the discipline of history, in anthropological studies a much more permeable boundary is adopted.
2 This is another instance where historical and anthropological practices differ. In the latter, sound sources often assume primacy and frequently are the only sources available.

18

EMBODYING DIFFERENCE: ISSUES IN DANCE AND CULTURAL STUDIES

Jane C. Desmond

A man and a woman embrace. Each stands poised, contained. They look past each other, eyes focused on distant points in the space. Like mirror images, their legs strike out, first forward, then back. As one, they glide across the floor, bodies melded at the hips, timing perfectly in unison. They stop expectantly. The woman jabs the balls of her feet sharply into the floor, each time swivelling her hips toward the leading foot. The man holds her lightly, steering her motion with the palm of this hand at her back. This is tango . . .

Most readers of this passage probably have some image of the tango in their minds, whether from dancing, watching others dance, or seeing representations of the tango in Hollywood films. Most, if pressed, could even get up in their living rooms and demonstrate some recognizable if hyperbolic rendition of the tango. Few of us, however, have given more than passing thought to such an activity or have chosen to include it in our scholarly work. Dance remains a greatly undervalued and undertheorized arena of bodily discourse. Its practice and its scholarship are, with rare exception, marginalized within the academy.

But much is to be gained by opening up cultural studies to questions of kinesthetic semiotics and by placing dance research (and by extension, human movement studies) on the agenda of cultural studies. By enlarging our studies of bodily 'texts' to include dance in all of its forms – among them social dance, theatrical performance, and ritualized movement – we can further our understanding of how social identities are signalled, formed and negotiated through bodily movement. We can analyse how social identities are codified in performance styles and how the use of the body in dance is related to, duplicates, contests, amplifies, or exceeds norms of non-dance bodily expression within specific historical contexts. We can trace historical and geographic changes in complex kinesthetic systems, and can

154

study comparatively symbolic systems based on language, visual representation and movement. We can move away from the bias for verbal texts and visual object-based investigations that currently form the core of ideological analysis in British and North American cultural studies.

Cultural studies remains largely text-based or object-based, with literary texts still predominating, followed by studies of film texts and art historical objects.[1] Even excursions into popular culture are concerned largely with verbal or visual cultural products, not kinesthetic actions. Much current work on rap music, for instance, focuses primarily on the spoken text or legal and economic aspects of the music industry. Even the now popular subfield of critical work on 'the body' is focused more on representations of the body and/or its discursive policing than with its actions/movements as a 'text' themselves. In part this omission reflects the historical contours of disciplinary development within the academy. In addition, the academy's aversion to the material body, and its fictive separation of mental and physical production, has rendered humanities scholarship that investigates the mute dancing body nearly invisible. That dancing – in a Euro-American context at least – is regarded as a pastime (social dancing) or as entertainment (Broadway shows), or, when elevated to the status of an 'art form', is often performed mainly by women (ballet) or by 'folk' dancers or non-whites (often dubbed 'native' dances, etc.) also surely contributes to the position of dance scholarship. However, these omissions signal reasons why such investigation is important. They mark clearly the continuing rhetorical association of bodily expressivity with non-dominant groups.

The rhetorical linkage of non-dominant races, classes, gender and nationalities with 'the body', to physicality instead of mentality, has been well established in scholarship on race and gender. But the implications of those linkages, their continuance or reworking within the context of daily bodily usage or within dance systems *per se*, have yet to be investigated fully. Nor have the complex effects of the commodification of movement styles, their migration, modification, quotation, adoption, or rejection as part of the larger production of social identities through physical enactment, been rigorously theorized.

Such analysis will be responsive to many of the tools already developed in literary theory, film theory, Marxist analysis and feminist scholarship, as well as ongoing theoretical debates about hierarchies based on racial, ethnic and national identities. Bourdieu (1977), for example, refers to the physical embodiment of social structures in his concept of 'the habitus', but this idea has not been greatly elaborated. But it will also require the acquisition or development of new tools as well – tools for the close analysis of movement and movement styles (already well developed in the dance field itself), just as such tools have been developed for detailed analyses of specific books and objects in literature and art history.

Dance scholarship, with a few notable exceptions, has until recently remained outside the influence of the post-structuralist shifts that have reshaped the humanities during the last twenty or so years. And conversely, cultural analysts have evidenced little interest in dance, although literary, filmic, and art historical texts have garnered great attention. But there is evidence that this is changing, both within the dance field itself and with isolated excursions into dance by literary critics and philosophers in the recent past.[2]

Movement style and meaning

Of the many broad areas of movement investigation sketched out above, I specifically want to discuss dance as a performance of cultural identity and the shifting meanings involved in the transmission of dance styles from one group to another.

Like Bourdieu's concept of 'taste' (1984), movement style is an important mode of distinction between social groups and is usually actively learned or passively absorbed in the home and community. So ubiquitous, so 'naturalized' as to be nearly unnoticed as a symbolic system, movement is a primary not secondary social 'text' – complex, polysemous, always already meaningful, yet continuously changing. Its articulation signals group affiliation and group differences, whether consciously performed or not. Movement serves as a marker for the production of gender, racial, ethnic, class and national identities. It can also be read as a signal of sexual identity, age, and illness or health, as well as various other types of distinctions/descriptions that are applied to individuals or groups, such as 'sexy'. Given the amount of information that public display of movement provides, its scholarly isolation in the realms of technical studies in kinesics, aesthetics, sports medicine and some cross-cultural communications studies is both remarkable and lamentable.

'Dance', whether social, theatrical, or ritually based, forms one subset of the larger field of movement study. And although we tend to think of dances, like the tango, lambada, or waltz, as distinctive aggregations of steps, every dance exists in a complex network of relationships to other dances and other non-dance ways of using the body, and can be analysed along these two concurrent axes.[3] Its meaning is situated both in the context of other socially prescribed and socially meaningful ways of moving and in the context of the history of dance forms in specific societies.

When movement is codified as 'dance', it may be learned informally in the home or community, like everyday codes of movement, or studied in special schools for social dance forms (like the Arthur Murray Studios) and for theatrical dance forms (like the School of American Ballet). In either case, formal or informal instruction, and quotidian or 'dance' movement, the parameters of acceptable/intelligible movement within specific contexts are highly controlled, produced in a Foucauldian sense by specific discursive practices and productive limitations.

To get at what the 'stakes' are in movement, to uncover the ideological work it entails, we can ask what movements are considered 'appropriate' or even 'necessary' within a specific historical and geographical context, and by whom and for whom such necessities obtain. We can ask who dances, when and where, in what ways, with whom, and to what end? And just as importantly, who does *not* dance, in what ways, under what conditions and why? Why are some dances, some ways of moving the body, considered forbidden for members of certain social classes, 'races', sexes? By looking at dance we can see enacted on a broad scale, and in codified fashion, socially constituted and historically specific attitudes toward the body in general, toward specific social groups' usage of the body in particular, and about the relationships among variously marked bodies, as well as social attitudes toward the use of space and time.

Were we to complete a really detailed analysis of social dance and its gender implications, for example, it could provide us with a baseline from which to pursue further questions that are much larger in scale. We might ask, for instance, how the concept of pleasure is played out in this kinesthetic realm. Who moves and who is moved? In what ways do the poses display one body more than another? What skills are demanded of each dancer, and what do they imply about desired attributes ascribed to men or to women? What would a 'bad' rendition of a particular dance, like the tango for instance, consist of? An 'un-Latin' or 'un-American' version? An 'improper' one?

These questions are useful for historical as well as contemporary analysis. For example, the waltz was regarded as too sexually dangerous for 'respectable' women in Europe and North America when it was first introduced in the nineteenth century. The combination of intoxicating fast whirling and a 'close' embrace was thought to be enough to make women take leave of their senses. Some advice books for women even claimed waltzing could lead to prostitution.

Nineteenth-century dance manuals included drawings showing 'proper' and 'improper' ways to embrace while dancing, specifying the position of the head, arms and upper body, and the required distance that should be maintained between male and female torsos. In manuals directed toward the middle and upper classes, bodies that pressed close, spines that relaxed, and clutching arms were all denigrated as signs of lower-class dance style. The postural and gestural maintenance of class distinction was a necessary skill to be learned, one that could even be represented with precision in 'yes' and 'no' illustrations of dancing couples.

Such detailed bodily analysis of the linkage of gender and class provides another discursive field through which to understand the shifting constitution of class relations and gender attributes during the nineteenth century. Changing attitudes toward the body as evidenced in the 'physical culture' movement, and changes in dress such as the introduction of 'bloomers', as well as new patterns of leisure activities and their genderedness provide part of the wider context through which such dance activities gain their meaning. Similarly, the rapid industrialization and class realignments that took place during the latter half of the century, giving rise to new ideas about the division between leisure and work, between men and women, and toward time and physicality are played out in the dance halls. As 'dance', conventions of bodily activity represent a highly codified and highly mediated representation of social distinctions. Like other forms of art or of cultural practice, their relation to the economic 'base' is not one of mere reflection, but rather one of dialogic constitution. Social relations are both enacted and produced through the body, and not merely inscribed upon it.

Appropriation/transmission/migration of dance styles

Obviously, ways of holding the body, gesturing, moving in relation to time, and using space (taking a lot, using a little, moving with large sweeping motions, or small contained ones, and so forth) all differ radically across various social and cultural groups and through time. If dance styles and performance practices are both symptomatic and constitutive of social relations, then tracing the history of dance styles and their spread from one group or area to another, along with the changes that occur in this transmission, can help uncover shifting ideologies attached to bodily discourse.

The history of the tango, for example, traces the development of movement styles from the dockside neighbourhoods of Buenos Aires to the salons of Paris before returning, newly 'respectable', from across the Atlantic to the drawing rooms of the upper-class portions of the Argentine population during the first decades of the twentieth century. As Deborah Jakubs (1991) has noted, the taste of the upper classes for 'a fundamentally taboo cultural form is a recurrent phenomenon', as evidenced by the passion for Harlem jazz exhibited by many wealthy white New Yorkers in the 1920s and 1930s.

A whole history of dance forms could be written in terms of such appropriations and reworkings occurring in both North and South America for at least the last two centuries and continuing today. Such practices and the discourse that surrounds them reveal the important part bodily discourse plays in the continuing social construction and negotiation of race, gender, class and nationality, and their hierarchical arrangements. In most cases we will find that dance forms originating in lower-class or non-dominant populations present a trajectory of 'upward mobility' in which the dances are 'refined', 'polished', and often desexualized. Similarly, improvisatory forms become codified to be more easily transmitted across class and racial lines, especially when the forms themselves become commodified and sold through special brokers, or dance teachers.

In studying the transmission of a form, it is not only the pathway of that transmission, but also the form's reinscription in a new community/social context and resultant change in its signification that it is important to analyse. An analysis of appropriation must include not only the transmission pathway and the mediating effects of the media, immigration patterns and the like, but also an analysis *at the level of the body* of what changes in the transmission. Often in the so-called desexualization of a form as it crosses class or racial boundaries, we can see a clear change in body usage, especially (at least in Europe, and North and South America) as it involves the usage of the pelvis (less percussive thrusting, undulation, or rotation for instance), and in the specific configurations of male and female partnering. For example, the closeness of the embrace may be loosened, or the opening of the legs may be lessened. In analysing some of these changes we can see specifically what aspects of movement are tagged as too 'sexy' or 'Latin' or 'low class' by the appropriating groups.[4] Of course, the same meaning may not at all be attached to the original movements by dancers in the community that developed the style.

Looking back to the early years of this century in North America, for instance, the case of the professional dance team of Vernon and Irene Castle provides a good example. The husband and wife duo became well known among the middle and upper classes through their exhibition ballroom dancing and their popular movies. They were so popular that Irene Castle set the standard for fashion and hairstyle and appeared in many magazines. Performing in elegant dance clubs, and running their own dance school in New York City, they built their reputations on popularizing (among the middle and upper classes) social dances that originated in the lower classes, especially within the black population. They 'toned down', 'tamed' and 'whitened' such popular social dances as the Turkey Trot and the Charleston. Such revisions tended to make the dances more upright, taking the bend out of the legs and bringing the buttocks and chest into vertical alignment. Such 'brokering' of black cultural products increased the circulation of money in the white community which paid white teachers to learn white versions of black dances.

But it would be a mistake to consider that such appropriations, while they seem to recuperate the potential contestatory power of cultural production by subordinate groups, do so monolithically. While markers of social 'difference' can be to some extent reduced to 'style' and repositioned from a contestatory marginality to more mainstream fashionable practice, both the specific practices themselves and their meanings shift in the process. Indeed, even in those instances where the recuperation seems very 'successful', there is some change in the dominant population's cultural production.

And, of course, appropriation does not always take the form of the hegemonic groups' 'borrowing' from subordinated groups. The borrowing and consequent refashioning goes both ways. To take just one example, the

'Cakewalk', a strutting couples dance performed by African Americans during the slavery era, is thought to have been based on a mimicry of European social dance forms, where (heterosexual) coupled dancing was prevalent, as opposed to the separate-sex dance traditions of West Africa. The meanings of the movement lexicons change when transported into the adopting group. While the notion of 'appropriation' may signal the transfer of source material from one group to another, it doesn't account for the changes in performance style and ideological meaning that accompany the transfer. Concepts of hybridity or syncretism more adequately describe the complex interactions among ideology, cultural forms and power differentials that are manifest in such transfers.

Concluding thoughts

I have argued throughout this piece for an emphasis on the continually changing relational constitution of cultural forms. Concepts of cultural resistance, appropriation, and cultural imperialism are important for the light they shed on the unequal distribution of power and goods that shape social relations. And indeed these inequities may form a kind of limit or substratum that ultimately determines the topography of cultural production. But an overemphasis on such concepts can obscure the more complex dialectics of cultural transmission. Such concepts can overemphasize formal properties that circulate or are 'lost' in the process of moving from one group to another, thus resulting in an inattention to the contextual specificity of meanings attached to or arising from the usage of formal properties, and obscuring as well the hybridization of such forms.

I have also argued for increased attention to movement as a primary not a secondary social text, one of immense importance and tremendous challenge. If we are to expand the humanities now to include 'the body' as text, surely we should include in that new sense of textuality bodies in motion, of which dance represents one of the most highly codified, widespread and intensely affective dimensions. And because so many of our most explosive and most tenacious categories of identity are mapped onto bodily difference, including race and gender, but expanding through a continual slippage of categories to include ethnicity and nationality and even sexuality as well, we should not ignore the ways in which dance signals and enacts social identities in all their continually changing configurations.

But to do so will require special tools. Although I have been emphasizing the larger theoretical level of analysis of the transmission and hybridization of cultural production in this essay, extended treatment of specific cases, both historic and contemporary, is clearly necessary. Such research will allow us to test the validity of these frameworks and to provide the data necessary for detailed accounts of exchange, change and circulation and the ways in which those are attached to the social production of identity. But if we are to talk about dancing in anything other than the broadest terms, we must be able to do close analysis of dance forms, just as we might of literary texts. While most scholars have spent years developing analytic skills for reading and understanding verbal forms of communication, rarely have we worked equally hard to develop an ability to analyse visual, rhythmic, or gestural forms. As cultural critics, we must become movement literate. Here is where skills drawn from the dance field become indispensable.

Systems of movement analysis developed in dance, such as Laban's Effort/Shape system, provide a good starting point. Effort/Shape methodologies employ abstract concepts of continuums in the use of the weight of the body (ranging from 'strong' to 'light'), in the body's attitude toward space (ranging from 'direct' to 'indirect'), and in the use of time (ranging from 'quick' to 'sustained'). In so doing, they can provide an analytical system as well as a language with which to speak about the body moving in time and space.

Although the Effort/Shape system does not code movements in terms of gender or cultural affinities, all analytical systems reflect the contours of their historical etiology and of the objects of analysis. The Effort/Shape system, for example, developed out of Rudolph von Laban's analysis of twentieth-century European movement patterns. Given the demands of cross-cultural and intracultural research, no one system will be sufficient. To keep our broader levels of analysis anchored in the materiality and kinesthesia of the dancing body, we need to generate more tools for close readings, and more sophisticated methodologies for shuttling back and forth between the micro (physical) and macro (historical, ideological) levels of movement investigation.[5] The difficulty of this research will repay us well, expanding understanding of the ways in which the body serves both as a ground for the inscription of meaning, a tool for its enactment, and a medium for its continual creation and recreation.

(An early version of this paper was presented at the conference 'Politics in Motion: Dance and Culture in Latin America' held at Duke University in the winter of 1991.)

NOTES

1 The debates about what 'cultural studies' is, should and should not be have intensified during the last ten years as the term has gained greater circulation and as its practitioners have gained increasing institutional power in the academy. I use this term in the sense of a group of self-nominated scholars who affiliate themselves and their work with such a term. Implicit in its usage is usually a concept of critique, antidisciplinarity, and of the importance of investigating the linkages between social/economic/political power and cultural production. See Johnson (1986–7), and Grossberg et al. (1992) for discussions about the scope of cultural studies. The American version of cultural studies is greatly influenced by the

pioneering work of Stuart Hall and the Birmingham Centre for Contemporary Cultural Studies in Britain.

2 Within the dance field, an excellent work by Foster (1986) marks the first full-length study situated within a structuralist/post-structuralist position, and increasingly articles and new books evidence a familiarity and willingness to engage ideological issues.

3 This is not to imply that the division between 'dance' and 'non-dance' is always clear, nor that it is always of primary importance in formulating research. Such a designation is subject to change historically and geographically. What may be particularly useful to note is what movements and what spatial sites are associated with 'dancing' when that concept is used, and what are not. By asking what constitutes 'dance' within a particular context, we can find out more about what values are associated with dance, whether as entertainment, social activity, ritual, or 'art'. The shifting dividing line between dance and non-dance activities and the moments of such an invocation are part of a political history of bodies and movement.

4 In asking what an 'un-Latin' rendition of a particular dance would be, for instance, we can begin to identify the movement parameters deemed necessary to identify it as such both within and outside of 'Latin' communities.

5 In the last few years, three new works have appeared which exemplify this approach of moving with assurance between the micro and macro levels of analysis. All three were written by scholars with extensive dance experience and/or with training in movement analysis in addition to their disciplinary training in the social sciences. See Ness (1992); Novack (1990) and Savigliano (1995).

19

AN INTRODUCTION TO DANCE ANALYSIS

Janet Adshead

The arts: the need for analysis

Although dance scholars are handicapped in analysis by the limited evidence of dances, particularly from previous centuries, other problems exacerbate this. Perhaps most important among them are the sometimes conflicting views of art educators, choreographers and dancers about the values and dangers of 'analysing' art works. These are views that find echoes in all arts disciplines despite much more firmly established traditions of detailed analysis of art works. It is fair to say that the idea of analysis is still greeted with reservations by some 'expert' listeners or spectators in all arts. This may be, perhaps, for the very reason that once the reader, spectator or listener is equipped with some means of access to the work s/he simply engages with it and sees or hears it in all its richness and complexity without conscious or deliberate recourse to specific techniques.

However, if the present position for dance is compared with that of music in the early part of this century, we are forced, by analogy, to accept that a greater richness of understanding is the inevitable consequence of analytical and scholarly study. It is possible to see, in the case of music, just how much of an impact the availability of recordings has had on scholarship with reference to today's record review programmes on the radio and to detailed critical articles where several interpretations of a single work are compared. The result is that performances of a single phrase or section of a work are discussed in depth. Yet in 1909 when Virginia Woolf heard Wagner's operas at Bayreuth she felt that there were immense problems in dealing with this new sound and that these problems arose directly from the fact that the music was heard once and once only. Even in the first decade of the twentieth century there was a wealth of notated scores for study although few recordings. At the present time dance has neither in abundance.

163

The commonplace remark that music is in its infancy is best borne
out by the ambiguous state of musical criticism. It has few traditions
behind it.

(Woolf 1909; repub. 1979: 31)

This comment seems strange to readers today when a comparison is made of
the quantity and quality of critical writing to which the music student has
recourse and that available for dance study. But Virginia Woolf's point is
that such critical comment, if made without the benefit of recordings to
study, tends to be simply descriptive with little of illuminating insight. She
continues by making a comparison, not with dance, but with literature.

A critic of writing is hardly to be taken by surprise, for he can
compare almost every literary form with some earlier form and can
measure the achievement by some familiar standard.

(*ibid.*)

Similarly, when a new dance form emerges, e.g. postmodern dance, the critic
has to be thoroughly familiar with existing forms in order to see how and in
what ways the new dance diverges from previous practices and how it draws
on them. Being familiar with the varied types of the art allows the spectator
to formulate criteria based on interpretative and evaluative principles. It is
then possible to make reasoned and reasonable statements instead of making vague noises of approval or disapproval. Virginia Woolf explains the
difficulty of making judgements in these terms:

the fact however that so little has yet been done to lay bare the
principles of the art accounts for the indecision which marks our
attempt to judge new music.

(*ibid.*)

In the intervening period much work of this kind has taken place in music,
both in the field of musical criticism and analysis of works and in the aesthetics of music, but little in dance. The musical parallel is not without problems. Despite the vigorous growth of 'theory' of music and a fairly strict
formal analysis there remains scepticism when the interest is broader than
this structural approach. The theory of Heinrich Schenker has provoked a
debate that is illuminating for its parallels with dance study. His aim, to link
'theory' in intimate connection with 'art', demands that students should be
capable of subtle discrimination in hearing and not simply able to read
scores and analyse them. The complexity of the enterprise is illustrated thus:

the finished work of art conceals within itself countless assumptions – imponderables that demand of those who would re-create

with understanding (and every higher act of comprehension is re-creation) a commensurate expenditure of effort.

(Jonas 1982: xiv)

The assumptions that he refers to are related both to knowledge of music (or dance) itself and to the cultural inheritance that we bring to understanding art; they develop from the traditions of that art and are the means by which art works are able to carry multiple and historical meanings as well as contemporary ones. As Jonas indicates, this makes engagement with the art an active, intense effort of understanding on the part of both the spectator and the performer.

The tradition of systematic analysis of musical works seems not to have dimmed appreciation of music any more than the scholar of literature or visual art has succeeded in destroying enjoyment of novels or poems or paintings. Fears that the work would disappear under the microscope or on the dissecting table seem unfounded. If there is something worthy of repeated viewing and sustained attention it will still be there at the end of the analytical process. The dance scholar knows this just as the musicologist does, but both would also acknowledge with passion that the only valid *purpose* or *reason* for doing it lies in the increased understanding and appreciation that may result. To listen to music, to hear its structure and understand how it creates particular effects provides an exquisite delight that using it as aural wallpaper cannot. To watch a dance and see and hear its complex interweaving of rhythms and patterns and to perceive the way in which these contribute to the imaginative significance of the whole construction is, similarly, both the excitement of, and justification for, engaging in analysis.

Criticism, in the form of short articles in newspapers and journals, is a related but not identical kind of activity. It is an important distinction since criticism has different purposes and enlightens different audiences. In literature, music and visual art the practical criticism of the newspaper critic serves the purpose of educating the layperson, the general audience, encouraging attendance at new performances or the reading of new books. The *scholarship* of literary criticism, musicology and art history and criticism serves the purpose of furthering knowledge in each domain and increasing the depth of response that is possible with full knowledge. In a crucial sense it is the vital reservoir from which the general critic works.

A degree of scepticism is to be expected with the development of new theory since theories exist to be challenged for their capacity to illuminate the activity that they chart. They cannot, however, justly be attacked simply for being 'theories' since this is patently what they are. This sometimes happens in the world of art, as though we would all be better off without theories, simply enjoying art works. The problems that would result for appreciation and education if we adopted this line in practice are well outlined by writers such as Best (1986b) and Smith (1977). 'Simple' enjoyment

165

and appreciation, it is argued, are the result of hard work, often combined with good teaching. People do not automatically and without guidance find enjoyment in complex works. They *learn* how to do this and are amply rewarded.

It should be apparent where our sympathies lie but the sceptic is right to point to the dangers of becoming overly analytic at the expense of engaging with the whole work and responding to it imaginatively. What we want to reinforce is the possibility of giving reasons for opinions, of providing evidence to support an interpretation, of ascribing qualities to the art work and offering some means of judging its value. Only then is there the chance, in consequence of this process, of guiding others towards greater enjoyment and understanding. Promoting one's own views in the name of 'criticism' or 'education' without giving reasons is simply not good enough.

The nature of dance analysis

If we apply these general principles specifically to dance then the notion of analysis has a relevance even at the level of looking at an example of human activity and calling it 'dance'. The perceiver has to have some idea of what a 'dance' is, and this, in turn, depends on having seen people doing something that has been labelled in this way. There are problems, of course, even in *recognizing* unusual forms of activity as dance, particularly from cultures other than the spectator's own, and in borderline activities such as ice dancing. A similar problem occurs when the spectator is presented with new forms of dance, whether performed for social or artistic purposes, since they tend to run counter to existing types of dance. They may fall outside accepted or given frameworks and may be less immediately accessible.

For the purposes of this discussion, however, the point is that as soon as someone talks about an activity as 'dance' this is to embark upon analysis, to pick out features of an event and to match them against assumptions about what a dance is. This ability can be refined until the individual recognizes the characteristics and distinguishing elements not only of dance (as distinct from drama or music) but of different styles of dance within general groupings of dances and, at the level of individual works, sees the uniqueness of each one.

Perhaps the first and most obvious necessity is to explain in outline what is meant by analysing individual dance works since the term 'analysis' can be understood in a number of different ways. Here it is used to describe a process which, if sympathetically taught, is crucial in coming to understand dance, to appreciate it more deeply and to value it. Far from destroying the dance it can illuminate it by increasing the ability to discriminate finely between the features of a single dance and to make comparisons between dances. Analysis provides a structure for the knowledge that is needed to frame interpretations and increases the possibility of becoming imaginatively and creatively involved in a work.

Dance analysis does this by taking account, in its conceptual structure, of the movements present in the dance, allowing the possibility of a *minutely detailed examination* of its parts, in the way that a notation score records it, but it also permits a *synthesis* of the results of detailed observation with contextual knowledge, which then furthers the process of *interpreting* and *evaluating* the dance. Dance analysis does not remain solely at the level of a description of movement as 'movement analysis' or a 'movement theory' might; nor is an 'effort-shape' theory (in the sense that some American theorists have developed Laban's work) seen to be adequate to answer the problem of interpretation in dance. The notion of interpretation requires that the character of the dance, its subject matter, the treatment of that subject matter and the qualities that might be ascribed are also understood. This is beyond the scope of theories that simply analyse movement.

Appreciating dance is a complex process which depends also upon the individual having certain skills, for example the skill of noting or observing separate movement components of the dance and being able to perceive them as related or unrelated happenings. Constructing a clear picture of the movements and the way in which they coexist, of the dancers, as individuals and as groups, of the performing environment, costumes and sound, is the basis of analysis.

Once these elements have been seen, and it is often no easy matter to grasp them as the dance rushes by, the spectator can proceed to make sense of them by drawing on all that s/he knows about dances, about the type of subject matter and about the conventions of that art, and engaging imaginatively with it in order to ascribe certain qualities and attribute meaning(s) to the dance. Then one could be said to appreciate the dance. It is not assumed that all dances have specific, identifiable 'meanings' in a simple sense but the term is used more widely to cover the 'significance' of the dance, or what it is 'about'.

Making sense of a dance requires, then, that an interpretation is made, derived from a rigorous description of the movement and supported by additional knowledge of the context in which the dance exists. But it is not just the historical or biographical facts of the work's provenance, nor simply the details of the movement and its structuring, but the cumulative effect of acquiring this knowledge and then seeing how these elements are transmuted in the whole. The dance may have a purpose or function, primarily as an art work or as a ritual act or as a form of entertainment, for example, or as more than one of these simultaneously. Understanding the individual circumstances of each dance is crucial to interpretation. Every dance is found in a particular cultural context just as, historically, it exists in a distinctive era and is made, performed and watched by specific, identifiable groups of people. These factors are relevant in understanding the significance of a dance and it is at this point that contextual knowledge of dance, embodied in studies from dance history, sociology, anthropology and theology, becomes valuable. It is worth highlighting here that the theory we outline is not art-specific but is capable of functioning across the many purposes of dance.

To start from direct engagement with the dance is to focus on the dance itself while acknowledging that other forms of scholarship contribute to the total picture. To take an anthropological or historical starting point is to conduct a different kind of study based primarily on the interests and methodologies of those disciplines. Many dance scholars start from such backgrounds and examine the dance as an expression or subversion of certain aspects of society or as part of an important historical event or period. Constructs central to those disciplines then underlie the study of dance.

While a report of a dance ritual or social event, an anthropological study of a dance form or a guide to understanding the historical significance of a dance, may contain important first-hand accounts, they embody a particular kind of interest that influences comments made about the dance. In other words, writings by historians and sociologists are already forms of analysis from the standpoint of the development of dance *through time* and in relation to *its place within a certain society*. The reader needs to be aware of this.

Our premise is that a satisfactory analysis which starts from the dance has yet to be fully worked out.

The uses of dance analysis

If analysis is seen as a close examination of the parts of a dance in order to make an interpretation of it and to evaluate it then this process would appear to be *the fundamental skill* required whatever one's specific interest in dance. The choreographer, performer, critic and notator all work with these same skills and concepts although they do so in different ways. Furthermore, the results of their skills, the choreography, the performance, the criticism and the score are all *understood* and *evaluated* using the same basic skills and concepts. Developing from this commonality, however, additional skills are required in each of the processes of making, performing, criticizing and notating the dance. These skills may, for example, be concerned with learning the symbol system of notation, or acquiring the facility with language which a writer needs, or the ability to manipulate movement in the case of the choreographer.

Although it is often maintained that choreography somehow springs fully fledged from intuition, or from unreasoned, inner experiences and that analysis is, therefore, irrelevant, this can readily be shown to be false. From the choreographer's point of view, s/he has to have a clear idea that a dance is being made and not a music piece, or any other kind of object, and this entails a notion of what the dance might look like. Inevitably this is based upon previous dances seen and made by the choreographer. A more or less explicit process of reasoning then occurs. Whether or not the choreographer's reasons for choosing to place one movement next to another are ever made public, or even put into words, we have to assume that there *are* *reasons*, that making a dance piece is a deliberate human act and not an accident. If the choreographer could not distinguish between different kinds of movements and then make decisions about how they should be placed, linking them to make longer sections in the creation of a whole dance, s/he would not be capable of making a dance. It may, of course, develop along unexpected lines and even the choreographer may be surprised by the result. In looking for 'surprise', artists sometimes intentionally try to escape human logic and the limitations of normal thinking patterns by chance or random methods. However, this is still a positive choice, a conscious decision about procedures, hence a deliberate act. The choreographer is inescapably engaged in an analytic process.

It can be demonstrated then that the skills of analysis are relevant not only to those involved in 'academic' studies but also that they are central in making the dance. Similarly, a performer has to observe the differences between separate steps and patterns or groups of steps, between spatial designs and dynamic qualities of different kinds in order to give an accurate and clearly pointed reading. *This involves analysis.* The spectator too, uses the same process although the end product is not a dance or a performance of one, but the enjoyment, understanding and appreciation of it. In a fundamental sense the choreographer and the performer share this spectatorial view of the dance.

Although the process can be demonstrated to be the same, the use to which it is put will vary. The *choreographer* uses analysis to further the end of making a dance, both as part of the creative process and by examining critically what s/he has made previously and what others have made. The *performer* uses analysis in order to improve technical skill and to facilitate understanding of the structure of the dance for the purpose of interpretation. In these two cases the analysis may rarely reach the stage of being put into words since it may be sufficient that it is only partly verbalized, i.e. to the extent that the dancers can pick up the steps and the choreographer explain them. For the spectator who is a casual theatre-goer, or for the social dance participant, the same may apply.

On the other hand, someone who *reconstructs* dances for the repertoire of theatre companies or revives dances from the original notation of the sixteenth or seventeenth centuries needs a much more articulated level of analysis in order to be able to put together the complete dance without the person who composed it being present to clarify what was intended.

The specialist spectator, i.e. the *critic*, uses analysis in order to provide the reasons for an interpretation and evaluation of a dance and to deepen her/his own response. An extension of this is found in dance education where, it is argued, it is only through articulating *what* has been learnt that understanding can be demonstrated to exist. This does not necessarily mean writing scholarly articles. Understanding of the requirements of performance might also be articulated through the *performance of a work* where this demonstrates skills of interpretation as well as purely technical abilities. An understanding of making dances could be articulated through the *composition of a dance*, for example, based on the principles which, through analysis, are found to characterize a particular period. Understanding of dance could also be articulated through *writing* about it. It is perhaps the dance student, or scholar, or theorist who pursues analysis in the intellectual sense of doing it simply for the sake of the knowledge that results rather than for a practical outcome. This kind of study brings with it requirements which may be somewhat different from those relevant to training a performer for the stage. By using analytic approaches, however, any dance student (in the widest sense) may have access to structures and meanings which were hitherto inaccessible.

20

DANCE, GENDER AND CULTURE

Ted Polhemus

At the most fundamental level of analysis, dance, gender and culture are one and the same thing. In order to demonstrate this provocative contention, however, it is necessary that we examine each of these subjects separately.

First *culture*. Putting aside a class-based view which presupposes that culture is possessed only by an educated élite, I will here use this term in a properly anthropological sense to encompass everything which the members of a social group (any social group) have in common – everything which they share and which contributes to and generates their sense of 'we-ness'. Culture is the glue which holds peoples together.

Worldview, religion, cosmology, an ethical system and language are some of the most obvious components of culture. Especially obvious to us is language which traditionally has been seen as the cornerstone, sometimes even the totality, of culture. It would, of course, be foolish to dismiss out of hand the significance of verbal language as an essential component of the social cement which is culture. Throughout human history verbal language has served as a marker of the boundaries of social groups and as a depository of any social group's tradition and history. It is, however, just as foolish to presume that verbal language is the only significant socio-cultural marker and depository.

Our own socio-cultural tradition (which for want of a better term is usually called 'the West') has always ascribed a particular importance to verbal language; an importance which some anthropologists have increasingly come to suspect is not shared by other peoples. There is, therefore, a growing suspicion that our 'In the beginning was the Word', logocentric worldview has biased our perception of *all* cultural systems (see Kristeva 1978). It is not my wish to debate here the relative importance of verbal communication or to suggest that verbal language is not a major component of culture. What does seem appropriate is to underline and celebrate the significance of non-verbal communicative systems – especially what might be termed *physical culture*.

From the moment of birth an individual begins the long and complex task of learning how to use his or her physical body. This is obvious and we note in 'baby books' significant moments of this process such as the first time a baby manages to stand or walk. What is less obvious, but by no means less important, is the fact that such physical development is a cultural as well as a biological phenomenon. *How* one should stand, walk, hold the body, etc. differs from one society to the next and in a fast changing society such as our own, from one era to the next.

Thus, for example, while everyone would readily agree that all physiologically normal human beings develop, for example, bipedal locomotion, it is less often appreciated that not only is the style of such locomotion specific to a given social group or era, but furthermore, that such stylistic differences – just like differences between verbal languages or dialects – are essential markers of 'Our Way of Life' and depositories of 'Our' tradition. To be a Masai, a Hopi, an Xingu, etc. is to comport oneself like a Masai, a Hopi or a Xingu. To put a foot wrong, that is, to move one's body in a stylistically inappropriate manner, is to step outside the boundaries of one's culture.

If it is difficult for us to accept the implications of this line of thought it is simply because we – like all the world's peoples – consign everything to do with our bodies to the domain of the 'natural'. That is to say, that territory which is beyond the reach of culture. Always and everywhere the way 'we' walk, sit, squat, lean against a wall, stand, sleep, copulate, and so forth is seen as *the* way the body *'naturally'* behaves. This is not only because one's physical self is existentially omnipresent, it is also because 'the body' is inevitably caught up in a symbolic congruence with 'the social body' of one's society; a congruence which is so complete that it has the effect of blinkering us to the cross-cultural relativity of corporal experience.

This is a complex problem which has been discussed at length by the anthropologist Mary Douglas (1970) and by myself in other works (1975, 1978, 1988). For our present purposes let us simply concentrate on the practical entailment of the interplay between the physical body and the social body; namely, that such symbolic interfacing inevitably consigns physiological behaviours to a domain which is 'natural' and, therefore, apparently outside of human intervention. (The precise, mirror-like replication of the human body in the social body – and vice versa – gives each of these levels of experience a patina of objective reality which is mutually reifying.)

In the terminology of our own culture's worldview, this means that physical behaviour is classified as biological and genetic rather than sociocultural and learned. Although this particular distinction may be unique to us, the bottom line of such classification is the same as that found in any traditional, tribal or peasant society – to consign physical behaviours to the realm of the 'natural' and immutable. But while the tendency to classify the physiological as 'natural' might itself be 'natural' it is rather amazing that we who have been uniquely exposed to so much cross-cultural experience should persist in this view. If not through first-hand experience, at least through the medium of ethnographic films we have seen how people from other societies use their bodies differently than we do and yet we persist in placing physicality outside the bounds of culture.

And most surprising of all, anthropologists who have studied other societies first hand and extensively are often the most persistent offenders. Indeed, anthropology itself has traditionally been divided between, on the one hand, 'physical anthropology' which deals with the evolution of the human body and, on the other hand, 'social' or 'cultural' anthropology which deals with human social organization and its products and artefacts. Thankfully there have been important exceptions and these individuals have pointed the way towards a study of humankind which would explore the interface between the socio-cultural and the physical levels of experience.

Margaret Mead, for example, in her work with Gregory Bateson (1942) and Francis Cooke Macgregor (1951) has shown not only that the members of traditional Balinese society learn to use their bodies in a style which is radically different from our own, but also that such physical behaviour is an intrinsic and fundamental part of Balinese culture. For Mead and her co-authors the essence of 'Balinese character' is Balinese style comportment.

In light of such work it seems pertinent that the social sciences re-examine the meaning of the word 'culture'. Culture is not exclusively nor, I would suggest, even primarily encoded and transmitted by means of words or artefacts. At least in so far as an individual's first and most rudimentary experience of his or her society is via bodily manipulation and physical education in its broadest sense, the deepest and most fundamental foundations of being a member of a particular society are inevitably corporal. Muscular tonus, stance, basic movement styles, gestures and so forth once learned are, like any physical activity, remarkably resistant to change and constitute not only the essential component of personal identity but of social and cultural identity as well. Furthermore, movement and other physical styles are in any society imbued with symbolic meaning with the result that how we use and move our bodies is inevitably the occasion for the transmission of all sorts and various levels of socio-cultural information including, most importantly, those meanings which exceed the limits of verbal language (see Polhemus 1978).

At its core, therefore, culture not only includes a physical dimension, it is a physical style system which signifies (embodies) what it means to be a member of a particular society. Mead and colleagues have shown how this works for the Balinese – that a particular way of holding one's body, of relaxing, of squatting, of walking and so forth is the very essence of being Balinese.

Our society is more complex and difficult to see in these terms because it is actually a loose conglomerate of many different, competing socio-cultural groups. Nevertheless, 'Western Society' offers us many examples of the central position of physical style within cultural systems. Consider, for example, the clash which occurred in the sixties between the hippies and 'Straight Society'. The essence of hippiness was symbolically expressed in the form of a physicality which was 'laid-back', 'loose' and 'easy' while 'Straight Society' was just that – 'rigid', 'up-tight', 'square' and 'up-right'. Where one personally stood in relationship to this clash of cultures was precisely encapsulated in how one walked down the street, sat in a chair, leaned against a wall or moved on a dance floor.

Which brings us to our second subject: dance. While physical culture may be viewed as a crystallization – an embodiment – of the most deeply rooted and fundamental level of what it means to be a member of a particular society, dance might be seen as a second stage of this process – a schema, an abstraction or stylizing of physical culture. There is impressive evidence to support both of these assumptions in the research which was generated by the Choreometrics Project.

Choreometrics, defined as 'the measure of dance or dance as a measure of culture' (Lomax 1968: 223), began as an offshoot of the cantometrics project which the anthropologist Alan Lomax set up to explore cross-cultural differences and similarities of music style.[1] In essays in their book *Folk Song Style and Culture* Lomax and his team tell us that the choreometrics project set out to test the hypothesis that 'dance itself is an adumbration of or derived communication about life, focused on those favoured dynamic patterns which most successfully and frequently animated the everyday activity of most of the people in a culture' (Lomax 1968: 223).

To test this hypothesis the choreometrics team created a coding system for scoring the primary parameters of dance (shape of transition, shape of main activity, energy of transition, energy of main activity, degree of variation, spread of flow through body). They then, after viewing film of dance from some forty-three cultures from around the world, scored each of these according to these parameters. There is not room here to discuss in detail either their methodology or their results,[2] but two principal findings deserve note: First, in all societies studied by the Choreometrics Project there was found to be an intrinsic relationship between dance styles and everyday movement styles. That is, dance could indeed be described as a stylization of everyday movement qualities. Second, the dance styles of the societies investigated by the Choreometrics Project seemed to reflect and embody the overall culture of that society. That is, dance styles, instead of being arbitrary, constitute a 'natural' expression of the cultural system within which they are found.

In other words: Dance is a stylized, highly redundant schema of a people's overall physical culture which is itself the embodiment of that particular people's unique way of life – their culture in the broadest sense of the term. Dance is the metaphysics of culture.

Lomax and his colleagues most frequently demonstrate this view in rather simplistic terms which seek to show how the movement patterns necessitated by a people's techniques of food gathering and preparation shape their styles of dance movement. Culture, however, is always a multi-faceted system which incorporates a complexity of symbolic codes which while inevitably 'practical' are rarely reducible to the straightforward practicality of obtaining and preparing something to eat.

A culture is a blueprint for a way of living. As such it must, of course, prescribe a means of obtaining foodstuffs, but it must also prescribe patterns of kinship, ethics, political organization, religion, cosmology and all the other systems which taken together organize and structure a way of life. If everyday movement patterns and dance are an embodiment of culture then one must expect that they embody *all* of these systems – many of which are far removed from the concrete techniques of food production and preparation and which, it could be argued, may even shape these techniques themselves.

The most important factor to emerge from the above is that to understand and appreciate the implications of even a single moment of dance movement it is necessary to possess a full understanding of the complexities of the socio-cultural system in which it is found. Because dance is a system of signification which possesses roots which permeate to the core of culture, it is necessary, if we wish to decode its meanings, to appreciate that a way of life (a culture) is much more than a way of filling one's stomach.

Thus far I have tried to show that dance is a liqueur which is distilled of the stuff of culture. It remains for us to explore the issue of gender in relation to dance and culture.

Traditionally, culture has been viewed as a single, coherent, objective entity; a 'thing' which exists on its own. Perhaps this view derives from a misunderstanding of Durkheim's axiom that a society is 'more than the sum of its parts' – a facile misinterpretation which credits socio-cultural systems with an objective reality (a 'thing-ness') which the French sociologist never intended (Durkheim 1982). For, ironically, while culture is the definitive shared, intersubjective experience its reality is, in the final analysis, always subjective – from the perspective of a particular individual. 'Our Culture' is always a synthesis of my or your or Joe Bloggs's understanding of 'Our Culture' and, obviously, if you or I or Joe (or Jane) Bloggs are experiencing 'Our' culture from radically different perspectives then this will in turn affect not only our vision of our culture, but – because culture exists only in our intersubjective visions of it – culture itself.

Let us, therefore, outline the most fundamental differences of perspective which generate a disjunction of that which we commonly take to be uniform and objective. In any society and at any point in human history there have always been two significant categories of experience which inevitably and profoundly distort any individual's subjective perception of cultural reality: age and gender.

In any society a 10-year-old will always perceive his or her culture differently than will a 70-year-old. However, given that a 70-year-old will have had the experience of having been a 10-year-old, the significance of this subjective distinction will eventually be diminished, at least for those individuals who reach old age. Gender, however, is more problematic. No matter how long we may live, no matter how rich and varied are our experiences, no matter how much we might strive to be 'objective', all of us are either male or female and none of us have ever truly experienced life from the perspective of the gender which we are not.[3] Even those few individuals in modern society who have changed sex can never know what it is like to have grown up as a member of the sex which – physiologically speaking – they have become.

Gender is a primary and insurmountable existential division which must inevitably define cultural experience and the perception of cultural reality. (Again, it is surprising how often this simple fact of life has been ignored by anthropologists and sociologists.) Logically, because life can only be experienced from the perspective of one particular gender and because culture (ultimately) exists only in the mind's eye of particular individuals, all of the world's cultures must be multiplied by two: the male culture and the female culture.

Because of this fact of life we must slightly revise our understanding of the interface between culture and dance. A culture is that which is shared by all of the members of a society. In practice, however, the possibilities of such intersubjectivity will always be limited by differences of gender. For this reason, it is necessary to distinguish between male and female cultural realities within the context of any social group. For both male and female cultural realities the processes of cultural expression and signification will be the same as those discussed above; culture in its broadest sense is embodied in the form of physical culture and this in turn is stylized and schematized in the form of dance. However, while this process itself may be unrelated to gender, the end results always are: the cultural reality which, for example, Masai (etc.) men express in their dance will be a different cultural reality than that which Masai (etc.) women express in their dance.

In emphasizing the obvious role that gender must play in the definition of cultural reality I do not want to fall into a physiological reductionism. Gender is itself, of course, culturally defined. We are not referring here simply to differences of genital equipment and so forth. However, the fact that, in any society, 'maleness' and 'femaleness' is a socio-cultural-physiological phenomenon and the fact that gender roles differ considerably from one society to another, do not alter the fact that *for any given individual* the experience of gender identity is an absolute boundary which is existentially insurmountable. Some distinction between the sexes is universal in all human societies, and inevitably, therefore, culture is bifurcated into male culture and female culture.

Dance – the distillation of culture into its most metaphysical form – always embodies and identifies this gender-generated division of cultural realities. Whenever men and women dance together, therefore, cultures collide: male culture and female culture. Nor is it necessary, of course, for men and women to actually dance together for such collisions to occur. In societies where men and women dance separately a simple comparison of their respective dance styles instantly alerts us (and them, the participants) to their intrinsic gender-culture differences. The men's dance style is a crystallization of what it means to be a male member of their culture. The women's dance style is a crystallization of what it means to be a female member of that culture. Indeed, in some tribal societies the cultures which the men and women dance are so different that it is as if the two sexes came from different worlds – which is, of course, precisely the case.

I do not doubt, on the other hand, that some 'unisex' cultures could be found in which dance and cultural realities exhibit few gender-specific differences. The majority of socio-cultural systems probably exist somewhere in the middle of this kline between the sexually dymorphic and the unisex. In our own culture, in recent times, we have seen the most unusual phenomenon: extreme fluctuations in the degree of gender differentiation of cultural systems. Such a phenomenon, especially given the comparatively short time-span within which it has occurred, must be unique in human history.

When I was a teenager growing up in an American suburb in the late 1950s and early 1960s I was taught to dance at school, against my will, I might add. Whether 'slow' or 'fast', these dance steps and the macho behavioural activities which framed dance movement *per se* had one thing in common: the male led. The male chose with whom he would dance. The male (if the female consented to dance with him – for she always had, if nothing else, the terrible power of rejection) physically supported the female. The male determined the rhythm and the style of their relationship in time and space. The female – as in 'real life' – followed his lead.

At the time that I had just about managed to do this, a social revolution occurred, a revolution of gender and culture which was spelled out on the dance floors of America and Britain long before such things were written or spoken about. Suddenly males did not ask girls to dance, nor did they define the rhythm and style of the encounter. As with hippy clothing and adornment styles, dance was heralding a brave new unisex world.

However, when the film *Saturday Night Fever* was released in the late 1970s, it became clear, beyond a shadow of a doubt, that this new world would never become a reality, if, indeed, it ever was such for even an alternative minority. Here we saw a complete return at least in terms of gender differentiation to the norms of dance, behaviour and culture which existed prior to the unisex experiments of the late 1960s. The male asks the girl to be his partner. The male physically supports the female. The male sets the pace and style of the dance; the male is the centre of attention.

'Disco', despite its 'alternative' popular connotations (i.e. one's parents saw it as completely opposed to the dance styles of their day), brought a return of Western society's traditional assumptions of gender. There may be less touching and therefore fewer possibilities of the male physically supporting the female and the business of males asking females to dance may be less verbal and formal, but simply by observing a disco dance floor in, say, the Costa Brava, it is clear that here we have returned to a dance/cultural system where men lead and women follow. For example, the male approaches the female on the dance floor, makes eye contact, checks for rejection or approval while the female, if and when the situation becomes one of a couple dancing together, marks time until she can respond to the style and rhythm of dance established by the male.

Disco and the male/female cultures which it embodies, however, are not all-embracing and since *Saturday Night Fever* we have also seen the rise of various alternative sub-cultures which continue the unisex direction of the hippies in dance, body decoration and worldview. One is thinking here of punks, gothics, the New Psychedelics and so forth. For example, the 'pogo' dance of the punks, like their adornment styles, makes little or no distinction between male and female.

This must serve to remind us that 'the West' is no longer, if indeed it ever was, a single cultural system. Aside from Normal Western Male Culture and Normal Western Female Culture there is also to be taken into consideration an ever-increasing cultural pluralism in the form of the new 'tribes' – each with its own values, beliefs, lifestyle assumptions, adornment styles and dance styles and in most cases, each with its own gender-specific sub-sub-culture.[4] These 'tribes', like any of the traditional tribal or peasant social systems we have discussed previously, achieve a cultural reality primarily and most fundamentally through the medium of style – physical cultural style as embodied in dress, adornment and dance.

For while the modern age may have provided us with communication media which can instantly broadcast and internationalize our dress and dance styles, even we have not succeeded in finding an alternative to stylistic expression as an embodiment of culture. In this regard we are, as our most distant ancestors were, dependent upon style, in our dress and dance, as the definitive means by which we can crystallize our social experiences into cultural realities. Whether our cultures are traditional or modern, male, female or (hypothetically) unisex, they would cease to exist if we did not wear them and dance them. At the most fundamental and significant level, to be a punk, as to be a Masai, is to dress and move as one. Words fail us in such metaphysical territory and while Wittgenstein may well be right that 'What we cannot speak about we must pass over in silence' (Wittgenstein 1961: 74), that has never stopped human beings from achieving some bottom-line, schematic cultural reality in their dress and dance. For even in a disco in Benidorm the movement of sweaty bodies in time and space can sketch out the schematic outlines of some much-longed-for Utopian society.

NOTES

1 This development became increasingly necessary as the realization grew that song could be best defined as 'danced speech'.
2 However, for critical assessments of these see Royce (1980), chapter 6, and Youngerman (1974).
3 It is perhaps useful to note that sex refers to biological maleness or femaleness whereas gender refers to features that are associated with being male or female which are socially constructed and defined.
4 It is important to state that no qualitative distinction is being made here between traditional and modern in terms of a unilinear evolutionary framework.

21

CHOREOGRAPHING HISTORY

Susan Leigh Foster

Manifesto for dead and moving bodies

Sitting in this chair; squirming away from the glitches, aches, low-grade tensions reverberating in neck and hip, staring unfocused at some space between here and the nearest objects, shifting again, listening to my stomach growl, to the clock ticking, shifting, stretching, settling, turning – I am a body writing. I am a bodily writing.[1] We used to pretend the body was uninvolved, that it remained mute and still while the mind thought. We even imagined that thought, once conceived, transferred itself effortlessly onto the page via a body whose natural role as instrument facilitated the pen. Now we know that the caffeine we imbibe mutates into the acid of thought which the body then excretes, thereby etching ideas across the page. Now we know that the body cannot be taken for granted, cannot be taken seriously, cannot be taken.

A body, whether sitting writing or standing thinking or walking talking or running screaming, is a bodily writing. Its habits and stances, gestures and demonstrations, every action of its various regions, areas, and parts – all these emerge out of cultural practices, verbal or not, that construct corporeal meaning. Each of the body's moves, as with all writings, traces the physical fact of movement and also an array of references to conceptual entities and events. Constructed from endless and repeated encounters with other bodies, each body's writing maintains a non-natural relation between its physicality and referentiality. Each body establishes this relation between physicality and meaning in concert with the physical actions and verbal descriptions of bodies that move alongside it. Not only is this relation between the physical and conceptual non-natural, it is also impermanent. It mutates, transforms, reinstantiates with each new encounter.

Today's creaking knee is not yesterday's knee jogging up the hill. The way one reaches toward that knee, as much a metaphor as any attempt to name or describe the knee, already presumes identities for hand and knee. But during their interaction identities for hand and knee become modified. Together they discover that the knee feels or sounds different, that the hand looks older or drier than yesterday. Comparisons between past and present knees provide some sense of continuity, but the memory is also unreliable.

180

Was it a year ago that the knee started creaking that way? Did it cease to make that noise during running, or after stretching? Why did it hurt yesterday and feel fine today?

The body is never only what we think it is (*dancers pay attention to this difference*). Illusive, always on the move, the body is at best *like* something, but it never is that something. Thus, the metaphors, enunciated in speech or in movement, that allude to it are what give the body the most tangible substance it has.

Organized collections of these metaphors, established as the various disciplines that scrutinize, discipline, instruct and cultivate the body, pretend permanence of and for the body. Their highly repetitive regimens of observation and exercise attempt to instantiate physical constants. Thousands of push-ups, pliés, or Pap smears later, the body appears to have consistent features, a clear structure, identifiable functions. If one is willing to ignore all subtle discrepancies and to uphold the statistical averages, one can almost believe in a body that obeys nature's laws. But then it suddenly does something marvellously aberrant: it gives out, comes through, or somehow turns up outside the bounds of what was conceivable.

This is not to say that the body's latest unanticipated gestures occur beyond the world of writing. On the contrary, the body's newest pronouncements can only be apprehended as *bricolages* of extant moves. A sudden facility at physical feats figures as the product of past disciplinary efforts to render the body faster, stronger, longer, more dexterous. The onset of illness signals deleterious habits, psychological repression, a cleansing process. Any new sensation of sex issues out of an expanded, but not alternative, sensorium. These new writings, even as they jar perceptions with their arresting inventiveness, recalibrate, rather than raze, bodily semiosis.

How to write a history of this bodily writing, this body we can only know through its writing. How to discover what it has done and then describe its actions in words. Impossible. Too wild, too chaotic, too insignificant. Vanished, disappeared, evaporated into thinnest air, the body's habits and idiosyncrasies, even the practices that codify and regiment it, leave only the most disparate residual traces. And any residue left behind rests in fragmented forms within adjacent discursive domains. *Still, it may be easier to write the history of this writing body than of the pen-pushing body. The pen-pushing body, after all, bears only the thinnest significance as an inadequate robotics, the apparatus that fails to execute the mind's will.*

What markers of its movement might a bodily writing have left behind? But first, which writing bodies? empowered bodies? enslaved bodies? docile bodies? rebellious bodies? dark bodies? pale bodies? exotic bodies? virtuoso bodies? feminine bodies? masculine bodies? triumphant bodies? disappeared bodies? All these genres of bodies first began moving through their days performing what they had learned how to do – these bodies' mundane habits and minuscule gestures mattered. These 'techniques of the body', as named by Marcel Mauss and John Bulwer before him, bore significance in the way they were patterned and the way they related with one another. Each body performed these actions in a style both shared and unique. Each body's movement evidenced a certain force, tension, weight, shape, tempo and phrasing. Each manifested a distinct physical structure, some attributes of which were reiterated in other bodies. All a body's characteristic ways of moving resonated with aesthetic and political values. The intensity of those resonances are what permit genres of bodies to coalesce.

Yet each body's movements all day long form part of the skeleton of meaning that also gives any aberrant or spectacular bodily action its lustre. Those everyday patterns of movement make seduction or incarceration, hysteria or slaughter, routinization or recreation matter more distinctively. The writing body in the constant outpouring of its signification offers up nuances of meaning that make a difference. The writing body helps to explicate the blank stare of the black man in the white police station, the raised shoulders and pursed lips of the rich woman walking past the home-less family, the swishing hips and arched eyebrows of gay men as a straight couple enters their bar, the rigid stance and frowning forehead of the single woman waiting at the bus stop next to the construction site. Or put differently: the writing body helps to explicate the blank stare of the black man in the white police station, the blank stare of the rich woman walking past the homeless family, the blank stare of gay men as a straight couple enters their bar, the blank stare of the single woman waiting at the bus stop next to the construction site. Each body's distinctive pronouncements at a given moment must be read against the inscription, along with others, it continuously produces. A blank stare does not mean the same thing for all bodies in all contexts.

How to get at this skeleton of movement's meaning for any given past and place? Some bodies' quotidian movements may have been variously recorded in manuals – ceremonial, religious, educational, social, amorous, remedial, martial – that instruct the body, or in pictures that portray it, or in literary or mythological references to its constitution and habits. In their movements, past bodies also rubbed up against or moved alongside geological and architectural constructions, music, clothing, interior decorations . . . whose material remains leave further indications of those bodies' dispositions. Insofar as any body's writings invited measurement, there endure documents from the disciplines of calculation addressing the body's grammatical makeup – its size, structure, composition, and chemistry – that tell us something about what shape a body was in.

These partial records of varying kinds remain. They document the encounter between bodies and some of the discursive and institutional frameworks that touched them, operated on and through them, in different ways. These documents delineate idealized versions of bodies: what a body was supposed to look like, how it was supposed to perform, how it was required to submit. Or they record that which was non-obvious, those details of bodily comportment construed as necessary to specify rather than those deemed self-evident. Occasionally, they reflect patterns of bodily deviance, whether ironic, inflammatory, inverted, or perverted, from the expected. Whatever their take on bodies, these documents never produce an isolatable and integral single physical figure, but instead stock an antiquarium storeroom with the sharded traces of bodily movement across the cultural landscape.

A historian of bodies approaches these fragmented traces sternum leading, a sign (*in the West since, say, the eighteenth century*) that his or her own body is seeking, longing to find, the vanished body whose motions produced them. Yes, the historian also has a body, has a sex, gender, sexuality, skin colour. And this body has a past, more or less privileged, more or less restricted. This historian's body wants to consort with dead bodies, wants to know from them: What must it have felt like to move among those things, in those patterns, desiring those proficiencies, being beheld from those vantage points? Moving or being moved by those other bodies? A historian's body wants to inhabit these vanished bodies for specific reasons. It wants to know where it stands, how it came to stand there, what its options for moving might be. It wants those dead bodies to lend a hand in deciphering its own present predicaments and in staging some future possibilities.

To that end historians' bodies amble down the corridors of documentation, inclining toward certain discursive domains and veering away from others. Yes, the production of history is a physical endeavour. It requires a high tolerance for sitting and for reading, for moving slowly and quietly among other bodies who likewise sit patiently, staring alternately at the archival evidence and the fantasies it generates. This physical practice cramps fingers, spawns sneezes and squinting.

Throughout this process historians' own techniques of the body – past practices of viewing or participating in body-centred endeavours – nurture the framework of motivations that guide the selection of specific documents. One historian's body is drawn toward domestic labour and the panoply of sexual practices. Another responds to etiquette, fashion and dance, but ignores training for sports and the military. Whatever the kinds and amounts of bodily references in any given constellation of practices, they will yield versions of historical bodies whose relation to one another is determined as much by the historian's body history as by the times they represent.

In evaluating all these fragments of past bodies, a historian's own bodily experience and conceptions of body continue to intervene. Those bodies of the past were 'plumper', 'less expansive in space', 'more constricted by dress' than our own. They tolerated 'more pain', lived with 'more dirt'. The 'ankle was sexier', the face 'less demonstrative', the 'preference for vertical equilibrium more pronounced', than in our time. Even the space 'between'

SUSAN LEIGH FOSTER

bodies and the codes for 'touching' and 'being touched' signalled differently from today.

These comparisons reflect not only a familiarity with corpo-realities but also a historian's interpretation of their political, social, sexual and aesthetic significance. Any of the body's features and movements – the space it occupies, its size and dispositions, the slowness, quickness, or force with which it travels, a body's entire physicality – reverberate with this cultural significance twice over: Physical actions embodied these values when the body was alive and kicking, whatever documentary apparatus registered its actions then re-evaluated as it re-inscribed the body's semiotic impact.

But if those bodies of the past incorporate a historian's bodily predilections, its political and aesthetic values, they also take shape from the formal constraints imposed by the discipline of history. Historians' bodies have been trained to write history. They have read widely among the volumes that compose the discourse of history and from them learned how to stand apart in order to select information, evaluate its facticity, and formulate its presentation in accordance with general expectations for historical research. From this more distant locale, they work to mould the overall shape of historical bodies by asking a certain consistency, logic and continuity from the many and disparate inferences of which they are composed. They have also listened to authorial voices within histories that strive to solidify themselves so as to speak with transcendental certainty. From these voices they have learned that pronouncements about the past should issue in sure and impartial tones. They have deduced that historians' bodies should not affiliate with their subjects, nor with fellow historians who likewise labour over the secrets of the past. Instead, those voices within past histories teach the practice of stillness, a kind of stillness that spreads across time and space, a stillness that masquerades as omniscience. By bestilling themselves, modestly, historians accomplish the transformation into universal subject that can speak for all.

But dead bodies discourage this staticity. They create a stir out of the assimilated and projected images from which they are concocted, a kind of stirring that connects past and present bodies. This affiliation, based on a kind of kinesthetic empathy between living and dead but imagined bodies, enjoys no primal status outside the world of writing.[2] It possesses no organic authority; it offers no ultimate validation for sentiment. But it is redolent with physical vitality and embraces a concern for beings that live and have lived. Once the historian's body recognizes value and meaning in kinesthesia, it cannot dis-animate the physical action of past bodies it has begun to sense.

Tensing slightly closed eyelids, some bodies dimly appear: glancing, grasping, running in fear, standing stoically, sitting disgraced, falling defiantly, gesturing enticingly. In that dream-like space that collects filmed or performed reconstructions of the past, visual images from the past, and textual references to past bodies, historical bodies begin to solidify. *The head tilts at an angle; the rib cage shifts to the side; the writing body listens and waits as fragments of past bodies shimmer and then vanish.*

If writing bodies demand a proprioceptive affiliation between past and present bodies, they also require interpretation of their role in the cultural production of meaning: their capacities for expression, the relationships between body and subjectivity they may articulate, the bodily discipline and regimentation of which they are capable, the notions of individuality and sociality they may purvey. The facts as documented in any recorded discourses, however, do not a body's meaning make. They substantiate the causal relationship between body and those cultural forces that prod, poke and then measure its responsiveness. They substantiate only bodily reaction. They lie askew from a body's significance and in its wake. And even a historian's movements among them cannot draw them together so as to fashion meaning for a past body's candid stance or telling gesture. The construction of corporeal meaning depends on bodily theorics – armatures of relations through which bodies perform individual, gendered, ethnic, or communal identities.[3]

Bodily theorics already exist embedded in the physical practices with which any given historian's body is familiar. Each of his or her body's various pursuits elaborates notions of identity for body and person, and these conjoin with the values inscribed in other related activities to produce steadier scenarios of who the body is in secular, spectacular, sacred, or liminal contexts. Any standardized regimen of bodily training, for example, embodies, in the very organization of its exercises, the metaphors used to instruct the body, and in the criteria specified for physical competence, a coherent (or not so coherent) set of principles that govern the action of that regimen. These principles, reticulated with aesthetic, political, and gendered connotations, cast the body who enacts them into larger arenas of meaning where it moves alongside bodies bearing related signage.

Theorics of bodily significance likewise exist for any prior historical moment. Circulating around and through the partitions of any established practice and reverberating at the interstices among distinct practices, theorics of bodily practices, like images of the historical body, are deduced from acts of comparison between past and present, from rubbing one kind of historical document against others. In the frictive encounters between texts, such as those expressing aesthetic praise, medical insights, proscriptive conduct, and recreational pursuits, theorics of bodily significance begin to consolidate.

The first glimmerings of body theorics put meaning into motion. Like the shapes that pieces from a puzzle must fit, theorics contour bodily significance within and among different bodily practices. Theorics allow

185

interpolation of evidence from one practice where meaning is specified to another where it has remained latent, thereby fleshing out an identity for bodies that informs a specific inquiry and also the larger array of cultural practices of which they are a part. Theorics make palpable ways in which a body's movement can enact meaning.

Not all writing bodies, however, fit into the shapes that such theorics make for them. Some wiggle away or even lash out as the historian escorts them to their proper places, resisting and defying the sweep of significance that would contain them. In the making of the historical synthesis between past and present bodies, these bodies fall into a no-man's-land between the factual and the forgotten where they can only wait for subsequent generations of bodies to find them.

I gesture in the air, a certain tension, speed, and shape flowing through arm, wrist, and hand. I scrutinize this movement and then feel my torso lift and strain as I search for the words that would describe most accurately this gesture's quality and intent. I repeat the movement, then rock forward insistently, pressing for a conversion of movement into words. A sudden inhalation, I haven't taken a breath in many seconds. I am a body yearning toward a translation. Am I pinning the movement down, trapping it, through this search for words to attach to it? This is what we thought when we thought it was the subject doing the writing. We thought any attempt to specify more than dates, places and names would result in mutilation or even desecration of the body's movement. We gave ourselves over to romantic eulogies of the body's evanescence, the ephemerality of its existence, and we revelled in the fantasy of its absolute untranslatability. Or else, and this is merely the complementary posture, we patted the mute dumb thing on the head and explained to it in clearly enunciated, patronizing tones that we would speak for it, thereby eviscerating its authority and immobilizing its significance.

It is one thing to imagine those bodies of the past, and it is another to write about them. The sense of presence conveyed by a body in motion, the idiosyncrasies of a given physique, the smallest inclination of the head or gesture of the hand – all form part of a corporeal discourse whose power and intelligibility elude translation into words. Bodies' movements may create a kind of writing, but that writing has no facile verbal equivalence. In commencing to write a historical text, discrepancies between what can be moved and what can be written require of historians yet another form of bodily engagement and exertion. Yes, the act of writing is a physical labour, rendered more vividly so, when the subject of that writing is bodily movement resurrected from the past by the imagination.

But to construe bodies' movements as varieties of corporeal writing is already a step in the right direction. Where bodily endeavours assume the status of forms of articulation and representation, their movements acquire a status and function equal to the words that describe them. The act of writing about bodies thereby originates in the assumption that verbal discourse cannot speak *for* bodily discourse, but must enter into 'dialogue' *with* that bodily discourse. The written discourse must acknowledge the grammatical, syntactical and rhetorical capacities of the moved discourse. Writing the historical text, rather than an act of verbal explanation, must become a process of interpretation, translation and rewriting of bodily texts.

How to transpose the moved in the direction of the written. Describing bodies' movements, the writing itself must move. It must put into play figures of speech and forms of phrase and sentence construction that evoke the texture and timing of bodies in motion. It must also become inhabited by all the different bodies that participate in the constructive process of determining historical bodily signification. How could the writing record these bodies' gestures toward one another, the giving and taking of weight, the coordinated or clashing momentum of their trajectories through space, the shaping or rhythmic patterning of their danced dialogue?

And what if the bodies I am writing about spring off the page or out of my imagination, I don't know which, and invite me to dance. And what if I follow and begin to imitate their movements. As we dance alongside one another – not the euphoric dance of the self-abandoned subject, not the deceptively effortless dance of hyperdisciplined bodies, but instead, the reflexive dance of self-critical bodies who none the less find in dancing the premise of bodily creativity and responsiveness – I'm not leading or following. It seems as though this dance we are doing is choreographing itself through me and also that I am deciding what to do next. Dancers have often described this experience as the body taking over, as the body thinking its own thoughts ... but this is as inaccurate as it is unhelpful; it is merely the inverse, again, of the pen-pushing body.

At some point, historical bodies that have formed in the imagination and on the written page can seem to take on a life of their own. The historical inquiry takes on sufficient structure and energy to generate meaning and to narrate itself. Its representational and narrational determinants, infused with their author's energy and with the vibrancy of dead bodies, begin to perambulate on their own. When this transformation in the nature of the inquiry occurs, a corresponding redefinition of authorial function also takes place: The author loses identity as the guiding authority and finds him or herself immersed in the process of the project getting made. *This is not mystical; it's really quite bodily. Rather than a transcendence of the body, it's an awareness of moving with as well as in and through the body as one moves alongside other bodies.*

The transformation in authorial identity shares nothing in common with the appearance of modest objectivity that the universal subject works to achieve. The universalist voice, even as it strives not to contaminate the evidence, not to neglect any point of view, none the less treats the historical subject as a body of facts. Similarly, the partisan voice, fervently dedicated to rectifying some oversight and to actively exposing an area of deficiency in historical knowledge, approaches the past as fixed sets of elements whose relative visibility needs only an adjustment. If, instead, the past becomes embodied, then it can move in dialogue with historians, who likewise transit to an identity that makes such dialogue possible.

In this dancing out of all the parts that have been created, historians and historical subjects reflect upon as they re-enact a kind of improvised choreographic process that occurs throughout the research and writing of history: As historians' bodies affiliate with documents about bodies of the past, both past and present bodies redefine their identities. As historians assimilate the theories of past bodily practices, those practices begin to designate their own progressions. As translations from moved event to written text occur, the practices of moving and writing partner each other. And as emerging accounts about past bodies encounter the body of constraints that shape the writing of history, new narrative forms present themselves.

To choreograph history, then, is first to grant that history is made by bodies, and then to acknowledge that all those bodies, in moving and in documenting their movements, in learning about past movement, continually conspire together and are conspired against. In the process of committing their actions to history, these past and present bodies transit to a mutually constructed semiosis. Together they configure a tradition of codes and conventions of bodily signification that allows bodies to represent and communicate with other bodies. Together they put pen to page. Together they dance with the words. Neither historian's body nor historical bodies nor the body of history become fixed during this choreographic process. Their edges do not harden; their feet do not stick. Their motions form a byway between their potential to act upon and be acted upon. In this middle ground they gesture toward one another, accumulating a corpus of guidelines for choreographic signification as they go, making the next moves out of their fantasies of the past and their memory of the present.

Bodily musings

I can see them now, Clio and Terpsichore, costumed in their combat boots and high-top sneakers, their lycra tights and baggy trousers, a leather jacket, a vest, under which can be glimpsed unshaven armpits, perhaps even a bow tie or some plastic bananas as a hairpiece . . . I can feel them spinning, lurching, sidling and smashing up against one another, laughing knowingly as they wipe the sweat off foreheads and from the skin between lips and nose; in a standoff, carefully calculating the other's weight and flexibility, careening toward one another, rolling as one body and then failing apart, only to circle around for a fast-paced repartee, trading impersonations of past historians and choreographers they have inspired. Wickedly realistic details of one caricature set the other muse in motion. These simulated bodies pop out of theirs, a kinetic speaking-in-tongues, only to be displaced by other corporeal quiddities. Finally, they run out of steam, collapse on the ground, adjust a sock, scratch an ear. But these pedestrian gestures, infused with the natural reflexiveness of all muses, doubly theatricalized by the attentive gaze of the partner, commence yet another duet: the crossing of legs in response to the lean on an elbow, a tossing of hair in response to a sniffle. This duet rejuvenates itself endlessly. It has an insatiable appetite for motion.[4]

But where are they dancing, Clio and Terpsichore? in what landscape? what occasion? and for whom? No longer capable of standing in contemplative and gracious poses, no longer content to serve as the inspiration for what others create, these two muses perspire to invent a new kind of performance, the coordinates of which must be determined by the intersection of historiographies of dance and of body. But what will they claim as their dance's origin? How will they justify their new choreographic/scholarly endeavour?

Sifting through images of originary bodies, Clio and Terpsichore stumble upon an account of the origins of dance and also of rhetoric, the discipline that, after all, spawned that of history, iterated in the introductions to several handbooks on rhetorical practices written after the third century AD and up until the Byzantine period. These mytho-historic anecdotes focus on the city of Syracuse at a moment when the tyrants Gelon and Hieron rule with savage cruelty. In order to ensure total control over the populace, they forbid Syracusans to speak. Initially, citizens communicate with the rudimentary gestures of hand and head that index their basic needs. Over time, however, their gestural language, now identified as *orchestike*, or dance-pantomime, attains a communicative flexibility and sophistication that leads to the overthrow of the tyrants. In the elated confusion that follows, one citizen, a former adviser to the tyrants, steps forward to bring order to the crowd. Integrating gestural and spoken discourses, he organizes his arguments into an introduction, narration, argument, digression and epilogue, the fundamental structural categories of rhetoric, the art of public persuasion.

In this account, the tyrant's eradication of speech – a levelling gesture that sweeps across public and private spaces – puts all citizens, male and female, those with expertise in logos and those who excel at chaos, on the same footing. From this common place, the rebellious bodies of the citizens slowly infuse movement with linguistic clout. They circulate around the tyrant, conspiring on a tacit and circumspect kinegraphy that not only indicates their expressive and physical needs but also a reflexive awareness of their predicament. Eventually, their collaborative subversion prevails, and the tyrant is overthrown. In this moment of political liminality (*and taking precisely the amount of time necessary to leap an epistemic fault*) the dancing body, forged in subversive communality, feeds/bleeds into the rhetorical body, a public and powerful figure. The reinstantiation of speech, however, does not return the community to speech as formerly practised. Instead, the speaking body attains new eloquence, a new fascination, a new and seductive hold over its listeners.

What seems so promising about this story, beyond its delicious obscurity or its singular pairing of dance and rhetoric, as an originary pretext for Clio and Terpsichore's duet? They are not immediately sure, for it takes the two muses hours of negotiation (danced and spoken) to arrive at an interpretation they can agree upon: Clio initially refuses to believe that the rhetorical body, once originated, had retained any resonances of the dancing body. Terpsichore sulkily retreats into silence, gesturing with dignity and disdain the absolute untranslatability of her art. Clio, attempting to dialogue, praises the primordial status of dance, mother of all the arts. Terpsichore, infinitely bored by this guilt-ridden and misguided tribute, accuses Clio of inspiring only desiccated, static drivel. Now, they're mad: they stomp; they shout; they hyperbolize; they posture; they pinch their faces, hunch their shoulders, and spit out the most absurd and hurtful provocations, then feign distress, victims of their own drama. But in the ensuing silence, the choreography of their combat in its full rhetorical glory stands out. Embarrassed by their excesses, but intrigued by the aesthetics of their anger, they cannot resist a candid glance at one another. Biting their lips to keep from laughing, they determine to continue their deliberations.

Terpsichore senses the need to rationalize choreography as persuasive discourse, and Clio realizes the need to bring movement and fleshiness into historiography. They both agree that they cannot help but admire the immense power in the resistive wariness of those bodies that have tangled with the demonic character of a tyrant. And they sense the strength of a choreographic coalition composed of multiple constituencies. They desire bodies capable of troping, that can render or depict, or exaggerate, or fracture, or allude to the world, bodies that can ironize as well as metaphorize their existence. Troping bodies do not merely carry a message or faithfully convey an idea, but also assert a physical presence, one that supports the capacity for producing meaning. Irresistibly, such bodies retain no authority over some transcendental definition of their being, but instead remain entirely dependent on their own deictic gestures to establish identity.

Clio and Terpsichore have watched this troping body emerge in their own collaborations. They believe in this body that fuses dance and rhetoric, but they also sense, just as the story predicts, its sinister potential. It can become powerful enough to sway other bodies, or even fix them in its hold. It cannot command such power if other bodies have learned the choreographic and rhetorical conventions through which meaning is conveyed. As long as every body works to renew and recalibrate these codes, power remains in many hands. But if any bodies allow this body of conventions to overtake them unawares, then the tyrannical body gains the upper hand.

Determined to keep such tyrants disembodied, *Clio and Terpsichore finish their coffee, roll up their sleeves, and begin to write (or is it dance?):*

Post-script

The claim for a writing-dancing body, formulated in response to political exigencies of this specific moment, dates itself in the kind of inscription it undertakes to make apparent. At another moment and given different political circumstances, the metaphor of a bodily tropology might well prove reactionary rather than resistive. At such a time Clio and Terpsichore might agree instead to reinvent a separation between body and writing so as to preserve the powers of both rhetoric and dance. In a world, for example, beyond script, one consisting only of screens of simulacra that invite us to don virtual reality gear and dive through ever-unfolding windows of images, what could give the body's presence or its vanishing urgency over other visions?

NOTES

1 Roland Barthes opened up for consideration this approach to bodily writing most palpably through his attention to the physical circumstances surrounding his own profession as a writer in, among other writings, his autobiography (1977a).
2 The concept of kinesthetic empathy is inspired by dance critic John Martin's conception of inner mimicry (1939).
3 The *Oxford English Dictionary* identifies two meanings for the archaic word theoric, one pertaining to the theoretical and the other to the performative. In resurrecting this term, I am trying to gesture in both directions simultaneously.
4 Cunningham's influence on this duet between Clio and Terpsichore is explicated more fully in my book *Reading Dancing: Bodies and Subjects in Contemporary American Dance* (1986).

PART V

LOCATING DANCE IN HISTORY AND SOCIETY

The relationship between dance and its socio-historical context is complex, for dance does not simply 'reflect' the value systems, customs and habits of a society but actively constructs them. It produces as well as re-produces; speaks about society, and to it. Helen Thomas' proposal for a sociology of dance that 'elucidates not only how dance is understandable as a feature of the socio-cultural context of its creation, but also how it constitutes reflexively a significant resource for understanding that context itself' (1995: 30) can also be extended to a study of its history.

Dance historiography has suffered, perhaps more than the recording of most other forms of cultural activity, from a glossy veneer of glamour, myth and mystery. There are, of course, exceptions, but the focus on the history of the stars, the often self-promoting mythologization of the performer/choreographer and the lack of any conscious attempt to locate dance within the broader aspects of its cultural context (see Carter 1995) have resulted in a rather rosy-cosy view of the prime movers of dance and the dance heritage itself. Writers are now beginning to examine their subjects with more critical distance, not in order to negate their achievements but to place those achievements within the real world of politics, economics and commerce. Lynn Garafola's work on Serge Diaghilev (1989); Susan Manning's on Mary Wigman (1993), both included in this anthology, and Ann Daly's on Isadora Duncan (1995) are examples of this more balanced and critically adroit view of dance history.

Many hypotheses about dance rest, explicitly or otherwise, on two fundamental beliefs about its evolution and its universality; these beliefs infiltrate both scholarly and commonsense discourse. They are, first, that dance has progressed from the 'primitive' through to the 'civilized' and the steps on this evolutionary ladder are embodied in various dance genres. Thus, for example, folk dance goes further 'back' and is more rooted in the culture of 'the everyday'; it is therefore (and paradoxically) perceived as of less value

193

than ballet, which is the apex of civilized Western achievement. Second, is the syllogism that as all human beings move, and dance is movement, then everyone dances. Andrée Grau undermines the certainty with which these beliefs are held and points to how deduction, inference and speculation about the beginnings of dance and the reasons why people dance have somehow become established as fact. Furthermore, our ethnocentric impositions as to what the origins, histories and meanings of dances of other cultures must be seen to be just that – impositions. Although the claims for a progressive development of dance and its transcultural practice might seem to enhance its status, these claims result in a hierarchical notion that privileges present over past, 'ours' over 'theirs'. Grau argues, however, that 'because dance can mean so many things to different people around the world, it is essential not to impose our beliefs and concepts on to others'. Unless supported by evidence, either empirical or phenomenological, claims about the origins of dance remain myths. Furthermore, by anthropomorphizing the movements of the natural world and according the status of 'dance' to a whole variety of human movement, different kinds of concepts and activities are falsely conflated.

Some periods in dance history have been more prone than others to a different kind of mythologizing, and the Romantic period is one of these. As Jowitt points out, ballet in Western Europe during the first part of the nineteenth century (predominantly between the 1830s and 1850s) was the site of considerable ambiguity. In those dance works which have become synonymous with the period, the ballerina was etherealized whilst her dance technique demanded more and more strength and concealed virtuosity. The ballet itself provoked poetic and impassioned response, yet was also considered a less respectable, and therefore less respected art. Women were put on a metaphorical pedestal but men would be enticed to the theatre so they could literally look up their skirts. In her exposition of the period, Jowitt locates ballet within the wider world of Romanticism, and her writing is significant for this breadth of perspective.

Breadth of perspective is also the keynote of Lynn Garafola's opus on Serge Diaghilev and the Ballets Russes. A considerable amount of literature already exists on this period; as previously discussed in the General Introduction, dance historiography in Britain developed apace with the key texts that were produced by those whose enthusiasm was fired by the experience of seeing the Ballets Russes. Garafola is more distanced in time and in place; standing back, she places her subject within a far broader context of politics, economics, business and art, noting how audiences were not only cultivated in taste but cultivated in their very composition. As her research on audiences shows, it is not just an aesthetic or artistic imperative which drives a dance company: money, fashion and the demands of the market were (and are) highly significant influences on the repertoire. The circumstances of production are inextricably tied to the politics of consumption.

Elizabeth Dempster's exposition demonstrates the difficulty of attempting a neat categorization of the literature which has evolved from recent dance scholarship. Dempster considers the body in both its conceptual and corporeal form, tracing attitudes to, or rejection of the 'natural' body in ballet, modern and postmodern dance. Her historical trajectory is supported by analyses of dance works in which she focuses on how the body is constructed – and deconstructed – in performance. An examination of how women 'write the body' offers Dempster the methodological framework of gender, but this does not limit her to one disciplinary allegiance or perspective. Although commonplace now, writings on women and dance heralded a new transdisciplinary approach which identified dance as a key performer in the construction and circulation of social hegemonies.

Nevertheless, despite these epistemological advances, the neglect of dance in the wider world of scholarship is well exemplified by the case of African American vernacular dance, even though, as Malone claims, 'dance touches upon almost every aspect of African American life' (and, of course, transgresses these cultural and geographical boundaries). While acknowledging the distinctiveness of dance, it can also be read as demonstrating cultural values – and creative processes – which are shared with activities of similar origins and contexts. Malone identifies several characteristics of what she terms African American cultural style, noting particularly the commonalities between dance and music. Such an analysis, however, does not hold culture or dance in stasis, but demonstrates what Desmond (Part IV) calls the transmission or migration of dance styles and their embodied ideologies.

As the writings in this Part demonstrate, locating dance in its historical and cultural context is a dynamic activity. New theories, perspectives or disciplinary approaches offer new readings; new sources emerge or old sources are resignified, and established 'facts' become malleable and transform into different kinds of knowledge about dance and society.

FURTHER READING

Dance and politics: Prickett (1989 and 1990)
Ballets Russes: Garafola (1989); Drummond (1997)
Romantic Ballet: Alderson (1987); Garafola (1997)
Gender and dance: Dempster (1988) and see Further Reading, Part IV
African American vernacular dance: Malone (1996); Emery (1988). Adamczyk (1989) offers an annotated bibliography on Black dance. *Dance Research Journal* (1983) includes four articles on popular dance in Black America
Cross-cultural perspectives: Khan (1990); Copeland (1992); Kirschenblatt-Gimblett (1995)

22

MYTHS OF ORIGIN

Andrée Grau

Where does dance come from? How did it all evolve, with the dawn of humanity? How does a child acquire the ability to dance? These questions seem to have been with us for as long as people have been writing about dance. The most prolific time for discussing the origins of dance was undoubtedly the Victorian era, when scholars were preoccupied with the origins of just about everything.[1]

The evolutionary fallacy

In *Ten Lectures on Theories of the Dance* (1991) semasiologist Drid Williams presents a thorough review of the dance literature available to dance scholars today.[2] She constructs a sort of intellectual genealogy, examining critically the manner in which various writers over the years have attempted to understand and account for danced behaviours and for the beliefs and practices of those who dance. She demonstrates quite clearly how inadequate, often ludicrous, is much of what has been written about dance. She shows that writers have seen the origins of dance in sex, in play, in animal behaviour, or in magic, to mention a few examples. This made her conclude that 'in short, the dance could have begun in nearly any primordium that anyone cares to postulate and its essence has been located nearly everywhere' (1991: 7).

Her examples could be regarded as amusing and eccentric pieces of dance theorizing, if one could see a progression throughout the years from ignorance to understanding.[3] Unfortunately this is not the case and many recent works are as ill-informed as earlier ones. One finds dance scholars in the 1960s and even the 1980s still using evolutionary theories, long discredited and outdated in the social sciences (for example, see Rust 1969 or Lonsdale 1981). Until fairly recently most dance history books started with a chapter on 'primitive' dancing, moved up the evolutionary ladder to 'folk' dancing, then on to non-European 'classical' forms, finally reaching the ultimate: Western theatrical dance! In these volumes human 'progress' is presented as

197

a given, an unchallengeable 'truth'. 'We' are at one end of the scale, the 'primitives' are at the other, and everyone else is somewhere on the continuum. Similarly, the dance taxonomies of today are rooted in Victorian beliefs and ideology. When dancers, teachers, critics or historians use the term 'ethnic dance', for example, they are separating 'our' dancing from 'theirs'. They are, probably unknowingly, perpetuating the evolutionary fallacy.

The universalist fallacy

Recently one could read these words:

> Under a father's eager palm, the taut skin of a mother's belly ripples once, then again, prodded from within by a force that only a mother and father could identify: 'It's a hand, no, a foot, an elbow, maybe a knee . . .' Whatever the limb, the happy parents take its stirring as a sure sign of new life; they attribute to the quickening foetus a command, however rudimentary, of a basic human impulse: the thrusts and flexions and twists and turns of self-generated movement . . . The impulse to move is the raw material that cultures shape into evocative sequences of physical activity that we call dance.
>
> (Jonas 1992: 12)

This supposedly profound statement is the opening of a beautifully produced book, *Dancing: the Pleasure, Power, and Art of Movement*, written by Gerald Jonas, a distinguished writer with the *New Yorker*. Is this the current popular belief that we are supposed to hold about the beginning of dance? The book was, after all, accompanying a multi-million US dollars television series about dance around the world, shown on prime time television.

These kinds of statement take us right back to the beginning of the twentieth century when Havelock Ellis (1923) argued that 'life is a dance' because the whole world is filled with unceasing movement or that 'the dance is the basis of all the arts that find their origins in the human body' (1914). Why should dancing be singled out in such a way? Why not walking, or eating? After all, most human beings engage in these activities more frequently than they do in dancing. To argue that since dancing is movement, and movement is universal, dancing is universal and therefore the basis for all the arts, is nothing but a false syllogism.

Speculations

Looking into the origins of the act of dancing is very difficult: we cannot even know the origins of some dance forms that are still in existence today, because of the absence of historical evidence. So how can we talk with authority about prehistorical times? Any discussion can only be speculative.

We know human beings have been on earth for over 300,000 years, but that language only evolved about 40,000 years ago with the emergence of *Homo sapiens sapiens*. How did the first men and women communicate? We have no way of knowing for sure, but informed by the work of prehistorians, physical-anthropologists, and biologists, we can make intelligent guesses. Livingstone, for example, suggested that since singing is a simpler system than speech, with only pitch as a distinguishing feature, human beings probably sang long before they could talk and that 'singing was in fact a prerequisite to speech and hence language' (1973: 25). Hewes, discussing the gestural origins of language, argued that 'the ability to acquire propositional language based on gesture is . . . an older innate character [of human beings]' and that 'manual communication may thus come closer to representing the deep cognitive structure on which not only language but all of our intellectual and technological achievements rest' (1973: 11). Thus one can reasonably assume that prior to the emergence of *Homo sapiens sapiens*, human beings communicated by gestures and sounds. Dance could well have been used as a way of communicating feelings and emotions, since dance is sometimes used in such a way today.[4]

Looking at early paintings or sculptures also fosters speculation, though of course it is likely that people danced before they started painting and sculpting. For example, in the cave of Trois-Frères in the Ariège, South West France, we can see a figure engraved and painted in the rock 10,000 years ago. It shows someone, man or woman, wearing a large horned mask, whirling. Throughout the world today we see whirling movements in 'religious' dances. Maybe the picture in Trois-Frères shows a religious dance performed by a healer. Similar engravings have been found in Southern Africa and other parts of the world. One could therefore postulate the idea that 10,000 years ago human beings, in many areas of the world, danced to contact the supernatural world.

Obviously one has to be very careful with these kinds of speculations and not enter the realm of fantasy. The French dance historian Paul Bourcier (1978), for instance, relates an interesting anecdote. Based on the evidence found in the cave of Pech-Merle, in the Lot region of France, some dance writers described a prehistorical danced ceremony: 12,000 years ago women would come, with their children, to dance in the cave in the hope of becoming fertile once more. Looking at the footprints in the clay, they argued that the women danced with their children in front of them, and that they used a binary rhythm, with the main beat onto the left foot. How easily one can imagine these women and children dancing by torch light . . . However, looking at the actual physical evidence in Pech-Merle, what does one find? Two footprints of a child, the right and the left, and slightly behind it, deep into the ground, one footprint of a woman's left foot! Not quite the image of pilgrims presented by the imaginative dance writers.

Dance writers have looked at the dances of people today who have economic systems similar to Neolithic ones, arguing that from these dances one could deduce how primeval dances looked. However, once again, one has to be very wary: one cannot look at the dances of people who have little technology and appear relatively primitive – such as the Australian Aborigines, or the San of Southern Africa, who used to be called Bushmen – and expect them to illustrate how early men and women danced. All the dances we see today, be they performed by the Venda people, one of the many African nations,[5] or by the members of the Royal Ballet, are contemporary dances, in the sense that they are performed by present-day people. The San or Aborigines are *not* Stone Age people, they are twentieth-century people who have developed in ways different from ours. In addition, why should there be a link between the complexity of a people's technology and the complexity of its dances? (In the late 1960s Choreometrics, an American research project led by Alan Lomax at Columbia University, tried to link dance styles and economic developments. It was criticized and discredited by many dance scholars such as Joanne Keali'inohomoku, Judith Lynne Hanna, and Drid Williams, because of its underlying evolutionary ideology.)

Every dance says something about the history of the people who created it, but every dance is also a re-invention. *Swan Lake* performed in, for instance, Birmingham in 1993, gives us clues as to what *Swan Lake* performed in Saint Petersburg in 1895 was like, but it is not the same *Swan Lake*. Similarly *Tjilati*, the brolga dance of the Tiwi people of Northern Australia, performed today at a ritual, may give us indications as to how it may have looked 10,000 years ago, but it is not the *same* dance.

For centuries, people have led varied life styles, sometimes even when living in neighbouring countries, and we cannot look at *one* history of *one* dance. We have to look at *many* histories of many dances. *Tjilati is not* the ancestor of *Swan Lake*!

Dance writers, inclined towards ethology (the study of the behaviour of animals in their normal environment), may look into animal dance-like behaviours as a way of discovering a primordium for the dance. An anthropologist, however, would argue that dance can only be a human activity. Animals may have a limited range of communication signals that may have a dance-like quality, such as the so-called mating dances found among a number of species, yet these are very different from human dances. They exist within tightly circumscribed biological and genetic constraints. They do not incorporate displaced references – the ability to communicate about things and persons outside of spatial and temporal contiguity – nor do they include metaphor, metonym, or reflexivity, all of which are intrinsically linked with human dances.

A global perspective

It is quite clear that, interesting as they may be, speculations about primeval dance do not lead us very far. More pertinent to our understanding of dance would be to ask dancers today where they believe dance comes from. The Tiwi, for example, would argue that Purukupali, the hero from the Dreamtime, the mythological time when the world was created, choreographed the first dance to mourn the death of his son Tinani. He then taught the Tiwi a sequence of dances so that they, too, could commemorate the dead. For the Venda, dance was created to express the spirit of community. By dancing together unique links were established between individuals. Yet in other societies dance is held to have existed before human beings and even been instrumental in the creation of the world. Shiva Nataraja, for example, danced the world into being according to Hindu mythology. In our own society dancers often say that dance comes from their unconscious, from deep down within them. They also talk about being 'inspired' into creating dances, as if there is someone, something, somewhere whispering in their ears, giving them glimpses of wonderful dances.

Because dance can mean so many different things to different people around the world, it is essential not to impose our beliefs and concepts onto others. In order to move away from the pervasive Eurocentric viewpoint dance scholars should investigate their biases and broaden their perspectives. They can leave theorizing on the origins of dance behind in the Victorian era, where it belongs, and concentrate on dance issues which can be substantiated by evidence. If, to use Judith Lynne Hanna's expression, 'to dance is human', then by opening out to a 'global perspective' of dance we may indeed throw light on the meaning of our humanity.

NOTES

1 Typical examples of 'Victorian dance scholarship' would be Grove (1895) or Harrison (1913). It is important to note that scientific/academic writing is never divorced from the context in which it is written and that the past is always evaluated in terms of the present. The preoccupation with 'origins' seen in much of Victorian writing is, in this respect, not that dissimilar from the preoccupation of 'postmodern' writers with 'fragmentation', 'collage' and so on.
2 The term semasiology is from a Greek source and can be defined as the study of 'signification'. Its nineteenth-century use referred to the branch of philology which dealt with the meanings of words. Williams uses it to refer to the study of human actions as sign signification (1991: 363–4).
3 Indeed some are quite extraordinary: Grove, for example, argued that dancing had its roots in 'pantomimes' intended to produce, by 'sympathetic magic', the events which they imitated. This could still be seen in the dancing of non-Western people of her days: 'what the savage mostly cares about are love, success in the chase, and prowess in war, and all these he thinks procurable by mimetic dancing' (1895: 67). Jeffrey, on the other hand, saw dancing as resulting from an over accumulation of

sex hormones! Having observed a religious movement in the Calabar region of Nigeria in the 1920s, he wrote 'in the same order of activity sponsored by the presence of excessive sex hormone would appear to be outbreaks of dancing mania. Young women . . . are the most often affected' (Jeffrey 1953: 105).

4 Anthropologist John Blacking, for example, took this approach in his stimulating article 'Dance, Conceptual Thought and Production in the Archaeological Record'. In Sieveking, *et al* 1976: 3–13.

5 One must remember that Africa consists of over fifty countries, so when people talk about 'African dance' as if it were a single entity, they are denying African peoples the panorama of creativity and individuality.

23

IN PURSUIT OF THE SYLPH: BALLET IN THE ROMANTIC PERIOD

Deborah Jowitt

A mortal man, consumed with passion for a supernatural creature, attempts to possess her. He loses her for ever. The subject enchanted Parisian audiences of 1832 and sparked a new trend in ballet. But although Filippo Taglioni's *La Sylphide*[1] seemed to strike like a flash of lightning, a number of practical inventions, decisions and developments facilitated the emergence of the aerial ballerina and her ardent partner in tales of gossamer and gloom. Less than a year after the July Revolution of 1830 installed Louis Philippe on the French throne, the Opéra ceased to be court property. Dr Louis Véron, as the new director of what was now a private enterprise with a government subsidy, wished quite naturally to make the Opéra's productions reflect both its new independence and the power of the bourgeoisie that had triumphed the previous summer. He wanted that confident middle class in his audiences. They were already flocking to the boulevard theatres to see fairy spectacles and pantomimes, to see plays that laid on Gothic horror – their effects rendered more magical by improved stage lighting and machinery. The astute Dr Véron could see that the public craved mystery and exoticism, that they would be thrilled to see on the Opéra stage the haunted German valleys and misty Scottish fens that they had long been reading about in ballads by Goethe or Heinrich Heine and in novels by Sir Walter Scott, to see vaporous, beckoning women – firing a man's imagination even as they chilled his flesh with long, pale fingers.

The magical *verismo* of these other worlds offered escape during a period of what must have seemed a dizzying succession of sweeping political changes, particularly in France. The present government's careful middle-of-the-road policies might as easily be swept away. Science was revealing more mysteries than it explained, and religion had lost much of its potency. On the one hand, instability and uncertainty as a condition of life; on the other, a complacent, plodding morality. No wonder that the Parisian public loved to see theatre that made enigma and restlessness thrilling, but at the same time tamed it and contained it through theatrical conventions.

Up-to-date lighting equipment transformed the ballet stage into a fitting habitation for sylphs and other ethereal creatures. According to ballet historian Ivor Guest, one of Véron's first innovations at the Opéra was the installation of oil lamps with large reflectors to soften and diffuse the light. For the moonlit cloister act of Meyerbeer's opera *Robert le Diable*, he ordered the house lights extinguished. In short, he did everything that could intensify the atmosphere of light and shadow and heighten the effects of trapdoors, wires, veils, explosive powder, smoke machines, waterfalls and other marvels of stage apparatus.

Gradual developments in ballet technique made possible what was generally considered a new style of dancing, one well suited to bring fantasies to life. From Marie Taglioni and other dancers, as gifted if not as innovative, came the lightness and mobility that not only made fantasy flesh, and vice versa, but created a symbol of the unattainable far more profound than most of the ballet plots that made it possible.

Several scholars have wondered whether what we call Romantic ballet was perceived in its heyday as a vital part of the Romantic movement that flourished in painting, sculpture, music and literature. Were the flittings of these dancers truly 'Romantic' in the sense of challenging academic traditions? Was ballet not, they argue, a 'juste milieu' phenomenon that, like some of the middle-of-the-road painting of the day, simply applied a patina of Romantic imagery to traditional theatrics and to the same dance techniques that served neoclassicism? They have observed that even the most ardent of balletomanes, Théophile Gautier, thought that 'dancing is little adapted to render metaphysical themes . . . ' (Gautier 1973: 17).

It is true that ballet choreographers that we consider Romantic exploited and developed a traditional vocabulary, but an arch-Romantic like Byron did not deviate from traditional poetic forms either. And the German poet Friedrich Schlegel viewed Romantic poetry as something that would open up 'a perspective upon an infinitely increasing classicism' (Rosen and Zerner 1984: 17). In all fields of art, it was only pointless academicism that was to be resisted – like the approved genres of painting, and ballet's traditional classifications of male dancers according to physique as *danseur noble*, *demi-caractère*, or *caractère*. The choreographers' choice of particular steps within the classical vocabulary and the freer way dancers performed them did indeed 'increase' the range of classicism.

Certainly the general public did not attend the ballet for spiritual enlightenment, and it naturally lapped up spectacle and technical prowess. The *Petit Courrier des Dames* correspondent must have alarmed his Parisian readers when he described a sumptuous production of the colourful ballet *La Gitana* in Saint Petersburg in 1838. There were, he exclaimed, 500 people in the last act's masked ball, 5,000 candles, and 120 chandeliers: 'Is Europe saying the Opéra is no longer the first theatre of the world for art and splendour?' (1839: 31). When Giselle was first seen in London in 1841 in the form of a play – with dances, set to the original Adolphe Adam music, for those dangerous and alluring ghosts, the wilis – a poster advertised in huge letters what was obviously a major attraction: FIRST NIGHT OF THE REAL WATER![2]

Certainly the leaders of the Romantic movement in literature and painting – the fiercest balletomanes among them – looked down on ballet even as they delighted in it. It was, they understood, an excuse for watching pretty, lightly clad women disporting themselves. Yet everywhere their prose betrays deeper responses. Writing of Giselle in Les Beautés de l'Opéra, Gautier luxuriates in his description of the opening of Act II, when the heroine has become a wili: 'And the rising moon that shows through the slashes of the leaves her sweet, sad, opaline visage, does her transparent whiteness not remind you of some young German girl who died of consumption while reading Novalis?' (1845: 15). If some have considered Gérard de Nerval insensitive for remarking that Giselle died of loving dancing too much (Chapman 1978), what more poetic fate could await anyone: the artist dying of excess devotion to art? The Romantic imagery in these ballets goes quite deep, and, whether spectators of the day realized it or not, the dark and mysterious currents within the plots, the edge of morbidity, the hallucinatory visions drew them to the ballet as much as did the acrobatic feats of dancers and their personal charm.

Everyone may have thought, with Gautier, that ballet was suited to express only passion and amorous pursuit, but it is passion darkened by the Romantic preoccupation with the dichotomy of flesh and spirit. Many of the ballets express the despairing notion that a perfect union between man and woman is possible only beyond the grave. Few supernatural ballets ended happily. In Filippo Taglioni's La Fille du Danube (1836) and August Bournonville's Napoli (1842), the lovers are united on earth because they have proved their incorruptibility – never sullying their ideals, never swerving in their devotion to each other, no matter how many temptations or gorgeous lookalikes are strewn in their paths.

The heroes of nineteenth-century ballets behaved according to the Romantic ideal of the hero, of the artist. Customs wearied them, and they would brook no restrictions except those that they imposed themselves. Frequently they cast aside attractive women of the correct rank, amiability and certified humanness to pursue their chosen sylph, undine, or even a fey and spiritual peasant girl ((Giselle). The crucial test to which the hero is often put exemplifies a highly Romantic dilemma. Will he be steadfast to his ideal, his true love, and not be taken in by a beguiling facsimile? When young Rudolph in La Fille du Danube becomes demented because his beloved (whom he takes to be mortal) has thrown herself into the river, his friends attempt to distract him by a veiled double who dances almost as well as does his darling. Weathering this deception, he plunges into the river and into a lively throng of veiled naiads, who 'dance their mazy fascinations around him' (Heath 1977: 80). But his love has given him a posy – a talisman which helps him to distinguish between truth and illusion. In Bournonville's *Napoli*, the faithful fisherman Gennaro, searching the grottoes of the sea for his supposedly drowned Teresina, is confronted with a bevy of beguiling sea nymphs, among whom sports his reluctant, magicked sweetheart. The stage image is a familiar one: the lone man threads his way through swirling flocks of identically dressed females, looking searchingly at each one. It persists through *Swan Lake* and *The Sleeping Beauty* into Balanchine's ballets and such modern fantasies as the scene in the 1937 movie *Shall We Dance?* in which Fred Astaire dances perplexedly down a line of fetching women in Ginger Rogers masks.

True and false confront the ballet hero in subtler forms too. The tragedy of *Giselle* is often presented as arising from a nobleman's thoughtless dalliance with a peasant girl, but there is another possible interpretation: Albrecht and Giselle are soulmates, made for each other, but issues of class prevent him from recognizing this. Certainly the several great performances given in our time by Gelsey Kirkland and Mikhail Baryshnikov brought this to almost unbearably poignant life.

But although the themes of truth versus illusion, ideal versus real, that pervade so many of these ballets link them persuasively to Romanticism, the choice of subject was not the crux of the matter. According to Baudelaire (Rosen and Zerner 1984: 22), anything could be viewed 'Romantically', and he cited as characteristics of such a vision, 'intimacy, spirituality, colour, aspiration toward infinity' – all of which distinguished Romantic ballet.

Realism, an instance of 'intimacy' and a feature of much painting, was an integral part of the Romantic ballet worlds too, especially those created by August Bournonville and Jules Perrot. Even in supernatural ballets, they prided themselves on the detail of their crowd scenes, the verisimilitude with which they evoked a Highland revel or a Naples dockside or a village festival. The admittedly theatricalized naturalism, with dances justified by parties or festivals, set off the spirit world where dancing was a given and a metaphor for the restlessness of spiritual longing.

The supernatural ballets also had connections with early nineteenth-century landscape painting. Although the popularity of this genre of painting reflected the desire to turn to nature as a constant in a bewildering world, the painter – imbuing nature with his own feelings – brought out its mysteriousness, its changeability. The play of light and shadow over a field could suggest conflict among the powers of nature. The mysterious landscapes of Caspar David Friedrich are tranquil, yet disturbing; Hugh Honour has pointed out how Friedrich occasionally 'painted the foreground in great detail, but sank an immeasurable chasm between it and the distant, almost visionary, horizon, tantalizingly out of reach, creating an uneasy mood of yearning for the unattainable' (1979: 78). And in Turner's sensuous vortexes of light, nature itself becomes a shimmering dreamworld.

The air, earth, fire and water spirits of ballet awakened their lovers to the beauty of the natural world, to that landscape glinting beyond the window. In the second act of *La Sylphide*, the sylph flies to a treetop to bring down a nest for James's inspection and offers him spring water in her cupped hands. The scene must have seemed to contemporary spectators almost a visualization of Victor Hugo's popular poem 'La Fée et la Péri' in which a fairy tries to win the soul of a dying child by promising to reveal nature's secrets.

In considering how these ballets were perceived in their day, one must – as always – allow for individual sensibilities. When Hans Christian Andersen saw the 'Ballet of the Nuns' in Act II of *Robert le Diable* at the Paris Opéra in 1833, he was overwhelmed by the thrilling atmosphere of death, misty female sensuality, forbidden pleasures and religious blasphemy:

> By the hundred they rise from the graveyard and drift into the clois-
> ter. They seem not to touch the earth. Like vaporous images, they
> glide past one another. Suddenly their shrouds fall to the ground.
> They stand in all their voluptuous nakedness, and there begins a
> bacchanal like those that took place during their lifetimes, hidden
> within the walls of the convent.
>
> (Aschengreen 1974: 15)

But for every Andersen, there was undoubtedly a Fanny Appleton (later Mrs Henry Wadsworth Longfellow), who remarked in a letter that the members of the corps de ballet 'drop in like flakes of snow and are certainly very charming witches with their jaunty Parisian figures and most refined pirouettes' (Guest 1980: 112).

Marie Taglioni's style of dancing, so enchanting to audiences, was the result, not just of her sensibility, but of changes in ballet technique. The manual of classical dancing produced in 1828 by the La Scala teacher and choreographer Carlo Blasis shows how the turnout of the hips had increased since the eighteenth century, making it possible for dancers to raise their legs higher, to execute more brilliant beats, to change directions more rapidly and more fluidly. Although dancing of the 1830s would probably not strike us as particularly expansive, it would have seemed to nineteenth-century balleto-manes much freer and larger in scale than what they had seen around the turn of the century.

In this development, fashion played a role. When the *ancien régime* toppled, with it fell the ponderous, ornate and constricting clothes that went with rank and power. The soft slippers and light, loose-fitting dresses and Grecian draperies that came with, or just after, the French Revolution enabled women dancers to increase the range of their movements significantly. By the time corsets returned, the dancers had already changed, and they never looked back. Even before *La Sylphide*, Taglioni was dancing onstage in simple light dresses similar to those her mother made for her to practise in. As historian Marian Hannah Winter (1974) has remarked, fashion freed dancers' thighs. Ecstatic reviews of the way Taglioni bent from side to side confirm that it made possible some freeing of the torso as well.

Pointe work, so crucial to the image of the supernatural female, was not a new technique in 1832, although it wasn't standard equipment for all female dancers when Taglioni came to the Paris Opéra. (The 1830 edition of Blasis's manual doesn't even mention it.) Geneviève Gosselin, people remembered, had danced on her toes in 1815, maybe earlier, and 'grotesque' (meaning acrobatic) dancers of both sexes did pointe work. It was viewed more as a feat than anything else – and often seems to have been performed as one. Engravings of the little company that Filippo Taglioni assembled for the Opéra in Stuttgart later in the 1820s show all the women on pointe. It is during those years that his daughter must have worked on perfecting her own approach – discovering ways to strengthen her feet and rise onto her toes without apparent effort.

Some of the impetus for pointe work might have come from the elaborate 'flying' techniques developed by Charles Didelot. His *Zéphire et Flore* astounded London balletgoers in 1796, Saint Petersburg audiences in 1804, and Parisians in 1815 (when Mlle Gosselin reputedly stood on her toes). It was still a favourite when Taglioni performed it in Paris with Jules Perrot in 1830. Didelot didn't simply fly down some heavenly personage on a cloud to clinch the plot. Any of his dancers might fly by means of individual wires and harnesses. They could take to the air, or be carefully lowered until only the tips of their toes touched the stage floor. For imaginative choreographers and ambitious dancers, it must have seemed natural to wish to echo that effect in passages where it wasn't possible to attach someone to a wire.

Circumstances, then, conspired to produce a style of dance and stage machinery ideal for supernatural subjects. Marie Taglioni's own attributes, her classes with Auguste Vestris in Paris, and her father's taste and inspired coaching defined that style. Not all dancers copied her purity, her coolness, or her de-emphasis of athleticism, but they studied her delicate attack, her simplicity, the fluidity of her arms and torso. For example, it was remarked – as if it were a novelty – that she often held her long arms down, gently curved, instead of flourishing them about; one characteristic of the style that August Bournonville perpetuated in Copenhagen is just such a *port de bras* for jumps. It tends to make dancers look lighter and to focus the audience's attention on their nimble feet.

*

Dancers have always been praised for 'lightness', but from the 1830s until late in the century, variants of the term saturated the metaphors and similes of writers on ballet. Light as weightlessness, light as luminosity; in English the same word serves both meanings. But even in languages where the words differ, the meanings intertwine in descriptions of ballerinas. *The Times* in London described Adèle Dumilâtre's dancing as being 'so ethereal . . . that she almost looked transparent' (Guest 1984: 92). The delight caused by airy and seemingly effortless dancing, set off by mysterious lighting and gauzy, billowing skirts, seems related to the century's uneasiness about the flesh. Praising the lighting for Perrot's *Eoline*, Gautier raved that it gave the illusion that 'Eoline is only the envelope, the transparent veil of a superior being, a goddess condemned by some fate to live among men' (Guest 1984: 311). The 'condemned' is telling, and it's interesting that it comes as if automatically from the pen of a cheerful hedonist like Gautier. Insubstantiality, then, is close to godliness.

Lightness in the sense of airiness complements the notion. The buoyancy of the female dancer helped her to embody a spiritual aspiration; the lightness of a male dancer suggested the hero's desires to transcend the limits of the flesh. It could also stand for the winging of his soul as he took on some of the qualities of the sought-after dream. Even the constant motion, the restlessness for which dancers were admired, can be seen as a dissatisfaction with present existence and a yearning for realms beyond. Also, in the Romantic era, the artist-as-rebel was a favoured image. By their apparent denial of gravity, the sylphs and their kin prettily demonstrated their exemption from laws governing human behaviour. So female dancers were enthusiastically compared to birds, butterflies, balloons, feathers, moonbeams, shadows, and criticized for showing too much vigour or attack. Male dancers, generally disprized during these years, succeeded the more they resembled the women in terms of style. It was 'the aerial Perrot, Perrot the sylph, Perrot the male Taglioni' (Guest 1984: 57).

The lithographers intensified the public's fantasies of supernatural heroines. The ballerinas – even when depicting real if exotic women – seem unstable, elusive. They hover on one improbably dainty toe, not in perfect equilibrium, but leaning slightly forward as if they're just passing through the pose. When shown in midair, their bodies are softly curved, legs barely apart – less as if they'd leapt than as if they'd been blown upward. Some of the poses may be artistic conventions rather than ballet reality but the conventions were dictated by the artists' perceptions of the ballets. And as refinements of dance technique helped create the airborne images onstage, techniques in lithography developed as if in response. As Charles Rosen and Henry Zerner have pointed out, drawing on the surface of the stone made possible subtle nuances of tone and images that 'vanish at the edges' (1984: 79). The dancer becomes the glistening focal point in an evanescent and cloudy world.

She may have been an abstraction, but she was unmistakably female. In expressing the ambiguous tensions they felt between reality and spiritual longing, the ballet librettists and choreographers – almost without exception male[3] – revealed confused emotions in regard to women. On the one hand, almost all the stories were told from the hero's point of view; on the other, the ballerinas dominated the stage. Even in ballets where the hero dreamed the heroine, she was clearly superior to him – enchanting, evasive, unrestricted by his codes, and able to drift about on her toes. Yet she flew into his arms of her own accord. In the thrilling, much-discussed dream sequence in *La Péri*, Carlotta Grisi leaped from the framed platform that contained 'her world' and was bravely caught by Lucien Petipa. The audience marvelled over his strength, but was more excited by her daring, and *The Times* critic commented of some lifts in the same ballet: 'She is supported by Petipa, but seems as if supported by air alone' (Cohen 1976: 85).

Only occasionally in these ballets does a male character obviously dominate a female one. Jules Perrot, a compelling performer as well as a brilliant choreographer, created intriguing demonic roles for himself in several ballets. August Bournonville, working in Copenhagen relatively isolated from Parisian fads, refused to cater to the general dislike of male dancers; like Perrot, he was a good dancer and wanted to perform. The fairy worlds were, as a rule, unbalanced in their populations. Gautier explained that Myrtha, the Queen of the Wilis, had only female subjects, since men were 'too heavy, too stupid, too in love with their ugly hides to die such a pretty death' (1845: 17).

These rather liberated creatures imagined by men stood opposed to the respectable middle-class wife and mother (also, to some extent, a male creation). In *La Sylphide*, James's betrothed, Effie, a woman of real weight and substance, with sensible shoes and domestic talents, is far less vivid than her rival. Despite their supposed purity, the supernatural creatures are *femmes fatales*, representing all that is erotically potent and compelling about women. They offer a double message, beckoning the hero both as the incarnation of an ideal and as a temptress luring him from the straight and narrow. It isn't for nothing that Erik Aschengreen called his fine monograph on Romantic ballet 'The Beautiful Danger'.

Balletomanes were awed by the effort it took to appear effortless. In 1839, when Lucile Grahn first performed *La Sylphide* in Paris, the house held its breath to see if she would do Taglioni's 'terrible pas' of Act II, which Elssler had cut: 'C'était une question de vie ou de mort' (*Petit Courrier* 1839: 207). And what applause when she triumphed in it! Because the preferred steps for spirits were bounding ones, the labour that went into becoming ethereal was considerable: the quantities of ballottés, brisés, temps-levés, emboîtés, assemblés, cabrioles, sauts de basque, and ballonés that packed the dances

210

required strong ankles and good wind. It was thanks to Amalia Ferraris's 'supple and sinewy foot' that she was able to 'beat the *entrechat huit* to perfection' (Beaumont 1938: 225).

In the days before the blocked pointe shoe was perfected, hovering on tiptoe required immense strength. Today's dancer, wearing a blocked and stiffened slipper, stands, in effect, on her toenails, on the very tip of her toe. The vertical equilibrium is so secure that, once up there, she is almost at rest. The ballerina of the mid-nineteenth century was stepping as high onto the toe pads as possible, and could stay there only by exertion of all her leg muscles and a tremendous lift in the body. Yet in 1846, in *Paquita*, Carlotta Grisi thrilled balletomanes by fancy hops 'on the tip of the toe with a turn of dazzling vivacity' (Guest 1980: 254).

In addition, female dancers, along with the men, had to be skilled at balancing on the flat foot or half-toe for extended periods of time. The choreography of the day featured elaborate *adagio* sequences that are uncommon now except in the Bournonville repertory. Standing on one leg, the dancer would revolve smoothly, make one pretty pose metamorphose into another, bend forward or back – all without wobbling. Taglioni is said to have worked for two-hour stretches three times a day with her father while preparing for her debut. Léopold Adice's syllabus of 1859 lists a barre in which exercises are performed one hundred times each. Bournonville dancers hoisted their legs in *grands battements* a total of 320 times. To be secure in *adagio*, a dancer might work at holding one leg in the air for a hundred counts, as Marie Taglioni did. Louise Fitzjames had her maid stand on her hips to increase turnout, and Carlotta Grisi said sourly that those times Jules Perrot stood on her hips while she lay face down on the floor with legs spread were the erotic high points of their liaison. Beginners forced their turnout by standing in a box with braces that could be adjusted via a series of grooves. (No wonder Marie Taglioni was easily able to pass off one of her pregnancies as knee trouble.)

The prose devoted to ballerinas during the heyday of Romanticism makes it clear that spectators found the paradox of a real, and probably available, woman playing an incorporeal nymph a titillating one. Gautier lingers lovingly over descriptions of ballerinas' knees, ankles, breasts, noses and chins. Fanny Cerrito 'knows how to curve and soften her plump arms like the handles of an ancient Greek vase' (Chapman 1978: 33). Classical allusion aside, the sentence is unabashedly sensual.

Besides the enraptured accounts, a beguiling detritus of poems, lithographs, curios and sheet music attest to the fervour dancers inspired. Portraits of the most famous ballerinas of the day assumed curious forms. A 1984 exhibit presented by the Theatre Collection of the Austrian National Library included the following mementoes of the wildly acclaimed Fanny Elssler: a porcelain cast of her left hand, her right foot sculpted in marble, portrait medallions naming her 'Terpsichore's Darling' and images of Fanny and her sister Therese as sylphides painted on a cup and on a pipe. In terms of the souvenirs and verbiage they generated, dancers – female ones, at any rate – were the rock stars of the nineteenth-century bourgeoisie.

For the unearthly heroines of the ballets, physical union with a mortal posed usually fatal danger. The sylph lost her wings and expired. Alma, the 'daughter of fire', a statue who comes to life by day, faces a vexing dilemma: if she falls in love, she will become a statue for ever. (Seldom was an audience more tantalized by the prospect of a lovely idol falling off her pedestal.) By these standards, the women dancers of the nineteenth century were not very sylphish offstage. Salaries for all but the stars were not high; a well-to-do protector, not hard to come by, was considered by many to be a necessity. Members of the Jockey Club frequented the green room and backstage areas of the Paris Opéra; at Her Majesty's Theatre, the bloods of London could obtain seats in the 'omnibus boxes' on the sides of the stage – the better to ogle, and perhaps to pinch and pass messages. Benjamin Lumley, the director of this theatre when *Ondine* was premiered there, related that backstage one evening when Fanny Cerrito was dancing the lovely 'Pas de l'Ombre', frolicking on the seashore with her newly acquired shadow, Adeline Plunkett aimed a kick at Elisa Scheffer, her rival for the favours of the Earl of Pembroke, missed, broke the cord holding the 'moon' lamp, and temporarily extinguished Cerrito's dance (Guest 1969).

Sometimes, of course, dancers married other dancers or formed liaisons with them – as did Jules Perrot and Carlotta Grisi, Arthur Saint Léon and Fanny Cerrito, Fanny Elssler and (briefly) Anton Stuhlmüller. However, these relationships in no way exempted female performers from the solicitations of others. Young corps dancers were particularly anxious to secure wealthy protectors or husbands. Out of their meagre salaries – often made even smaller by fines levied for various infractions – they had to pay for classes, obtain practice clothes, scheme for advancement. Many came from poor families. In *Les Petits Mystères de l'Opéra* (1844), Albéric Second's satirical look at the backstage world of the Paris Opéra, one *petit rat* wears a capacious pocket under her sylph costume, into which she packs useful objects she's picked up, including a pack of cards, five or six cigar butts, a squeezed half lemon, some cheese, a scrap of soap, and a necklace. Furthermore, she says, the bulging pocket gives her a 'Spanish shape' pleasing to the gentlemen in the stalls. The same girl relates how the dancing master Cellarius lures coryphées – who rank above the girls of the quadrilles – to come to his place the three times a week when they're not performing and partner gentlemen who are ostensibly learning to waltz: five francs to dance with a chair, ten to dance with a *figarante* at the Opéra. Supper on the town afterward, where a girl can gorge . . .

Given the lack of birth control, it's not surprising that many female dancers became mothers. Ballerinas often danced well into their pregnancies. Sometimes their offspring accompanied them on their numerous tours or guest appearances. More often, the babies were brought up by grandparents or aunts or friends. 'Well, Fanny, send the brat to me,' Elssler's English friend Harriet Grote wrote cheerfully, when Fanny decided not to take her seven-year-old Therese to America. It was four years before Fanny retrieved her daughter (Guest 1972: 67).

The nineteenth-century female dancer would probably not have struck us as looking ethereal, considering her diet, childbearing, and the kind of muscles she had to develop. Fanny Elssler, to judge from her pink satin and black lace 'Cachucha' costume, was a woman of medium height with a trim, but not tiny waist and a full, curving bust. A sylph could hardly be ethereal enough in her dancing, but the woman who played her could be too ethereal to suit public taste. Gautier couldn't abide shoulder blades that stuck out ('two bony triangles that resemble the roots of a torn-off wing' – the analogy is revealing). Poor Louise Fitzjames was constantly criticized for her thin-ness. A caricaturist presented her as a dancing asparagus, and Gautier said that she wasn't 'even substantial enough to play the part of a shadow' (1973: 21). Being substantial enough to play a shadow . . . it might be considered the mission of the Romantic ballerina.

Such ballerinas were among the first to embody abstract qualities, which not all of the spectators who flocked to adore them recognized. These per-formers didn't *represent* Beauty or Music or Fecundity as had their counter-parts in earlier centuries, yet their light, fleeting, ardent dancing could suggest something larger than their stage personas and more ineffable than the roles they played.

Most of the supernatural ballets of the early nineteenth century – along with a host of other ballets of the period – have perished. The only works in this genre that can be experienced today are *Giselle* and the Danish August Bournonville's version of *La Sylphide*, his *Napoli* and *A Folk Tale* (in the last two, the heroines were not supernatural, but were temporarily in thrall to supernatural forces). All have been altered to some degree, and the *Giselle* we see today was largely re-choreographed by Marius Petipa in 1884. The poetic image of a mortal man lured by a filmy female vision into a magical world didn't perish with the decay of Romanticism, however. Trans-formed by new ideas and new styles in dancing, it bloomed again in Saint Petersburg, and years later in London and New York City. It is with us still.

NOTES

1 See original text for a fuller discussion of this ballet.
2 Playbill for Sadler's Wells Theatre, week beginning 23 August 1841.
3 Some of the exceptions are Lucile Grahn; Fanny Elssler's sister Therese; and Marie Taglioni, who choreographed *Le Papillon* in 1860 for her protégée, Emma Livry.

24

DIAGHILEV'S CULTIVATED AUDIENCE

Lynn Garafola

The forging of a new ballet audience actually began before the fabled season of 1909. Diaghilev's Paris ventures of 1906–8 usually receive short shrift. Yet from the first these magnificent events – the Exhibition of Russian Art in 1906, the Russian concert series of 1907, and the complete *Boris Godunov* in 1908 – captured the city's imagination. In these years, Diaghilev acquired a growing legion of partisans, the embryo of the cultivated elite that formed his most important public up to the War. At the same time, he assembled a band of influential critics, publicists and patrons who embraced his successive Russian enterprises and ultimately championed his ballet. The sensational triumph of the 1909 *saison russe* stemmed, in part, from the rising tide of enthusiasm for Diaghilev's previous accomplishments and the ever increasing breadth of his audience.

At the centre of this following stood the diplomats and high public officials who presided over Diaghilev's early career in the West, underscoring its political character and importance. But these alone did not suffice to create a self-sustaining audience. The public that took the Russian dancers to heart was, overwhelmingly, a musical one, a community of concert- and opera-going professionals and aficionados. The Russian Historical Concerts presented at the Paris Opéra in 1907 stirred enormous interest in that community, as did the production of *Boris Godunov* the following year. The importance of these seasons cannot be overestimated. Not only did they bring together the core public of the Ballets Russes, but as musical and, in the case of *Boris*, decorative preludes to the 1909 enterprise, they set its aesthetic tone. Composers such as Alexander Borodin and Nikolai Rimsky-Korsakov and visual artists such as Alexander Golovin, Alexandre Benois, Leon Bakst and Nicholas Roerich all contributed to the opera and ballet repertory; in both media, they reiterated the blend of sumptuousness, decorative harmony and historical veracity so appealing to audiences of *Boris*. Visually as well as musically, Diaghilev aligned his earliest ballet ventures with the aesthetic of his lyric theatre.

214

Diaghilev's initial venues emphasized this connection. Even more, they reinforced the elitist aura that Diaghilev sought to confer on ballet. If this was the stepchild of the Belle Epoque, opera was its favourite son. Wagner's lucubrations and innovative productions elevated opera from mere social pleasure to an intellectually compelling art. At the same time, his theatre at Bayreuth became the centre of a cult, a shrine to which the wealthy, cultivated tastemakers of the Belle Epoch made pilgrimage annually until World War I. Here, among the throng who crowded the Teutonic rituals of Bayreuth in the 1890s and early 1900s was the cultured, cosmopolitan and knowledgeable audience to which Diaghilev laid claim in his early years in the West. The overnight triumph of the Ballets Russes reflected Diaghilev's success in attracting this sophisticated following to his dance enterprise.

In appropriating this audience for ballet, no one proved more instrumental to Diaghilev than Gabriel Astruc. Publisher, editor, sometime playwright, and impresario of vision, Astruc moved through the many Paris worlds that came together in Diaghilev's seasons, along with a score of other enterprises that successfully located the Ballets Russes on the social and artistic landscape of Paris.

Crucial to Diaghilev's enterprise was a group of investors approached by Astruc in the spring of 1909. French by birth and nationality, this group was mostly Jewish in origin and connections. It included the most distinguished names in Jewish banking circles and many of the era's outstanding patrons, collectors and artistic dilettantes; by marriage it embraced 'regilded' aristocrats who had bartered their threadbare titles for a fortune. There is more than a touch of irony in the outpouring of Jewish wealth and Jewish support for an enterprise aimed at restoring the prestige of a regime so notoriously anti-Semitic as the Russia of Nicholas II.

Astruc's notes listing possible sources for raising the Fr.100,000 guarantee capital for Diaghilev's 1909 season amply document these overlapping interests. High on the list are bankers and financiers with a passion for the arts: Baron Henri de Rothschild, who wrote plays under the *nom de plume* of André Pascal; Camondo, who composed as well as collected and presided over the Society of Friends of the Paris Opéra; Otto Kahn, chairman of the board of the Metropolitan Opera and Henri Deutsch de la Meurthe, an international oil magnate and composer. Other names are equally revealing. Bardac, Heine, Ganay, Clermont-Tonnerre, Leonino, and Lyon were all prominent names in the arts with links to leading Jewish families and fortunes.

The core of Diaghilev's ballet public lay in the *haute bourgeoisie* that supported his own and Astruc's musical undertakings. Thanks to the booking lists (*feuilles de location*) surviving in the Archives Nationales for all seven performances of Diaghilev's 1908 production of *Boris Godunov* at the Paris Opéra, the configuration of this basic audience can now be established.[1] These documents, which indicate the occupants of boxes, loges and orchestra seats, confirm Diaghilev's overwhelming success in appropriating the serious French musical audience for the Ballets Russes. They also reveal that his public was not primarily an aristocratic one, despite the Proustian-sounding titles reported in the society columns of *Figaro*. Rather, Diaghilev's audience was an amalgam of financiers, bankers and diplomats, members of the city's foreign and Franco-Jewish communities, and personalities from the worlds of fashion, music, entertainment and the press.

Wealthy foreigners added a distinctive note to this cosmopolitan milieu. By the late nineteenth century Americans like the Princesse de Polignac and her sister the Duchesse Decazes (*née* Isabelle Singer), Comtesse Boni de Castellane (*née* Anna Gould, the railroad heiress), and Princesse Joseph de Caraman-Chimay (*née* Clara Ward of Detroit) had penetrated the barriers of the French aristocracy, restoring with their millions its threadbare façade. Other English-speaking millionaires like Mrs Bertha Potter Palmer, the Chicago biscuit manufacturer's wife, W.K. Vanderbilt, a New York railroad magnate, and James Hennessy of champagne and cognac fame, took to spending long periods in Paris, where they frequented such glamorous events as *Boris*, high points of the city's *grand saison*. This Anglo-Saxon presence, which came at a time of intense Anglophilia among the Parisian upper classes, was not the only national strain embellishing *le tout Paris*. In the decades immediately preceding World War I, the French capital became an international pleasure ground, the haunt of Argentine playboys and Indian rajahs, and a mecca for nobilities from Europe's southern and eastern periphery. Although intensely Russian, *Boris* won the ardent support of the city's Polish colony. Little love was lost between the Godebskis, Potockis, and Czartoryskis, Polish national families long resident in France, and the Russian colossus occupying their homeland. For the Poles, however, Mussorgsky transcended politics: his work sprang from the Slavic East, that cauldron of festering nationalism. In the stateless cosmopolitans who figured so prominently in Diaghilev's public, one finds an analogue to the supranationalist sensibility of his exotic fare.

The ethnic, national and cultural interests of Astruc's brilliantly fabricated audience made it particularly susceptible to both the exoticism and musical sophistication of Diaghilev's earliest dance productions. Not only did the move from opera to ballet demand relatively minor artistic shuffling, but exoticism – or more properly speaking, orientalism – was a thread woven into the high and popular art of the *fin de siècle* even if theatrical fashion and design awaited the inspiration of Bakst, Golovin and Roerich to discover it. The late nineteenth century witnessed a resurgence of interest in Far Eastern art with entrepreneurs such as Isaac de Camondo, Henri Cernuschi and Emile Guimet amassing great collections of Chinese, Japanese and Indian antiquities. Notwithstanding the influence of *japonisme* on painters and decorative designers, the substance of French orientalism

216

derived from the ancient biblical and Islamic lands that stretched from North Africa to Iran, following the course of French imperialism. Beginning in mid-century, writers, painters and interior designers found in these new spheres of European influence a rich vein of exotica that provided both motifs and thematic material for their work. With the dawn of the new century, orientalism made its appearance in dance, thanks in large part to occidental foreigners on the French stage who extended the familiar pale of exotica eastward to India. The most famous – or infamous – of these performers was Mata Hari (alias Margaretha Zelle MacLeod), who made her Paris debut at the Musée Guimet of Asiatic Arts in 1905 and subsequently appeared as Salomé and Cleopatra on the international opera house circuit. Her spectacular success (a horseback performance *au naturel* before a Sapphist gathering attended by Colette is legendary) induced other 'Hindu' dancers to try their luck in the French capital. Among these was Ruth Saint Denis, who appeared at the Théâtre Marigny in the autumn of 1906; at the Olympia a rival 'danseuse hindique' entertained audiences with an imitation of Miss Ruth's *Radha* ballet.

Despite the widespread interest in orientalia, the fashionable craze for 'oriental' colour and costume on the eve of World War I dated from Diaghilev's first ballet performances. Almost overnight, the highly colouristic and sensual vein of orientalism identified with the Ballets Russes became decorative and fashion commodities. 'The taste for oriental art came to Paris as a Russian import, through ballet, music and decoration,' commented *Figaro* in 1913. 'Russian artists have acted as intermediaries between the East and us, and they have given us a rather greater taste for oriental colour than a taste for their own art' (Delhi 1913: 1).

In subtle ways the audience that followed Diaghilev through the byways of Ballets Russes orientalia shifted the aesthetic emphasis of the company's repertory, narrowing, by virtue of its taste, the field of artistic possibilities. Exoticism wove a vivid thread in Fokine's early work, but it was only one of several colouring his imagination. Hellenism and neoromanticism were equally vivid, and in the ballets conceived outside Diaghilev's purview, these other themes and styles held their ground. Paris, however, remained cool to them. What thrilled Diaghilev's audience was the exoticism of *Cléopâtre*, *Schéhérazade*, and *Firebird*, whose visual opulence, luxurious costuming and flamboyant effects mirrored, as Paul Morand later observed, 'the boldness of the audience's dress, its immodesties, extravagant coiffures, depilated bodies, cosmetics' (Morand 1925: 154). Such opulence had been second only to music in the impression created by *Boris*, and it remained the single most important production value up to the war. The proliferation of orientalia on Diaghilev's stage between 1909 and 1914 is more than a sign of Fokine's spent imagination. Rather, it betrayed a willingness on Diaghilev's part to cater to the tastes of his public and transform a genre of limited possibilities into a commercially exploitable formula. As early as 1910 the charge of pandering to the demands of a sensation-seeking Paris audience was raised in the Saint Petersburg press by Vladimir Telyakovsky, Director of the Imperial theatres.[2] Although scarcely an unbiased source, given the history of his relations with Diaghilev and the inevitable competition between the latter's seasons and the Imperial Ballet, Telyakovsky's barbed remarks underscore a central paradox of artistic endeavour in the market-place. For if removal of institutional constraints opens the field of artistic choices, the loss of financial security imposes its own set of imperatives.

A master publicist, Diaghilev used every means possible to create an artistic and social 'splash', pressing salons, newspapers and embassy contacts into service for *Boris* and his early dance seasons. With each succeeding year, however, the need to surpass previous successes became more urgent. With the formation of a permanent company, it became an economic necessity. Diaghilev now set out to entice the merely fashionable to grand 'celebrity' events.

Charity galas and other special performances were among the ways Diaghilev created that aura of social-cum-artistic uniqueness that became his company's trademark. The first *répétition générale* of the 1910 season marked the occasion of an extremely fashionable charity event, although because of a mishap to the scenery en route from Berlin, it had to be cancelled. Two weeks later, however, the company gave *The Polovtsian Dances* and *Le Festin* on a gala Opéra programme that also included Richard Strauss's *Salomé* and a *Coppélia* in which the Opéra's Mlle Léa Piron *en travesti* partnered Carlotta Zambelli as Swanilda. On July 1 Russians and French again pooled their talents. For this unique event, *Cléopâtre* shared a bill with *Rigoletto* and the ballet divertissement from *Thaïs*. Events of this kind, duly reported in the society columns of *Figaro*, added immeasurably to the cachet of Diaghilev's enterprise.

Open rehearsals were another device calculated to bring fashionable Paris to the theatre. In June 1910 *Figaro* carried notices of three *Firebird* rehearsals, reporting the ballet's 'most considerable effect' upon the audience and anticipating the work's future success (*Courrier des Théâtres* 1910). These 'sneak previews' served many purposes. Diaghilev's practice of inviting friendly critics like Robert Brussel and Raoul Brevanne of *Figaro*, Ricciardo Canudo of *Montjoie!*, and Jean-Louis Vaudoyer to observe new works in the final stage of preparation ensured favourably disposed articles up to the day of the actual premiere. (Another way of accomplishing this was to 'plant' commissioned texts – like Cocteau's 1911 panegyric 'Le Ballet russe' – in influential newspapers and magazines (Steegmuller 1970: 74–5).) Here, Astruc's connections proved invaluable. In addition to creating advance press, rehearsals fuelled the gossip mills. Diaghilev distributed vast numbers of free tickets, recalled Stravinsky, to the hand-picked audience of 'actors, painters, musicians, writers, and the most cultured representatives of society' (1936: 47) that attended his *répétitions générales*. In the case of *Giselle* only 203 of the 1,967 spectators who attended the *répétition générale* actually paid for tickets. With their access to salons, these unofficial publicists sent news of company events rippling among Diaghilev's target audience, while preparing the ground for works that might otherwise have risked financial failure.

With the advent of ballet, another new element was added to the audience, one that sent a whiff of notoriety across the theatre. Beginning in 1909 and accelerating as the war approached, the demi-monde, that glamorous half-world of courtesans, actresses, rakes and tabloid journalists, whose amorous intrigues and tragic suicides so fascinated the Belle Epoque, found a place alongside the connoisseurs and collectors of high society. Like actresses, dancers gravitated almost automatically to the demi-monde: no amount of artistry could wipe the stigma of low-class origins and sexual impropriety from the followers of Terpsichore. With the exception of Rosita Mauri, a former *étoile* teaching at the Opéra school, and Mathilde Kchessinska, Saint Petersburg's *prima ballerina assoluta*, dancers had shied from *Boris*. In 1909, by contrast, they occupied a place of honour, with such celebrated personalities on hand as Carlotta Zambelli, the Opéra's reigning *étoile*, Madame Mariquita, ballet mistress of the Opéra-Comique, Isadora Duncan and Natalia Trouhanova. But Astruc's efforts to introduce a specifically dance element into the audience did not stop with notables. From the Opéra and Comedie Française, he commandeered a 'frieze' of 'bediamonded' beauties, a *corbeille* of alternating blondes and brunettes, whom he sat in the front of the dress circle. Nor was this the only means by which Astruc reiterated ballet's traditional association with sexual impropriety. Among the other celebrities in the audience were actresses such as Louise de Mornand and Madeleine Carlier, who doubled offstage as demi-mondaines.

The popularity of the Ballets Russes among Paris pleasure-seekers also reflected the renaissance of dance as a public social pastime. In 1911 and 1912 the tango invaded fashionable tearooms, while at chic supper clubs exhibition dancers like Vernon and Irene Castle entertained a cosmopolitan mélange of Argentine millionaires, Russian grand dukes, French aristocrats, and New York's 'Four Hundred'. Among the pleasure-minded habitués of the Café de Paris, the audience for ballet and social dancing overlapped, as it did at the races and across the footlights. But there were other connections as well. At one of Anthony Drexel's parties in London, the Castles shared the limelight with Nijinsky, while at Deauville, the Casino engaged both the star couple and the Ballets Russes to headline the resort's inaugural season. Leaving no stone unturned in its quest for elegance and cachet, the Casino had Gabriel Astruc prepare the guest list for Deauville's official opening.

In private entertaining, too, ballet overlapped with fashions in recreation. In June 1913 the cream of Paris society turned out for the 'leçon de danse' organized by Princesse Amédée de Broglie. That same month the Marquise de Ganay, a longtime Diaghilev supporter, gave a brilliant fête that featured lords and titled ladies in a programme of 'dances of yesteryear'. With backgrounds that ranged from Byzantine to Empire (Josephine's rose garden at Malmaison was the setting for a tableau to the music of *Le Spectre de la Rose*), the event was styled a *répétition générale*. Still another entertainment that June drew inspiration from ballet. At Comte Aynard de Chabrillan's, guests in Romantic-era tarlatans à la *Les Sylphides* performed a 'Fantaisie sur des valses de Schubert' staged by Opéra ballet master Léo Staats. All these events coincided with Diaghilev's most brilliant prewar season.

Isadora Duncan's success, moreover, spawned a host of 'interpretative' imitators, who, like the fashionable converts to eurythmics, added to the heterogeneity of Diaghilev's audience. The dancer Caryathis was among the growing number of Paris teachers who catered to this new clientele of amateurs and the figure-conscious. A former dressmaking apprentice with a studio in Montmartre, she taught an unorthodox blend of eurythmics and ballet and gave recitals of dances choreographed to Ravel and Satie. In a poster for one such event, Bakst drew a tunic-clad figure weaving Duncanesque movements among serpentine lengths of exotic cloth.

Unlike the painters who were her neighbours, Caryathis did not confine her activities to Montmartre. A part-time demi-mondaine, she ventured into the limelight of fashionable Paris, and with another 'kept' woman, her pupil Gabrielle Chanel, and two of her lovers, attended the premiere of *Sacre*. Caryathis's appearance that night added still another sensation to that sensation-filled occasion: the fringe across her forehead, all that was left of tresses clipped off in a fit of romantic pique, gave Paris its first sight of bobbed hair.

By 1913 Diaghilev had certainly put ballet on the artistic map of fashionable Paris. His mixed dance and opera season that spring at Astruc's recently inaugurated Théâtre des Champs-Elysées was a 'stupendous success'. On the morning of the fourth performance, not a seat was to be had, and on June 11 Astruc announced that seven performances had been added to the season.

Despite the glowing record of triumphs, dance itself remained the least appreciated ingredient of Diaghilev's recipe. Indeed, among the outpouring of press reports and articles, Jacques Rivière's attempts to analyse choreographic form, particularly in his impassioned articles about *Le Sacre du Printemps*, stand out as unique. Critics lavished attention on composers and designers who awoke on the morrow of a premiere to find themselves instant celebrities, while stars like Nijinsky and Karsavina inspired the passion of company devotees. Under the pressure of financial necessity, Diaghilev eschewed the task of educating his Parisian public. Instead, he sought to dazzle and tantalize it, counting on the allure of fashion and scandal to establish a niche for his enterprise on the Parisian firmament.

Diaghilev's early seasons held a special appeal for Slavic, Jewish and other notables of foreign descent living in the French capital. By 1913, however, this relatively assimilated group was overshadowed as fresh arrivals from abroad crowded Diaghilev's seasons. Not all these foreigners were as sophisticated as Carl Van Vechten, who shared a loge with Gertrude Stein at a performance of *Sacre*. Many critics decried the enormous influx of tourists who flocked to the Ballets Russes and other spectacles during the *Grande Saison de Paris*. To this status- and pleasure-seeking public, which descended, as Astruc wrote, 'upon our caravansaries, our restaurants, our theatres, and our racetracks' and willingly paid 'three times the normal price for the same hotel room, the same mutton chop, the same orchestra stalls which are offered at a saving – but to no avail during the rest of the year' (Astruc in Bullard 1971: 105), reviewers sought to lay the blame for the outrageous behaviour of the *Sacre* audience.

'A good half of the so-called Parisian audience,' wrote Léon Vallas in *La Revue française de musique*:

> is made up of people who are as foreign to France as they are to art, and that more than a quarter of the remainder are socialites who are incapable of being moved by a daring artistic venture. We are constrained to believe that the audience which ordinarily frequented the *théâtres lyriques* and concerts was not heavily represented in the shocking racket that has been heard throughout all the performances of *Le Sacre du Printemps*.
>
> (Vallas in Bullard 1971: 108)

Vallas and his confrères undoubtedly exaggerated the role of foreigners. Certainly, at the premiere, some of the noisiest spectators – Madame Mühlfeld, Comtesse René de Pourtalès, the woman who called Ravel 'a dirty Jew' – were French. But critics were right in discerning a connection between the riotous events of 1913 and the changing composition of Diaghilev's audience. By 1913 the Diaghilev enterprise inevitably prompted thoughts of fashion and scandal, along with artistic daring. The noisy, untutored mob of fashionable and demi-monde Paris had largely overshadowed the musically sophisticated community of Diaghilev's early seasons. That community had been one of connoisseurs bred in the habits of aristocracy, even if they were not bluebloods themselves. The Rothschilds, Camondos, Doucets, Singers and Reinachs, names enshrined as the 'grands donateurs' of the Louvre and Jeu de Paume, allied the collector's instinct with the spirit of the connoisseur. Their superb collections of eighteenth-century and impressionist art found their way not into the marketplace but to the halls of museums.

Diaghilev's newly crystallizing public, by contrast, was one of consumers. The keynote of the connoisseur is disinterested appreciation and taste; that of the consumer 'good value'. The first seeks beauty; the second judges quality by rarity and price. Where repetition might offer the connoisseur further occasion for contemplation, for the consumer it merely lessens the value of the original. By 1913 the company's de luxe programmes had become collector's items, and as bibliographic rarities, these beautifully illustrated publications were sold independently of performances. With the emergence of the ballet consumer, the props, programmes, costumes, designs, and even performances of the Ballets Russes were transformed from objets d'art to articles whose value was determined by their scarcity in the marketplace.

With its high-sounding titles and unexpected connections, Diaghilev's French public certainly makes for lively reading. But antiquarian interest aside, it has an importance that far transcends historical chit-chat. The culti-vated audience coaxed into being from 1906 to 1914 elucidates two long-standing puzzles. It explains the speed with which the Ballets Russes put down roots in Western Europe and the obsession with exoticism and luxury that became Diaghilev trademarks. That ballet re-entered the cultural consciousness of the West via the French upper class is equally a matter of import. The idea of privilege synonymous with the Ballets Russes in its most legendary era remains, even today, branded into the identity of classical dancing.

NOTES

1 'Feuilles de location', AJ13/1292, Archives Nationales.
2 Valentin Serov, Letter to the Editor, *Rech'*, 22 Sept. 1910. Serov's letter is an attack on the position articulated by Telyakovsky in an interview published in *Birzhvye vedomosti* (Stock Exchange Gazette) a short time before. I am grateful to the late Professor Ilya Zilbershtein for providing me with a copy of Serov's letter.

25

WOMEN WRITING THE BODY: LET'S WATCH A LITTLE HOW SHE DANCES

Elizabeth Dempster

Major innovation in dance has occurred largely outside the ballet academy. The radical redefinition of concert dance which began at the turn of the century was a movement initiated by women artists working independently of traditional structures to develop new languages of physical expression. The early modern dance was a repudiation of the tenets of nineteenth-century ballet, including its emphasis on spectacle and virtuoso display. It was an avowedly female-centred movement, both with respect to the manner in which the body was deployed and represented and in the imagery and subject matter employed. The early modern dancers were asking that the body and its movement, along with the place and context of dance, be looked at in new ways. They inherited no practice; the techniques and the choreographic forms they developed were maps and reflections of the possibilities and propensities of their own originating bodies.

In the early 1900s dancers such as Isadora Duncan, Loie Fuller, Maud Allen and Ruth St Denis constructed images and created dances through their own unballetic bodies, producing a writing of the female body which strongly contrasted with classical inscriptions. These dancers, creating new vocabularies of movement and new styles of presentation, made a decisive and liberating break with the principles and forms of the European ballet. The modern dance genre is now most closely identified with the choreographic output of the second generation of modern dancers – Mary Wigman, Doris Humphrey, Martha Graham – and the training systems they developed. It is to this body of work that the following discussion refers.

Modern dance is not a uniform system, but a corpus of related though differentiated vocabularies and techniques of movement which have evolved in response to the choreographic projects of individual artists. Common to these contrasting styles of dance – and it is this that allows us to group otherwise disparate works under the banner of 'modern dance' – is a conception of the body as a medium and vehicle for the expression of inner forces. The spatial and temporal structure of these dances is based on emotional and psychological imperatives. The governing logic of modern dance is not pictorial, as in the ballet, but affective.

For the modern dancer, dance is an expression of interiority: interior feeling guiding the movement of the body into external forms. Doris Humphrey described her dance as 'moving from the inside out' (Cohen 1972); for Graham it was a process of 'making visible the interior landscape' (Graham 1950: 21–2). This articulation of interior (maternal) spaces creates forms which are not, however, ideal or perfected ones. The modern dancer's body registers the play of opposing forces, falling and recovering, contracting and releasing. It is a body defined through a series of dynamic alternations subject both to moments of surrender and moments of resistance.

In modern dance the body acts in a dynamic relationship with gravity. For Humphrey the body was at its most interesting when in transition and at a moment of gravitational loss, that is, when it was falling. Modern dance has often been termed 'terrestrial', that is, floor-bound and inward-looking. As such it has been negatively compared to the ballet and the aerial verticality and openness of that form. But as Graham has stressed, 'the dancers fall so that they may rise'. It is in the *falling*, not in being down, that the modern body is at its most expressive.

The modern body and the dance which shapes it are a site of struggle where social and psychological, spatial and rhythmic conflicts are played out and sometimes reconciled. This body – and it is specifically a female body – is not passive but dynamic, even convulsive, as Deborah Jowitt sees it:

> In many of [Graham's] important works of the forties and fifties, you felt the dancing shuddering along in huge jerks, propelled by the violently contracting and expanding bodies. When I first saw Graham in 1955, I was stunned by the whiplash of her spine; by the way, as Medea in *Cave of the Heart* she writhed sideways on her knees – simultaneously devouring and vomiting a length of red yarn.
>
> (Jowitt 1977: 72)

Jowitt concludes that Graham's dancing was like no other she had witnessed, 'a body language consisting solely of epithets'.

Modern dance posits a natural body in which feeling and form are organically connected. Graham, for example, conceived the body as a conduit, a responsive channel through which inner truths are revealed. The body has a revelatory potential and technique is the means by which the outer manifestations of the body are brought into alignment with the inner world of the psyche.

Through all times the acquiring of technique in dance has been for one purpose – so to train the body as to make possible any demand made upon it by that inner self which has the vision of what needs to be said. No one invents movement; movement is discovered. What is possible and necessary to the body under the impulse of the emotional self is the result of this discovery.

(Graham in Cohen 1974: 139)

The function of technique in modern dance is, as Graham has described it, to free the socialized body and clear it of any impediment which might obscure its capacity for 'true speech'. Ironically, perhaps, this concept of the 'natural' body was expounded in support of highly systemized and codified dance languages and training programmes which inscribe relationships – necessarily conventional and arbitrary – between the body, movement and meaning.

Modern dance's valorization of the 'natural' and its positing of an individualized presymbolic subject are not features of the classical system of training. Ballet training shapes, controls, improves upon and perfects the body's given physical structure; in this process both the natural body and the individualized subject are erased. As the principles of modern dance have become progressively codified into systematic techniques, the concept of a 'natural' body, pre-existing discourse, can no longer be sustained. Modern dance, now distant from its creators' originating ideas, is passed on through highly formalized training programmes; and like the classical system, this training involves erasure of naturally given physical traits and processes of reinscription.

How are the body and 'the feminine' inscribed by the female-devised languages of modern dance? Graham's dances sacralize and mythologize the female body, a body shown to be subject to forceful emotional, unconscious and libidinal impulses. In Foster's reading it is the body of the hysteric:

The action begins in the abdomen, codified as the site of libidinal and primitive desires. The symbolic contents of the abdomen radiate through the body, twisting and empowering the body with their message. Graham's characters seem to be subject to the psychological mechanism of repression. The powerful message from the unconscious makes its way only with difficulty through the emotional and intellectual centers of the person and into the world. Graham depicts the tense conflict between corporeal and psychological elements.

(Foster 1986: 81)

Graham's location of 'the feminine' may seem uncomfortably close to the space traditionally ascribed to the body, women and dance within patriarchy. Her choreographies, however, represent the inner world as a dynamic, outward-flowing, conflictual force; 'the feminine' is not passive but voluptuously and sometimes violently active. It is a force which shapes the outer world. Graham's work reflects the psychoanalytic preoccupations of her time, but the public and performative nature of Graham's articulation of these concerns, and the power she ascribes to the female body, significantly distinguish her representation of the feminine from that associated with clinical practice.

As early as the 1930s Graham and her fellow artists were presenting a newly defined dance practice in the public arena and in so doing they created spaces for dance and for women which had not existed before. But this form of dance, once an oppositional practice, is now offered as a second language supplementing classical ballet in the training of the professional dancer. In my judgement modern dance's gradual codification, its identity as a formularized technique, has rendered it susceptible to colonization; and it is this codification rather than any inherent ideological complicity which permits elements of modern dance to be subsumed into the ballet.

Lincoln Kirstein, the founding father of the New York City Ballet, has cursorily dismissed modern dance as the 'minor verse' of theatre. He considers it timebound, nostalgic and lacking the 'clear speech acts' and universal legibility of the ballet. He is one of a number of critics who have argued that ballet is the only enduring Western concert dance form (Kirstein 1935). In Kirstein's view, ballet's pre-eminence is assured because modern dance has failed to produce a stable lexicon and is therefore lacking in consequence.

But modern dance has clearly developed vocabularies and syntactical conventions; and Kirstein's perceptions are misplaced. He would be less inaccurate if his subject had been postmodern dance. The postmodern is not a newly defined dance language but a strategy and a method of inquiry which challenge and interrogate the process of representation itself. Once the relation between movement and its referent is questioned, the representational codes and conventions of dance are opened to investigation. Analysis, questioning and manipulation of the codes and conventions which inscribe the body in dance are distinguishing features of the postmodern mode.

In the 1940s Merce Cunningham had already begun to demonstrate that dance could be primarily about movement. In contrast to the expressionism of modern dance, in which movement is presumed to have intrinsic meaning, Cunningham choreographies emphasize the arbitrary nature of the correlation between signifier and signified. In his deconstruction of existing choreographic codes Cunningham challenged the rhetoric of 'the natural' which surrounded modern dance. The political dimensions of this deconstructive project have been addressed more directly in the work of some of the later postmodern choreographers.

Susan Foster defines two stages/modes of postmodern dance practice: objectivist and reflexive. The first is the precondition for the second, but the two modes were coextensive in the 1960s and 1970s and together constitute the genre. Foster differentiates the two stages of postmodern dance as follows:

> Objectivist dance focuses on the body's movement, allowing any references to the world to accrue alongside the dance as a byproduct of the body's motion. The reflexive choreography [. . .] assumes that the body will inevitably refer to other events, and because of this asks how those references are made. Whereas objectivist dance has laid bare the conventions governing representations to allow the body to speak its own language, reflexive choreography works with these same conventions to show the body's capacity to both speak and be spoken through in many different languages.
>
> (Foster 1986: 188)

Like Cunningham, the postmodern choreographers emerging in the 1960s distinguished themselves from both the classical tradition and the then firmly established modern dance in that their focus was on the fundamental material and medium of dance, the moving body itself. The body was no longer to be trained to the task of interpreting or illustrating something other than its own material reality. Postmodern dance does not present perfected, ideal or unified forms, nor bodies driven by inner imperatives, but bodies of bone, muscle and flesh speaking of and for themselves.

> The dances are about what they look like. Because [objectivist dances] simply present individual people in motion, the dancers clearly do not presume to represent idealized experience or experience that might be common to all people.
>
> (Foster 1986: 185)

In *Work 1961–1973* (1974) Yvonne Rainer writes of her 'chunky' body not conforming to the traditional image of the female dancer. Elsewhere she recalls a Boston reviewer, writing in the 1960s, disdainfully commenting on the 'slack' bodies of (the later-termed) postmodern dancers (Brown and Rainer 1979). A democratization of the body and of dance was heralded in the postmodern work of the 1960s and 1970s. Whilst Cunningham pursued a deconstruction of choreographic conventions through technically trained bodies – bodies which maintained the 'look' of the dancer – postmodern works of this period featured both trained and untrained performers, in short 'any-old-body'. Widely used choreographic devices such as rule games, task-based and improvisational structures provided a frame for the

227

perception and enjoyment of bodies in action – trained or untrained, old or young, thick or thin, male or female.

The play of oppositions and the gender stereotyping embodied in the ballet and perpetuated in modern dance traditions were systematically de-emphasized in the postmodern work of this era. Within the selection, structuring and performance of movement strong contrasts and oppositions were reduced or eliminated. Rainer speaks here of *The Mind is a Muscle*, *Trio A* (1966):

> The limbs are never in a fixed, still relationship and they are stretched to the fullest extension only in transit, creating the impression that the body is constantly engaged in transitions. Another factor contributing to the smoothness of the continuity is that no one part of the series is made any more important than any other. For four and half minutes a great variety of movement shapes occur, but they are of equal weight and are equally emphasized.
>
> (Rainer 1974: 67)

The postmodern dancer's range and style of movement were not determined by gender, and sex-specific roles were rare – notable exceptions being a number of works by Yvonne Rainer in which issues of gender, sexual identity and seduction in performance were addressed directly (see Rainer 1974). The early postmodern focus on non-hierarchical and non-genderized use and organization of the body and its movement continues in current postmodern dance.

Postmodern dance, as Foster has indicated, also involves the reworking and reassessment of earlier forms of bodily inscription – drawing from, quoting, subverting and manipulating classical and other lexicons. Referring to Rainer's *Trio A* (1966) and Trisha Brown's *Accumulation* (1971), *With Talking* (1973) and *Plus Watermotor* (1977), Foster has noted the tensions which arise when (at least) two disparate modes of representation are juxtaposed or brought into dialogue (Foster 1986: 186). In these works the body is present as an instrument concerned simply with physical articulation, but at the same time it also alludes to other discourses: Rainer's *Trio A* contains references to earlier dance forms and Brown's dance presents speaking and dancing as simultaneous but independent texts. The play of contrasting discourses and the use of quotation in postmodern compositional process produce layered and complex dance works open to multiple readings. Yvonne Rainer, in conversation with Trisha Brown, discusses this effect in Brown's *Glacial Decoy* (1979):

> The costumes bring in another dimension [. . .] of, not exactly a persona, but an association with personae created elsewhere and earlier, somewhere between *Les Sylphides* and *Primitive Mysteries*,

maybe even *Antic Meet*, which has that take-off on *Primitive Mysteries*. And it is the dress that produces this association. There's a recurring, fleeting transformation from a body moving to a flickering female image. I think that because the dress stands away from the body the image is never totally integrated or unified, so one goes back and forth in seeing movement-as-movement, body-inside-dress, dress-outside- body, and image-of-woman/dancer, which is not the same thing as seeing or not seeing your work in terms of your being a woman. Femaleness in *Glacial Decoy* is both a given, as in your previous work, and a superimposition.

(Brown and Rainer 1979: 32)

The process of deconstruction and bricolage commonly associated with postmodern dance also describe an attitude to physical training. The development of what might be termed the postmodern body is in some senses a deconstructive process, involving a period of de-training of the dancer's habitual structures and patterns of movement. The dancer brings intelligence to bear on the physical structure of her/his body, focusing close attention upon the interaction of skeletal alignment and physiological and perceptual processes. Through this process the dancer reconstructs a physical articulation based on an understanding of what is common to all bodies and what is unique to her/his own. Our bodies evolve in dialogue with a complex physical and social world, so training systems which have informed postmodern dance are based on a conceptualization of the body as an organism in flux. The postmodern body is not a fixed, immutable entity, but a living structure which continually adapts and transforms itself. It is body available to the play of many discourses. Postmodern dance directs attention away from any specific image of the body and towards the process of constructing all bodies.

If postmodern dance is a 'writing' of the body, it is a writing which is conditional, circumstantial and above all transitory; it is a writing which erases itself in the act of being written. The body, and by extension 'the feminine', in postmodern dance is unstable, fleeting, flickering, transient – a subject of multiple representations.

26

'KEEP TO THE RHYTHM AND YOU'LL KEEP TO LIFE': MEANING AND STYLE IN AFRICAN AMERICAN VERNACULAR DANCE

Jacqui Malone

Through art we celebrate life. As Albert Murray says, 'Our highest qualities come from art; that's how we know who we are, what we want, what we want to do.'[1] The attainment of wholeness, rather than the amassing of power, is what ultimately makes people happy, and the goal of art is to help achieve that wholeness by providing humanity with basic 'equipment for living' (Burke 1957). Among African Americans that equipment is partially rooted in a vital and dynamic cultural style.

African American vernacular dance, like jazz music, mirrors the values and worldview of its creators. Even in the face of tremendous adversity, it evinces an affirmation and celebration of life. Furthermore, African American dance serves some of the same purposes as traditional dances in western and central African cultures: on both continents black dance is a source of energy, joy and inspiration; a spiritual antidote to oppression; and a way to lighten work, teach social values and strengthen institutions. It also teaches the unity of mind and body and regenerates mental and physical power. The role of dance as a regenerative force is echoed in the words of Bessie Jones of the Georgia Sea Islands: 'We'd sing different songs, and then we'd dance a while to rest ourselves' (Jones and Hawes 1987: 124).

Much has been written about the role of music and folklore among black people in the United States, but the meaning and the pervasiveness of dance have been sorely neglected despite the fact that dance touches almost every aspect of African American life. As Melville Herskovits tells us, 'The dance itself has in characteristic form carried over into the New World to a greater degree than almost any other trait of African culture[s].' Since the publication of Herskovits's groundbreaking work, *The Myth of the Negro Past*

(1941), the identification of African continuances in African American culture has been a source of much debate among American studies scholars. Fortunately, the discourse has evolved beyond a search for specific elements to the recognition of shared cultural processes of creativity, based on the notion that 'art moves within people' and that cultural continuity is never completely broken (Vlach 1978: 148). The composer and scholar Olly Wilson suggests that African and African American music and dance share similar 'ways of doing things, although the specific qualities of the something that is done varies with time and place and is also influenced by a number of elements outside the tradition' (Wilson 1990: 29). Recognition of the strong relationship between the dances of traditional African cultures and the dances of black Americans is now a commonplace among students and scholars of American history, music and dance.

A distinctive and characteristic style is manifest in the artistic expression of black dancers, singers and musicians. Style is an attitude, a mechanism for sizing up the world, and a mode of survival (Murray 1983: 55). 'Behind each artist,' writes Ellison, 'there stands a traditional sense of style, a sense of the felt tension indicative of expressive completeness; a mode of humanizing reality and of evoking a feeling of being at home in the world' (Ellison 1972: xvii).

Nowhere is African American style more manifest than in dance. The six definitive characteristics of African American vernacular dance are *rhythm, improvisation, control, angularity, asymmetry* and *dynamism*.

The importance of rhythm to human existence is an ongoing theme in the writings of Katherine Dunham. She understood as early as the 1950s that the breaking of *rhythm* in an individual or society results in disintegration, malaise and energy diffusion. It is the key to human potential for social and personal integration. Rhythm, asserts Léopold Senghor, is 'the architecture of being, the inner dynamic that gives it form, the pure expression of the life force. Rhythm is the vibratory shock, the force which, through our sense, grips us at the root of our being. It is expressed through corporeal and sensual means; through lines, surfaces, colours, and volumes in architecture, sculpture or painting; through accents in poetry and music, through movements in the dance [. . .] In the degree to which rhythm is sensuously embodied, it illuminates the spirit' (Senghor in Jahn 1990: 164).

African American vernacular dance is characterized by propulsive rhythm. Coming from dance-beat-oriented cultures, black Americans demand a steady beat in their dance music. Although the beat can be embellished, the basic rhythm provides the dancer with dramatic exits and entrances. The jazz dancer James Berry comments: 'The rhythmic motion on the beat with the music has something. You feel free to do what you want and you can't get lost, because you can always come in, you can dance with abandon but still you are encased within the beat. That is the heart of dancing' (Berry 1976–7: 24).

Improvisation, an additive process, is a way of experimenting with new ideas; that mind-set is Africa's most important contribution to the Western Hemisphere. One offshoot of that mind-set is the tendency toward elasticity of form in African American art. When Duke Ellington asked a candidate for his orchestra if he could read music, his reply was: 'Yeah, I can read, but I don't let it interfere with my blowing!' That point of view is prevalent among jazz musicians, who thrive on improvisation. 'True jazz is an art of individual assertion within and against the group. Each true jazz moment (as distinct from the uninspired commercial performance) springs from a contest in which each artist challenges all the rest; each solo flight, or improvisation, represents (like the successive canvases of a painter) a definition of his identity: as individual, as member of the collectivity and as a link in the chain of tradition' (Vlach 1978: 150).

Improvisation, for the black idiomatic dancer, functions in much the same way. It is one of the key elements in the creation of vernacular dance. From the turn-of-the-century cakewalk through the Charleston of the twenties and the lindy of the thirties and forties, black dancers inserted an improvisational 'break' that allowed couples to separate at various points so that they could have maximum freedom of movement. According to Thompson, 'breaking the beat or breaking the pattern in Kongo is something one does to break on into the world of the ancestors, in the possession state, precisely the rationale of drum-breaks (*casée*) in Haiti' (Thompson 1991: 8). From the 'breakdown' of colonial slave frolics to the break dancing of the twentieth century, the improvisational interlude has remained a cornerstone of African American dance in the United States. Indeed, throughout the Kongo-influenced communities of the African diaspora, there are many styles of 'breaking to the earth'. For example, the 'Break Out' or 'Break Away' is the main section in Jamaican Jonkonnu performances during which several dancers execute solos simultaneously.

All African American social dances allow for some degree of improvisation, even in the performance of such relatively controlled line dances as the Madison and the stroll of the fifties. In this dance tradition, the idea of executing any dance exactly like someone else is usually not valued. When vocal groups perform choreographed dance movements, the audience expects each singer to bring his or her own personality to the overall movement style, thereby creating diversity within unity. Contrary to popular opinion, black idiomatic dancers always improvise with intent – they compose on the spot – with the success of the improvisations depending on the mastery of the nuances and the elements of craft called for by the idiom.

Within the context of vernacular dance performance, the 'aesthetic of the cool' functions to help create an appearance of control and idiomatic effortlessness. What vernacular dance celebrates is a 'unique combination of spontaneity, improvisation, and control'. According to Murray, blues-idiom dance movement has nothing to do with sensual abandonment. 'Being always a matter of elegance [it] is necessarily a matter of getting oneself together.' Like all good dancers, practitioners of this style do not throw their bodies around; they do not cut completely loose. When the musical break comes, it is not a matter of 'letting it all hang out', but a matter of proceeding in terms of 'a very specific technology of stylization' (Murray 1982: 50, 90, 126). A loss of control and a loss of coolness place one *squarely* outside of the tradition.

Angularity is a prominent feature of African American body language, dress, and performance. Thompson has identified several Bakongo[2] angulated gestures and body postures that show up in the sports, musical performances, religious expressions, and day-to-day conversations of African Americans. Black nonverbal communication is rife with angles. We see them in female and male stances, walking styles, and greetings. In *Jazz Masters of the 30s*, Rex Stewart contends that the 'insouciant challenge' of Louis Armstrong's personal style was conveyed to the world by 'his loping walk [and] the cap on his head tilted at an angle, which back home meant: "Look out! I'm a bad cat – don't mess with me!" ' (Stewart 1982: 40). Zora Neale Hurston identified this characteristic as early as the 1930s: 'After adornment the next most striking manifestation of the Negro is Angularity. Everything that he touches becomes angular. In all African sculpture and doctrine of any sort we find the same thing. Anyone watching Negro dancers will be struck by the same phenomenon. Every posture is another angle. Pleasing, yes, but an effect achieved by the very means which a European strives to avoid' (Hurston 1981: 54).

Hurston also identified asymmetry as a significant feature of African arts and black American literature and dance:

> It is the lack of symmetry which makes Negro dancing so difficult for white dancers to learn. The abrupt and unexpected changes. The frequent change of key and time are evidences of this quality in music (note the St Louis Blues). The dancing of the justly famous Bo-jangles and Snake Hips are excellent examples. The presence of rhythm and lack of symmetry are paradoxical, but there they are. Both are present to a marked degree. There is always rhythm, but it is the rhythm of segments. Each unit has a rhythm of its own, but when the whole is assembled it is lacking in symmetry. But easily workable to a Negro who is accustomed to the break in going from one part to another, so that he adjusts himself to the new tempo.
>
> (Hurston 1981: 55)

The participatory nature of black performance automatically ensures a certain degree of dynamism because the demands of the audience for dynamic invention and virtuosity prevent the performer from delivering static reproductions of familiar patterns or imitations of someone else's hard-earned style.

When performers demonstrate their knowledge of the black musical aesthetic, the responses of audiences can become so audible that
they momentarily drown out the performer. The verbal responses of
audiences are accompanied by hand-clapping; foot-stomping; head,
shoulder, hand, and arm movement; and spontaneous dance. This
type of audience participation is important to performers; it
encourages them to explore the full range of aesthetic possibilities,
and it is the single criterion by which black artists determine
whether they are meeting the aesthetic expectations of the audience.

(Maultsby 1990: 195)

The folklorist Gerald Davis (1985) calls this phenomenon of African
American performance 'circularity': a dynamic system of influences and
responses whose components include performers, audiences, and their traditions. Davis's model begins with an ideal form – a preacher's sermon, for
example – and ends with a realized form that is shaped by all three components of the circular interchange. Davis's study concentrates on sermons
but he also observes circularity in certain musical forms, selected expressions of material culture, and – quite significantly for our purposes – in
some types of dance.

The African American aesthetic encourages exploration and freedom in
composition. Originality and individuality are not just admired, they are
expected. But creativity must be balanced between the artist's conception of
what is good and the audience's idea of what is good. The point is to add to
the tradition and extend it without straying too far from it. The circle in
black social dance is a forum for improvising and 'getting down' but the
good dancer does not go outside the mode established by the supporting
group. 'DO YOUR OWN THING,' explains the playwright Paul Carter
Harrison, 'is an invitation to bring YOUR OWN THING into a complementary relationship with the mode, so that we all might benefit from its
power' (Harrison 1972: 72–3). When a dancer enters the magic circle it is a
way of renewing the group's most hallowed values.

Among African Americans, the power generated by rhythmical movement has been apparent for centuries in forms of work, play, performance
and sacred expression. Rhythmical movement as a unifying mechanism and
a profound spiritual expression is poetically voiced in an excerpt from
Ellison's short story 'Juneteenth'. The speaker, Reverend Hickman,
addresses a crowd at an Emancipation Day celebration:

Keep to the rhythm and you'll keep to life. God's time is long; and
all short-haul horses shall be like horses on a merry-go-round. Keep,
keep, keep to the rhythm and you won't get weary. Keep to the
rhythm and you won't get lost [. . .] They had us bound but we had
our kind of time, Rev. Bliss. They were on a merry-go-round that

they couldn't control but we learned to beat time from the seasons [. . .] They couldn't divide us now. Because anywhere they dragged us we throbbed in time together. If we got a chance to sing, we sang the same song. If we got a chance to dance, we beat back hard times and tribulations with a clap of our hands and the beat of our feet, and it was the same dance [. . .] When we make the beat of our rhythm to shape our day the whole land says, Amen! [. . .] There's been a heap of Juneteenths before this one and I tell you there'll be a heap more before we're truly free! Yes! But keep to the rhythm, just keep to the rhythm and keep to the way.

(Ellison 1965: 274–6)

NOTES

1 Albert Murray, lecture, Center for Afro-American Studies, Wesleyan University, Middletown, Conn., spring 1985.
2 The Bakongo are descendants of an ancient classical civilization, Kongo, that included modern Bas-Zaire and neighbouring lands in modern Cabinda, Gabon, Congo-Brazzaville and northern Angola (Thompson 1983: 103).

PART VI

ANALYSING DANCE

As discussed in the General Introduction, the activities of analysing dance and locating it within its context are now inextricably linked. It could be argued, therefore, that to make the distinction that is reflected in these final two discrete Parts is no longer tenable as it reflects boundaries of knowledge which cannot be sustained. There is, however, a large body of scholarship which takes a dance(s) or a choreographic *oeuvre* as its prime focus, and examples of these are included here. Jordan and Thomas identify their methodology; in other writers, the analytic approaches are implicit and frame different purposes.

Using Siobhan Davies' *Duets* (1982) and Ann Daly's analysis of the third theme from Balanchine's *The Four Temperaments* (1946), Stephanie Jordan and Helen Thomas exemplify the various perspectives offered by formalism, structuralism and semiotics. Taking gender as their theme, they illustrate ways in which these differing analytical strategies offer possibilities for multiple readings. Furthermore, they argue that an interplay between the 'poetic' and semiotic approaches can result in a richer appreciation of dance.

Feminist perspectives have produced new ways of looking (in every sense) at cultural phenomena, and central to the feminist agenda has been the imperative to expose ways in which constructs of femininity are embodied in dance. Inevitably, perhaps, the construct of masculinity then came under scrutiny. Ramsay Burt (1995) not only considers the cultural meanings inscribed on the body of the male dancer but deals with theatre dance forms other than the oft-targeted classical or Romantic ballet. Examining Nijinsky and the Ballets Russes, Burt takes a broad approach to his subject, dealing with Nijinsky's persona as a performer and his choreographic *oeuvre*. He argues that Nijinsky's choreography was more radical than Fokine's not only in aesthetic terms but also in its representations of masculinity. Whilst his stage image presented 'a limited but contained expression of homosexual experience', overall the 'norms of traditional masculinity remained intact'. Nijinsky's appeal to a wide audience can partly be located in this ambiguity

237

of persona; he conformed with images of male prowess yet, in his exotic, sensual and androgynous roles, subverted those very images.

Writings are rare which locate dance within the prevailing political context, in the conventional sense of 'politics'; even more rare is an examination of the dance works themselves from this perspective. Susan Manning's analysis of Wigman's *Totenmal* (1930) leads her to claim not only that the dance can be read, in retrospect, as an example of protofascist theatre but that it also marked a turn away from the feminism which can be discerned in Wigman's earlier work. Although the political message of *Totenmal* was ambivalent in its confusion of pacifism and militarism, and in its attempt to degender which resulted in a reinforcement of gender, the dance actually concealed 'a highly politicized theatre within an apolitical aura'. Paradoxically, it was the *The Green Table* (Jooss 1932) which was not only conventionally staged but also presented within the traditional venue of the opera house, which affirmed the politics of the political left. Manning's scholarship demonstrates how dance works which are no longer extant in their complete form can be the subject of analysis, thus placing the dance itself central to historiography. Furthermore, here is a clear example of how different readings can be made when a dance is located retrospectively within the context of its production and reception.

Joan Acocella also integrates examples of detailed formal movement analysis with the circumstances of production in order to explore characteristics of Mark Morris's choreography. Using examples from a range of works, she considers the paradox of his vocabulary: dance which stresses the humanity of the body, with its earthy utilization of buttocks and crotch, revealed through movement which demands a high level of technical skill to accomplish. Struggle, toil and effort are not disguised, but used in an aesthetic endeavour very different from that of, say, Pina Bausch (see Part I).

The dance forms which have been the focus of study in the formal sectors of education tend to have been those practised in the theatre, and other genres have suffered from comparative neglect. Theresa Buckland's analyses of music videos exemplify an increasing interest in the close examination of dance which serves other, not entirely dissimilar functions from theatre dance, but which are presented in the context of 'entertainment'. Using the work of Kate Bush and Michael Jackson, she demonstrates the relationship between this genre and wider popular culture, exploring how, for example, dance on pop videos contributes to the construction of gender and the star persona. Buckland, as do Jordan and Thomas, explicitly calls for analysis which addresses both the aesthetic and cultural dimensions of the work, and, furthermore, accommodates the voices of producers and performers.

Richard Dyer's and John Mueller's analyses of 'Dancing in the Dark' from *The Band Wagon* (1953) are included here as examples of the generally rare consideration given to the choreography of dance in films. Dyer hints at the potential for readings informed by gender perspectives, which is the subject

238

of the much longer chapter from which this brief extract is drawn. Mueller focuses on the narrative of the film, explicating the way in which a significant change in the relationship between the two protagonists (Astaire and Charisse) is charted not by words, but in dance.

Whether dance analysis focuses on the poetic, aesthetic or intrinsic elements of a work, or whether it is read with more overt attention to cultural or extrinsic factors (all similar if not synonymous concepts), as Adshead (Part IV) argues, the purpose of dance analysis is to enhance our knowledge and enrich our experience. For, as Buckland suggests, 'in the desire to decode and render ideologies visible, the lure of the experiential should not always be treated with suspicion. Words and intellectual discourse cannot substitute for all modes of human experience, particularly in the realm of the nonverbal.' Or, as Mueller shares with us, when the script writers of *The Band Wagon* place into Astaire's mouth the notion that human speech is 'the greatest means of communication', Astaire delivers the line – 'and then calmly proceeds to show how much more richly dance can communicate'.

FURTHER READING

Gender and dance: See Further Reading for Part IV
Vaslav Nijinsky: Buckle (1971); Hodson (1986 and 1996)
Mary Wigman: Manning (1993); Wigman (1966); Partsch-Bergsohn (1994)
Mark Morris: Acocella (1993 and 1994)
Dance on camera: Jordan and Allen (1993). Three articles on film and video in *Dance Research Journal* (1987–8) 19, 2: 3–26
Fred Astaire/The Hollywood Musical: Delameter (1981); Mueller (1986); Dyer in Thomas (1993). The extract 'Dancing in the Dark' from *The Band Wagon* can be seen on *That's Entertainment*, Part 1, video ref: MGMUA/WHV R11/90. VHS S 050007 (1974). The full version of the film is on *The Band Wagon* MGM 5052147 (1953)

27

DANCE AND GENDER: FORMALISM AND SEMIOTICS RECONSIDERED

Stephanie Jordan and Helen Thomas

The following paper was specifically intended as a collaboration between two writers whose work on dance incorporates different disciplinary frameworks: dance practice/history/criticism (Jordan), and sociology of dance/culture (Thomas). Thus, our interest in and our observations on dance are coloured by the theoretical and methodological positions we inhabit in our respective disciplines. We have sought to use these differences, as well as points of overlap, to our advantage. Through the process of writing and re-writing the other's writing, we have attempted to generate a more kaleidoscopic view of the topics and themes under discussion in this paper than we would have been able to do individually.

The two starting points for our paper might hardly seem compatible, Ann Daly's analysis of the third Theme from Balanchine's *The Four Temperaments* (1946) in her article 'The Balanchine Woman' (1987) and the work of the choreographer Siobhan Davies.[1] The latter is a leading British contemporary dance choreographer, one of the first generation of contemporary choreographers to emerge in Britain in the 1970s. But Daly's feminist analysis of *The Four Temperaments*, we found, suggested an interesting additional perspective for viewing Davies' work, and a consideration of that perspective reminded us of some fundamental issues inherent in reading art.

Daly reads the third Theme of *The Four Temperaments* as an example of a man manipulating a powerless and vulnerable woman. It is a duet based on doublework, lifts and supports. Daly's view is that the goal of this joint venture is the display of the line of the woman's body, but that there are also violent, sadomasochistic undertones. The duet is an instance of ballet representing an ideology that denies women their own agency. Of course, it goes without saying that many other writers have seen very different things in this duet, and some have not seen any of what Daly saw.

Jordan (1987) described Davies' duet form as democratic, two people equally active, often presenting two distinct lines of dance in counterpoint, and with the woman motivating the man as much as vice versa. Davies' duet form seemed democratic in relation to most ballet and other established styles of contemporary dance. A closer examination revealed that most of the contact ideas introduced in Davies' duets use the man once again as the physically stronger and more powerful of the two. Even some moves which the woman could quite easily have achieved are given to the man. The woman lightly pushes the man's arm or foot or just touches him as a signal for him to move on. The man uses his strength to lift her or pull her up from the ground, but also acts as her support, which may not necessarily require much strength at all.

Is Davies' duet behaviour a mere token gesture towards the women's movement, giving the woman some agency, 'democratic', but really only superficially so? Perhaps we need now to see what else her duets contain, information that emerged from the early viewings of Davies' work.

Our example is a series of related duets from *Rushes*, a piece that Davies made for Second Stride in 1982. These duets, performed by the grey couple in the piece, have been selected because they are in many ways typical of Davies' duet style of the mid and late 1980s. They can also be compared with *The Four Temperaments* duet, being likewise part of a non-narrative piece. Seen as a whole, *Rushes* progresses towards a violent rush of activity. The six dancers move slowly at the beginning, later dash from one spot to another, until at the end, in a state of tension, it is as if they have to leave the stage. A mob develops: solos and duets give way to quartets and sextets as the piece progresses. There is tension, even violence, but nothing as specific as character or story.

An important image that emerges in these duets is that of the body being pulled or pushed onwards, 'rushed', not stopping and being placed, but always going somewhere. Sometimes the dancers, each in turn, give the impetus or signal to move on to their partner and, as we have seen, the man more forcibly than the woman. But that is only one way in which this image arises: the dancers often carry it within their own bodies, as if they propel themselves or are propelled by an external imaginary force.

Another feature is the imaginary lines that seem to pull out from the dancers, as gestures, for instance, project beyond the body. Often there is counterpull, forces pulling in different directions to create spatial tension. This can occur within one body: in the second duet in the series, the woman arches and throws one arm way back, but her weight pulls her forward to become the force that wins. At other times there are pulls in opposing directions between the dancers who function independently: back to back (the moment occurs in both duets 2 and 3), the woman stretches one arm out to pull directly upwards, while the man pulls away horizontally. There are instances too when the spatial pull involves contact: in duet 1, the man pulls the woman back in an arch, while both take their hips forwards until they eventually fall and release the spatial tension into a run. This last example also emphasizes an important line within the structure of this duet, the diagonal line which is the territory of the duet. Physical manipulation of a partner to move him or her on or to hold the person back is therefore part of the general force-field of the series of duets, and indeed of the piece as a whole, a powerful expression of tension, but nevertheless an ingredient in the general style of the work, one that complements and is complemented by other ingredients. It has implications well beyond those of the relationship between man and woman.

Lifts too take their place within the formal logic of the duets, expressing climax in more than one sense. There is the climax of level – there are no major jumps to compete as elevation. There is also a peak of dynamic excitement – lifts look especially energetic as lifts combined with turns, and the second lift in duets 2 and 3 raises the dynamic level one stage higher, each turning further than the last. These lifts can also be seen as climaxes of resolution, after counterpoint and spatial tensions between the couple. But they are temporary resolutions, as the dancers return immediately afterwards to expressing the tensions that are so characteristic of this piece.

So far, we have looked at the *Rushes* duets from a formalist perspective, which is what early viewings suggested. Many of the concerns behind such a perspective have a parallel in the analysis of music, but perhaps the most significant parallel lies in the linguistic analysis of literature which emerged from the Russian formalist school of literary criticism in the 1920s. The formalists were concerned to analyse how words were used and combined in a particular manner to generate a desired aesthetic effect, in much the same way as we have illustrated here. One of the problems with this kind of analysis, however, is that it is somewhat one-sided, and we would want to maintain that the words themselves or, in this case, the movements themselves, cannot be studied without any reference to meaning or in isolation from the whole work. When we say then that, despite the absence of a specific story or plot in *Rushes*, the work conveys tension and even violence, the concern becomes to ask how the work manages to achieve this. To that extent, we see ourselves as moving from a strict formalist perspective towards what might be more appropriately termed a structuralist analysis of *Rushes*.

It is important to note that structuralism does not embody a single theoretical framework, but, rather, it can be best described as a method of inquiry. As a mode of analysis, structuralism seeks to explain surface events, in this case a dance, in terms of the structures that lie below the surface level and that underscore it. Moreover, from this viewpoint, the art work is treated as a structure that functions as an emerging coherent whole, constantly in the process of structuration through its own determinate internal rules. The art work is not simply an aggregate of individual parts, rather, the parts conform to the same set of internal rules that determine the whole. The parts, then, have no existence outside the structure in which they are brought into being and through which they are ordered. But the structure is not static, because it is able to use transformational rules that provide for the possibility of new material being brought into existence to effect change and movement. So the concern becomes to look at the art work in terms of its specificity, dynamics, form, content and so forth in order to draw out the complex sets of interrelationships at work in it, which, combined together, help to create the aesthetic effect and give rise to the emerging integrated whole. Thus, individual movements in a dance have no meaning in and of themselves. Rather, meaning is determined by the relationship of the movement to all other aspects that are involved in the dance work. Consequently, although we are separating out certain sections of *Rushes*, to illustrate particular points, the concern is always to integrate these back into the emerging whole.

Our analysis, in general, privileges what Jakobson (1972) terms the 'poetic function' of language. Jakobson sets out six linguistic functions of communication which can be applied fruitfully to other modes of communication apart from verbal language: the referential, the emotive, the cognitive, the phatic, the metalinguistic, and the poetic function. The various functions run together and, in the same message, they can be seen to exist in various proportions. The dominant function is reliant upon the type of communicational expression. If, for example, the aim is to prevent confusion between the sign and the object or the message and the reality it refers to, then the referential or cognitive function will predominate. However, if the message ceases to be the instrument of communication and becomes the object of communication, as in works of art, then the poetic function will predominate. There are two major forms of semiotic expression, the referential (objective, cognitive) function on the one hand, and on the other, the emotive (subjective, expressive) function. These two functions are closely related and yet antithetical to each other. They combine what Jakobson (1972) calls 'the double function of language'. Each function involves different modes of perception, one with understanding, the other with feeling and, as a result, they embrace two different modes of meaning. The logical and the expressive signs have different and opposing characteristics and comprise two forms of signification that coincide with the polarity between the sciences and the arts. Where the referential function predominates, the concern will be with denotation or signing and conversely, where the poetic function is the determining function, then the focus will be on connotation or symbolizing.

Daly's semiotic analysis of *The Four Temperaments* is largely denotative in character. That is, she looks at the work to demonstrate how it reflects existing gender relations in the 'real world' outside the dance. The analysis points to, in a somewhat literal manner, a symmetry between the dancers' movements and the ways in which women are subordinated by the 'male gaze' or look, in a society seen to be organized on the basis of patriarchal relations.

244

This type of semiotic analysis is largely extrinsic in orientation as opposed to ours which seeks to focus on the intrinsic, structural and connotative features of a dance work where the poetic function is treated as primary. Of course, this does not mean that the referential function is absent, but rather that it is subservient to the aesthetic dimension where the focus is on the symbol which is self-referring, as opposed to the sign which is concerned with denotation.

If we wished to read the first example we gave of the duet form in *Rushes* in a denotative manner, we might begin by considering the symmetrical and asymmetrical relations between the male and female dancers. As we suggested earlier, there is a symmetry between the man and woman in terms of physical activity, in the two distinct lines of counterpoint and in the reciprocity of movement motivation. However, when the contact element of the work is taken into account, these relations of symmetry are counterposed by other asymmetrical relations, with the male dancer taking on the traditional role of being physically stronger and more powerful than the female. In other words, 'democracy's body' in dance co-exists with its opposite, the traditional use of men and women's bodies within dance and without in the 'real world'. We could suggest that these relations of symmetry and asymmetry speak to and of the changes and continuities in contemporary gender relations in our culture. While there has been a movement towards women's liberation and equality of the sexes at least in certain aspects of social life, these have been underpinned by the continuation of the status quo insofar as the traditional power bases in society remain male dominated.

This kind of analysis privileges the referential function of communication as opposed to the poetic function. Sometimes, or at least at some points during a piece, as we suggested before, one reading might conflict with or even cancel out another. Indeed, this is likely to happen in work, like that of Davies, where there is a good deal of analytical interest other than the gender relations. We consider that when other formal relationships come into play along with the man/woman relation, then analysis should be directed towards the interrelation of the parts to the whole work.

On reflection, perhaps it is significant that gender aspects of the piece seemed so quiet at early viewings (Jordan's). Conventional behaviour can so easily become invisible behaviour. Often, it is only when the rules of behaviour have been broken that we come to understand that indeed, they constitute conventions of behaviour which are rule bound and subject to sanctions. As we pointed out earlier, it is important to get underneath the surface of appearances to reveal the hidden structural interrelations. However, it is interesting to speculate that, if Davies had shifted from the physical conventions between man and woman more than she did, the duet could well have developed into a statement about gender, and obscured her formal issues (and the poetic function) in the process. If she had taken this idea to the extreme, the dance could have been reduced to a piece of agitprop with the concomitant loss of what Marcuse calls art's 'otherness' (Marcuse 1977). By using the conventions of male/female behaviour in dance, Davies might be seen not to have put gender on the agenda.

So far, we have deliberately avoided talking about Davies' intentions as a choreographer, primarily because we have been focusing on the dance as an entity in itself, rather like a text, which is viewed as not being reducible to its creator and/or its viewers. Nevertheless, there is a tripartite relation at work here (author/text/reader(s), choreographer/dance/viewer(s)) that we feel requires consideration. So, it might be pertinent to introduce Davies' claim that she sees her dancers first and foremost as people, with dance person-alities, not as men and women. Lifts, she describes as fulfilling 'a visual and dynamic need as much as anything else', like 'the rise and fall of a melody [. . .] I don't want to restrict myself to not using that' (Davies 1989).

Davies then seems to have been touched by the consciousness of the women's movement – the relative democracy of her duet style demonstrates this – but only insofar as this does not reduce the richness of her formal content, which celebrates the poetic function of dance.

From what he said and accounts of his behaviour, Balanchine was cer-tainly not touched by the women's movement, and it is crystal-clear that women and men in his ballets are used as contrasting elements. In *The Four Temperaments*, this continues to be the case. However, we use the word 'elem-ents', because it is possible to see the opposition of men and women as one part of the formal content of the piece. Other writers have read the ballet as a whole in formalist terms: as an essay about scale, the expansion and con-traction of vision (Croce 1979), or as a piece about the construction of a ballet body (Copeland 1990). When we looked at the ballet as a whole (Daly does not do this – she generalizes from an examination of one section of the ballet, the one that can be most easily read in terms of man manipulating woman), we saw fragmentation and small-scale activity leading to a mass assertion of power in geometrical configurations, modernist architectural solidity after early waywardness, uncertainty and even occasional absurdity. Choleric, the last and the most powerful, self-sufficient of the four tem-peraments is a woman! She becomes the leader of the mass into the final, highly formal, highly architectural, machine-imaged, aeroplanes-taking-off-from-a-runway apotheosis.

Given this analysis, which privileges the abstract, we see that lifts and supports can be read primarily in terms of increasing the effect of power. Two bodies combine to extend and dramatize the line of verticality, the pull between sky and earth, to create counter-tensions in a horizontal plane, to enlarge a movement idea, to use the off-vertical (of the woman's body) as a metaphor for danger and the assertion to overcome that danger.

At the same time, however, if we probe underneath the surface of the final Theme a little more, we suggest that this abstract relation of woman to the mass and to modernist forms can also be read analytically as a counterpoint to the historically perceived role of women as producers and consumers of denigrated cultural forms.

During the nineteenth century, women became increasingly associated with 'mass' culture, while real 'high' culture remained the privilege of men. Women were excluded from authentic high culture before the nineteenth century but, during the industrial revolution and cultural modernization, this exclusion took on new overtones. In the late nineteenth and early twentieth centuries, the idea of the threat of the masses 'rattling at the gate' led to cries of the loss of civilization and culture and the underlying view that it was the rise of mass culture (the masses) which had caused this decline. But there was yet another hidden subject underneath this – woman. Women were also rattling at the gate, but their battle was with a male-dominated society.

As artistic realism gave way to aesthetic modernism, so the identification of woman with mass culture came to take on new dimensions. Time and time again in the political and artistic discourses of the turn of the century, woman is associated with mass culture, while 'high' modernist culture remains firmly in the privileged realm of the male. Ultimately, according to Huyssen (1986), mass culture as woman comes to stand as modernism's other. So, it is interesting that Choleric in Balanchine's work becomes the leader of the mass, a symbol of danger, which forms into strong, abstract, modernist-like configurations. In this instance, the mass, with woman at its head, actively advances into the shape of modernism rather than adopting its prescribed role as modernism's denigrated other. We suggest that woman, here, as a metaphor for danger, is active, not passive, and not merely being supported.

Even in Theme 3, one can see these features and effects: the colossal circlings of the legs one after the other taking the woman into the shape of a ship's prow, enlarged movement and shape enabled by the man's support. Or there are the high lifts with pointes pulling together underneath the woman, then shooting out arrow-sharp to the floor, a movement that contributes to the geometrical content of the apotheosis. Then, in the 'drag step', with the man reaching out and upwards, the effect of energy and work is increased by the woman clinging aggressively to his back. We do not read this as Daly does: 'the man literally carries the ballerina on his back.' Nor do we see her stretched legs and points pushing into the floor as 'lifeless, following after her like limp paws' (Daly 1987).

In the context of the whole ballet and the expressiveness derived from abstract features, we begin to read gender relations differently from Daly, and we would rather agree with Edwin Denby's (1986) observation of 'girls dancing hard and boys soft' in The Four Temperaments. Even in Theme 3, the woman shows her own work: she is not simply the manipulated, passive woman. Elsewhere, women show rather than mask the power of pushing themselves upwards, as well as being supported into huge lifts. True, there are instances of women being manipulated blatantly like marionettes, turned and strummed like a cello in Theme 3, for instance, but these are just brief touches of humour, not used to build a character, or to be fixed like a label to a dancer, and, in the same ballet, it is just as easy to find examples of men being mocked, played with, again as brief touches of expression. Just as often too, women and men work together to produce image and effect.

Yet, still, like Davies, we do not feel that Balanchine is making any major point about gender, at least in *The Four Temperaments*. Gender is not really on his agenda either. He uses ballet's gender conventions as invisible conventions, fascinated by the particular content of ballet language, its emphasis on line, stretch and verticality and the extension of these features in doublework, and wanting to use that content for every expressive purpose other than to comment on gender relations.

Balanchine's comments, often chauvinistic comments, about women are famous. Several of his dancers have spoken in support of them. The ballet culture as a whole supports them. In one sense, he said too much. In another, he said far too little, but then, he was not given to talking much at all, and certainly not to the sophisticated analysis of his work that would have placed his comments on women in a very different perspective. However, it is clear that many of his dancers have invested their roles with quite different and wide-ranging representations of women, like Merrill Ashley, Kyra Nichols, Suzanne Farrell and Darci Kistler, and possibly these dancers in the light of changing representations of women in life around them. 'In spite of the choreography,' Daly suggests (1987: 17), referring to Ashley's autonomy in the *Symphony in C* adagio. We would suggest that the choreography has the formal richness and potential that have encouraged these interpretations, that it was a text created in dialogue with its original cast, and that is now a text that has an independent life from that of its creators. We refer again to the tripartite structure here, choreographer/dance/viewer, and bring the performer into the picture as well. We believe too that Balanchine dancers today might also do well to research their own image, beyond the immediacy of their own roles and in relation to the whole poetic context of a ballet.

We are not denying that Balanchine can be read as Daly reads him – only that there are many other possibilities, many yet to be discovered as new interpretations emerge, if we admit the poetic function of art. The picture becomes far more complex and, we think, more intriguing. We suggest that the same ideas can be readily applied to other ballet choreographers.

A richness emerges when we consider the interplay of both the poetic and semiotic perspectives. So often, work is examined from one or other of these two perspectives, and analysis is only the poorer for this. We are open to the possibility of multiple readings on the basis of intertextuality (author(s)/text(s)/reader(s)) which poststructuralist and postmodernist approaches celebrate. However, we do not wish to suggest that any account will do, as is often the case in postmodernist and poststructuralist approaches which place stress on the relativization of accounts and a seemingly endless play of signifiers. Ultimately, both perspectives are structuralist in orientation, because they maintain that the world is made up of relationships between objects rather than the things themselves. Semiotic analysis, for example, is founded on the notion that there is an arbitrary relation between the sign and its referent, between the elements that comprise the sign, the signifier and signified, and an arbitrary relation between the signs which, by virtue of their difference from each other, make up the system of signs in question. Both perspectives together can now enhance our understanding of all kinds of dance, work that we feel questions traditional male/female roles as well as work that does not seem to do this.

NOTE

1 Daly's work draws on developments in feminist film theory, which incorporates semiotics and psychoanalysis. One of the reasons why the authors have chosen to focus on Daly's writing is that it has often been used rather uncritically by other writers who adopt a feminist stance. There is a chapter on Davies' work in Jordan (1992).

28

NIJINSKY: MODERNISM AND HETERODOX REPRESENTATIONS OF MASCULINITY

Ramsay Burt

Male prowess in Nijinsky's roles

A much reproduced drawing by Jean Cocteau shows Nijinsky in the wings after *Le Spectre de la Rose* (1911). Like a boxer between bouts, he lies back exhausted on a chair holding a glass of water while Vassili, Diaghilev's valet, fans him with a towel. In the background, looking concerned, are Diaghilev, Bakst and Misia Edwards (later Sert) and her husband. Part of the mythology about Nijinsky concerns his incredible leap out through the window at the end of this piece and, in general, the extraordinary agility and elevation of his jumps. Michel Fokine, however, talked down Nijinsky's leap (Fokine 1961: 180–1). Anton Dolin claims that he had danced most of Nijinsky's roles either with the Ballets Russes or subsequently and with many dancers from the original casts. In his opinion Nijinsky's roles were not that demanding technically. This is perhaps to miss a crucial point about the attitude towards technical feats shared by Nijinsky, Pavlova, Fokine and other dancers of their generation from the Imperial Theatres. They disliked the *tours de forces* performed by the older generation of ballerinas and male dancers, feeling that these looked mechanical and were unsympathetic to the creation of an artistic feeling in performance. (But the younger dancers had all been trained to perform and all did perform the virtuoso roles in the Petipa repertoire.) Nijinsky's sister Bronislava, in her *Early Memoirs*, gives us several very detailed accounts of her brother's performances and how he prepared for them. She tells how his daily practice was geared towards developing his strength and that he would practise much more difficult feats than were needed for his roles. She also says that he would practise to minimize the preparations for jumps, and that he worked at finding how to land softly afterwards, so that when he was on stage his performance would appear effortless and flowing.

The description that Rebecca West gives us of the effect, is echoed in many other accounts:

> The climax of his art was his jump. He leaped high into the air, and there stayed for what seemed several seconds. Face and body suggested that he was to mount still further, do the Indian rope trick with himself as rope, hurl himself up into space through an invisible ceiling and disappear. But then he came down – and here was the second miracle – more slowly than he had gone up, landing as softly as a deer clearing a hedge of snow.
>
> (quoted Buckle 1975: 390)

It would seem that Nijinsky did possess extraordinary strength and agility but that this was accompanied by hard work at creating an illusion of effortlessness. As Nijinska remarked: 'Do you remember how many transitions, how many nuances there were during the course of his leap? These transitions and nuances created the illusion that he never touched the ground' (Nijinska 1986: 86). What all this amounts to is that whatever Dolin may have believed, Nijinsky did produce a spectacle of famed and mythologized agility on stage. While it was Diaghilev who commissioned these roles, it was Fokine who came up with the steps. As Lynn Garafola (1989) points out, Fokine is a transitional figure between the nineteenth-century ballet tradition and twentieth-century modernism. Judging by survivals like *Le Spectre de la Rose*, or from descriptions of ballets like *Narcisse* (1911), as far as the steps of Nijinsky's solos are concerned, these were fairly traditional. Compared with Nijinsky's subsequent innovations, Fokine's choreography is conventional, in phrasing and use of space: aided by Fokine and Nijinsky's musicality, jumps and effects coincide with appropriate musical climaxes, while spatially there are circles that boldly encompass the stage, and strong diagonals to give Nijinsky the appearance of mastering the space. These are devices for displaying traditional male virtuosity. The film theorist Steve Neale has proposed that 'women are a problem, a source of anxiety, of obsessive enquiry; men are not. Whereas women are investigated, men are tested. Masculinity, as an ideal, at least, is implicitly known. Femininity is, by contrast, a mystery' (1983: 15–16). The evidence suggests that in these virtuosic roles, Nijinsky passed the test. Fokine himself was keen to dance Nijinsky's roles himself in 1914 after the latter's break with Diaghilev and the company. Fokine's male solos clearly conformed to conventional expectations of male strength and prowess, and supported the notion that the Russian male dancers were less tainted by civilization and more in touch with 'natural' masculinity than their western contemporaries.

Nijinsky as genius

Nijinsky was not just famous for his strength, agility and for his exceptional skill in partnering a ballerina. He was also hailed for his extraordinary expressiveness and the uncanny way he 'got into' his roles. His performance as Petrouchka is the prime example of this. Nijinsky's role contained both dynamic dancing and demanding mime. His sister records:

> When Petrouchka dances, his body remains the body of a doll; only the tragic eyes reflect his emotions, burning with passion or dimming with pain [. . .] Petrouchka dances as if he is using only the heavy wooden parts of his body. Only the swinging, mechanical, soul-less motions jerk the sawdust-filled arms or legs upwards in extravagant movements to indicate transports of joy or despair [. . .] Vaslav is astonishing in the unusual technique of his dance, and in the expressiveness of his body. In *Petrouchka*, Vaslav jumps as high as ever and executes as many *pirouettes* and *tours en l'air* as he usually does, even though his petrouchkian wooden feet do not have the flexibility of a dancer's feet.
>
> (Nijinska 1981: 373–4)

It was for his dramatic expressiveness in roles like Petrouchka and the sensuality of his performance of roles like the Golden Slave in *Schéhérazade* (1910), as well as for his technical abilities that Nijinsky was acclaimed as a genius. As Christine Battersby has argued, the idea of genius has sometimes been invoked to allow male artists to give expression to emotions that, over the last two centuries, have been characterized as feminine (1989: 74). In Nijinsky's case, the description is, in the hands of some writers, a back-handed compliment. Prince Peter Lieven for example suggested:

> I think the neatest and at the same time the truest estimate of Nijinsky's intellect was given me by Misia Sert, one of Diaghilev's best friends. She called him an 'idiot of genius'. This is no paradox. In our enthusiasm over the 'entity of genius' our admiration goes to the dancer's creative instincts and not to the conception of his brain, as for example, his role in *Petrouchka*.
>
> (Lieven 1980: 89)

Alexandre Benois is even more dismissive of Nijinsky's intelligence. For him Nijinsky was someone who only came alive for the stage: 'Having put on his costume, he gradually began to change into another being, the one he saw in the mirror [. . .] The fact that Nijinsky's metamorphosis was predominantly subconscious is in my opinion, the very proof of his genius' (1941: 289).They are surely both putting Nijinsky down retrospectively. Both disapproved of the radicalism of his choreography, and are writing with benefit of hindsight, knowing of his subsequent mental illness. But the idea that Nijinsky was a genius in his dancing and in his on-stage creation of roles such as Petrouchka is a comparatively safe and unthreatening one. It can easily be recuperated within conservative definitions of masculinity.

Nijinsky's heterodox roles in Fokine's ballets

But Nijinsky's roles were nevertheless transgressive. Most of them presented a spectacle of male sexuality. This raises the question of who this spectacle was intended for, as gender ideologies enforce that the dominant point of view is male, presuming that men are attracted to the spectacle of female sexuality but repelled by the male body. Heterosexual male norms are generally maintained through keeping male sexuality invisible. Any explicit expression of male sexuality was against the conventions of nineteenth-century middle-class gender ideologies. How far therefore did Nijinsky's roles in ballets like *Narcisse*, *Schéhérazade*, *Le Spectre de la Rose* and in his own *L'Après-Midi d'un Faune* (1912) break with the nineteenth-century tradition, and to what extent were they still open to acceptable interpretation as essays on classical or 'oriental' themes?

Many contemporary descriptions of Nijinsky ascribe androgynous qualities to his dancing, stressing its male power and strength but female sensuousness. Richard Buckle quotes several descriptions of Nijinsky's performance of the Golden Slave in *Schéhérazade* including Fokine's comment that 'the lack of masculinity which was peculiar to this remarkable dancer [. . .] suited very well the role of the negro slave' (Fokine 1961: 55). Fokine then likens Nijinsky to a 'half-feline animal' but also to a stallion 'overflowing with an abundant power, his feet impatiently pawing the floor'. Alexandre Benois, who wrote the libretto for this ballet, described Nijinsky's performance as 'half-cat, half-snake, fiendishly agile, feminine and yet wholly terrifying' (Buckle 1975: 160). It has already been pointed out that, within the technical range of male ballet dancing of his day, Nijinsky was considered to perform considerable technical feats. His roles often therefore allowed him to express sensuality and sensitivity (conventionally feminine) with extraordinary strength and dynamism (conventionally masculine).

None of the descriptions of Nijinsky suggest that he was actually effeminate. Moreover, according to Anton Dolin, Diaghilev disliked obvious homosexuality and hated any signs of effeminacy (Dolin 1985: 50). Garafola suggests that the androgynous quality of Nijinsky's dancing may have related to the image of the androgyne in the work of many homosexual visual artists of the Aesthetic movement at the end of the nineteenth century (1989: 56). The androgyne presented the image of a graceful, innocent, often languid youth, unspoilt by the world. Emmanuel Cooper (1986) has suggested that many homosexual artists of the Aesthetic movement saw in the androgynous male a positive image of the homosexual as a third sex. According to the 'scientific' explanation of homosexuality initially proposed by Karl Ulrichs, homosexual men were women born in men's bodies, and constituted a third sex. Those homosexuals who subscribed to the notion of a third sex saw this as a slightly effeminate 'in-between' man or woman (see Dyer 1990).

The role of Narcisse which Nijinsky created in Fokine's *Narcisse* can be interpreted as a straight piece of classical mythology, but is also open to interpretation as an image of the third sex. The figure of Narcissus is an image that has a history of use by homosexual artists that goes back to Caravaggio. Nijinska's description of Narcisse exemplifies all the qualities associated with the Aesthetic androgyne – grace, innocence and unspoiltness:

> His body of the youth in love with his own image emanated health and the athletic prowess of the ancient Greek Games. It could have been dangerous to portray in a dance the sensual and erotic Narcisse, driven to ecstasy by his own reflection in the water. Vaslav had so interpreted this scene that all such implications disappeared, dissolved in the beauty of his dance. Each pose on the ground, each movement in the air was a masterpiece.
>
> (Nijinska 1981: 366–7)

Alternatively the vigorous classicism of Nijinsky's presentation of the role might be interpreted from another, different homosexual perspective that looked back to Classical Greece as an example of a robust, manly culture in which male homosexuality was normal (see Dyer 1990: 22–5).

What made *Narcisse* acceptable to straight audiences, apart from its classical origins, was the fact that it is a moral fable that warns against the dangers of self-obsession. For transgressing social norms, Narcissus is punished. On another level he also has to be punished for being the erotic subject of the (male) spectator's gaze, as must the Golden Slave in *Schéhérazade*. In the Slave's case the discourse through which Nijinsky's highly ambiguous and exotic roles might nevertheless have appeared acceptable was that of Orientalism. As Edward Said (1978) has pointed out, for the nineteenth-century European (and by implication for the Ballets Russes' audiences) the Orient was associated with the freedom of licentious sex. In the Romantic imagination, Mario Praz (1967) identifies a literary and artistic tradition which combined the imagery of exotic places, the cultivation of sadomasochistic tastes, and a fascination with the macabre. *Schéhérazade*, with its orgy and subsequent execution, is clearly an example of this. All of this is within the discourse of Orientalist art, with the qualification that Nijinsky, the Golden Slave, could, as a Russian dancer (though actually Polish by birth), claim to be part 'oriental'.

254

Those involved in the Ballets Russes, as Russians, were ambiguously both of the East and West. Peter Wollen points to the ambiguous nature of the identity of the Russian ballet: it was a fusion of French ballet traditions and indigenous Russian Orientalist traditions. Drawing on dancers and visual artists from Saint Petersburg, it was part of European Russia in contrast to more 'eastern' Moscow. 'Yet by a strange reversal the trend was turned around and, in the form of the Ballets Russes, Paris (cultural capital of Europe, the "west") began to import Russia, the "east", in a deluge of exaggerated Orientalism' (Wollen 1987: 21).

The Ballets Russes never performed in Russia and both Diaghilev and Nijinsky were dismissed from the service of the Imperial Theatres. Bakst, Benois and Roerich never worked for the Imperial Theatres after 1909, Fokine leaving in 1918. After 1911, Nijinsky was unable (or Diaghilev may have encouraged him to believe he was unable) to return to Russia because he had defaulted from his military service. Yet these artists claimed, as Benois put it, to be presenting Russian ballet to Europe, making new works that would embody 'all the beloved old with a fresh and stimulating manner of presentation' (Benois 1936: 194). One can therefore conclude that the project of the artists and intellectuals in Diaghilev's circle was to define through the ballet their identity as Russians, in ways that were impossible within and oppositional to the hegemonic Russian establishment.

For Diaghilev and Nijinsky as homosexual men, this marginal position also enabled a limited but contained expression of homosexual experience. Nijinsky's homosexuality was signified primarily through ambiguities within the stories, and through qualities of costume and decor. It was not signified by the virtuosic solos for which he became famous. In the case of the Golden Slave, Fokine's innovatory methods of combining mime and dance into expressive movement (Garafola 1989) were a vehicle for expressing a transgressively sensual and eroticized male image, but in a context within which transgression was seen to be punished. Punishment in the form of the violent ending of *Schéhérazade* might be appreciated as an erotic spectacle, but was made acceptable by being displaced from 'normal' Europeans onto 'oriental' 'Others'. The status quo of norms of traditional masculinity thus remained intact. It is only through the modernism of his own choreography that Nijinsky actually challenged and disrupted conservative gender ideologies.

Nijinsky's ballets and gender representation

Nijinsky's *Jeux* has not survived, and can only be glimpsed through descriptions, from the evidence of photographs and from drawings by Valentine Gross. It was the first 'modern' ballet to take a modern theme (tennis and a triangular relationship) and use a modern set and costume. Nijinsky was interested in Gauguin's paintings while working on *Jeux* (see Nijinska 1981:

442). Buckle points to ways in which the surviving drawings and photographs of *Jeux* resemble the monumental, sculptural qualities of Gauguin's compositions (1975: 339). But Nijinsky's attraction must also surely have been thematic. Gauguin rejected the sophisticated social mores of nineteenth-century Europe in preference for what he saw as the innocent freedom of social and sexual relations in Tahiti. In doing so Gauguin contributed to the European myth of the 'primitive'. To the Western 'orientalist' imagination 'primitive' people were less inhibited about sexuality. *Jeux* was set in the present, and its theme was surely modern, uninhibited social and sexual relationships. His other ballets at the time, *Faune* and *Sacre*, deal with similar themes and are both set in the 'primitive' and mythic or mythological past.

Nijinsky's *L'Aprés Midi d'un Faune* is set to Debussy's *Prelude à L'Aprés Midi d'un Faune* of 1894 that was itself inspired by Mallarmé's poem of 1876. The poem presents the reveries of a young Faune. These include an encounter with two beautiful nymphs which may be recollected from a dream, a fantasy or a real event. Mallarmé was one of the poets that Verlaine dubbed 'les poètes maudits', pure of heart but despised and rejected by both mother and society, and accursed (maudits) by God. Nijinsky's amoral interpretation of the poem is surely within this tradition. The ballet's first performance provoked heated debate in the French press, and charges of indecency (Buckle 1975: 284–9). These largely concern the ballet's ending. The Faune, having surprised a group of nymphs, carries back to his rock a veil that one of them has dropped. As it is usually performed now, the Faune stretches out on top of the veil while making a couple of pelvic thrusts, jerks his head back in pleasure and then lies still. The first performance may have been more sexually explicit than this, or, as Richard Buckle suggests, he may have been lying on his right arm and thus appear to be masturbating (Buckle 1975: 284). According to *Figaro* the ending was changed after the first performance, thus eliminating the 'indecency'.

As a classical male role, the Faune superficially resembles the title role of Fokine's *Narcisse*. The difference, however, is in its attitude towards morality. Underlying the myth of Narcissus is a warning about unnatural behaviour – being unmoved by the love of Echo, being obsessed with personal appearance. The Faune, however, is 'pure', 'natural' and innocent. The movement style of the ballet is simple walking steps and jumps, dance stripped of every vestige of balletic style. This exquisite surface thus, by being outside of balletic convention, created an ideological space for the ballet that was outside of social convention. The Faune, as Nijinsky shows him, is amoral, and the piece a deliberate provocation to society to condemn such spontaneous sexual behaviour, as if he were saying only a depraved mind could see anything depraved in this. It was surely Nijinsky's homosexual point of view that allowed him to produce a representation of 'natural' masculinity that ran so strongly against convention. As Sokolova, who danced in the ballet with Nijinsky, recalls,

> Nijinsky as the Faune was thrilling. Although his movements were absolutely restrained, they were virile and powerful, and the manner in which he caressed and carried the nymph's veil was so animal that one expected to see him run up the side of the hill with it in his mouth.
>
> (1960: 41)

Nijinska's (1981) description of his other ballet for Diaghilev, *Sacre*, also stresses the animality of the male dancers. In the reconstruction that Millicent Hodson produced for the Joffrey Ballet the men look bestial. They characteristically make their entrances leaning forward; their postures are like those of the figures in the famous nineteenth-century Russian painting of *The Volga Boatmen* by I. Repin (1844–1930). The angle at which the men in *Sacre* lean, and the slightly pointed hats they wear, make them look as if they are about to jump forwards and upwards, and penetrate into one of the massed groups of women. In the first act men fight each other in the Games of the rival clans. The Ancients, in the second act, wear bear skins with the animals' heads fitting on their own like hoods. Grouped with other men round the circle in which the Chosen One is trapped and will dance herself to death, they perform a dance sequence which includes a movement where they drag their left foot across the floor like an animal pawing the ground. Throughout the Chosen One's sacrificial solo, they wait for her death spasm, the signal for them to rush in and grab her, hoisting her high in the air. All these are instances of the bestial quality in the male roles in *Sacre*.

Sokolova recalled the heat on stage every time *Sacre* was performed (Sokolova 1960: 44). Millicent Hodson suggests this may have been partly due to the ritualistic nature of the movement – circle dances that generated altered mental states (Hodson 1985: 41). It must also have come from the effort expended by both sexes in jumping, throwing themselves on the ground and straight away springing back up again, running, stamping. Within this, the male dancers have more dynamic leaps and jumps than the female ones. These are the sorts of movements for which Nijinsky himself was famous in his roles in other men's ballets. In *Sacre*, rather than hiding effort and exhaustion, these are if anything exaggerated. There is no way that the male dancers in *Sacre* could have been thought of as effeminate. If *Faune* presented a pure, 'natural' masculinity, in *Sacre* Nijinsky has stripped this of its acceptable classical setting, to produce a representation of masculinity at its nastiest and most abject. The first performance of *Sacre* on 29 May 1913 at the Théatre des Champs-Elysées has gone down in history for the disturbance that split the audience; that what split them was the revolutionary character of the choreography and not the music is proved by the fact that the latter was ecstatically received when performed on its own in a concert in Paris early in 1914. It was Nijinsky's choreography, including the ways in which masculinity was represented in the ballet, that surely caused the most offence.

Modernism and the male body

Jacques Rivière (1983) argued that the difference between Nijinsky's work and that of Fokine was a new focus on the body: Fokine was too artful, vacillating and vague, but Nijinsky did away with artificiality in 'a return to the body'. Fokine had nevertheless, in his roles for Nijinsky, expanded the range of male dance to include both sensitive and sensual movement, and strong and dynamic expression. Fokine's ballets might hint at aspects of male sexuality whose expression had not previously been acceptable, but these occurred within exotic, 'oriental' or classical settings that were far enough removed from contemporary, modern European ones to defuse any potential threat. In addition Nijinsky as a dancer was so dynamic and skilful that he was hailed as a (male) genius. This in itself was a convenient excuse for any eccentricities. Thus although Fokine may have been introducing types of representation that were new to dance, they could nevertheless be fitted into existing conservative gender ideologies.

It is these two aspects of Nijinsky's star persona – the dynamic solo and the homoerotic spectacle – that have left an active legacy for much of the twentieth century. First, the myth of Nijinsky's leap has fascinated many male ballet dancers and set a standard to which they have aspired. Second, photographs and drawings of Nijinsky in revealing costumes were a prototype for a genre of homoerotic images of male ballet dancers.

It is only in the last few years that Nijinsky's contribution to radical dance practice has been rediscovered by dance historians. *Sacre* can now be seen to have revealed the division in the audience for early modernism – between liberals and radicals who were sympathetic to changing social mores and those conservatives who responded to the anti-bourgeois sentiments of modernism. If the re-emergence of the male body in dance and ballet at the beginning of the twentieth century can be seen as a disruptive force, it was not through the renewal of bravura male dancing nor the founding of a homoerotic tradition but through the radicalism of early modernism. By denaturalizing and destabilizing the representation of gender in theatre dance, Nijinsky was using the kinds of deconstructive strategies that are more familiarly associated with the work of the postmodern choreographers.

29

DANCES OF DEATH:
GERMANY BEFORE HITLER

Susan Manning

In June 1930, Wigman realized her vision of 'communal theatre' in collaboration with Albert Talhoff. Together they staged *Totenmal* (*Call of the Dead*), a multimedia spectacle memorializing soldiers killed in the First World War. Premiered at the Third Dancers' Congress held in Munich, the production combined a speaking choir and movement choir. Talhoff borrowed the form of the speaking choir from the working-class theatre movement, while Wigman borrowed the form of the movement choir from the populist wing of the modern dance movement. Having disbanded her all-female dance company two years before, the choreographer cast students drawn from her Dresden school, the Munich branch school, and the Dorothee Günther school in Munich. She later commented on the transition from her dance company to the movement choir in *Totenmal*:

> It was no longer a matter of the play of forces with and against one another [. . .] The potential matter of conflict was no longer to be solved within the group itself. What was of concern here was the unification of a group of human beings [that] strove from a unified viewpoint toward a common aim recognized by everyone; a viewpoint which no longer permitted any splitting into single actions [. . .]
> In the same way as the choric creation demands its antagonist – whether or not it takes actual shape or takes effect as thematic idea above and beyond the events – in many cases it also asks for a leader [*Anführer*] chosen by the chorus, for the one who conveys the message powerfully, who, supported and carried by the entire chorus, advances the thematic idea and brings it to its final execution.
>
> (Wigman 1966: 92–3)

Totenmal occasioned more critical debate than any of Wigman's earlier group works. Although some critics considered the production an ambitious realization of the Wagnerian *Gesamtkunstwerk* (total work of art), others found it a disappointment, more hype than substance, and outdated as well. Many saw the work as a sign of the stagnation of the modern dance movement as a whole. What contemporary observers could not see, of course, was the extent to which *Totenmal* modelled a prototype for Nazi theatre – in its theme, the cult of the fallen soldier; in its format, the combination of a movement choir and a speaking choir; and, above all, in its strategy of not appearing 'political'. Only in retrospect can one see how Talhoff and Wigman, perhaps unintentionally, staged not a 'theatre above politics', as they believed, but a protofascist theatre. Revising the tradition of festival, borrowing forms from the left and reorienting them toward the right, *Totenmal* set a precedent for Nazi dramaturgy.

In the preface to the published script Talhoff stated his intent to create an 'alternative' to the 'political theatre' of Erwin Piscator, Bertolt Brecht, Kurt Weill and others, 'an alternative that points toward the universally human essence of existence, at once timely and timeless' (Talhoff 1930a: 12). But Talhoff's script contradicted his preface, sounding 'the cult of the fallen soldier' familiar from nationalist and militarist rhetoric of the time. Wigman's staging then obscured this association by lending the production an almost religious aura. The apparent contradiction between Talhoff's script and Wigman's staging was itself a protofascist gesture, projecting the illusion of community (*Gemeinschaft*) as a way of erasing the very real divisions of society (*Gesellschaft*).

The turn toward fascism evident in *Totenmal* accompanied a turn away from the feminism implicit in earlier dances. In this production Wigman again employed actual facial masks, carved by a Munich artist named Bruno Goldschmitt. But the masks functioned to confer gender rather than to blur gender, as a masked choir of men – representing the spirits of men fallen in battle – confronted a masked choir of women – representing the men's wives, mothers, sisters and lovers. The action turned on the women's attempt, led by Wigman, the only unmasked figure, to call the dead back to life.

For the first time since staging *The Queen* (c.1917) on Monte Verità, Wigman cast men as dancers in a group work, and the male presence for the first time cast women in traditional roles. The women no longer defined themselves as a self-sufficient female community but derived their identities from their relations with men. Their masks no longer refused the male gaze, but rather assigned them stereotypical female identities. That Wigman alone remained unmasked reversed the dynamic of earlier masked dances such as *Dance Fairy Tale* (1925) and *Dance of Death* (1926). In those dances the mask had allowed both Wigman and her dancers to defy the antitheses of male and female, human and demonic, living and dead. But in *Totenmal* Wigman's unmasked presence mediated between the women's chorus, the chorus of the living, and the men's chorus, the chorus of the dead. Her unmasked persona embodied her near superhuman stature.

As in *Dance of Death*, Wigman's leadership became associated with self-sacrifice. Through the first half of *Totenmal* she led through the example of action, confronting the spirits of the dead again and again, even though the other women fled. But at the crux of the work she subordinated herself to the Demon, the personification of war, and thereafter the strength of her acquiescence became an example to the other women. For the first time since staging *The Seven Dances of Life* (1921), Wigman externalized the demonic principle in the form of a male performer. Opposing herself to the male demon, she redefined leadership as female endurance. That she appeared unmasked reinforced the new gendering of her *Führerschaft* (leadership).

In the tradition of festival, the production of *Totenmal* took place in a specially designed hall, seating sixteen hundred spectators, built with a generous subsidy from the city of Munich. Also in the tradition of antibourgeois theatre, the spectacle featured a mass of performers, about a hundred in all, divided between the speaking and movement choirs. Talhoff's script was performed in a mode halfway between speech and song, a sort of chanting that employed varied techniques for breath control. A few speakers were concealed in booths surrounding the auditorium. During interludes in the action these seemingly invisible voices read letters from soldiers killed in the war. The programme alerted spectators that these letters were taken from actual collections published in Germany, France and England. The remaining speakers were divided into two groups on platforms placed on both sides of the stage. Accompanying the speaking choir was a percussion orchestra (scored by Talhoff) as well as a colour organ that coordinated sound and light effects.

The spectacle divides into eight sections.[1] In the first, *Hall of Summons* (*Raum des Rufs*), the women enter up a ramp from the orchestra pit to the central platform, pausing one by one under a spotlight. Each dancer assumes a physical attitude corresponding to her mask. The masks are individualized yet stereotyped, suggesting the stages of a woman's life from youth to old age. Once all the women gather on the platform, Wigman directs them to huddle together. Fused into an anonymous mass, they set off the choreographer's larger-than-life quality. Suddenly, the spirits appear on an upstage platform, frightening the women. According to the stage directions, all the women except Wigman flee.

In *Totenmal* the opposition between femininity and masculinity corresponds to the opposition between life and death, or in movement terms, between mobility and immobility, animation and stasis. The women's masks and movement styles are individualized (however stereotypically), but the men's costumes are identical, their masks nearly so, and they move in unison with a uniform quality. According to the stage directions: '[The men] wear cothurni. Their gestures are stenographically monotonous. Each spirit figure executes inexhaustible repetitions of the same assigned movement'

(Talhoff 1930a: 62). Wigman's dancing mediates between the oppositions of life and death, femininity and masculinity. Her performance embraces the extremes of mobility and immobility, encompassing a far broader range of movement qualities than either the male or female chorus.

Subsequent sections repeat and intensify the fundamental action of the first section: again and again the women encounter the spirits, and all except Wigman flee. During interludes in the action the voices of soldiers killed in the war resound through the space, each of their letters punctuated by the entire choir reciting, 'From one who fell in Flanders . . . From one who fell at Ypres . . . From one who fell in Arras' (Talhoff 1930b: 24).

The leader resumes her mission in *Hall of Oblivion* (*Raum der Vergessenheit*). At first Wigman dances alone, flanked by the group of women. Finally, they join her, magnifying her invocation of the dead. But as soon as the chorus of spirits reappears, the women flee once again. The choreographer remains, continuing her attempt to animate the chorus of spirits, but darkness soon blots out her figure and evokes the invisible voices of the fallen soldiers.

In *Hall of Conjuration* (*Raum der Bannung*) the choreographer renews her attempt to conjure the dead. The stage directions describe her dance as 'the struggle between space and figure, between space-light and conjuring movement' (Talhoff 1930a: 45). Finally, the chorus leader imitates her gesture, and it seems as if Wigman has succeeded in rousing the dead. Yet her success proves illusory; the chorus of spirits turns away from the pair, and the demon figure suddenly appears and jumps between the two. The section ends with a tableau of the Demon threatening Wigman. At this point her leadership shifts from actively confronting the spirits to enduring her defeat.

The choreographer makes a final effort to call the spirits back to life in *Hall of Echoes* (*Raum des Gegenrufs*). At first her steps are reverent, then agitated. Finally, the spirits are set in motion, and she withdraws into the shadows, her life-force drained by their coming to life. According to the stage directions, the chorus of the dead stamps in unison, and the rhythm of their stamping synchronizes with the voices of the speaking choir. At a sudden cry darkness falls, cutting short the spirits' dance. Wigman revives and dances, first summoning reserves of energy, then weakening, finally whirling herself into exhaustion. She falls to the side as the spirits rush forward, waving their heavy gown like flags. The rhythmic movements of the spirits synchronize with the voices of the speaking choir, which accuses the spectators of forgetting the dead. Then the spirits retreat to their original formation. Wigman responds with a dance of sorrow, her movements nearly devoid of energy. She rises to standing, growing into the shape of a cross then collapses, breaking the shape, and lies still as if dead. As in the earlier *Dance of Death*, her leadership becomes identified with sacrifice, and the cross associates her with the sacrificial leadership of Christ.

Extending this religious association, the final section, *Hall of Devotion* (*Raum der Andacht*), shifts the mode of presentation and focuses on images of sound and light. Voices alternately herald a new beginning through the power of God's love and damn the destructiveness of war and man's inability to break the vicious cycle of hate. Ultimately, faith triumphs over despair. An American journalist described the 'emotional crescendo' of the end: 'The light organ changed from dull to high, strong colors, the chanting grew in volume, the cymbals crashed, the organ blared red, and the mourners [the speaking choir] stood straight with their arms held high in token of victory and belief. An emotionally exhausted audience staggered to its feet.'[2]

Why in the end cannot the living and the dead, the female chorus and the male chorus unite? Examined separately, the script and the staging suggest overlapping and contradictory answers. But when examined in tandem, the script and staging project a coherent ideological strategy, which retrospect reveals as protofascist.

The choreography posited an exchange of energies between the choreographer and the chorus of the fallen soldiers. Conjuring the dead to life, Wigman spent her own life-force. The duality of motion and stillness, animation and stasis, governed the world of the dance. Within this world arousing the inanimate required extinguishing the animate. Hence, there seemed a kinesthetic barrier between the living and dead, the male chorus and the female chorus.

The staging overlaid this kinesthetic barrier with religious import. As the dance images gave way to images of sound and light, the action suggested the fusion of living and dead not in actuality but in imagination. This imagined union analogized the ritual of Christian communion, the merging of the worshipper with Christ. That Wigman's final dance enacted the image of a cross underscored the religious import of the action.

The production's kinesthetic design and overt religiosity realized Talhoff's stated intent of creating 'an alternative . . . to the political theatre'. But the script contradicted the staging and pointed not to a theatre above politics but to a theatre of ambivalent politics. Playing off what historian George Mosse (1979) has termed 'the cult of the fallen soldier', the script confused militarism and pacifism.

The speaking choir suggests that Wigman's attempt to bring the fallen soldiers back to life fails because the living community of spectators does not sufficiently remember the dead. In this way the text reinforced nationalist rhetoric that accused the home front of 'backstabbing' the soldiers on the front and called for the nation to atone for and avenge the loss by taking up arms again. The wordplay of the title underscored this implication, for *Totenmal* plays on the connotations of both *Denkmal* (monument or memorial) and *Kainsmal* (Cain's mark, i.e., a symbol of guilt).

But the socialists also exploited the emotional impact of the memory of the war dead. Inverting nationalist rhetoric, socialists evoked the image of the fallen soldier as a warning against future militarist adventures. The script accorded with this pacifist programme, by including letters written by soldiers of all nations – not just German soldiers – killed in the First World War.

The script's confusion of militarism and pacifism was obscured by the production's personification of war in the figure of the Demon. Given human form, war seemed more a natural phenomenon than a sociopolitical event. Like the kinesthetic barrier between the living and the dead, war became a given, beyond human control and beyond human decision-making. From this perspective, the distinction between militarism and pacifism appeared irrelevant.

The evidence suggests that most contemporary spectators considered *Totenmal* a pacifist statement. This is how it appeared to spectators and participants interviewed decades later, who remembered especially the haunting voices reading the soldiers' letters. Presumably, these 'invisible voices' made the greatest impression on many other spectators as well, who easily might not have understood the chanted script or recognized its covert support for militarism. (However, the text was available for sale, in English and French translation in addition to the original German.) Certainly, the reviewer for the *Völkischer Beobachter*, organ of the Nazi party, interpreted the production as a statement of support for pacifism. The reviewer commented: 'Thalhoff [sic] doesn't appear to be a Jew [. . .] but that his piece is dedicated to all soldiers fallen in the World War alone demonstrates his internationalist-pacifist orientation' (anon. 1929). Only a few spectators were as perceptive as Ernst Iros, who wrote in *Die neue Zeit*: 'The seemingly straightforward progression of the action is confusing, because it takes all sides, both affirming war and negating war. It is not above politics, as Talhoff believes, but rather feeble-minded and speculative' (Iros 1930: 12).

The ambivalent politics of *Totenmal* take on a particular significance in the context of contemporary political developments. Nineteen thirty was a year of crisis for the Weimar Republic. Under pressure of mounting unemployment and worldwide economic collapse, the precarious coalition of Social Democrats and conservatives that had governed through the twenties fell apart. Political factionalism gave way to political extremism. In March the coalition cabinet resigned, and in September the Nazis scored their first victory at the polls. Thus, during the summer that *Totenmal* played in Munich, an electoral battle raged between socialists and nationalists. Against this backdrop the production's dual advocacy of militarism and pacifism projected middle-class desire not to have to choose between the extreme left and the extreme right. The spectators that longed for a 'middle way' between nationalism and socialism also longed for a 'theatre above politics', and *Totenmal* seemed to provide both. The staging of the war memorial obscured its contradictory politics, effacing the necessity of choice. The protofascism of the spectacle lay in its strategy of concealing a highly politicized theatre within an apolitical aura.

Kurt Jooss's *The Green Table* (*Der Grüne Tisch*), premiered in 1932, presents an illuminating comparison with *Totenmal*. Like Wigman's collaboration with Talhoff, Jooss's work staged a dance of death employing masks. But there the resemblance ends. In contrast to *Totenmal*, which protested the conventions of bourgeois theatre, *The Green Table* embraced the possibilities for 'dance theatre' (Tanztheatre) within the opera house. Set to a score by Fritz Cohen and designed by Hein Heckroth, the production cast dancers from the Essen Opera, where Jooss worked as ballet director.

Although originally a student of Laban, Jooss had little interest in the form of the movement choir. Rather he believed in the synthesis of modern dance and ballet. In 1927 he wrote: 'The creative adventures of expressionism lie behind us, also the convulsive cries of early jazz, the primeval tones of expressionist poetry, and the free – in its way barbaric – *Ausdruckstanz*. We are living in an age which is rediscovering artistic form [. . .] A creative compromise between free personal expression and formal compliance with objective, intellectual laws is developing' (Markard 1985: 15). At the Essen Opera, Jooss was responsible for choreographing operettas and opera interludes as well as creating independent works for the dance ensemble such as *The Green Table*. Addressing the Second Dancers' Congress, he noted:

> Economic possibilities for the practice of dance on any larger scale today almost only exist in the opera houses and to a lesser degree in the drama theatres. The dance world of today must therefore take two major aspects into account: satisfying the needs of the theatre on the one hand, but on the other hand, and at the same time, working unceasingly [. . .] on the overall idea of dance theatre.
>
> (Markard 1985: 17)

The Green Table departed from *Totenmal* not only in its adherence to the conventions of bourgeois theatre but also in its unambiguous alignment with leftist politics. Although the protofascism of *Totenmal* becomes clear only in retrospect, the political affiliation of *The Green Table* was more apparent in 1932 than decades later, when the generalizing power of the work and its survival in the repertory have supported multiple interpretations. Created during the last year of the Weimar Republic, the production affirmed leftist politics through a simple structural device, the juxtaposition of framed and framing sections. While the framed sections associate the dance of death with war, the framing sections assign responsibility for war's dance of death to the Gentlemen in Black and to the Profiteer.[3]

The traditional dance of death exists outside chronological and geographical coordinates. As visualized by the fifteenth-century frescoes depicting the dance of death on the walls of a church in Lübeck, known as the Lübecker Totentanz and one of Jooss's sources for his work, the personification of death inhabits a generalized locale, symbolic of all times and places. Within this symbolic world-space he leads representatives of all classes of society – beggar, peasant, bishop, king – to their end. Revising this traditional conception, Jooss localized the dance of death within the arena of war. Within the framed sections Death summons his victims – young soldiers and their idealistic leader, an old woman, a young girl, and a female revolutionary. The action suggests that war destroys not only those who go off to fight but also those who stay home awaiting their loved ones.

The Gentlemen in Black, masked and tuxedoed, appear in the opening and closing sections, framing the remainder of the action with their deliberations around a large green table. Although they gesture in disagreement, their debate reveals them going through the motions, as they repeat exactly the same steps at the end as at the beginning. The logic of sequence sets their ritualized discussion as the continuing cause of war. Undeterred by the destruction of the dance of death, they continue their machinations.

Who are the Gentlemen in Black? This is a key question for a political interpretation of the work. In the postwar period Jooss insisted upon the ambiguity of their identity. In an interview conducted in 1976, the choreographer noted that they represented 'all the powers which can gain in a war, which in the end, through their machinations, cause a war'. He added: 'I didn't know and I still don't know who "The Gentlemen in Black" are, I don't think they are diplomats. There may be one or two diplomats among them' (Markard 1985: 49).

That the choreography left the exact identity of the Gentlemen in Black ambiguous and open to interpretation has led to multiple interpretations of the work. When Jooss's company-in-exile toured the work during the years of the Second World War, the masked dancers were widely seen as Nazi leaders. When the Joffrey Ballet revived the ballet in 1976, they were associated with the American 'military-industrial complex' responsible for the Vietnam War. In other words, successive generations of spectators have identified the Gentlemen in Black in terms of contemporary notions of a power elite. Thus The Green Table has survived in repertory, its message of continuing relevance.

The work did carry a particular import in the context of 1932, however, and in this context contemporary spectators clearly saw Jooss's alignment with leftist politics. As the choreographer later noted, the work had two sources, his viewing of the Lübecker Totentanz and his reading of the leftist journal Die Weltbühne, which featured the political satire of Kurt Tucholsky. Jooss remembered one recurring refrain in Tucholsky's writing: '"Don't believe it, don't believe it, these peace talks. It's all rubbish, it's all fake, they are secretly preparing a new war." He had true secrets which could prove that he was right' (Markard 1985: 49). According to Tucholsky and other leftist intellectuals associated with *Die Weltbühne*, a coalition of industrialists and conservatives wielded the real power in the Weimar government, just as they had during the Wilhelmine Empire. Capitalism and militarism were allies.

The choreography supports the thesis of an alliance between capitalism and militarism by drawing a connection between the Gentlemen in Black and the figure of the Profiteer. Through the framed sections, the Profiteer lurks as an evil presence, presiding over the brothel, stealing from the corpses of slain soldiers, profiting from the social disruption and carnage of war. Significantly, the Profiteer is the only figure within the framed sections to escape Death, dropping to the floor and rolling offstage just before the blackout that precedes the reappearance of the Gentlemen in Black. As Marcia Siegel has pointed out, although the Profiteer's movement qualities – the way he 'shrinks, angles, hides' – contrast the movement qualities of Death – 'imposing, contained, direct and strong' – the Profiteer shares the quality of indirectness with the Gentlemen in Black (Siegel 1989: 20). Within the framed sections the Profiteer represents the workings of entrepreneurial capitalism, thus functioning as the Gentlemen's surrogate. His actions realize the large designs of capitalism on a day-to-day level.

Given the temper of leftist politics in the closing years of the Weimar Republic, such a reading of *The Green Table* was inescapable. The Nazis correctly interpreted Jooss's leftist leanings, and after they came to power, they harassed the choreographer. The municipal government of Essen dismissed Fritz Cohen and several other Jewish members of the company, and an article appeared in the local newspaper branding Jooss as 'Moses' temple dancer'. The attack read in part: 'In the new Germany the artist has the damned duty to exercise spiritual and national discipline due to his public mission. If he cannot do this, he must leave the fairground of German art and display his creations where he finds spiritually and racially kindred souls!' (Markard 1985: 51). Jooss took the hint and, along with members of his company, slipped across the border to Holland. The next day the local Gestapo arrived at his house with an arrest warrant. The company took up exile in England, and the choreographer did not return to Germany until 1949.

NOTES

1 My reconstruction derives from Talhoff's published script (1930a and b), Wigman's prompt book (available at the Academy of Arts in Berlin), and a brief silent film. The original film is available at the Federal Film Archive in Koblenz; a

substantial excerpt is included in Snyder and Macdonald's documentary *Mary Wigman, 1886–1973: 'Where the Fire Dances between the Two Poles'*.
2 Ripley, 'Music and the Dance', NYPL-DC.
3 The analysis presented here is based on viewing the work in performance and on the 1982 'Dance in America' video of the Joffrey production.

30

MARK MORRIS: THE BODY AND WHAT IT MEANS

Joan Acocella

One of the things that has endeared Mark Morris to his audience is the emphatically human look of his company. In the troupe's early days, the women tended to be large – the 'girls' basketball team', someone commented at a 1983 concert – and the men small. In other words, they looked more like regular people than like a dance company, where size differences between the sexes are greater than the human norm. But what is most striking about the lineup of dancers who have passed through the Morris company is simply the physical variety within the group. Some of the women are large, and have discernibly female bodies. Others are tiny. One of the men, Guillermo Resto, looks like a wrestler; others are delicately built. One man is grey-haired, another balding. Two have dreadlocks. Morris's dancers are also older than the average American dancer. For most of the company's existence, the majority of its members have been over thirty. And they are a vivid ethnic assortment. No one wears glasses onstage, but otherwise they look a lot like the crowd one might meet at the bank or the grocery store.

They also move like human beings. On occasion they perform the kind of 'ordinary movement' – plain walking, sitting down in a chair – that was introduced into dance in the sixties by the Judson Dance Theater. For the most part, however, what they do is not ordinary movement but a carefully designed choreography that stresses qualities we think of as ordinary, such as weight and effort. Weight above all. 'Gravity is our friend,' Morris said to an interviewer in 1989. 'At least, we modern dancers like it.' This love of gravity is one of the things that make people, when they look at his work, think of the early modern dancers, such as Isadora Duncan, who reintroduced weight into concert dancing at the turn of the century. Morris's dancers tend to stand in *demi-plié* (on slightly bent knees), with their bare feet flat on the floor. They look solid; you can feel their weight in your mind. And often, when they jump, they don't cushion the landing by bringing the foot down in stages (ball, then heel). They land with a thud.

Indeed, they are always thudding, falling, smacking the floor. In *Gloria*

(1981), the prayer-for-mercy section begins with a man crashing onto the stage from somewhere high in the wings, as if he had been dropped down by a backhoe. In *Dido and Aeneas* (1989), when the wicked Sorceress (played by Morris) comes running onstage along a balustrade, her feet smack the wood loudly with each step. A reviewer once commented that Morris used his feet as if they were webbed, a remark that reportedly annoyed him very much but which had some justice. Flesh against hardness – he loves this sound.

In insisting on the relationship of the body to the floor, Morris is telling not just a hard truth – the earth is beneath us, we're mortal – but a delicate truth, about what the body is. Never has flesh seemed more human than when, in Morris's dances, we hear it come up against the unyielding floor. In *Behemoth* (1990), his most terrifying work, he turns the screw even tighter: a lone dancer, lying on his back, moves slowly upstage by pushing himself with his feet, and the traction of his sweaty back against the floor makes a low moaning sound. We cannot see the man's face; we only hear this moan, the report of what is tender and alive against what is hard and cold.

What Morris is interested in is exposure, and this helps to explain another curiosity of his choreography, his love of the buttocks. 'People have always said we have big butts,' he commented to Christine Temin of the *Boston Globe* in 1989. 'We *do* have big butts.' As it happens, only a few of the dancers (including Morris) have big butts – that is, normal butts, not dancer-thin – but what all of them have is choreography that emphasizes the buttocks. *Demi-plié*, to begin with, tends to push the buttocks out. (According to company wisdom, Morris's heavy use of *demi-plié* actually increases the size of the buttocks.) Beyond that, Morris is constantly showing the buttocks. In the Waltz of the Flowers in *The Hard Nut*, Morris's 1991 version of *The Nutcracker*, seven dancers lie down on their backs with their heads to us and execute a half-somersault, so that we look directly at their back ends – seven of them, all in a row, blandly greeting the audience: an image all the more remarkable in that these people are supposed to be flowers. They repeat the manoeuvre four times, lest we miss the point. The costumes aid in the exposure. In a number of Morris's early pieces, what the dancers wore was simply underwear: jockey shorts, boxers, jogging bras. Elsewhere too, the costumes he has favoured – smocks that end at the crotch, tights and jumpsuits that end at mid-thigh, like long-line girdles – tend to be revealing.

'I love to see their butts,' says Morris. That love is not erotic, or not mostly. If it were, their butts would look sexier and presumably the men's buttocks would be more in evidence than the women's, which they are not. No, what he is after is the thing that is *underneath*, both literally and meta-phorically. The buttocks are an innocent, hardworking part of the body – soft and round, the seat of humility, the place that gets kicked. To Morris they seem to represent something modest and tender and unacknowledged, the body's vulnerability. At the same time, what they represent in dance terms is the body's dignity, for they are the motor of action: they contain the pelvis, from which the movement originates. So in both senses the buttocks harbour a fundamental truth, and one that in Morris's eyes is validated by the fact that it requires exposure. For him, truth is always hard to find. Veils have to be dropped. Once, describing to a journalist why he loved conduct-ing choreographic workshops, he said, 'It's like we all pull our pants down' – a telling metaphor. In one of his dances, *Striptease* (1986), the performers do pull their pants down.

And it's not just the buttocks he is interested in. He also makes heavy use of the crotch. In his *L'Allegro, il Penseroso ed il Moderato* (1988), when the vocal text speaks of a goddess giving birth, three women lie down on the floor and spread their legs. In his *Lovey* (1985), we see a woman in baby-doll pyjamas on all fours, butt out, with her back to us – a startling sight. In *Gloria*, in the middle of a slow, plangent, here-is-my-soul passage, the dan-cers bend down and, with one arm in front and one behind, clasp their hands at their crotches. The effect is not at all sexy. This is not the crotch grabbing of rock singers ('Look what I have here') or of alley mime ('Screw you'). On the contrary, there is often a note of pain – the dancers in *Gloria* look as though they are hanging on to their crotches for dear life. Elsewhere, the point, again, is simply exposure: something private being revealed, something inside being forced out.

Another way Morris exposes the body is by refusing to refine effort out of his choreography. Most dance is designed, and cast, in such a way that however difficult the steps, they can be executed with a look of ease. Indeed, this is one of the great pleasures of watching dance: to see something so hard be done, it seems, so effortlessly. Morris's logic is the opposite. He gives the dancers steps that cannot be performed with a look of ease – turns so hard-flung that they can't be finished neatly, steps that must be completed in one count when, to be done without rush, they need two, stretchings and reachings that push the dancers beyond any control over their appearance. 'In a lot of the movement,' says Donald Mouton, who danced with the company for nine years, 'your job is to push one extremity as far as you possibly can. It's not just step right, step left. You have to bring your left leg all the way around until you can't go any farther, so you have to go to the next place. It's not a decorative thing at all.'

On the contrary, it is a struggle. Toward the end of *The Hard Nut* Morris has about half the cast of the ballet come onstage to do *pirouettes à la seconde*. *Pirouette à la seconde* is a virtuoso ballet step in which the dancer – almost always a man (Baryshnikov was famous for this step) – sticks one leg out at a 90-degree angle to the body and then performs a pumping turn in place. The more turns, the more spectacular the step: the dancer looks like a pneumatic drill. But the extended leg must be kept absolutely straight and at 90 degrees, and the dancer's balance must not waver. For this reason, there is usually some allowance in the choreography for the dancer to end the pirou-ette when he chooses (that is, before he starts to fall over). Furthermore, the

271

pirouette à la seconde is normally done solo; if two people tried to do it together, they would tend to go out of unison and thus rob the step of its look of focused perfection. Morris, however, has not just one or two people but ten people – none of them professional ballet dancers, many of them struggling to keep the leg from drooping – perform *pirouettes à la seconde* in unison, with no allowance for ending early. The effect, and the goal, is not a look of perfection but one of good-humoured effort. It is like watching ten people trying to climb a flag-pole simultaneously. In other pieces the dancers show a kind of blunt purposefulness that, combined with the kind of steps they perform, makes them seem like children in a Christmas pageant. They are trying to do their job, and that's all. No matter how proficient the company has become, they have never lost this look of innocence.

Morris often underlines the quality of effort by casting his dancers against type, against ease. 'I remember, when he gave us a step in rehearsal,' Mouton says, 'and we all did it, if he said to you, "That's a natural for you", that meant you weren't going to get to do it.' Morris doesn't always cast against type, but he does it often, and deliberately, 'so they can't do imitations of themselves,' as he once explained in an interview.

What he is trying to get at through all this exposure can be seen in his 1982 *New Love Song Waltzes*, a work that became a big audience favourite. Set to Brahms's song cycle *Neue Liebeslieder*, the piece is a love dance, but whereas most love dances are transfiguring, moulding the human form into longer lines, sweeter harmonies, as if love naturally made us superhuman, *New Love Song Waltzes* tells the opposite story: love makes the dancers human.

The opening is thrilling. As the lights go up, we see a single woman, Ruth Davidson, crouching at the back of the stage. She runs toward us, jumps into *demi-plié*, leaps upward, executes a full turn in the air, her skirt flying up meanwhile to show her strong thighs, and then lands, bam, in *demi-plié*, facing us straight on. This is an explosive announcement, and what it announces is what the vocal text is telling us at that moment: 'Abandon hope of rescue, O heart, / when you venture on the sea of love.' It is a declaration, in bodily terms, of the violence of love and the sheer, exposing effort love puts us through: how it turns our heads, lifts our skirts, makes us tear around.

The rest of the piece follows in the same vein. There are fifteen sections – a ring dance, a cascade dance, an exploding down-the-middle-of-the-stage dance, and so on – each with a lesson about love. But in all of them, the force of love is to make the dancers struggle. They hang by their legs from each other's necks. They haul each other around by the armpits. They fall, and others step over them. At other times they don't so much struggle as simply move with utter bluntness. They take hard little hops; they stoop; they squat; they sit on each other's arms.

In what is always the audience's favourite section, the dancers, in pairs, take to the floor and embrace, but not in a poetic manner. They lie smack on top of each other, tangling their legs together, letting their skirts hike up, showing us the insides of their thighs. Looking at them, we can feel the actual heaviness of another human body, the warmth of the flesh, the burden of it. They feel the burden too, and as the dance proceeds, the dancers get up one by one and move over into other pairs of arms. They are always restive, always searching.

New Love Song Waltzes, like *A Midsummer Night's Dream*, is about love not as something that two people feel for each other and can therefore resolve – this may be the only love dance in the world that contains no partnered duet – but as something that one person, or all humanity, feels: love as a goad, a yearning, changeable in its object but not in its force. This is an extension of Morris's concern with human vulnerability, and the voice of that vulnerability is the body. Somebody trying with all his might to hook himself onto somebody else by a body part that can't hold him, and in the process showing his bulging tendons, his clamped gluteals: that, for Morris, is romantic love, its comedy and its sorrow.

It is no accident that *New Love Song Waltzes* is set to vocal music. Since 1980, half of Morris's entire repertory has been set to vocal music – an extraordinary percentage. There are probably a number of reasons for this, but according to him, the main reason is that singing comes out of the body: 'When you have a person reading music and playing the violin, you have the sound of that, but it's one generation removed from the body. Singing is like dancing. It's the body, the body in the world, with nothing in between, no instrument between.' The closer something is to the body, the more interesting it is to him. And of course the voice comes from *inside* the body – the lungs, the throat, the mouth – and sounds like it: liquid, fleshly, urgent. It too is a private part.

This intensely visceral idea of dance is something for which there are obvious sources in Morris's early life. Both the main styles of dancing in which he was trained as a boy, flamenco and Balkan folk dance, are stamping styles. They give an oral report of the rhythm, not just a visual report, and it was from them that Morris learned to love the sound of the foot coming down on the floor. Folk dance – and, in particular, the Koleda Folk Ensemble, a commune-like troupe with whom Morris performed as a teenager – is also the obvious model for effort in dancing, for the image of dance as a bunch of regular people trying to do something together. Indeed, the Morris company in their *pirouettes à la seconde* in *The Hard Nut* look like a flashback to Koleda: a big group, a hard step, a good will. Another possible model is the annual recitals staged by Verla Flowers, Morris's first dance teacher. In those recitals every child got a part – got to be a cowboy or a sugar plum – and worked hard at it. As for the love of vocal music, Morris grew up on singing. He came by it all naturally.

But for the particular way that the Morris troupe looks – human, unglamorized, naked almost – there is another source, the troupe itself. As with all dance companies, what they are onstage is something like what they are offstage, and what they are offstage is unusually unassuming and comradely. The troupe began as a group of friends, and though some of those people have since departed and been replaced by people hired from auditions, they are still a group of friends. Of course there is competition within the group, and there are resentments over who gets what role. Rehearsal is not democratic; Morris says what he wants, and the dancers do it. But there is a spirit of common cause. According to Morris, the reason he chose the dancers he did for his early company was not just that they were friends: 'They were learning how to dance at the same time that I was learning how to choreograph. It happened at the same time.' That is one of the reasons that over the years the dancers have tended to be older. Simply, they are his age, because they started out with him. In turn, the fact that they are close to him in age makes the troupe more democratic. 'Nothing in this company is ever mandatory,' says Tina Fehlandt, one of Morris's original dancers, 'and when it is, I'm gone.' Of course, some things, if not mandatory, are strongly recommended, and the troupe today is not as democratic as when they were starting out. Still, the feeling of fellowship is strong. Within two salary levels, based on seniority, all the dancers are paid the same, and many of them are to be found at the same bar after the show, with Morris at their centre, ordering another round and keeping everybody up too late.

With this sense of equality comes a certain humility. In his troupe, Morris says, 'you can't be that selfish, and you can't be that important, because you're just not. Neither am I.' Again, his humility is not what it used to be, but it is still a philosophical conviction, and you can see it projected onstage: human bodies toiling, and toiling together.

That humility may have a darker side. Several of the older members of the troupe claim that Morris sees himself as ugly. This is not an uncommon emotion in the dance world. Having to go out night after night and show their bodies to large groups of strangers, many dancers are very sensitive about what they imagine to be their physical imperfections. And what others feel but do not say, Morris does say. He says that he felt ugly as a child. The fact that he has given himself so many grotesque roles suggests that he may also have felt ugly as an adult, a condition that, according to some of his dancers, he generalizes to them. 'He wants to show off how odd we are,' says Erin Matthiessen, another company veteran. 'He sees himself as odd and broken.'

But because this matter so closely touches their self-esteem, the dancers probably overstate the case. If Morris wanted to make the dancers look ugly, he could do so, whereas they usually look immensely appealing. What Morris is intent on is not ugliness but, again, exposure and struggle. According to Jon Mensinger, he conducts auditions on the same principle, looking for people who seem somewhat awkward or unconfident: 'If there isn't something about them that's a little vulnerable, they don't have a chance.' We have seen the same principle in his casting: those for whom the dance being rehearsed is a natural are the ones who won't get to do it.

For Morris, a look of mastery, of taken-for-granted achievement, is the face of false pride. 'The big thing,' he told a critic in 1989, 'is not to tell lies [. . .] I can tell in shows when other choreographers, pieces, dancers, audiences are lying. I can tell it in my own dancers. And in myself.' According to Keith Sabado, one of Morris's most frequent corrections in rehearsal is 'You're *fa*-king!'

This phobic sensitivity to falseness may have something to do with being homosexual and thus having had to operate in false situations. (He has said that part of the reason he left the Eliot Feld Ballet, where he danced from 1976 to 1977, was that he 'got tired of pretending to be a straight guy in love with a ballerina'.) Presumably, it also has something to do with his family – with their high moral standards – of which this is a carryover, and with their unremitting kindness, against which this is a reaction. And of course it has to do with the times in which he grew up, the sixties and seventies. Both Morris and his company – or its older members, the ones who started out with him – show many of the incidental manners of the sixties youth culture. They are warm, informal, down-to-earth, anti-genteel.

But whatever his horror of falseness, Morris does not base his work on any claim to a restorative 'trueness', nor does he offer the kind of woolly naturalism that in the art of the sixties (and later) was so often put forward as the alternative to the fraudulence of bourgeois life. Asked about the effortfulness of his style of dancing, he answers, 'It's not effortfulness. It's non-effortlessness [. . .] I'm not stating the opposite of something else, like, "Here, check this out, it isn't conventional beauty". The thing I'm making, I think it's beautiful. I'm not doing an "anti" anything.'

The exposed look of the body on his stage might look like an 'anti' something, and in some of the early dances it probably was, at least in part. *Gloria*, which has ten dancers in grey street clothes dragging themselves across the floor on their stomachs to Vivaldi's exalted *Gloria in D*, has something in common with Jerome Robbins's *Dances at a Gathering* and Paul Taylor's *Esplanade*, those benchmark works of the sixties/seventies youth cult, with their gangs of fresh-faced young folk skipping and running and falling to the accompaniment of sanctified high-art music. Like them, *Gloria* shows a certain Franciscanism, an exaltation of what is plain and openhearted and innocent, as opposed to what is fancy and fake.

But despite this moral balm, most of Morris's work is free of sentimentality and also of naturalism. However natural the dancers' bodies may look, what they are doing is not natural. Leaving aside the extreme complication of the patterns they are making – the structure of the choreography, all of it pinned to the structural complications of the score – the steps themselves, plain though they may look, are highly artificial, 'made up'. People do not naturally fall onto their stomachs and drag themselves across the floor by their arms, let alone do this in a line of seven, in canon. Weight, exposure, struggle: all of these, in Morris's work, are carried far beyond what is normal. They are artistic strategies. For Morris, they give the dance its vividness and edge, its sheer specificity – this image, no other – and hence its symbolic force.

In 1987 Morris created a piece called *Strict Songs*, to a score by Lou Harrison that involved a large chorus singing adaptations of Hopi chants. *Strict Songs* is a hymn to the holiness of the world – the chorus sings of the deer on the mountains, the fantail goldfish, the falling stars – and it is full of dancers dressed in brown, green and blue (for earth, plants and sky) skimming across the stage. At the same time, it is clearly about death, and images of pain and struggle are interspersed among the more ecstatic moves. In the last moment of the piece, those two strands come together in a culminating image. Five couples (the full cast) are onstage. In each couple, one person lies down on the floor on his back, and the other person, placing the first person's feet against his stomach, launches himself into the air, where he levitates, balanced atop the first person's legs, as the curtain comes down.

This is a hellishly difficult manoeuvre. For the second person – the 'flier' – not to fall, the feet must be placed exactly right on the abdomen, and the takeoff into the air must be done with exactly the right thrust. We watch the dancers going through all this with immense care and deliberation. But then, once fliers are launched, we are shown an amazing sight: five people floating in the air. They have died and gone to heaven. At the same time, in the effort they have gone through – some of them are still trembling as they float there – we see how hard it is to die, how hard to get to heaven. Or rather, we feel it in the body, because it is the body's struggle we have witnessed.

This is merely an extreme case of what goes on in all of Morris's choreography. The quality of the body's effort has changed as the work has developed. In the early dances there is more fumbling, more awkwardness, and also more sweeping, more emotionalism. In the later dances the body is neater, more exact in its action. But in all of them the facts of the body are made very clear. This is partly because Morris loves those facts and partly because they accord with his idea of truth. But above all it is because he needs the full force of the body in order to show the force of the soul. Only in the body's resistance to its intention – the fact that the thighbone can only rotate so far in the hip socket, the fact that it is almost impossible to balance a 130-pound body horizontally in the air on somebody's feet, the fact that whatever you are trying to do up or out, your body is at the same time pulling you in and down – can he outline starkly enough that intention: somebody trying to *do* something.

Insofar as he is interested in ugliness and toil, it is for the same reason. What he is really after is beauty and mastery, but he wants them exactly at the moment when they come into being – when they emerge from what was not beautiful or mastered – so that we can see them clearly. There are many, many ways for a dancer to get into the air, and most of them are designed to look easy. By making the dancers of *Strict Songs* struggle to get in the air, Morris catches that action in the moment of its birth; we see something appear that wasn't there a moment ago. The sheer unexpectedness of that event gives it a miraculous character, or, rather, reveals its miraculous character. The dance is launched into metaphor, and what were dancers become angels.

31

DANCE AND MUSIC VIDEO: SOME PRELIMINARY OBSERVATIONS

Theresa Buckland[1]

Over the last decade, the increased TV transmission and commercial availability of music videos have undoubtedly augmented the accessibility of dance via the media. In the music video, dancing frequently forms a clearly discernible element, from the loose improvised rhythmic behaviour of the band and singers, to the strictly choreographed and drilled presentations of both professional dancers and pop stars.

In Britain, specialist cable TV channels, and programmes devoted to pop music such as the perennial *Top of the Pops*, afford abundant opportunity to view music videos. Even the non-aficionado can easily glimpse dancing images on music video, in the domestic context of TV advertisements, or on visits to particular pubs or discos, where the transmission of music videos contributes to an overall atmosphere.

The recent development of the music video has already attracted considerable scholarly attention. A diverse body of literature exists, drawing its analysts primarily from the schools of cultural studies, film theory, feminism and popular music studies. Yet the phenomenon of dancing as a fairly frequent element within the music video has received virtually no direct attention.[2] Film theory, with its emphasis on the constructed image, has tended to dominate, although some balance is being redressed by due regard for the affect and context of the music. None the less, the relationship between sound and dancing image, as transcribed by the camera, remains under-explored. Initial forays into the flourishing, yet hugely complex interrelations of popular dance culture, of which the music video is but one aspect, have highlighted the urgent need for the accumulation of ethnographic, bibliographic and, of course, videographic data. Here is a fascinating and rich field for sustained research. Any future research will, hopefully, not only explore the considerable questions and issues raised by studies in the media and in popular music, but take on board issues of human agency and creativity within the discipline of dance itself.

Preliminary reflections on dance and music video

A first point when examining the appearance of dance on pop music video was to query its function. A possible line of inquiry was the relationship between the dancing on the videos and that performed to the music in clubs and discos.

Today, the pop music industry provides the dominant musical context for social dancing in Britain. Video images of people dancing to music may, perhaps, be construed as merely reflecting or reinforcing the uses to which pop music might be put. Yet a large number of representations of dancing on video do not just suggest a typical party or club scene. Nor are the rhythmic images restricted to the epiphenomenal movements of the musicians. On the contrary, the dancing may frequently appear quite distinctive and deliberate. Performed either by the musicians or by specialist dancers, many routines reveal compositional skill and knowledge of stylized movement which highlight the dance content, as a focused rather than an unstructured activity.

Perhaps these video images of dancing relate to a convention lifted from stage performances of pop songs, where dancers are foregrounded as a substitute for lyrics in the instrumental sections. Rawkins's view that a 'dance sequence has become almost compulsory these days, and ranks highly in the cliché collection' (1984: 14), may well be true of the specific music video she discusses. But the continued use of dance routines, on the videos of well-established and rising pop celebrities, and the fact that the industry places a high premium on image and innovation, would suggest something more than cliché. In any case, the pop music video's dual capacity as advertisement and art work would agitate against any consistent artistic failure to innovate. The consumer's attention has to be attracted by some semblance of originality. Dance sequences, *per se*, do not suggest artistic sterility, but obviously their content and composition require some care to be in line with aesthetic and commercial demands of prevailing fashions.

My first thoughts on dance in pop video led to speculation that the more intellectually reflective end of the spectrum of pop music would eschew the use of dance in its promotional videos. Musicians, or their producers, might prefer either to present the music as played live, or to interpret the music by drawing on filmic devices, particularly from avant-garde films. Following this line of argument, images of dancers would best be deployed in the marketing of music intended for the dance club scene. In practice, this dichotomy of pop music and video functions breaks down, although it is fair to say that there is a kernel of truth in it.

Choreographers of Western theatrical dance are generally accorded individual recognition as authors of their dance works. In the context of the music video, however, anonymity for the choreographer appears to be the norm, especially if they do not already enjoy a public reputation as a choreographer. Where credit is given for the choreography, the star's own expertise as a dancer, or indeed as choreographer, is likely to be a major aspect of their appeal as an entertainer, as in the obvious case of Michael Jackson. In this preliminary investigation of dance on music video, it is no accident that our attention has been mostly drawn to the dancing pop star. Such a phenomenon is arguably more evident in the American pop industry, although a British example, who early pioneered the music video, is Kate Bush. Her multi-media stage performances included carefully crafted dance sequences, as an extension of the lyrical content of her songs. It is interesting to note that Bush's work emerged at a time when dancing gained wider currency, fuelled by the media, as a desirable means of achieving both healthy fitness and the *body beautiful* (usually female it must be said).

Inspired by Hollywood and the trappings of stardom, the recycling of images of women in the concert and video work of Madonna, in particular, continues to grab media attention and, indeed, that of scholars, fascinated by the chimera of a post-feminist woman who controls her own signification in the media. Dance, in this context, veers between authenticating Madonna's street cred in her use of the latest dance club craze, as in the video *Vogue*, and highlighting her images of female temptress, as in the videos of *Like a Virgin* (although the dance content is limited in extent here) and *Open Your Heart*. Madonna's own dancing, clothes, facial expression, and choice of camera angles exploit cultural conventions of soft pornography, the seductive body knowingly objectified in a range of movement codes, tied to the archetype of Salome.

One of the earliest music videos to be made in Britain for wide public consumption also foregrounded woman as dancer. Interestingly enough, dance was not utilized as a potential means of sexual stimulation for male gratification, nor was it intended to purvey the latest movement styles from the discos. Arising from her primary interest as a song-writer and not as a performer, Kate Bush's video of *Wuthering Heights* in 1977 employs dance as an expressive tool to underline the emotional state of the revenant heroine from the Emily Brontë novel of the same title. Influenced by the British mime artist Lindsay Kemp and trained as a dancer for two years after leaving school, Bush has continued to include dance in her music videos, as one element in interpreting the song text.

The pop star as dancer on music video: Kate Bush and Michael Jackson

Kate Bush – *The Whole Story*

In the late 1970s, not only was Bush unusual for the wide range of vocal pitch, barely approached never mind highlighted in regular pop music records, but also the accompanying movements to her singing were drawn, not from conventional disco routines, but from a more experimental expressive base. Her presentation of the song, which earnestly seeks to conjoin word, movement, sound and sentiment, appears perhaps a little too literal for present-day tastes, experienced in reading a multitude of simultaneous and disjunctive images. Nevertheless, Bush was an innovator of note in her attempt to communicate the concept of a song, to an audience outside the traditional domain of musical theatre, through the personal performance of a visual and aural holistic spectacle.

Wuthering Heights, as presented on the 1986 compilation, *The Whole Story* (1986), is essentially a video version of a stage performance, using effects of duplicate and inverted mirror images, tricks of colour changes, and strobing to complement the sense of otherworldliness inherent in the subject. Cathy's ghost is remarkably agile, as she cartwheels and spins in slow motion, trailing multiple images of outstretched legs and arms across the screen in the instrumental sections. Soft focus and dry ice heighten our cultural reading of this slender girl-like figure, in gauzy long white dress with untamed long dark hair, as a spectre with the same Romantic pedigree as Gautier's Wilis in *Giselle*. Bush's movements, although not strictly from the classical ballet canon, owe more to this European tradition of lyricism, augmented with expressive actions from a Grahamesque influence, than to the popular Afro-American derived vernacular of jazz dance.

Similar sources of movement vocabulary and compositional structuring can be viewed in *The Man with the Child in his Eyes* (1978), in which Bush selects a limited amount of material, to be repeated in tandem with chorus and verse. Arguably, this somewhat predictable marrying of musical and choreological structure at this level enables the audience to focus on the song's lyrics, suggesting the singing subject's recurrent fascination with the object of the song's title. As viewers, we are invited to view Bush as a secretive yet knowing girl child, beginning and concluding in foetal position, who draws and lulls us into her confidences. The camera moves us in from the initial overhead shot, into a close-up of Bush's face, made-up as innocent temptress, eyes appealing yet canny, as she addresses us in an intimate yet knowing way. The soothing, long, rounded sound of the opening of the chorus is echoed in the movement, as both arms draw a half-circle outwards from her body, as if casting a spell. Singing subject and object of the song blur, as she takes on characteristics referred to in the words, expressing them through the colour of her voice, her wide open and occasionally dreamy eyes, and through the seemingly unselfconscious, yet intimate, movements circling her body. Tight camera shots and the primarily static choice of position from which to address us augment the sense of intimacy and voyeuristic pleasure we derive from being told emotional secrets.

The choice of a duet to visualize *Running Up That Hill* (1985) reveals Bush in her most dancerly mode on this video compilation. A heterosexual

281

emotional relationship is played out through the movement, in a style reminiscent of London Contemporary Dance Theatre during the 1970s. *Running Up That Hill* commences in hazy purple light with a female hand reaching directly out to grasp a man's neck. As he rhythmically rocks his head jerkily from side to side, the beat begins. The shadowy features of this man are succeeded by the inverted face of Bush, eyes closed, and the camera pulls slightly back to reveal her, in a descending wrap around the man's body. From a low cradling position, he lifts her as she sings 'It doesn't hurt me – do you want to feel how it feels' before she reaches out with spread fingers, away from engagement with the man. Once again, Bush takes the protagonist's role, interpreting the situation and emotional sense of the lyrics, through movement and spatial relationships, enhanced by the camera shots and lighting which directly focus the viewer's gaze. The man appears either in shadow, with his back to us, behind Bush, or with his face averted from her and from us. Through such means, the viewer is manipulated to concentrate on the 'I' of the song, the difficulties of the relationship are expressed through this woman's point of view. The choice of full-length baggy culottes over dance leotards attempts to lessen the specificities of time and place with regard to the two actors, alerting the viewer to focus on the essence of their relationship, aside from any contextual factors.

Unlike the other tracks on the video, Bush does not lip-synchronize the lyrics, with the result that the visual content of the video appears more as a reflective and stylized expression of a personal relationship. Unusually then, the treatment of the star's role in this video operates outside the usual conventions of popular musical theatre, where the bodily production of movement and words are perceived as congruent. Instead the foregrounding of the movement together with a costume, designed to facilitate ease of action rather than specify a social time and context, orientate the video more towards the conventions of twentieth-century Western dance theatre as an art, rather than popular commodity.

When Bush employs dance movement in her later video collection, *The Sensual World* (1990), she again draws from a lyrical, expressive base in her interpretation of the title song. In *Love and Anger* (1989), she turns to the world of classical dance, as an emotionally passive corps de ballet, almost lifted from a white act of *Swan Lake*, merely provide a background of a visual, vertical pulse, to her contrasting image of a contemporary female vocalist, in what appears to be a TV studio. Bush's eclectic theatricality, crossing the worlds of mime, art dance, musical and opera with pop music, contrasts sharply with the dance vision of most American music videos in the 1980s. American female pop stars, whose dance expertise has been highlighted in their videos, have tended to position themselves in relation to the screen tradition of dance and to current popular forms. In that screen tradition of dance (and its feeder, the American stage musical) cross-overs between the vocabularies of ballet, jazz, folk, social and modern dance have a long pedigree, as the musical theatre works of Balanchine, Astaire, Pan, Holm, de Mille, Robbins and Fosse illustrate. In the American music video, the contemporary dance styles of street and disco share existing screen images of dance and sometimes older dance traditions, as in the work of choreographer and pop artist Toni Basil who, in the early 1980s, juxtaposed vocabularies of ballet and hip-hop.

Michael Jackson – *Smooth Criminal*

Jackson's gifts as a solo dancer came to video prominence with *Billie Jean*, directed by Steve Barron, but more particularly with *Beat It*, choreographed by Michael Peters and directed by Bob Giraldi. Peters' choreography, together with that of Jackson himself, is evident on arguably the most successful pop music video of all, *Thriller*, in which the Hollywood ideal of synthesizing plot, character, costume, locale, music, dance and lyrics is realized in an integrated whole (Delameter 1981: Ch. 6).

In his full-length feature film *Moonwalker*, Jackson's acting ambitions are pursued through another stereotypical cinematic role, that of the do-gooder stranger with superhuman powers. This metaphoric treatment of Jackson's own image and relationship with his fans is emphasized through a narrative which casts the threatened as children who perceive and react to Jackson as saviour and pop star. As a vehicle to celebrate his star persona whilst projecting an anti-drugs message to children, *Moonwalker* suffers from a weak plot line, almost absurd transformation scenes, and a somewhat raunchy concert delivery of the final song. The most highly structured dance content in the film, however, occurs in *Smooth Criminal*. It begins with the child stars of the film (two boys and a girl) peeping over a fence at Jackson who, in a blaze of light, enters a club. The scene is a mix of gangster movie and western as Michael Jackson enters the underground city club, occupied by men in thirties-style suits and homburgs and women in moll-like evening dresses. A cautious silence greets his entry, temporarily halting the club activities, while close-ups switching between tense watching faces and a whispered 'watch him' set the mood. Suddenly moving sharply, as if going for his gun, in classic *stranger in town* style, Jackson instead spins a coin in slow motion towards the (anachronistic) juke box. The music, and his obvious command of it vocally and bodily, are the signal for action. What follows is a dance drama on a theme once popular in cabaret, variety entertainment and TV, where the locale and situation permit a series of small staged episodes to be expressed through dance.

Throughout this demonstration, Jackson's skills as a dancer are uppermost, although lip-synching to his own voice ensures the viewer's attention on his actions within each frame. *Reading* the text plays upon the viewer's knowledge of Jackson's image and particularly his kinetic and vocal hallmarks. The shouted gasp which initiates the song is accompanied by a percussive upper chest contraction, so distinctive of Jackson's personal dancing style, together with both knees oscillating in and out as he skilfully and swiftly swivels his feet. No wonder the club hostess nods her approval for entry as he jauntily but stylishly walks on from his concluding leg kick. From here on we are treated to a virtuoso performance of fluid sensuous grace which is always under precise rhythmic control and which merges almost imperceptibly back and forth between everyday gestural interaction and dance structures. This is of course the ideal of dance drama whether under stage or cinematic conventions but none the less the frame is broken to underline Jackson's prowess as a dancer through drawing attention to his real life status in the pop world. As the watching children admire Jackson's feline controlled flow, one of them claims to be the source of all Jackson's kinetic skill. He begins to perform a sequence of Jackson's highly idiosyncratic movements and his point is seemingly substantiated by a cut into the club where Jackson is performing the same sequence. The context beyond the film is that of Michael Jackson as exemplary model for youngsters; Jackson not only provides a cute moment which reminds us of his watching film audience, but underscores his influential and innovative status as dancing star on audiences beyond the frame.[3]

Smooth, rapid spins, further percussive upper body contractions, moonwalking, head nods, and low rotated asymmetrical leg kicks provide further celebratory examples of his style in which he is not averse to the occasional use of hidden mechanical effects to achieve spectacular leans and fast turns. In Jackson's videos, the Barthesian concept of the voice's grain (the body in the voice) combines with the visuals of the feline flow of the centred body which can channel the eruption of explosive rhythm into patterned yet seemingly improvisational expression in response to the energy and texture of the instrumentation (Barthes 1977b: 179–89). The process creates a particular pleasure which results in surrender to a seduction more compelling than intellectual analysis. Watching Jackson videos can be a singularly absorbing activity. In the desire to decode and render ideologies visible, the lure of the experiential should not always be treated with suspicion. Words and intellectual discourse cannot substitute for all modes of human experience, particularly in the realm of the nonverbal.

Personal talent and knowledge as a dancer inevitably contribute to the decisions of pop artists such as Kate Bush and Michael Jackson, to emphasize the choreographic elements of their music videos. Yet the inclusion of dance images on the music videos of pop artists, who perceive themselves primarily as musicians, warrants attention, even if dancing may appear less systematically across their output.

Popular culture, dance and radical art

In live performance, the strong visual energy of dance may often complement a noisy, rhythmic beat, adding spectacle and variety to what might
otherwise be a dominantly static display. Such excitement for the audience
may be provided by highly acrobatic or virtuoso dancing, as in the break
dancing of the greatly influential Rock Steady Crew in the early 1980s or,
more recently, in the accompanying hip hop spectacle of M.C. Hammer's
performances. A number of music videos aim to capture the excitement of
the live spectacle by rapid editing of dancing figures, alongside techniques
of jump cuts, fast zooms, spins, shrinks, dissolves, dolly shots and Dutch
angles. The flatness of the screen image and the slow passage of real time, so
evident in long, documentary-style shots of energetic live concerts, are
counteracted by video techniques which heighten visual perception in a
heady, hallucinatory fashion, seeking to emulate the transformative experience of live audience participation for the spatially distanced video viewer.
New technological facilities combine with filmic techniques already established as intentionally disruptive and as hallmarks of the avant-garde, where,
arguably, radical perception rather than passive seduction on the part of the
viewer is intended.

Given the close personal links between the world of visual arts and pop
entertainment since the 1960s, the incorporation of high and avant-garde art
techniques and images within the music video is not at all surprising (Frith
and Horne 1987). Beyond this though, the recycling of representations and
styles, from the once opposing worlds of high and popular cultures,
contributes to the consideration of music video as quintessentially postmodernist in its content, and, in shifting between artistic and commercial
product, postmodernist in its very form.

Following this line of argument, any dance content may appear in a music
video purely for its surface attraction and, indeed, apparently throwaway
glimpses of dancing flash on screen, in the fast edit visual equivalent
of House music, where cutting and splicing of readymade sounds is a
compositional technique.

Occasionally, the dance style, rather than the filmic procedures, may be
associated with the avant-garde and enlisted alongside the popular. Certain
innovatory notaries of the pop world may collaborate with elements of the
radical fringe of the contemporary dance world. David Bowie, for example,
has employed the physically challenging work of Louise Lecavalier whose
sheer strength, energy and visible muscle power question stereotypical roles
of female dancers. Certainly, the interrogation of gender construction and
sexuality has featured strongly in Western performance work of the 1980s,
across both popular and art entertainment. Music video is no exception,
exploiting the technology in its self-conscious play with image and metamorphosis. Torn from their seemingly once fixed high or popular contexts,

images are accorded equal valence in the bricolage of music video. Such 'free-floating images' (Fiske 1986: 75) should not, however, prevent the viewer from reflecting on the role of the music video in the construction of the overall image of specific pop artists.

Conclusion: some avenues for exploration

The relative eclecticism of dance sources for the Hollywood musical has already been noted, but it is evident that, in emulating and paying tribute to that model, pop artists such as Michael Jackson have striven to realize the concept of the integrated dance musical. Codified movement is regarded as one complementary element in the communication of that overall aim, working conjunctively with the other expressive systems of sound, word and visuals in the formulation of a clear narrative.

Underpinning our approach to dance in music video has been the concept of the *integrated text* which concerns any text which employs different systems of communication. In general parlance, the term 'integration' implies wholeness or unity, as in Delameter's notion of the integrated dance musical mentioned above. In our usage, the degree of wholeness or unity in the integrated text will depend upon the kinds of relationship that can be found between the different systems. The traditional Hollywood film musical thus aims to employ the systems conjunctively, creating a classic realist text which renders the reader passive in its promise of closure. Even though Michael Jackson's *Thriller* uses two Hollywood genres, the narrative works in a linear fashion at an overall level, unlike, for example, New Order's *True Faith* video (1989) where the reader's attempts to unravel a scenario are continually thwarted.

With regard to the role of dance in the music video, at one end of a continuum is a dramatic mode, where dance operates prominently as an expressive tool. At the other is the fragmentary, unrelated dance image, non-diegetic, unconnected to the musical producers, and perhaps only flitting briefly across the scene. Here the moving body interacts with the technology to form abstract visual and rhythmic patterning. It is perhaps not surprising that this style appears rarely in the presentation of the dancing pop star. Even when the dancing is not deployed to illuminate text, character, or situation, the filmic treatment of the dancing pop star is constrained primarily by the constructive techniques of stardom. To treat the body of a star, even in its surface screen formulation, as entirely manipulable material for video effects is potentially to deny the readily perceivable movement skills of the performer. Clear recognition of the star's identity and physical prowess are essential ingredients in the media transmission of a pop artist, already celebrated as a dancer from his or her live act. Whether these features will continue as technology (which has already robbed us of the genuinely acoustic) progresses further, remains to be seen.

Initial investigations into dance and music video reveal a wealth of research to be undertaken. Far more extensive surveys of the range and deployment of dance styles, examining their interaction with video techniques, need to be launched. Detailed analyses of filmic and choreographic devices, from a formalist perspective, ought not, though, to exclude the voices of the producers and performers of these music videos. Too little is known of the creative aspects of dance on pop video and of how it is initially conceived, then delivered, with respect towards other channels of communication in the integrated text. Within the academic debate on music video, a tendency towards the textual analysis of popular texts, without regard for their use in society is, happily, being addressed, but such an approach need not concentrate exclusively on the examination of music videos to reveal socio-cultural factors of race, gender, class, or youth culture, alone. In addressing such ideological factors, there may often be a danger of overlooking the aesthetic dimensions of such work, reducing the production and reading of texts, positioned as popular culture, to mere ciphers of some grand theory. Studies of dance and the media must, of necessity, engage with current theoretical debate, but not to the exclusion of developing methodologies which illuminate the phenomenon of dancing in all its aspects.

NOTES

1 With acknowledgement to Elizabeth Stewart for her initial input into the original chapter.
2 Exceptions include Mercer (1986) and Saint Clair Harvey (1990).
3 This analysis was written before Jackson's reputation was dented by media exposure of his alleged relationships with children.

32

TWO ANALYSES OF 'DANCING IN THE DARK' (*THE BAND WAGON*, 1953)

RICHARD DYER

'I seem to find the happiness I seek'

Couple-dances in the MGM musicals of the forties and fifties play variations on the construction of heterosexuality, but with a greater emphasis, compared to Rogers and Astaire, on both difference and female-on-male dependency. 'Dancing in the Dark' from *The Band Wagon* suggests an idea of a fusion of difference within heterosexuality, which then leads to a sense of enabling dependency. Fred Astaire and Cyd Charisse, entirely within the one number, 'Dancing in the Dark', reach a different-but-equal arrangement through a sense of the fusion of differences, achieved through both an accommodation to each other's (dance) style and a use of (dance) ground uncommon to both.

The dancers, as characters and stars, represent two different sets of values explicitly embodied in their dancing styles. He is the old Hollywood musical, his dance based on vaudeville, his idea of the purpose of the thing 'pure entertainment'; she, with her background in ballet, represents the new Hollywood musical of the forties, with its infusion of American Ballet Theatre and its aspiration to be meaningful as well as entertaining. The film is very deliberate in its use of Astaire and Charisse and poses them the question of whether they can dance together (with all that implies). 'Dancing in the Dark' is the demonstration that they can. It follows a series of disastrous and quarrelsome rehearsals for the show they are both to appear in; having at last discussed the fact that they both feel inadequate in relation to the other, they go at his suggestion to Central Park to see if they are capable of dancing together. They walk through a public dance floor of couples and into a clear space. The setting is important. It is not the theatre, it is not professional dance of any kind, it is the recreational space and dance of 'ordinary people'. This both provides neutral territory for these two professional dancers and also suggests the idea of doing what they feel like, rather than what, as in rehearsal, they are being required to do. The joy, naturally, is that they discover that when they are themselves and ordinary, they can indeed dance together.

To achieve this the dance has to give the impression of spontaneity and intuition. She initiates the idea of dancing by idly sketching an expansive, balletic movement out into the area, establishing it as a space to dance in. He initiates the idea of dancing together by then doing a nimble turn which ends up with him posed facing her. As characters, both are spontaneously trying out the possibility of dancing. There then follows a longish sequence of mirroring, moving from side to side facing each other, looking into each other's eyes. There is no sense of one being the reflection of the other: one does not start a movement a moment before the other, neither looks at the other's body. It is perfect intuition, pure transparency of understanding between them. The steps here and throughout are a combination of ballet and hoofing, equally shared, practically impossible to disentangle. In other words, the perfect fusion, through spontaneity, intuition and transparency, of difference.

As the number develops, there is an increase in mutual holding and her-on-him dependency positions. Out of the fusion of what they really are/want develops a new awareness of difference and dependency. The instances of the latter are enabling; he spins her out or pulls her up in ways that allow her to flourish, to extend exhilaratingly upwards or outwards, with an energy and expansiveness at odds with the contained and inward movement associated with pretty femininity in showbiz dance. This is not to say that her movements connote masculinity, they are far too graceful for that; rather they suggest the ideal of womanhood confidently flowering in the ground of male support.

'Dancing in the Dark' accomplishes the movement from courtship (getting to know one another) to consummation (reaching a peak of passion) within one number.

JOHN MUELLER

Astaire dancing

A hefty percentage of the musicals produced in Hollywood in the 1930s were of the backstage variety – musicals in which putting on a show provided the major impetus for the plot. Astaire's first film, *Dancing Lady*, was one of these, but thereafter, except for *The Band Wagon* (1953), he avoided them. Although the setting for most of his films is show business in one form or another, almost all of his films are primarily love stories – romances about two people who happen to spend a great deal of time singing and dancing, usually with each other.

It was difficult to develop fully more than one plot line in the Hollywood musicals of Astaire's era, because the films were short and so much of their time had to be given over to musical numbers. Although most backstage musicals also involve a love story, the putting-on-a-show theme tends to dominate, the love story to become incidental. This happens in *The Band Wagon*, too, though the script is perhaps slightly more successful than most in giving each plot line its due. In part this is because both revolve around the Astaire character. He plays a washed-up Hollywood hoofer who is trying to make a comeback on Broadway in a new show written for him by his friends, played by Oscar Levant and Nanette Fabray. At first the show is a disaster, run by a director (Jack Buchanan) who insists on making it 'intellectual'. When it fails, Buchanan willingly turns things over to Astaire, who achieves success by excising the pretentiousness and stressing that the show should be 'fun set to music' – to borrow a line from an earlier Comden–Green fable, *The Barkleys of Broadway*.

The love story concerns Astaire and his ballerina partner in the show, played by Cyd Charisse. Wary of each other at the beginning, they gradually become attracted, and finally sink into a clinch at the end. In some respects it's unfortunate that the love story must be given subplot status, for the problems that beset the Astaire–Charisse romance are interesting and have considerable potential for development. The two are kept apart not by contrived plot devices like mistaken identity but for reasons that derive directly from fundamental plot premises: self-consciousness about the differences in their ages (Astaire was fifty-four in 1953, Charisse thirty) and about their different backgrounds (the high art world of ballet, the lowly world of tap). In addition, Charisse is already 'taken' – she is the girlfriend of the show's choreographer, played by James Mitchell.

At first Astaire and Charisse have little interest in each other offstage and evince a considerable incompatibility during rehearsals. Eventually, however, they talk over their differences and, with tension reduced, resolve to see if they can dance together. The resulting romantic duet, 'Dancing in the Dark', is the film's highlight. Not only do they discover they can dance compatibly, but, in some remarkably ingenious choreography, they begin inadvertently to fall in love.

Charisse and Astaire meet at a party for the show's backers and he tries, without her noticing, to make sure she is not too tall for him. Although they soon find themselves arguing over his age and her artistic pretensions, Buchanan is able to dragoon them into the show.

Things do not go well at rehearsals. Astaire feels out of place and has difficulty managing the lifts and other feats urged on him by the show's high-pressure, patronizing choreographer, James Mitchell. Frustrated and furious, Astaire finally throws a tantrum and walks out. At the instigation of the choreographer, Charisse visits Astaire in his room at the Plaza Hotel and awkwardly tries to calm him down. In a scene that strains Charisse's acting ability to the limit, the two dancers finally talk things out and are able to smooth over many of their differences, most of which have been caused, they discover, by their defensiveness toward each other. Charisse asks, 'Can you and I really dance together?' To find out, they take a horse-drawn cab to Central Park where they seek out a place to dance.

Eventually they come across a secluded open-air dance floor. The music of the most famous Schwartz–Dietz song of all, 'Dancing in the Dark', wafts through the trees, and to its accompaniment they do discover, to no one's great surprise, that they can indeed dance together, and quite well.

This dance is often seen as a crucial metaphor for the central problem in the putting-on-a-show plot: the successful blending of the high art of the ballerina with the low art of the hoofer and ballroom dancer. This notion should not be pushed too far, however, since, after all, the show is *not* a success when Buchanan attempts to blend high art with popular art, but only when Astaire takes over and throws out all the high art pretensions. Besides, the ballroom/ballet blend characterizes all of Astaire's romantic duets with ballet-trained partners: Vera-Ellen, Leslie Caron, the Charisse of *Silk Stockings*, even Audrey Hepburn. The duet is remarkable not so much for its ingenious blending of art forms as for the way it develops a subtle emotional transformation. Astaire and Charisse, now wary friends, set out with a task before them that seems straightforward: to discover if they can dance together even though they come from different worlds and different generations. In the course of the dance, however, something unexpected happens: quite contrary to their wills and intentions, they begin to fall in love. Two choreographic devices are used to trace this: an elaborate game of touching and partnering, and the use of stunned hesitations.

The progress of the romance in the dance is most clearly charted in the way the dancers touch each other. At first they are distant and reluctant to touch. However, as the dance, and the romance, build, the partnering gradually becomes closer and progressively more confident and joyous, and lifts and elaborate partnered spins are worked into the texture. Finally, the climax of the dance is reached during an elaborate progression across the floor in which Charisse makes a great, deliberate show of wrapping her arms around Astaire's back rapturously. Touching, in fact, is used neatly to mark out the emotional change in the scenes that frame the dance: as they ride to the park in the horse-drawn cab, Astaire and Charisse are steadfastly *not* touching – to emphasize this, Astaire has his arms folded across his chest; in the ride *from* the park, by contrast, they are holding hands.

At the same time, the second choreographic device is being developed. One of the most remarkable aspects of Astaire's dancing and choreography is his ability to alter and shade the tempo within a single phrase. In 'Dancing in the Dark' these modulations of tempo are used to dramatic purpose: several times the dancers sink to the floor and hesitate in apparent surprise and wonder at what is happening to them; then they are impelled back into the dance. Later, when romantic inhibitions have been overcome, the idea is reprised, altered now to suit the dancers' new relationship: the sinking and rising are done in cooperation – as if the pair are mocking their earlier uncertainty and hesitancy.

The arrangement and orchestration of the music, by Conrad Salinger, is quite beautiful: sensual and dramatic, avoiding the tendency toward sappiness or lugubriousness that so often prevailed in MGM musicals. Another special appeal of the number is its attractive, understated decor, which contrasts markedly with the gaudy excess of the Broadway show Buchanan is trying to put on. Especially impressive is the simple, becoming costume Charisse wears, a copy of a $25 dress that had been purchased from an Arizona supplier by costume designer Mary Ann Nyberg. It cost the MGM wardrobe department $1,000 to make copies of the dress for the dance number.

At the beginning of the number, Astaire and Charisse leave the cab to wander silently through Central Park in search of a place to dance. They cross a crowded ballroom floor (where a band is playing the contemplative 'High and Low' from 1930) and eventually come upon a secluded dance area. Their walk is sombre, reflective; they are obviously ill at ease with each other. They do not touch; Astaire, in fact, mostly keeps his hands in his pockets.

Entering the dance area, Charisse, without looking at Astaire, inserts a brief, swooning dance phrase into the stroll, by way of invitation. Astaire answers with a danced turn that causes him to pull his hands from his pockets. But then he realizes that he doesn't know what to do with his hands; he reaches out, splays his fingers, and uncertainly pulls his hands back toward his body. Rather than touch her, he deliberately clasps his hands behind his back. In this tense and strangely restrained pose, the 'Dancing in the Dark' melody enters, and the dance begins.

In the first phrases the dancers flow sometimes with the melody (richly rendered by cellos), sometimes with the counter-melody. Astaire's hands are finally freed in a turn, and he reaches out to touch Charisse – from a distance – and sends her into some quick spins. This leads to turns that begin with the dancers close but soon develop into a remote embrace. Separating, they glide back to the edge of the dance floor.

The music now returns to the opening phrase, and the dancers repeat their reflective, musically intricate dance-walk, but with an important difference – Astaire is now loosely partnering Charisse, hand to hand. She turns in his arms, and they resume the walk in a tighter pose, with him partnering her from behind. Out of this emerges a partnered pirouette (the first of several in the dance), which Charisse ends by sinking to the ground. The dancers hesitate in this pose, in apparent bewilderment, and then return to the dance.

They sweep liltingly side by side around the floor, and then once again Charisse spins into a fall. This time the fall emerges not from a partnered pirouette but from a lift, and this leads to the second bewildered hesitation. They are again pulled back into the dance by the music and are soon moving across the floor, Astaire firmly partnering Charisse from behind. The themes of touching and of hesitancy are intricately linked here as Charisse's right hand slowly moves upward – as if it were being impelled, reluctantly, by an outside force – to take Astaire's hand.

Another partnered pirouette leads to the third of the fall-hesitations, and then, all hesitation gone, the dancers flow across the floor, their progress punctuated by a pair of exultant lifts. At the far end of the floor (after the first of the two camera cuts in the dance), there are more partnered pirouettes, now elaborated with shifts of direction and extensions of arm and leg. After the dancers separate briefly, Charisse sinks down on a bench, her back to Astaire. Unlike her previous falls, this one does not suggest bewilderment or uncertainty. She simply waits, proffering her hand with full confidence that Astaire will come around behind her, take it, and pull her back into the dance. This he does, exactly as the orchestra returns full-throatedly to the main theme. He pulls her upward and then off the bench and into his arms.

After more partnered pirouettes comes the emotional climax, in a final progression across the floor that displays to advantage Charisse's remarkable arms. (It is of interest that, where other choreographers were understandably mesmerized by Charisse's long, shapely legs, Astaire saw the choreographic possibilities in her long, shapely arms.) Charisse turns in Astaire's arms and then locks her left arm around his neck. In that position she performs two voluptuous backbends. Then she pauses, leaning against him, and finally, with great deliberateness, wraps her other arm around his neck in an embrace that is at once dramatic and intimate as he presses her tightly to his body.

With that, the dance and the dancers have made their statement, and all that remains is to blend the dance back into the story. After a camera cut, Astaire and Charisse dart toward some stairs that lead up from the dance floor and spin their way up them – one of those difficult steps that look so easy in Astaire's work. At the top they form dramatic poses with diagonal arms, first in opposition, then together. Charisse sinks to the floor for a final mocking reprise of her earlier falls; where those were uncertain and bewildered, this one is confident and trusting. Astaire pulls her to her feet again, and they climb back into the cab – Astaire pausing to dance his re-entry. As the music fades, they settle back into the seat of the cab, contentedly holding hands. The thing that Astaire, not notably a sentimental person, remembered most about the duet twenty-seven years later was the trouble he had 'getting back into that dammed cab'. Salinger's musical arrangement at the end of the number is very fine: the 'Dancing in the Dark' melody for violins, and a bold, dramatic counter-melody for brasses, blend effortlessly into some jaunty, quietly contented phrases for strings as the dancers reboard the cab and sit back.

In the hotel-room scene that precedes the 'Dancing in the Dark' duet, the scriptwriters had Astaire call 'human speech' the 'greatest means of communication'. Astaire delivers the line dutifully – and then calmly proceeds in this duet to show how much more richly dance can communicate.

BIBLIOGRAPHY

Acocella, J. (1992) 'Twyla Tharp's bottom line', *The New Yorker*, November 30
—— (1993) *Mark Morris*, New York: Farrar Straus Giroux
—— (1994) 'Mark Morris: the body and what it means', *Dance Now* 3, 2: 38–47
Adair, C. (1992) *Women and Dance: Sylphs and Sirens*, London: MacMillan
Adamczyk, A. (1989) *Black Dance: an Annotated Bibliography*, New York: Garland Publishing Inc.
Adamson, A. and Lidbury, C. (1992) *Kurt Jooss: 60 years of The Green Table*, Birmingham: University of Birmingham
Adshead, J. (1981) *The Study of Dance*, London: Dance Books
Adshead, J. (ed.) (1986) *Choreography: Principles and Practice*, Proceedings of The Study of Dance Conference 4, Guildford: University of Surrey
Adshead, J. (ed.) (1988) *Dance Analysis: Theory and Practice*, London: Dance Books
Adshead-Lansdale, J. (1993/4) 'Dance and critical debate: towards a community of dance intellectuals', *Dance Theatre Journal* 11,1: 22–4, 33
—— (1994a) *Guide to Dance in European Higher Education*, European League of Institutes of the Arts Dance Section. Pub.: London: *Dance Theatre Journal*
—— (1994b) 'Dance analysis in performance', *Dance Research* 12, 2: 15–20
—— (1996) 'Dance history: current methodologies', *Dance Research Journal* 28,1: 3–4
—— (1997) 'The "congealed residues" of dance history: a response to Richard Ralph's "Dance Scholarship and academic fashion" – one path to a predetermined enlightenment?', *Dance Chronicle* 20,1: 63–86
Adshead-Lansdale, J. and Layson, J. (eds) (1983, 1994) *Dance History: an Introduction*, London: Routledge
Alderson, E. (1987) 'Ballet as ideology: Giselle, Act II', *Dance Chronicle* 10, 3: 291–304
Anon. (1929) 'Wer ist Albert Thalhoff [sic]', *Völkischer Beobachter* 163, 17 July
Aschengreen, E. (1974) trans. Patricia N. McAndrew, 'The beautiful danger: facets of Romantic ballet', *Dance Perspectives* No. 58
Au, S. and Peter, F-M. (eds) (1989) *Beyond Performance: Dance Scholarship Today*, Federal Republic of Germany Centre of the International Theatre Institute
Banes, S. (1980, 1986) *Terpsichore in Sneakers: Postmodern Dance*, Middletown, Conn.: Wesleyan University Press
—— (1994) *Writing Dancing in the Age of Postmodernism*, Hanover: Wesleyan University Press

Barthes, R. (1977a) *Roland Barthes by Roland Barthes*, New York: Hill and Wang
—— (1977b) trans. S. Heath, 'The grain of the voice', in *Image–Music–Text*, London: Fontana
Bateson, G. and Mead, M. (1942) *Balinese Character*, Special Publications of the New York Academy of Sciences, Vol. II
Battersby, C. (1989) *Gender and Genius*, London: The Women's Press
Beaumont, C. (1938) *The Complete Book of Ballets*, New York: G.P. Putnam's Sons
Benois, A. (1936) 'The decor and costume', in Brahms, C. (ed.) *Footnotes to the Ballet*, London: Lovat Dickinson
—— (1941) *Reminiscences of the Russian Ballet*, London: Putnam
Berg, S. (1993) 'The real thing: authenticity and dance at the approach of the millennium', in (ed.) Palfry, B., with Gitelman, C. and Mayer, P., *Dance Reconstructed: Modern Dance Art, Past, Present and Future*, Rutgers: State University of New Jersey
Berry, J. with Dehn, M. (1976–7) 'Jazz Profound', *Dance Scope* 11, 1
Best, D. (1985) *Feeling and Reason in the Arts*, London: Allen and Unwin
—— (1986) 'Culture consciousness: understanding the arts of other cultures', *Dance: a Multicultural Perspective*, Report of the Third Study of Dance Conference, University of Surrey. Guildford: National Resource Centre for Dance
Bhabha, H. (1994) *The Location of Culture*, London: Routledge
Birdwhistell, R. (1971) *Kinesics and Context*, London: Allen Lane, 1971
Bopp, M.S. (1994) *Research in Dance: a Guide to Resources*, New York: G.K. Hall
Border Crossings: Dance and Boundaries in Society, Politics, Gender, Education and Technology (1995) Riverside: University of California
Border Tensions: Dance and Discourse (1995) Proceedings of the Fifth Study of Dance Conference, Guildford: University of Surrey
Bourcier, P. (1978) *Histoire de la Danse en Occident*, Paris: Seuil
Bourdieu, P. (1977) trans. Richard Nice, *Outline of a Theory of Practice*, Cambridge: Cambridge University Press
—— (1984) trans. Richard Nice, *Distinction: a Social Critique of the Judgement of Taste*, Cambridge: Harvard University Press
Brecht, B. (1977) *Kleines Organon für das Theater*, in *Gesammelte Werke*, 16 (Frankfurt/Main)
Brennan, M. (1993/4) 'Ways of seeing dance', *Dance Now* 2, 4: 18–21, 55
Brown, C. (1968) 'An appetite for motion', *Dance Perspectives* No. 68
Brown, Carol (1994) 'Retracing our steps: the possibilities for feminist dance histories', in Adshead-Lansdale, J. and Layson, J., *Dance History: an Introduction*, London: Routledge
Brown, T. and Rainer, Y. (1979) 'A conversation about *Glacial Decoy*', *October* No. 10: 29–37
Buckland, T. and Stewart, E. (1993) 'Dance and music video', in Jordan, S. and Allen, D., *Parallel Lines: Media Representations of Dance*, London: John Libbey
Buckle, R. (1971) *Nijinsky*, New York: Simon and Schuster and (1975) Harmondsworth: Penguin
Bullard, T.C. (1971) 'The first performance of Igor Stravinsky's *Sacre de Printemps*', Unpub. Diss. Eastman School of Music (Rochester, USA)
Burke, K. (1957) *The Philosophy of Literary Form*, New York: Vintage Books

Burt, R. (1995) *The Male Dancer: Bodies, Spectacle, Sexualities*, London: Routledge

Carroll, N. (1992) 'Theatre, dance and theory: a philosophical narrative', *Dance Chronicle* 15, 3: 317–31

Carter, A. (1994) 'Man as creative master, woman as responsive muse', *Dance Now* 3, 1: 34–9

—— (1995) 'Blonde, bewigged and winged with gold', *Dance Research* XIII, 2: 28–46

—— (1996) 'Bodies of knowledge: dance and feminist analysis', in Campbell, P. (ed.) *Analysing Performance*, Manchester: Manchester University Press

Chapman, J. (1978) 'An unromantic view of nineteenth-century Romanticism', *York Dance Review*, 7: 28–40

—— (1979–80) 'The aesthetic interpretation of dance history', *Dance Chronicle* 3, 3: 254–74

Cohen, S.J. (1972) *Doris Humphrey: an Artist First*, Middletown, Conn.: Wesleyan University Press

—— (ed.) (1974) *Dance as a Theatre Art: Source Readings in Dance History from 1581 to the Present*, New York: Dodd Mead

—— (1976) 'The English critic and the Romantic ballet', *Theatre Survey* XVII, 1: 82–91

Cooper, E. (1986) *The Sexual Perspective: Homosexuality and Art in the Last Hundred Years in the West*, London: Routledge & Kegan Paul

Copeland, R. (1990) 'In defence of formalism', *Dance Theatre Journal* 7, 4: 4–7, 37–9

—— (1992) 'The black swan and the dervishes: cross cultural approaches', *Dance Theatre Journal* 9, 4: 11–13, 41–3

—— (1993) 'Dance criticism and the descriptive bias', *Dance Theatre Journal* 10, 3: 27–32

Copeland, R. and Cohen, M. (1983) *What is Dance? Readings in Theory and Criticism*, Oxford: Oxford University Press

'*Courrier des Théâtres*' (1910) *Figaro* 19, 23 and 25 June

Croce, A. (1977) *Afterimages*, New York: Alfred A. Knopf and (1979) Vintage Books

—— (1981) 'Oh, that pineapple rag!', *The New Yorker* October 12

—— (1987) *Sightlines*, New York: Alfred A. Knopf

Daly, A. (1987) 'The Balanchine woman: of hummingbirds and channel swimmers', *The Drama Review* (TDR) 31, 1: 9–19

—— (1991a) 'What revolution? The new dance scholarship in America', *Ballett International* 14, 1: 49–50

—— (1991b) 'Unlimited partnership: dance and feminist analysis', *Dance Research Journal* 23, 1: 2–5

—— (1995) *Done into Dance: Isadora Duncan in America*, Bloomington: Indiana University Press

Dance Research Journal (1982) 15, 1: Three articles on philosophy and dance

Dance Research Journal (1983) 15, 2: Four articles on popular dance in Black America

Dance Research Journal (1987–88) 19, 2: Three articles on film and video

Dance Theatre Journal (1989) 7, 2: Issue on dance and sexual politics

Davies, S. (1989) 'The artist's view', *Dance Theatre Journal* 7, 2 Autumn

Davis, G. (1985) *I Got the Word in Me and I Can Sing it, You Know: a Study of the Performed African-American Sermon*, Philadelphia: University of Pennsylvania Press

Delameter, J. (1981) *Dance in the Hollywood Musical*, Michigan: UMI Research Press

Delhi (1913) 'La vie de Paris. Le Goût Oriental', Figaro 4 June: 1

Dempster, E. (1988) 'Women writing the body: let's watch a little how she dances', in Sheridan, S. (ed.) Grafts: Feminist Cultural Criticism, London: Verso

—— (1994) Preface, Writings on Dance Issue 10

Denby, E. (1986) Dance Writings, London: Dance Books

Desmond, J. (1994) 'Embodying difference: issues in dance and cultural studies', Cultural Critique 26: 33–63

de Valois, N. (1957) Come Dance with Me: a Memoir 1898–1956, London: Hamish Hamilton

Diffey, T.J. (1969) 'The Republic of Art', British Journal of Aesthetics 9: 145–56

Dolin, A. (1985) Last Words, London: Century

Douglas, M. (1970) Natural Symbols, London: Barrie and Rockliff

Drama Review (1986) 30, 2: Several articles on Pina Bausch

Drummond, J. (1997) Speaking of Diaghilev, London: Faber

Duncan, I. (1927) My Life, New York: Boni and Liveright

Durkheim, E. (1982) ed. Lukes, S., The Rules of the Sociological Method, London: Macmillan

Dyer, R. (1990) Now You See It, London: Routledge

—— (1993) 'I seem to find the happiness I seek', in Thomas, H., Dance, Gender and Culture, London: Macmillan

Elias, N. (1976) Über den Prozeb der Zivilisation, 2 vols. Frankfurt/Main

Ellis, H. (1914) 'The philosophy of dance', Atlantic Monthly, May

—— (1923) The Dance of Life, Boston: Houghton Mifflin

Ellison, R. (1965) 'Juneteenth', Quarterly Review of Literature 13, 3–4: 274–6

—— (1964, 1972) Shadow and Act, New York: Vintage Books

Emery, L. (1988) Black Dance: from 1619 to Today, New York: Dance Horizons

Farjeon, A. (1994) 'Choreographers: dancing for de Valois and Ashton', Dance Chronicle 17, 2: 195–206

Farrell, S. with Bentley, T. (1990) Holding on to the Air: an Autobiography, New York: Summit Books

Fiske, J. (1986) 'MTV: post structural post modern', Journal of Communication Inquiry 10, 1: 74–9

Fokine, M. (1961) Memoirs of a Ballet Master, London: Constable

Foster, S. (1986) Reading Dancing: Bodies and Subjects in Contemporary American Dance, Berkeley: University of California Press

—— (1995) Choreographing History, Bloomington: Indiana University Press

—— (1996) Corporealities, London: Routledge

Fraleigh, S. (1987) Dance and the Lived Body, Pittsburgh: University of Pittsburgh Press

—— (1991) 'A vulnerable glance: seeing dance through phenomenology', Dance Research Journal 23, 1: 11–16

Friedland, L-E. (1983) 'Disco: Afro-American vernacular performance', Dance Research Journal 15, 2: 27–35

Frith, S. and Horne, H. (1987) Art into Pop, London: Methuen

Garafola, L. (1989) Diaghilev's Ballets Russes, Oxford: Oxford University Press

—— (1997) Rethinking the Sylph: New Perspectives on the Romantic Ballet, Middletown, Conn.: Wesleyan University Press

Gautier, T. (1973) trans. Cyril Beaumont, The Romantic Ballet as seen by Théophile Gautier, New York: Dance Horizons

Gautier, T. Chasles, P. and Janin, J. (1845) *Les Beautés de l'Opéra*, Paris: Soulié

Getz, L. (1995) *Dancers and Choreographers: a Selected Bibliography*, USA: Aspodel Press

Gouldner, A. (1982) 'The dialectic of ideology and technology', in Culler, J., *On Deconstruction*, Ithaca: Cornell University Press

Graham, M. (1950) 'Martha Graham is interviewed by Pierre Tugal', *Dancing Times* October: 21–2

—— (1991) *Blood Memory: an Autobiography*, New York: Doubleday

Grau, A. (1993/4) 'Myths of origin', *Dance Now* 2, 4: 38–43

—— (1994) 'Feminist ethnography and performance: a review essay', *Dance Research* XII,1: 12–19

Grossberg, L., Nelson, C., Treichler, P. (eds) (1992) *Cultural Studies*, New York: Routledge

Grove, L. (1895) *Dancing*, London: Longman and Green

Guest, I. (1954, 1972) *The Romantic Ballet in London: its Development, Fulfilment and Decline*, London: Pitman Publishing

—— (1960, 1980) *The Romantic Ballet in Paris*, London: Dance Books

—— (1969) 'Dandies and Dancers', *Dance Perspectives* 37

—— (1984) *Jules Perrot: Master of the Romantic Ballet*, London: Dance Books

Hardy, T. (1974) *Under the Greenwood Tree; or, the Mellstock Quire* (1872), London: Macmillan

Harrison, J.E. (1913) *Art and Ancient Ritual*, Oxford: Oxford University Press

Harrison, P.C. (1972) *The Drama of Nommo: Black Theater in the African Continuum*, New York: Grove Press

Hazzard-Gordon, K. (1983) 'Afro-American core culture social dance: an examination of four aspects of meaning', *Dance Research Journal* 15, 2: 21–6

Healey, K. (1993/4) 'Expanding minds', *Dance Now* 2,4: 10–17

Heath, C. (1977) *The Beauties of the Opera and Ballet*, New York: Da Capo Press

Hecht, R. (1973/4) 'Reflections on the career of Yvonne Rainer and the values of minimal dance', *Dance Scope* 8, 1: 12–25

Heidegger, M. (1962) trans. Macquarrie, J. and Robinson, E., *Being and Time*, New York: Harper & Row

Herskovits, M.J. (1990) *The Myth of the Negro Past*, Boston: Beacon

Hertz, R. (1960) 'The pre-eminence of the right hand: a study in religious polarity', in Hertz, R., *Death and the Right Hand*, Aberdeen: Cohen and West

Hewes, G.W. (1973) 'Primitive communication and the gestural origin of language', *Current Anthropology* 14

Hodson, M. (1985) 'Ritual design in the new dance: Nijinsky's *Le Sacre du Printemps*', *Dance Research* 3, 2: 35–45

—— (1986) 'Ritual design in the new dance: Nijinsky's choreographic method', *Dance Research* IV, 1: 63–77

—— (1996) *Nijinsky's Crime Against Grace: Reconstruction Score of the Original Choreography for* Le Sacre du Printemps, Stuyvesant, New York: Pendragon Press

Honour, H. (1979) *Romanticism*, New York: Harper & Row (Icon Editions)

Humphrey, D. (1959) *The Art of Making Dances*, New York: Holt, Rinehart and Winston

Hurston, Z.N. (1981) 'Characteristics of Negro expression', in *The Sanctified Church: The Folklore Writings of Zora Neale Hurston*, Berkeley: Turtle Island

Husserl, E. (1931) trans. Boyce Gibson, W.R., *Ideas: General Introduction to Pure Phenomenology*, New York: Humanities Press

Huyssen, A. (1986) *After the Great Divide*, London: Macmillan

Iros, E. (1930) 'Uraufführung von Albert Talhoff's *Totenmal*', *Die neue Zeit* 12

Jackson, N. (1994) 'Dance analysis in the writing of Janet Adshead and Susan Foster', *Dance Research* XII, 1: 3–11 and Adshead-Lansdale's (1994) response 'Dance analysis in performance', *Dance Research* XII, 2: 15–20

Jahn, J. (1990) *Muntu: African Culture and the Western World*, New York: Grove Weidenfeld

Jakobson, R. (1972) 'Linguistics and poetics', in De George, R. and F. (eds) *The Structuralists: from Marx to Lévi-Strauss*, New York: Anchor Books

Jakubs, D. (1991) 'The history of the tango', in *Politics in Motion: Dance and Culture in Latin America Conference*, Durham: Duke University

Jeffrey, M.D.W. (1953) 'African tarantula or dancing mania', *Eastern Anthropologist* 6: 2

Jeyasingh, S. (1990) 'Getting off the Orient Express', *Dance Theatre Journal* 8, 2: 34–7

—— (1992) 'What is dance?, *Dance Now* 1, 1: 21–2 Spring

—— (1995) 'Imaginary homelands: creating a new dance language', in *Border Tensions: Dance and Discourse*, Proceedings of Fifth Study of Dance Conference, Guildford: University of Surrey

Johnson, R. (1986–7) 'What is cultural studies anyway?', *Social Text* 16: 38–80

Jonas, G. (1992) *Dancing: the Pleasure, Power and Art of Movement*, London: BBC Books

Jonas, O. (1982) *Introduction to the Theory of Heinrich Schenker: the Nature of the Musical Work of Art*, New York: Longman

Jones, B. and Hawes, B.L. (1987) *Step it Down: Games, Plays, Songs and Stories from the Afro-American Heritage*, Athens: University of Georgia Press

Jordan, S. (1992) *Striding Out: Aspects of Contemporary and New Dance in Britain*, London: Dance Books

Jordan, S. and Allen, D. (1993) *Parallel Lines: Media Representations of Dance*, London: John Libbey

Jordan, S. and Thomas, H. (1994) 'Dance and gender: formalism and semiotics reconsidered', *Dance Research* XII, 2: 3–14

Jowitt, D. (1977) *Dance Beat: Selected Views and Reviews, 1967–1976*, New York: Marcel Dekker

—— (1985) *The Dance in Mind: Profiles and Reviews 1977–83*, Boston: D.R. Godine

—— (1988) *Time and the Dancing Image*, Berkeley: University of California Press

Kael, P. (1965) *I Lost it all at the Movies*, Boston: Little, Brown and Co.

Kaeppler, A. (1992) 'Theoretical and methodological considerations for anthropological studies of dance', *Ethnographica* 8: 151–7, 25

Kavanagh, J. (1996) *Secret Muses: the Life of Frederick Ashton*, London: Faber

Khan, N. (1993) 'Changing concepts versus traditional forms', *Dance Now* 2, 2: 72–4

Kinney, T. and Kinney, M.W. (1914, 1936) *The Dance: its Place in Art and Life*, New York: Tudor

Kirkland, G. (1987) *Dancing on my Grave: an Autobiography*, London: Hamish Hamilton

Kirschenblatt-Gimblett, B. (1995) 'Making difference: mapping the discursive terrain of multiculturalism', *Writings on Dance* 13: 56–61

Kirstein, L. (1935) *Dance: a Short History of Classical Theatrical Dancing*, New York: G.P. Putnam's Sons

Koner, P. (1993) *Elements of Performance: a Guide for Performers in Dance, Theatre and Opera*, Switzerland: Harwood Academic Publishers

Koritz, A. (1996) 'Re/moving boundaries: from dance history to cultural studies', in Morris, G., *Moving Words: Rewriting Dance*, London: Routledge

Kostelanetz, R. (1992) *Merce Cunningham: Dancing in Space and Time*, London: Dance Books

Kozel, S. (1994) 'Spacemaking: experiences of a virtual body', *Dance Theatre Journal* 11, 3: 12–13, 31, 46–7

—— (1995a) 'The virtual world: new frontiers for dance and philosophy', in *Border Tensions: Dance and Discourse*, Proceedings of the Fifth Study of Dance Conference, Guildford: University of Surrey

—— (1995b) 'Reshaping space, refocussing time', *Dance Theatre Journal* 12, 2: 3–7

Kraus, R. (1969) *History of the Dance in Art and Education*, New Jersey: Prentice Hall

Kreemer, C. (1987) *Further Steps: Fifteen Choreographers on Modern Dance*, New York: Harper & Row

Kristeva, J. (1978) 'Gesture: practice or communication', in Polhemus, T. (ed.) *Social Aspects of the Human Body*, Harmondsworth: Penguin

Laban R. (1948, 1963, 1975) *Modern Educational Dance*, London: MacDonald & Evans

Lavender, L. (1995) 'Understanding interpretation', *Dance Research Journal* 27, 2: 25–33

Lawler, J. (1964) *The Dance in Ancient Greece*, London and Middletown, Conn.: A. and C. Black and Wesleyan University Press

Layson, J. (1983, 1994) 'Dance history source materials', in Adshead-Lansdale, J. and Layson, J. (eds) *Dance History: an Introduction*, London: Routledge

Leppart, R. and McClary, S. (eds) (1987) *Music and Society: the Politics of Composition, Performance and Reception*, Cambridge: Cambridge University Press

Lesschaeve, J. (1985) *The Dancer and the Dance: Merce Cunningham in Conversation with Jacqueline Lesschaeve*, New York: Marion Boyars

Lieven, Prince P. (1980) 'Vaslav Nijinsky', in Steinberg, Cobbett (ed.) *The Dance Anthology*, New York: New American Library

Livingstone, F.B. (1973) 'Did the Australopithecines sing?', *Current Anthropology* 14

Lomax, A. (ed.) (1968) *Folk Song Style and Culture*, Washington DC: American Asscn. for the Advancement of Science, Pub. No. 88

Lonsdale, S. (1981) *Animals and the Origins of Dance*, London: Thames & Hudson

Lunn, J. (1994) 'Speak up!', *Dance Now* 3, 1: 26–7

Macaulay, A. (1987) 'Notes on dance classicism', *Dance Theatre Journal* 5, 2: 6–9, 36–9

—— (1992) 'Spring', *The New Yorker*, 25 May

—— (1997) 'Further notes on classicism', *Dance Theatre Journal* 13, 3: 25–30

Malone, J. (1996) *Steppin' on the Blues: the Visible Rhythms of African American Dance*, Illinois: University of Illinois Press

Manning, S. (1993) *Ecstasy and the Demon: Feminism and Nationalism in the Dances of Mary Wigman*, Berkeley: University of California Press

—— (1994) 'Borrowing from feminist theory', in *Retooling the Discipline: Research and Teaching Strategies for the 21st Century*, Proceedings of the Society of Dance History Scholars, Riverside: University of California

Marcuse, H. (1977) *The Aesthetic Dimension*, London: Macmillan

Markard, A. and H. (eds) (1985) *Jooss*, Cologne: Ballett-Bühnen-Verlag

Martin, J. (1939) *Introduction to the Dance*, New York: Norton

Marwick, A. (1970, 1989) *The Nature of History*, London: Macmillan

Maultsby, P. (1990) 'Africanisms in African American Music', in Holloway, J.E. (ed.) *Africanisms in American Culture*, Bloomington: Indiana University Press

Mauss, M. (1973) 'Techniques of the body', *Economy and Society* II, 1: 70–88

Maynard et al. (1995) 'Francis Sparshott's Philosophy of Dance', in *Border Crossings: Dance and Boundaries in Society, Politics, Gender, Education and Technology*, Proceedings of the Society of Dance History Scholars, Riverside: University of California

McFee, G. (1992) *Understanding Dance*, London: Routledge

McGehee, H. (1989) *To be a Dancer*, USA: Editions Heraclita

McLuhan, M. (1964) *Understanding Media*, London: Routledge

Mead, M. and Macgregor, F.C. (1951) *Growth and Culture*, New York: Putnam

Mercer, K. (1986) 'Monster metaphors – notes on Michael Jackson's *Thriller*', *Screen* 27, 1: 26–43

Merleau-Ponty, M. (1962) trans. Smith, C., *Phenomenology of Perception*, London: Routledge & Kegan Paul

Morand, P. (1925) 'Paris letter. May 1925', *Dial* June: 154

Morris, G. (ed.) (1996) *Moving Words: Rewriting Dance*, London: Routledge

Morrison Brown, J. (ed.) (1979) *The Vision of Modern Dance*, USA: Princetown Book Co.

Mosse, G. (1979) 'National cemeteries and national revival: the cult of the fallen soldier in Germany', *Journal of Contemporary History* 14, 1: 1–20

Mueller, J. (1986) *Astaire Dancing: the Musical Films*, London: Hamish Hamilton

Murray, A. (1982) *Stomping the Blues*, New York: Vintage

—— (1983) *The Omni-Americans: Black Experience and American Culture*, New York: Vintage Books

Neale, S. (1983) 'Masculinity as spectacle', *Screen* 24, 6: 2–19

Ness, S. (1992) *Body, Movement and Culture: Kinesthetic and Visual Symbolism in a Philippine Community*, Philadelphia: University of Pennsylvania Press

Newman, B. (1992) *Striking a Balance: Dancers Talk about Dancing*, New York: Limelight Editions

Nijinska, B. (1981) *Early Memoirs*, London: Faber & Faber

—— (1986) 'On movement and the school of movement', in Baer, N., *Bronislava Nijinska: a Dancer's Legacy*, San Francisco: The Fine Arts Museums of San Francisco

Nijinsky, V. (1937) *The Diary of Vaslav Nijinsky*, ed. by R. Nijinsky, London: Gollancz

Novack, C. (1990) *Sharing the Dance: Contact Improvisation and American Culture*, Wisconsin: University of Wisconsin Press

Partsch-Bergsohn, I. (1974) *Modern Dance in Germany and the United States*, Chur, Switzerland: Harwood Academic Publishers

Petit Courrier des Dames (1839–[41]) Paris: Imprimerie de Dondy, Dupré

Polhemus, T. (1975) 'Social Bodies', in Benthall, J. and Polhemus, T. (eds), *The Body as a Medium of Expression*, London: Allen Lane

—— (ed.) (1978) *Social Aspects of the Human Body*, Harmondsworth: Penguin

Polhemus, T. (1988) *Body Styles*, Luton: Lennard

Polhemus, T. and Procter, L. (1978) *Fashion and Anti-Fashion*, London: Thames & Hudson

Polhemus, T. (1993) 'Dance, gender and culture', in Thomas, H., *Dance, Gender and Culture*, London: Macmillan

Potter, L. (1993) 'Where does responsibility lie?', *Dance Now* 2, 3: 60–1

Praz, M. (1967) *The Romantic Agony*, London: Thames & Hudson

Prickett, S. (1989) 'From workers' dance to new dance', *Dance Research* VII, 1: 47–64

—— (1990) 'Dance and the workers' struggle', *Dance Research* VIII, 1: 47–61

Rainer, Y. (1974) *Work 1961–1973*, New York: New York University Press

—— (1983) 'A quasi survey of some "minimalist" tendencies in the quantitatively minimal dance activity midst the plethora, or an analysis of *Trio A*', in Copeland, R. and Cohen, M., *What is Dance?*, Oxford: Oxford University Press

Ralph, R. (1995) 'On the light fantastic toe: dance scholarship and academic fashion', *Dance Chronicle* 18, 2: 249–60

Rawkins, S. (1984) *Video Rock*, London: Hamlyn

Redfern, H.B. (1973) *Concepts in Modern Educational Dance* (reprinted London: Dance Books, 1982)

Redfern, B. (1983) *Dance, Art and Aesthetics*, London: Dance Books

Regitz, H. (1996) 'Cunningham in conversation with Regitz', *Ballett International* 8/9: 26

Retooling the Discipline: Research and Teaching Strategies for the 21st Century (1994) Proceedings of the Society of Dance History Scholars, Riverside: University of California

Rheingold, H. (1991) *Virtual Reality*, London: Mandarin

Rieff, P. (1966) *The Triumph of the Therapeutic*, New York: Harper & Row

Rivière, Jacques (1983) 'Le Sacre du Printemps', in Copeland, R. and Cohen, M., *What is Dance?*, Oxford: Oxford University Press

Robbe-Grillet, A. (1953) *Les Gommes*, Paris: Editions de Minuit

—— (1967) 'A future for the novel', in Hall, J.B. and Ulanov, B. (eds) *Modern Culture and the Arts*, New York: McGraw Hill

Roose-Evans, J. (1970) *Experimental Theatre*, London: Studio Vista

Rosen, C. and Zerner, H. (1984) *Romanticism and Realism: the Mythology of Nineteenth Century Art*, New York: W.W. Norton and Co.

Rothfield, P. (1994) 'Points of contact: philosophies of movement', *Writings on Dance* 11/12: 77–86

Royce, A.P. (1980) *The Anthropology of Dance*, Bloomington: Indiana University Press

Ruskin, J. (1843) *Modern Painters*, in Braudy, L. (1976) *The World in a Frame*, New York: Anchor Press/Doubleday

Rust, F. (1969) *Dance in Society*, London: Routledge & Kegan Paul

Sachs, C. (1933) trans. B.Schönberg (1937), *World History of the Dance*, New York: W.W. Norton

Said, E. (1978) *Orientalism*, London: Routledge & Kegan Paul

St Clair Harvey, L. (1990) 'Temporary insanity: fun, games and transformational ritual in American music video', *Journal of Popular Culture* 24, 1: 39–64

Savigliano, M. (1995) *Tango and the Political Economy of Passion*, Boulder, Colorado: Westview Press

Sayers, L.-A. (1992) 'The interpretation of movement', *Dance Now* 1, 3: 42–9

Second, A. (1841) *Les Petits Mystères de l'Opéra*, Paris: G. Kugelmann/Bernard–Latte

Servos, N. (1984) trans. P. Stadié, *Pina Bausch: Wuppertal Dance Theatre or the Art of Training a Goldfish*, Cologne: Ballett-Bühnen-Verlag

—— (1995) 'Pina Bausch talks to Norbert Servos', *Ballett International* 112: 37–9

Seymour, L. (1984) *Lynn: the Autobiography of Lynn Seymour*, London: Granada

Shawn, T. (1954, 1963) *Every Little Movement: a Book about François Delsarte*, Pittsfield: Eagle Printing Co. Republished 1974 New York: Dance Horizons

Sheets-Johnstone, M. (1966, 1979) *The Phenomenology of Dance*, London: Dance Books

Siegel, M. (1989) 'The Green Table – sources of a classic', *Dance Research Journal* 21, 1

—— (1991) *The Tail of the Dragon: New Dance 1976–1982*, Durham: Duke University Press

—— (1995) 'On multiculturality and authenticity: a critical call to arms', in Gere, D. (ed.) *Looking Out: Perspectives on Dance and Criticism in a Multicultural World*, New York: Schirmer Books

—— (1996) 'Virtual criticism and the dance of death', *The Drama Review (TDR)* 40, 2: 60–70

Sieveking, G. de G., Longworth, I.H. and Wilson, K.E. (eds) (1976) *Problems in Economic and Social Archaeology*, London: Duckworth

Sklar, D. (1991) 'On dance ethnography', *Dance Research Journal* 23, 1: 6–10

Smith, B. (1994) 'A dancing consciousness: interview with Rebecca Hilton', *Writings on Dance* 10: 23–33

Smith, R.A. and Smith, C.M. (1977) 'The artworld and aesthetic skills', *The Journal of Aesthetic Education* 11, 2: 117–32

Sokolova, L. (1960) *Dancing for Diaghilev*, London: John Murray

Sontag, S. (1966) *Against Interpretation*, New York: Dell Publishing Co.

Sorley-Walker, K. (1987) *Ninette de Valois: Idealist without Illusions*, London: Hamilton

Sparshott, F. (1988) *Off the Ground: First Steps to a Philosophical Consideration of Dance*, New Jersey: Princeton

Sparti, M. (1996) 'Dance history: current methodologies', *Dance Research Journal* 28, 1: 3–4

Steegmuller, F. (1970) *Cocteau: a Biography*, Boston: Little, Brown

Stewart, R. (1982) *Jazz Masters of the 30s*, New York: Da Capo Press

Stravinsky, I. (1936) *Stravinsky: an Autobiography*, New York: Simon and Schuster

Talhoff, A. (1930a) *Totenmal: Dramatisch-chorische Vision für Wort, Tanz, Licht*, Stuttgart: Deutsche Verlags-Anstalt

—— (1930b) trans. M.A. Moralt, *The Call of the Dead*, Stuttgart: Deutsche Verlags-Anstalt

Taylor, M. and Saarinen, E. (1994) *Imagologies*, London: Routledge

Theodores, D. (1995/6) 'Formalist and feminine: the New York school', *Dance Theatre Journal* 12, 3: 40–6

Thomas, H. (1993) *Dance, Gender and Culture*, London: Macmillan

—— (1995) *Dance, Modernity and Culture*, London: Routledge

—— (1996) 'Do you want to join the dance? Postmodernism/poststructuralism, the body and dance', in Morris, G., *Moving Words: Rewriting Dance*, London: Routledge

Thompson, R.F. (1983) *Flash of the Spirit: African and Afro-American Art and Philosophy*, New York: Random House

Thompson, R.F. (1991) 'Coming down the body line: Kongo Atlantic gestures and sports', in Dawson, C.D. (ed.) *Dancing between Two Worlds: Kongo-Angola Culture and the Americas*, New York: Ragged Edge

Trotter, H. (ed.) (1995) 'Is technology the future for dance?', in *The Green Mill Dance Project Papers*, Canberra: Ausdance

Van Vechten, C. (1955) *Fragments from an Unwritten Autobiography*, New Haven: Yale University Library

Vaughan, D. (1977) *Frederick Ashton and his Ballets*, New York: Alfred A. Knopf

Vlach, J.M. (1978) *The Afro-American Tradition in Decorative Arts*, Cleveland: Cleveland Museum of Arts

Warner, Marina (1994) *Managing Monsters*, London: Barrie & Jenkins

Wigman, M. (1966) trans. W. Sorell, *The Language of Dance*, Middletown, Conn.: Wesleyan University Press

Williams, D. (1991) *Ten Lectures on Theories of the Dance*, New Jersey: Scarecrow Press

Wilson, O. (1990) 'The influence of jazz on the history and development of concert music', in Baker, D.N. (ed.) *New Perspectives on Jazz*, Washington DC: Smithsonian Institution Press

Winter, M.H. (1974) *The Pre-Romantic Ballet*, London: Sir Isaac Pitman and Sons

Wittgenstein, L. (1953) trans. G.E.M. Anscombe, *Philosophical Investigations*, Oxford: Blackwell

—— (1958) *The Blue and the Brown Books*, Oxford: Blackwell

—— (1961) *Tractatus Logico-Philosophicus*, London: Routledge and Kegan Paul

Wollen, P. (1987) 'Fashion/Orientalism/The Body', *New Formations* 1: 5–33

Woolf, V. (1909) 'Impressions at Bayreuth', *The Times* 21 August. Republished in *Books and Portraits* (1979) London: Triad/Panther

Writings on Dance (1993) 'Thinking Through Feminism' (whole issue), No. 9

Youngerman, S. (1974) 'Curt Sachs and his heritage: a critical review of world history of the dance with a survey of recent studies that perpetuate his ideas', *Cord News* 6, 2: 6–17

Videography

Bush, K. (1986) *The Whole Story*, Picture Music International, Noverica/EMI Records MVP 9911432

—— (1990) *The Sensual World. The Video*, EMI Pictures Music International MVP 991 2533

Jackson, J. (1989) *Janet Jackson's Rhythm Nation*, 1814 A. and M. Records, Channel 5 Video Distribution AMV 855 089 855–3

Jackson, M. (1988) *Moonwalker*, Ultimate Productions, Guild Home Video GH 8580

Jordan, S. (1987) *Rushes (Davies): Analysis of Three Duets*, University of Surrey: National Resource Centre for Dance

Madonna (1990) *The Immaculate Conception*, Warner Music Vision, Sire Records 7599 38214–3

New Order (1989) *Substance*, Virgin VVD 627

INDEX

A Folk Tale (Bournonville) 213
Aborigines and dance 200
Accumulation (Brown) 228
Acocella, Joan 105, 106, 238, 269–77
adagio sequences 211
Adair, C. 11
Adam, Adolphe 205
Adice, Léopold 211
Adshead, Janet 5, 121, 163–70, 239
aesthetics 8, 54, 87–8, 96, 141
African American vernacular dance 159–60, 195, 230–5
age 156, 175–6
Agon (Balanchine) 104
Alexander technique 74
Allegro, il Penseroso ed il Moderato, L' (Morris) 271
Allen, Maud 223
Alonso, Alicia 53, 58–61
Alston, Richard 48
Amacher, Maryanne 34
American Ballet Theater 113, 116
American music video 282–3
analysis, dance 2, 12–13, 19, 121, 163–70, 237–9
anatomy 54, 74–5
ancestry, 'blood' 54, 69–71
Andersen, Hans Christian 207
androgyne 253–4
angularity of black dance 231, 233
animality 256–7
animals and dance 125, 132–3, 200
anthropology 12, 93–4, 173
Apollo (Balanchine) 54, 62–5, 115–17
Appleton, Fanny 207
appreciation, dance 9, 121, 133, 165–7, 169

Après-Midi d'un Faune, L' (Nijinsky) 253, 256–7
Argyle, Pearl 26
Armstrong, Louis 233
Arnold, Matthew 104
art, concept of 125–34
arts 125–34, 136, 147, 163–6, 199, 204–6, 285
Aschengreen, Erik 207, 210
Ashley, Merrill 248
Ashton, Frederick 19, 23–8, 90; *Symphonic Variations* 113–17 *and see individual ballets*
Astaire, Fred 206, 239, 283, 288–93
Astruc, Gabriel 215–16, 218–21
asymmetry of black dance 231, 233
Atlas, Charles 34
Au, S. 2
audience 21, 38–43, 61, 169, 194, 214–22, 233–4
Ausdruckstanz 20, 36–7, 44
Australia, dance studies in 6–7
authenticity 89, 92–3, 97, 120, 151–2
autobiographies 150–2

Baiser de la Fée, Le (Ashton) 26
Baker's Dozen (Tharp) 110
Bakst, Leon 214, 216, 220, 250, 255
Balanchine, George 54, 61–5, 96, 100, 104–6, 113–16, 206, 237, 241, 246–8, 283
ballet: as art form 92, 96–7, 155; classical 27, 29–30, 33, 57–9, 113–14; Diaghilev and audience for 214–15, 217–20; gender and 241–2, 248; German 36–7, 265; influence on Cunningham 138–9; modern dance and 131, 223–6, 228; music video

283; Romantic 58–60, 203–13;
Russian 251, 255–6, 258; as tradition
146, 149; as Western achievement 194
Ballet Nacional de Cuba 58–9
Ballets Russes 3, 194, 214–17, 219,
221–2, 237, 250, 254–5
Band Wagon, The 238–9, 288–93
Banes, S. 20, 35, 53
Barron, Steve 283
Bartenieff, Irmgard 94
Barthes, R. 284
Baryshnikov, Mikhail 106, 206, 271
Basil, Toni 283
Bateson, Gregory 173
Battersby, Christine 252
Baudelaire, Charles Pierre 206
Bausch, Pina 20–1, 36–45, 100, 238
Bayadère, La (Petipa) 110, 117
Beat It (Jackson) 283
Beaumont, C. 211
Beauvoir, Simone de 136, 143
Behemoth (Morris) 270
being-in-the-world 136, 138–9
Benois, Alexandre 214, 252, 253, 255
Bentley, Eric 99
Berry, James 231
Best, D. 165
Bhabha, Homi 47–8, 49
Bharata Natyam 21, 47, 49–52
Billie Jean (Jackson) 283
black dance 159–60, 195, 230–5
Blackmur, R.P. 99, 105
Blake, William 25
Blasis, Carlo 207, 208
Bliss, Arthur 24
Bluebeard (Bausch) 37, 41
body: attitude to 140; Bausch and use of
38–9, 432; Bharata Natyam 50; dance
studies and 12; historian and 121–2,
180–91; historical context and cultural
studies 154–5, 157, 159–60; as
instrument 66–70, 78, 228; Laban
theory 94; mind and 1, 13; Morris
and use of 269–77; phenomenology
and 136; physicality 36–7, 54, 172–3;
range of movement 33; training 73–4,
77, 80; virtual reality spacemaking
81–8; women and modern dance
223–9
Bohner, Gerhard 36
Bolm, Adolph 58
Boris Godunov (Mussorgsky) 214–19

Borodin, Alexander 214
Boswell, James 125
Bourcier, Paul 199
Bourdelle, Antoine 147
Bourdieu, Pierre 155, 156
Bournonville, August 114, 205, 206,
208, 210, 211, 213
Bowie, David 48, 285
Brae, June 27
Brahms, Johannes 272
Brahms' Paganini (Tharp) 111
break, musical and improvisation 232–3
Brecht, Bertolt 39–40, 42, 260
Brevanne, Raoul 218
Britain, dance studies in 3–5, 8–9
Broglie, Princesse Amédée de 219
Brontë, Emily 280
Brooks, Frederick 85
Brown, Trisha 77, 227, 228, 229
Brussel, Robert 218
Buchanan, Jack 290, 291, 292
Buckland, Theresa 238, 239, 278–87
Buckle, Richard 251, 253, 256
Bullard, T.C. 221
Bulwer, John 182
Burke, K. 230
Burt, Ramsay 11, 237, 250–8
Bush, Kate 238, 280–3, 284
buttocks, use of in work of Morris 238,
270–1
Byrne, David 108, 109; 111
Byron, Charles Gordon 6th Baron 204

Cage, John 34
Camondo, Isaac de 215, 216
Canudo, Ricciardo 218
Caraman-Chimay, Princesse Joseph de
216
Carlier, Madeleine 219
Carnations (Bausch) 44
Caron, Leslie 291
Carrafa, John 110
Carter, A. 193
Caryathis 220
Castellane, Comtesse Boni de 216
Castle, Vernon and Irene 159, 219
Catherine Wheel, The (Tharp) 90, 108–12
Cernuschi, Henri 216
Cerrito, Fanny 148, 211, 212
Chabrillan, Comte Aynard de 220
chance, Cunningham and use of 20,
30–1

Chanel, Gabrielle 220
Chapman, J. 205, 211
Chapman, Wes 116
Chappell, Billie 114
characterization 57, 63, 65
Charisse, Cyd 239, 288, 290–3
Checkmate (de Valois) 23–5
choreography: analysis 19, 146, 168–9;
  Ashton 26–8, 113, 115–16; Astaire
  291; Balanchine 248; Bausch 37;
  concept and 76–7; criticism and 100;
  Cunningham 20, 29–34, 226–7; as
  dance discipline 9, 11; Davies 241,
  246; de Valois 24–5; Fokine 237, 251,
  255; Graham 54, 226; Jeyasingh 48–
  50; Jooss 266–7; modern dance 223;
  Morris 238, 269–71, 274–6; music
  video 279–81, 283–4; Nijinsky 237,
  253, 255, 257; Petronio 75–6;
  Romantic ballet 204; study of 2;
  Tharp 109–11; Tudor 57; Western
  94, 96; Wigman 263; writing history
  as 180–91
Choreometrics 94, 174, 200
Christie, Linford 51
Clark, Michael 72
class, social 120–1, 155–9, 171, 287
classical dance 36, 49, 110–11, 204, 207,
  222, 225, 227–8
classical, the 93, 223, 253, 257–8
classicism 90, 113–15, 117, 254
Cléopâtre (Fokine) 217, 218
Cocteau, Jean 218, 250
Cohen, Fritz 265, 267
Cohen, S.J. 210, 224, 225
communication: black 233; classical
  dance language 49, 51; dance as 68,
  174, 239, 293; dance theatre 38, 40,
  42, 44; language 171, 244–5; origins
  of 199–200; popular music video
  281, 286–7
company, dance 73, 269, 274
concept of dance 119–22
Concerto Barocco (Balanchine) 104
consciousness 72–80, 120, 136–40,
  142–3
contemporary dance 241–2
context: analysis and 167, 237–8; art as
  concept 127, 129–31, 133; criticism
  and 89, 99; meaning and 77, 156–60;
  modern dance 223; physicality 94;
  socio-historical 90, 193–5

continuity of African American dance
  231
control in black dance 231–3
Cooper, Emmanuel 253
Copeland, Roger 89, 90, 98–107, 246
Coppélia (Saint-Léon) 218
Cornfield, Ellen 33
corps de ballet 19, 23–4, 29, 207, 212,
  282
cosmopolitanism of prewar Paris 216,
  221
costume 44, 61–2, 78, 108–11, 207–9,
  217, 228–9, 258, 261, 270, 282, 292
Coton, A.V. 117
Covent Garden Theatre, London
  115–17
Cranko, John 36
creative dance 4, 7
criticism 88–90, 91–7, 98–106, 127, 139,
  153, 164–6, 169
Croce, Arlene 90, 96, 105–6, 108–12,
  246
crotch, use of in work of Morris 238,
  271
cultural studies and dance studies 120,
  154–61
culture: African American 230–1; art as
  concept 126, 129–32; arts and 10–11;
  body and 180; criticism and 89, 91–7,
  99–101; dance and 12, 121, 166–7;
  dance and context 193–5; gender
  247–8; inheritance and analysis 165;
  meaning and 185–6; oral history and
  151; past and present 70;
  phenomenology and 141, 143;
  popular dance 238, 278, 280, 282,
  285–7; virtual reality 87; West 222
Cunningham, Merce 20, 29–34, 48, 100,
  137, 138, 139, 226, 227

Daly, Ann 11, 193, 237, 241, 244, 247,
  248
Dance of Death (Wigman) 260–2
Dance Fairy Tale (Wigman) 260
dance studies 1–12
dance theatre 20, 36–43, 265, 282–3
Dance Theatre Wuppertal 36–44
dancer-choreographer relationship
  79–80
Dances at a Gathering (Robbins) 275
dances of death, Germany before Hitler
  259–67

Danceworks 72
Dancing in the Dark (*The Band Wagon*) 238, 288–93
Dancing Lady 289
Dante Sonata (Ashton) 27–8, 114
Davidson, Ruth 272
Davies, Siobhan 237, 241–2, 245–6, 248
Davis, Gerald 234
de Valois, Ninette 19, 23–8
Debussy, Claude 256
Decazes, Duchesse 216
deconstruction 19, 195, 226–7, 229, 258; descriptive criticism and 89–90, 98–107
definitions of art 126–7
degree courses in dance 4–7, 9
Delameter, J. 283, 286
Delhi 217
Delsarte, François 4, 152
demi-monde 219–20
demi-plié 269–70, 272
Dempster, Elizabeth 1–2, 12–13, 195, 223–9
Denby, Edwin 98, 102, 247
Denis, Ruth St 69, 96, 217, 223
Denishawn dancers 148
dependency and difference, Astaire and Charisse duets 288–9
description 89–90, 98–107, 138–42, 167, 187
desire 67–70
Desmond, Jane C. 120, 154–61, 195
Deuce Coup (Tharp) 108
Deutsch de la Meurthe, Henri 215
Devi, Rukmani 48
Diaghilev, Serge 193, 194, 250, 251, 253, 255, 257; audience cultivation 214–22
Didelot, Charles 208
Dido and Aeneas (Morris) 270
Diffey, T.J. 134
discipline, dance studies as academic 2, 4, 8–10
disco 177–8, 283
Dolin, Anton 250, 251, 253
Doubles (Cunningham) 139
Douglas, Mary 172
Draper, Paul 112
Drexel, Anthony 219
duets 64, 241–3, 245–6, 288–93
Duets (Davies) 237
Dumas, Russell 72
Dumilâtre, Adèle 209

Duncan, Isadora 4, 13, 77, 147, 152, 193, 219, 220, 223, 269
Dunham, Christine 117
Dunham, Katherine 231
Durkheim, Emile 175
Dyer, Richard 238, 254, 288–9
dynamism 147, 224, 231, 233–4, 243, 258

education, dance and 3–9, 11
effort 238, 269, 271–3, 275–6; -lessness 210, 250–1; -shape theory 161, 167
Einstein, Albert 29
El Greco 70
Eleven (Cunningham) 137–8
Eliot Feld Ballet 275
Eliot, T.S. 71, 98, 115
elitism 105, 214–15, 222
Ellington, Duke 232
Ellis, Havelock 198
Ellison, R. 231, 234–5
Elssler, Fanny 211, 212, 213
Elssler, Therese 212
emotion 28, 39–42, 50, 63–4
86
entertainment 41, 96–7, 155, 219–20
Eoline (Perrot) 209
Esplanade (Taylor) 275
Essen Opera 265
essence 67–8, 115–16, 126, 128, 137–8, 140, 150
ethereality 204–5, 209–10, 213
ethnography and phenomenology 143
Europe: as centre of dance 77–8; dance studies in 5–6
evaluation 139, 150–3, 164, 166–9
evolution of dance 193, 197–8
existential phenomenology 119, 135–6, 139–40, 142–3
experience: analysis and 121–2; culture and 175–6; dance theatre 20, 38–9, 41–2, 44; life 54; phenomenology and 120, 135–40, 142
exposure as theme of Morris 271–2, 274–6

Fabray, Nanette 290
Façade (Ashton) 114
Farjeon, Annabel 19, 23–8
Farrell, Suzanne 248
fashion 207–8, 220–1, 279
Fedorovitch, Sophie 117

Fehlandt, Tina 274
femininity 225–6, 229, 237, 251, 261–2, 289
feminism 10, 12, 136, 142–3, 237, 241, 260; post- 280
Ferrari, Amalia 211
Festin, Le (Fokine) 218
Fille du Danube, La (Taglioni) 205–6
film 102–3, 148
Firebird (Fokine) 58, 217, 218
Fiske, J. 286
Fitzjames, Louise 211, 213
Flaxman, John 27
floor, use of 50, 74–5, 224, 270
Flowers, Verla 273
Fokine, Michel 217, 237, 250–6, 258
folk dance 3, 155, 193, 197, 273, 283
Fonteyn, Margot 24, 27, 58, 114
formalism 12, 100, 128, 241–9
Forti, Simone 77
Fosse, Bob 283
Foster, Susan Leigh 11, 13, 19, 121–2, 180–91, 225, 227, 228
Foucault, Michel 156
Four Temperaments, The (Balanchine) 54, 61–2, 104–6, 237, 241–2, 244, 246–8
Fraleigh, Sondra 119, 135–43
Franck, César 114, 115
free association 38, 41
Freud, Sigmund 104
Friedrich, Caspar David 206
Frith, S. 285
Fuller, Loie 223
function: of analysis 165; of arts 129; of black dance 230; of dance 89, 167; of dance analysis 168–70, 239; of dance on music video 279, 286; of theory 106

Ganay, Marquise de 219
Garafola, Lynn 11, 193, 194, 214–22, 251, 253, 255
Gasset, Ortega y 102
Gauguin, Paul 255, 256
Gaunt, Hilda 24, 26
Gautier, Théophile 60, 98, 204, 205, 209, 210, 211, 213, 281
gender: body and 195; cultural and dance studies 120–1, 155–8, 160–1; culture and dance 171–8; dance and 237–8, 241–9; ideology and Nijinsky

253, 255–8; Petronio and 78; popular music video 280, 285, 287; status of dance 1; use of masks in German dance 260; virtual reality 87
generalization, critical 99, 106
genius: curiosity as 70–1; Nijinsky as 252–3, 258
German dances of death 259–67
Gilroy, Paul 47
Giraldi, Bob 283
Giselle (Coralli/Perrot) 23, 53, 58–61, 110, 205, 206, 213, 218, 281
Gitana, La (Taglioni) 204
Glacial Decoy (Brown) 228–9
Glasner, Katie 109
Gloria in D (Vivaldi) 275
Gloria (Morris) 269–70, 271, 275
Gluck, Christoph Willibald von 37
Gods Go a-Begging, The (de Valois) 25
Goldschmitt, Bruno 260
Golovin, Alexander 214, 216
Gosselin, Geneviève 208
Gouldner, Alvin 106
Goyen, William 69
Graham, Martha 13, 27, 54, 66–71, 153, 223–6
Grahn, Lucile 210
Grau, Andrée 194, 197–201
Green Table, The (Jooss) 238, 265–7
Greenberg, Clement 99
Grisi, Carlotta 210, 211, 212
Gross, Valentine 255
Grote, Harriet 213
Guest, Ivor 204, 207, 209, 211, 212
Guimet, Emile 216

Hammer, M.C. 285
Hanna, Judith Lynne 200, 201
Hard Nut, The (Morris) 270, 271, 273
Hardy, Thomas 147
Harper, Meg 33
Harrison, Lou 276
Harrison, Paul Carter 234
Harvey, Cynthia 117
Hawes, B.L. 230
Heath, C. 206
Heckroth, Hein 265
Heidegger, Martin 135, 136
Heine, Heinrich 60
Helpmann, Robert 25, 27
Hennessy, James 216

Hepburn, Audrey 291
Her Majesty's Theatre, London 212
heritage 1–2, 48
hero in Romantic ballet 205–6, 209–10, 212
Herskovits, Melville 230
Hewes, G.W. 199
hierarchy of dance 92–3, 97
Hilton, Rebecca 54, 72–80
Hinduism and dance 201
historian and the body 180–91
historical characteristics of art 119–20, 129–32, 134
historiography 120, 122, 190, 193–4, 238
history 2, 8, 96, 144–53
Hitchcock, Alfred 109
Hodson, Millicent 257
Hogarth, William 25
Honour, Hugh 206–7
Horne, H. 285
Hugo, Victor 207
Humphrey, Doris 104, 223, 224
Hurston, Zora Neale 233
Husserl, Edmund 136, 137
Huyssen, A. 247

identity 13, 47–8, 82, 97, 137–8, 142, 154–6, 160, 173, 185–8
imagery 42–3, 76, 81, 88
imagination 68, 141–2
Imperial Theatres 218, 250, 255
improvisation 21, 51, 54, 72–3, 76, 80–5, 158, 231–4, 284
information 59–62, 73, 79, 94
institutional framework and concept of art 129–30
instrument: body as 66–70, 78, 228; dancer as 57
intellectuals and dance criticism 103–4, 107
intelligence, physical 74–5
intentionality 132–3, 140–1
interaction, human and virtual reality 81–2, 86–7
interiority, dance as expression of 201, 224
interpretation 63–4, 98–9, 101–5, 139, 164, 166–70
interviews 149–50
intimacy 82–5
Iros, Ernst 264

Jackson, Michael 238, 280–4, 286
Jahn, J. 231
Jakobson, R. 244
Jakubs, Deborah 158
jazz 92, 158, 230, 232, 283
Jeux (Nijinsky) 255–6
Jews as patrons of Diaghilev 215
Jeyasingh, Shobana 21, 46–52
Job (de Valois) 25
Joffrey Ballet 257, 266
Jonas, Gerald 198
Jonas, O. 165
Jones, Bessie 230
Jooss, Kurt 37, 238, 265–7
Jordan, Stephanie 237, 241–9
Jowitt, Deborah 11, 98, 99, 100, 102, 194, 203–13, 224
Judson Dance Theater 269
jumps 116, 208, 243, 250–2, 257–8, 269

Kael, Pauline 103
Kahn, Otto 215
Karsavina 220
Kauffer, E. McKnight 24
Kaye, Nora 53, 57–8
Kchessinska, Mathilde 219
Keali'inohomoku, Joanne 200
Keats, John 115
Keersmaeker, Anna Teresa de 78
Kemp, Lindsay 280
Kierkegaard, Soren Aabye 142
Kinney, T. and M.W. 145
Kirkland, Gelsey 206
Kirstein, Lincoln 105, 226
Kistler, Darci 248
Klein, Susan 73–4, 79
Koleda Folk Ensemble 273
Komar, Chris 33
Kovich, Robert 33
Kozel, Susan 12, 54–5, 81–8
Kracauer, Siegfried 103
Kraus, R. 4
Kresnik, Hans 36
Kreutzberg, Harald 36
Kristeva, J. 171
Krueger, Myron 87, 88
Kurshals, Raymond 109

Laban, Rudolf von 5, 36, 94, 161, 167, 265
Lambert, Constant 25, 27

landscape painting and Romantic ballet 206–7
language 10, 12–13, 21, 46–52, 150, 171–3
Lawler, J. 147
Layson, June 120, 144–53
Lecavalier, Louise 285
LeClercq, Tanaquil 53, 61–2
Leppart, R. 10
Lesschaeve, Jacqueline 29–34
Levant, Oscar 290
Levinson, André 105
lexicon, dance 94–5, 226, 228
Lieven, Peter 252
Lifar, Serge 114
life, dance of 66–70
lifts 78, 116, 241, 243, 246–7
lighting 109, 204, 209
Like a Virgin (Madonna) 280
Liszt, Franz 27, 28
literature 8–9, 11, 147, 204–5
living/dead as theme 260–2, 263–4
Livingstone, F.B. 199
Lomax, Alan 174, 200
London Contemporary Dance Theatre 4, 282
Lonsdale, S. 197
Loquasto, Santo 108, 109, 111
Louis Philippe, of France 203
Love and Anger (Bush) 282
Lovey (Morris) 271
Lübecker Totentanz 266
Lumley, Benjamin 212
Lunn, Jonathan 53

Macaulay, Alastair 90, 105, 113–17
McClary, S. 10
Macdonald, Alistair 48
Macgregor, Francis Cooke 173
McLuhan, Marshall 84
Madonna 280
Mahler, Barbara 73–4, 79
Making of Maps (Jeyasingh) 48–50
male/female 78, 116, 121, 176–8, 205, 241–9, 260–3
Mallarmé, Stéphane 256
Malone, Jacqui 195, 230–5
Man with the Child in his Eyes (Bush) 281
Man, Paul de 101
Manning, Susan 193, 238, 258–67
Marcel, Gabriel 136
Marcuse, H. 246

Mariquita, Mme 219
Markard, A. and H. 265, 266, 267
Marquez, Gabriel Garcia 51
Martins, Peter 54, 62–5
Marvell, Andrew 115
Marwick, A. 3, 151
masculinity 237–8, 261–2, 289; Nijinsky and representations of 250–8
masks, use of 260–1, 266
Mata Hari 217
Matthiessen, Erin 274
Maultsby, P. 234
Mauri, Rosita 219
Mauss, Marcel 182
Mead, Margaret 173
Mensinger, Jon 274
Merleau-Ponty, Maurice 135, 136, 140
methodology of dance studies 12–13
Meyerbeer, Giacomo 204
Michelangelo 62
militarism and German dance 238, 260, 264, 267
Milton, John 115
mime 58, 108
Mind is a Muscle, Trio A, The (Rainer) 228
Mitchell, James 290
modern dance 4–5, 9, 27, 29–30, 36–7, 53–4, 92, 96–7, 131, 195, 223–9, 259–60, 265, 269, 283
modernism 246–7, 251, 255–6, 258; post- 10, 20, 54, 77, 97, 248–9, 258, 285
Monotones (Ashton) 117
Monson, Jennifer 80
montage 21, 38, 40
Moonwalker (Jackson) 283
morality 1, 41, 256
Morand, Paul 217
Mornand, Louise de 219
Morris, G. 12
Morris, Mark 95, 96, 115, 238, 269–77
Mosse, George 263
Mouton, Donald 271–2
movement: analysis 167, 169; ballet as 114; body and 180–7; body work and 74–5, 77–80; characterization 57; Cunningham 20; dance and 5, 8, 66, 68, 194, 198; dance as art 129, 133; dance theatre 40–4; description 98; formalism 100; identity 154; intentionality 140–2; Laban theory

94; meaning and 156–8, 244, 246–7; modern dance 223–9; music 63; music video 279, 281–2, 284, 286; 'ordinary' 269; rhetoric and 122; shapes and 19, 26–7; as social text 156, 160; space and 30–3; and speaking choirs in *Totenmal* 259–63, 265; style and culture 173–5; virtual reality 81–4, 87; vocabulary 52
Movement Research 72
MSG (Petronio) 76
Mueller, John 238, 239, 289–93
Mühlfeld, Mme 221
multiculturalism 21, 89–90, 96–7, 100, 178
Murray, Albert 230, 231, 232–3
music 33–4, 40, 63, 108–9, 111–12, 163–5, 204, 273, 276; video and dance 238, 278–87
musicals, Hollywood 286, 288–90, 292
Mussorgsky, Modest Petrovich 216

Napoli (Bournonville) 205–6, 213
Narcisse (Fokine) 251, 253–4, 256
nationalism and German dance 260, 263–4
nationality 155–8, 160
naturalism 121, 172, 225–6, 275
Nazism and theatre 260, 266–7
Neale, Steve 251
Negri, Pola 58
Nerval, Gérard de 205
New Love Song Waltzes (Morris) 272–3
New Order 286
New York as centre for dance 72, 77–8
New Zealand, dance studies in 7
Newman, Barbara 53, 57–65
Nicholas II, of Russia 215
Nichols, Kyra 248
Nietzsche, Friedrich Wilhelm 142
Nijinska, Bronislava 26, 250–2, 254–5, 257
Nijinsky, Vaslav 71, 115, 152, 219, 220, 237; representations of masculinity 250–8
Novack, C. 11
Nutcracker, The (Ivanov) 23, 270
Nyberg, Mary Ann 292

Ondine (Perrot) 212
Open Your Heart (Madonna) 280
openness 54, 69

oral history 149–50
Orbs (Taylor) 112
organisations and dance research 2–3, 6
orientalism 216–17, 222, 253–6, 258
origins of dance 193–4, 197–201

pacificism and German dance 238, 264
Palmer, Bertha Potter 216
Palucca, Gret 36
Paquita (Mazilier) 211
Paris Opéra 114, 203–4, 207–8, 212, 214–15, 218
partnering 76, 78, 139, 159, 241, 243, 248, 291–3
pattern 80, 85, 117, 165
Paulay, Forrestine 94
Pavlova, Anna 48, 49, 250
Paxton, Steve 77
Pech-Merle, France 199
perfection 66, 70
performance: analysis and 170; black dance 232; as dance discipline 9, 11; dancers and 57–65; identity and 156; intentionality 141; Nijinsky 253; physicality 94; popular music video 279–80, 285; as practice 66–7, 95; Russian artistic 250–1; as source material 146, 148; special and Diaghilev 218
Péri, La (Coralli) 210
Perrot, Jules 206, 208, 209, 210, 211, 212
Perse, St John 70
personality 42, 49, 58, 67
Peter, F.-M. 2
Peters, Michael 283
Petipa, Lucien 210
Petipa, Marius 113–14, 213, 250
Petits Mystères de l'Opéra, Les (Second) 212
Petronio, Stephen 54, 72–5, 78–80
Petrouchka (Fokine) 58, 252
phenomenology 54–5, 81–8, 119–20, 135–43
philosophy 119–20, 125–7, 134, 135–6, 140, 142
photocopies as source material 146–7
photography as source material 147–8, 151
phrases, dance 20, 29–32, 73, 75–6, 78
physical culture 121, 171–4, 176, 178
physicality 82, 85, 88, 94, 104, 155, 180, 184